# The
# JIM CORBETT
# Omnibus

OUP India's Omnibus collection offers readers
a comprehensive coverage of works of enduring
value, attractively packaged for easy reading.

# The
# JIM CORBETT
## Omnibus

Man-eaters of Kumaon

The Temple Tiger and
More Man-eaters of Kumaon

The Man-eating Leopard of
Rudraprayag

OXFORD
UNIVERSITY PRESS

# OXFORD
UNIVERSITY PRESS

YMCA Library Building, Jai Singh Road, New Delhi 110 001

Oxford University Press is a department of the University of Oxford.
It furthers the University's objective of excellence in research, scholarship,
and education by publishing worldwide in

Oxford   New York
Auckland   Cape Town   Dar es Salaam   Hong Kong   Karachi
Kuala Lumpur   Madrid   Melbourne   Mexico City   Nairobi
New Delhi   Shanghai   Taipei   Toronto

With offices in
Argentina   Austria   Brazil   Chile   Czech Republic   France   Greece
Guatemala   Hungary   Italy   Japan   Poland   Portugal   Singapore
South Korea   Switzerland   Thailand   Turkey   Ukraine   Vietnam

Oxford is a registered trade mark of Oxford University Press
in the UK and in certain other countries.

Published in India
by Oxford University Press, New Delhi

ISBN-13: 978-0-19-562762-6
ISBN-10: 0-19-562762-8

Illustrated by Prashanto, Sanjib Singha, S.Das, Nilabho, and Dean Gasper

Typeset in Lapidary333BT, 12.5/14
by Eleven Arts, Keshav Puram, Delhi 110 035
Printed in India by Pauls Press, New Delhi 110 020
Published by Manzar Khan, Oxford University Press
YMCA Library Building, Jai Singh Road, New Delhi 110 001

# CONTENTS

## The Man-eating Leopard of Rudraprayag

# MAN-EATERS OF KUMAON

# CONTENTS

# AUTHOR'S NOTE

As many of the stories in this book are about man-eating tigers, it is perhaps desirable to explain why these animals develop man-eating tendencies.

A man-eating tiger is a tiger that has been compelled, through stress of circumstances beyond its control, to adopt a diet alien to it. The stress of circumstances is, in nine out of ten cases, wounds, and in the tenth case old age. The wound that has caused a particular tiger to take to man-eating might be the result of a carelessly fired shot and failure to follow up and recover the wounded animal, or the result of the tiger having lost his temper when killing a porcupine. Human beings are not the natural prey of tigers, and it is only when tigers have been incapacitated through wounds or old age that, in order to live, they are compelled to take a diet of human flesh.

A tiger when killing its natural prey, which it does either by stalking or lying in wait for it, depends for the success of its attack on its speed and, to a lesser extent, on the condition of teeth and claws. When, therefore, a tiger is suffering from one or more painful wounds, or when its teeth are missing or defective and its claws worn down and it is unable to catch the animals it has been accustomed to eating, it is driven by necessity to killing human beings. The change-over from animal to human flesh is, I believe, in most cases accidental. As an illustration of what I mean by 'accidental' I quote the cases of the Muktesar man-eating tigress. This tigress, a comparatively young animal, in an encounter with a porcupine lost an eye and got some fifty quills, varying in length from one to nine inches, embedded in the arm and under the pad of her right foreleg. Several of these quills after striking a bone had doubled back in the form of a U, the point, and the broken-off end being quite close together. Suppurating sores formed where she endeavoured to extract the quills with her teeth, and while she was lying up in a thick patch of grass, starving and licking her wounds, a women selected this particular patch of grass to cut as fodder for her cattle. At first the tigress took no notice, but when the woman had cut the grass right up to where she was lying the tigress struck once, the blow crushing in the woman's skull. Death was instantaneous, for, when found the following day, she was grasping her sickle with one hand and holding a tuft of grass, which she was about to cut when struck, with the other. Leaving the woman lying where she had fallen, the tigress limped off for a distance of over a mile and took refuge in a little hollow under a fallen tree. Two days later a man came to chip firewood off this fallen tree, and the tigress who was lying on the far side killed him. The man fell across the tree, and as he had removed his coat and shirt and the tigress had clawed his back when killing him, it is possible that the smell of the blood trickling down his body as he hung across the bole of the tree, first gave the idea that he was something that she could satisfy her hunger with. However that may be, before leaving him she ate a small portion from his back. A day after she killed her third victim deliberately and without having received any provocation. Thereafter she became an established man-eater and killed twenty-four people before she was finally accounted for.

A tiger on a fresh kill, or a wounded tiger, or a tigress with small cubs, will occasionally kill human beings who disturb them; but these tigers cannot, by any stretch of imagination, be called man-eaters though they are often so called. Personally I would give a tiger the benefit of the doubt once, and once again, before classing it as a man-eater, and whenever possible I would subject the alleged victim to a post-mortem before letting the kill go down on the records as the kill of a tiger or a leopard, as the case might be. This subject of post-mortems of human beings alleged to have been killed by either tigers or leopards or, in the plains, by wolves or hyenas, is of great importance, for, though I refrain from giving instances, I know of cases where deaths have wrongly been ascribed to carnivora.

It is a popular fallacy that *all* man-eaters are old and mangy, the mange being attributed to the excess of salt in human flesh. I am not competent to give any opinion on the relative quantity of salt in human or animal flesh; but I can, and I do, assert that a diet of human flesh, so far from having an injurious effect on the coat of the man-eaters, has quite the opposite effect, for all the man-eaters I have seen have had remarkably fine coats.

Another popular belief in connection with man-eaters is that the cubs of these animals automatically become man-eaters. This is quite a reasonable supposition; but it is not borne out by actual facts, and the reason why the cubs of man-eaters do not themselves become man-eaters, is that human beings are not the natural prey of tigers, or of leopards.

A cub will eat whatever its mother provides, and I have even known of tiger cubs assisting their mothers to kill human beings: but I do not know of a single instance of a cub, after it had left the protection of its parent, or after that parent had been killed, taking to killing human beings.

In the case of human beings killed by carnivora, the doubt is often expressed as to whether the animal responsible for the kill is the tiger or leopard. As a general rule—to which I have seen no exceptions—tigers are responsible for all kills that take place in daylight, and leopards are responsible for all kills that take place in the dark. Both animals are seminocturnal forest-dwellers, have much the same habits, employ similar methods of killing, and both are capable of carrying their human victims for long distances. It would be natural, therefore, to expect them to hunt at the same hours; and that they do not do so is due to the difference in courage of the two animals. When a tiger becomes a man-eater it loses all fear of human beings and, as human beings move about more freely in the day than they do at night, it is able to secure its victims during daylight hours and there is no necessity for it to visit their habitations at night. A leopard, on the other hand, even after it has killed scores of human beings, never loses its fear of man; and, as it is unwilling to face human beings in daylight, it secures its victims when they are moving about at night or by breaking into their houses at night. Owing to these characteristics of the two animals, namely, that one loses its fear of human beings and kills in the daylight, while the other retains its fear and kills in the dark, man-eating tigers are easier to shoot than man-eating leopards.

The frequency with which a man-eating tiger kills depends on (a) the supply of natural food in the area in which it is operating; (b) the nature of the disability which has caused it to become a man-eater, and (c) whether it is a male or female with cubs.

Those of us who lack the opportunity of forming our own opinions on any particular subject are apt to accept the opinions of others, and in no case is this more apparent than in the case of tigers—here I do not refer to man-eaters in particular, but to tigers in general. The author who first used the words 'as cruel as a tiger' and 'as bloodthirsty as a tiger' when attempting to emphasize the evil character of the villain of his piece, not only showed a lamentable ignorance of the animal he defamed, but coined phrases which have come into universal circulation, and which are mainly responsible for the wrong opinion of the tigers held by all except that very small proportion of the public who have the opportunity of forming their own opinions.

When I see the expression 'as cruel as a tiger' and 'as bloodthirsty as a tiger' in print, I think of a small boy armed with an old muzzle-loading gun—the right barrel of which was split for six inches of its length, and the stock and barrels of which were kept from falling apart by lashings of brass wire—wandering through the jungles of the terai and *bhabar* in the days when there were ten tigers to every one that now survives; sleeping anywhere he happened to be when night came on, with a small

fire to give him company and warmth, wakened at intervals by
the calling of tigers, sometimes in the distance, at other times
near at hand; throwing another stick on the fire and turning
over and continuing his interrupted sleep without one thought
of unease; knowing from his own short experience and from
what others, who like himself had spent their days in the jungles,
had told him, that a tiger, unless molested, would do him no
harm; or during daylight hours avoiding any tiger he saw, and
when that was not possible, standing perfectly still until it has
passed and gone, before continuing on his way. And I think of
him on one occasion stalking half-a-dozen jungle fowl that were
feeding in the open, and on creeping up to a plum bush and
standing up to peer over, the bush heaving and a tiger walking
out on the far side and on clearing the bush, turning round
and looking at the boy with an expression on its face which
said as clearly as any words, 'Hello, kid, what the hell are you
doing here?' and, receiving no answer, turning round and walking
away very slowly without once looking back. And then again I
think of the tens of thousands of men, women and children who,
while working in the forests or cutting grass or collecting dry
sticks, pass day after day close to where tigers are lying up and
who, when they return safely to their homes, do not even know
that they have been under the observation of this so called 'cruel'
and 'bloodthirsty' animal.

Half a century has rolled by since the day the tiger walked
out of the plum bush, the latter thirty-two years of which have
been spent in the more or less regular pursuit of man-eaters,
and though sights have been seen which would have caused a
stone to weep, I have not seen a case where a tiger has been
deliberately cruel or where it has been bloodthirsty to the extent
that it has killed, without provocation, more than it has needed
to satisfy its hunger or the hunger of its cubs.

A tiger's function in the scheme of things is to help maintain
the balance in nature and if, on rare occasions when driven by

dire necessity, he kills a human being or when his natural food has been ruthlessly exterminated by man he kills two per cent of the cattle he is alleged to have killed, it is not fair that for these acts a whole species should be branded as being cruel and bloodthirsty.

Sportsmen are admittedly conservative, the reason being that it has taken them years to form their opinions, and as each individual has a different point of view, it is only natural that opinions should differ on minor, or even in some cases on major, points, and for this reason I do not flatter myself that all the opinions I have expressed will meet with universal agreement.

There is, however, one point on which I am convinced that all sportsmen—no matter whether their viewpoint has been a platform on a tree, the back of an elephant, or their own feet— will agree with me, and that is that a tiger is a large-hearted gentleman with boundless courage and that when he is exterminated—as exterminated he will be unless public opinion rallies to his support—India will be the poorer, having lost the finest of her fauna.

Leopards, unlike tigers, are to a certain extent scavengers and become man-eaters by acquiring a taste for human flesh when unrestricted slaughter of game has deprived them of their natural food.

The dwellers in our hills are predominately Hindu, and as such cremate their dead. The cremation invariably takes place on the bank of a stream or river in order that the ashes may be washed down into the Ganges and eventually into the sea. As most of the villages are situated high up on the hills, while the streams or rivers are in many cases miles away down in the valleys, it will be realized that a funeral entails a considerable tax on the man-power of a small community when, in addition to the carrying party, labour has to be provided to collect and carry the fuel needed for the cremation. In normal times these rites are carried out very effectively; but when disease in epidemic form sweeps through the hills and the inhabitants die faster than they can be disposed of, a very simple rite, which consists of placing a live coal in the mouth of the deceased, is performed in the village and the body is then carried to the edge of the hill and cast into the valley below.

A leopard, in an area in which his natural food is scarce, finding these bodies, very soon acquires a taste for human flesh, and when the disease dies down and normal conditions are established, the animal very naturally, on finding his food supply cut off, takes to killing human beings.

Of the two man-eating leopards of Kumaon, which between them killed five hundred and twenty-five human beings, one followed on the heels of a very severe outbreak of cholera, while the other followed the mysterious disease which swept through India in 1918 and was called 'war fever'.

# THE CHAMPAWAT MAN-EATER

## I

I was shooting with Eddie Knowles in Malani when I first heard of the tiger which later received official recognition as the 'Champawat man-eater'.

Eddie, who will long be remembered in this province as a sportsman *par excellence* and the possessor of an inexhaustible fund of *shikar* yarns, was one of those few, and very fortunate, individuals who possess the best of everything in life. His rifle was without equal in accuracy and striking power, and while one of his brothers was the best gunshot in India, another brother was the best tennis player in the Indian Army. When therefore Eddie informed me that his brother-in law, the best *shikari* in the world, had been deputed by the Government to shoot the Champawat man-eater, it was safe to assume that a very definite period has been put to the animal's activities.

The tiger, however, for some inexplicable reason, did not die and was causing the Government a great deal of anxiety when I visited Naini Tal four years later. Rewards were offered, special *shikaris* employed, and parties of Gurkhas sent out from the depot in Almora. Yet, in spite of these measures, the toll of the human victims continued to mount alarmingly.

The tigress, for such the animal turned out to be, had arrived in Kumaon as a full-fledged man-eater, from Nepal, from whence she had been driven out by a body of armed Nepalese after she had killed two hundred human beings, and during the four years she had been operating in Kumaon had added two hundred and thirty-four to this number.

This is how matters stood, when shortly after my arrival in Naini Tal I received a visit from Berthoud. Berthoud, who was Deputy Commissioner of the Naini Tal at that time, and who after his tragic death now lies buried in an obscure grave in Haldwani, was a man who was loved and respected by all who knew him, and it is not surprising therefore that when he told me of the trouble that man-eater was giving the people of his district, and the anxiety it was causing him, he took my promise with him that I would start for Champawat immediately on receipt of news of the next human kill.

Two conditions I made, however: one that the Government rewards be cancelled, and the other, special *shikaris*, and regulars from Almora, be withdrawn. My reasons for making this conditions need no explanation for I am sure all sportsmen share my aversion to being classed as a reward hunter and are as anxious as I am to avoid the risk of being accidentally shot. These conditions were agreed to, and a week later Berthoud paid me an early morning visit and informed me that news had been brought in during the night by runners that a women had been killed by the man-eater at Pali, a village between Dabidhura and Dhunaghat.

In anticipation of start at short notice, I had engaged six men to carry my camp kit, and leaving after breakfast, we did a march the first day seventeen miles to Dhari. Breakfasting at Mornaula next morning, we spent the night at Dabidhura, and arrived at

Pali the following evening, five days after the women had been killed.

The people of the village, numbering some fifty men, women and children, were in the state of abject terror, and though the sun was still up when I arrived, I found the entire population inside their homes behind locked doors, and it was not until my men had made a fire in the courtyard and I was sitting down to a cup of tea that a door here and there was cautiously opened, and the frightened inmates emerged.

I was informed that for five days no one had gone beyond their own doorsteps—the insanitary condition of the courtyard testified to the truth of this statement—that food was running short, and that the people would starve if the tiger was not killed or driven away.

That the tiger was still in the vicinity was apparent. For three nights it had been heard calling on the road, distant a hundred yards from the houses, and that very day it had been seen on the cultivated land at the lower end of the village.

The Headman of the village very willingly placed a room at my disposal, but as there were eight of us to share it, and the only door it possessed opened on to the insanitary courtyard, I elected to spend the night in the open.

After a scratch meal which had to do duty for dinner, I saw my men safely shut into the room and myself took up a position on the side of the road, with my back to the tree. The villagers said the tiger was in the habit of perambulating along this road, and as the moon was at the full I thought there was a chance of getting a shot—provided I saw it first.

I had spent many nights in the jungle looking for game, but this was the first time I had ever spent a night looking for a man-eater. The length of road immediately in front of me was brilliantly lit by the moon, but to the right and left the overhanging trees cast dark shadows, and when the night wind agitated the branches and the shadow moved, I saw a dozen tigers advancing on me, and bitterly regretted the impulse that had induced me to place myself at the man-eater's mercy. I was too frightened to carry out my self-imposed task, and with teeth chattering, as much from fear as from cold, I sat out the long night. As the grey dawn was lighting up the snowy range which I was facing, I rested my head on my drawn-up knees, and it was in this position my men an hour later found me—fast asleep; of the tiger I had neither heard nor seen anything.

Back in the village I tried to get the men—who I could see were very surprised I had survived the night—to take me to the places where the people of the village had from time to time been killed, but this they were unwilling to do. From the courtyard they pointed out the direction in which the kills had taken place; the last kill—the one that had brought me to the spot—I was told, had taken place round the shoulder of the hill to the west village. The women and girls, some twenty in number, who had been out collecting oak leaves for the cattle when the unfortunate woman had been killed, were eager to give me details of the occurrence. It appeared that the party had set out two hours before midday and, after going half a mile, had climbed into trees to cut leaves. The victim and two other women had selected a tree growing on the edge of a ravine, which I subsequently found was about four feet deep and ten to twelve feet wide. Having cut all the leaves she needed, the woman was climbing down from the tree when the tiger, who had approached unseen, stood up on its hind legs and caught her by the foot. Her hold was torn from the branch she was letting herself down by, and, pulling her into the ravine, the tiger released her foot, and while she was struggling to rise, caught her by the throat. After killing her it sprang up the side of the ravine, and disappeared with her into some heavy undergrowth.

All this had taken place a few feet from the two women on the tree, and had been witnessed by the entire party. As soon as the tiger and its victim were out of sight, the terror-stricken women and girls ran back to the village. The men had just come in for their midday meal and, when all were assembled and armed with drums, metal cooking-pots—anything in fact that would produce a noise—the rescue party set off the men leading and the women bringing up the rear.

Arrived at the ravine in which the woman had been killed, the very important question of 'what next?' was being debated when the tiger interrupted the proceedings by emitting a loud roar from the bushes thirty yards away. As one man, the party turned and fled helter-skelter back to the village. When breath had been regained, accusations were made against one another of having been the first to run and cause the stampede. Words ran high until it was suggested that if no one was afraid and all were as brave as they claimed to be, why not go back and rescue the woman without loss of more time? The suggestion was adopted, and three times the party got as far as the ravine. On the third occasion the one man who was armed with a gun fired

it off, and brought the tiger roaring out of the bushes; after this the attempted rescue was very wisely abandoned. On my asking the gun man why he had not discharged his piece into the bushes instead of up into the air, he said the tiger was already greatly enraged and that if by any mischance he had hit it, it would undoubtedly have killed him.

For three hours that morning I walked round the village looking for tracks and hoping, and at the same time dreading, to meet the tiger. At one place in the dark heavily wooded ravine, while I was striking some bushes, a covey of *kalege* pheasants fluttered screaming out of them, and I thought my heart had stopped beating for good.

My men had cleared a spot under a walnut tree for my meals, and after breakfast the Headman of the village asked me to mount guard while the wheat crop was being cut. He said that if the crop was not harvested in my presence, it would not be harvested at all, for the people were too frightened to leave their homes. Half an hour later the entire population of the village, assisted by men, were hard at work while I stood on guard with a loaded rifle. By evening the crop from five large fields had been gathered, leaving only two small patches close to the houses, which the Headman said he would have no difficulty in dealing with the next text day.

The sanitary condition of the village had been much improved, and a second room for my exclusive use was placed at my disposal; and that night, with thorn bushes securely wedged in the doorway to admit ventilation and exclude the man-eater, I made up for the sleep I had lost the previous night.

My presence was beginning to put new heart into the people and they were moving about more freely, but I had not yet gained their confidence sufficiently to renew my request of being shown round the jungle, to which I attached some importance. These people knew every foot of the ground for miles round, and could, if they wished, show me where I was most likely to find the tiger, or in any case, where I could see its pugmarks. That the man-eater was a tiger was an established fact, but it was not known whether the animal was young or old, a male or a female, and this information, which I believed would help me to get in touch with it, I could only ascertain by examining its pugmarks.

After an early tea that morning, I announced that I wanted meat for my men and asked the villagers if they could direct me to where I could shoot a *ghooral* (mountain goat). The village was situated on the top of a long ridge running east and west, and just below the road on which I had spent the night the hill fell steeply away to the north in a series of grassy slopes; on these slopes I was told *ghooral* were plentiful, and several men volunteered to show me over the ground. I was careful not to show my pleasure at this offer and, selecting three men, I set out, telling the Headman that if I found the *ghooral* as plentiful as he said they were, I would shoot two for the village in addition to shooting one for my men.

Crossing the road we went down a very steep ridge, keeping a sharp look out to right and left, but saw nothing. Half a mile down the hill the ravines converged, and from their junction there was a good view of the rocky and grass-covered slope to the right. I had been sitting for some minutes, scanning the slope, with my back to a solitary pine which grew at this spot, when a movement high up on the hill caught my eye. When the movement was repeated I saw it was a *ghooral* flapping its ears; the animal was standing in grass and only its head was visible. The men had not seen the movement, and as the head was now stationary and blended in with its surroundings it was not possible to point it out to them. Giving them a general idea of the animal's positions I made them sit down and watch while I took a shot. I was armed with an old Martini Henry rifle, a weapon that atoned for its vicious kick by being dead accurate—up to any range. The distance was as near 200 yards as made no matter and, lying down and resting the rifles on a convenient pine root, I took careful aim, and fired.

The smoke from the black powder cartridge obscured my view

and the men said nothing had happened and that I had probably fired at the rock, or a bunch of dead leaves. Retaining my position I reloaded the rifle and presently saw the grass, a little below where I had fired, moving and the hind quarters of the *ghooral* appeared. When the whole animal was free of the grass it started to roll over and over, gaining momentum as it came down the steep hill. When it was halfway down it disappeared into heavy grass, and disturbed two *ghooral* that had been lying up there. Sneezing their alarm call, the two animals dashed out of the grass and went bounding up the hill. The range was shorter now, and, adjusting the leaf sight, I waited until the bigger of the two slowed down and put a bullet through its back, and as the other one turned, and made off diagonally across the hill, I shot it through the shoulder.

On occasions one is privileged to accomplish the seemingly impossible. Lying in an uncomfortable position and shooting up to an angle of sixty degrees at a range of 200 yards at the small white mark on the *ghooral*'s throat, there did not appear to be one chance in a million of the shot coming off, and yet the heavy lead bullet driven by black powder had not been deflected by a hair's breadth and had gone true to its mark, killing the animal instantaneously. Again, on the steep hillside which was broken up by small ravines and jutting rocks, the dead animal had slipped and rolled straight to the spot where its two companions were lying up; and before it had cleared the patches of grass the two companions in their turn were slipping and rolling down the hill. As the three dead animals landed in the ravine in front of us it was amusing to observe the surprise and delight of the men who never before had seen a rifle in action. All thought of the man-eater was for the time being forgotten as they scrambled down into the ravine to retrieve the bag.

The expedition was a great success in more ways than one; for in addition to providing a ration of meat for everyone, it gained me the confidence of the entire village. *Shikar* yarns, as everyone knows, never lose anything in repetition, and while the *ghooral* were being skinned and divided up, the three men who had accompanied me gave full rein to their imagination, and from where I sat in the open, having breakfast, I could hear the exclamations of the assembled crowd when they were told that the *ghooral* had been shot at a range of over a mile, and that the magic bullets used had not only killed the animals—like that— but had also drawn them to the *sahib*'s feet.

After the midday meal the Headman asked me where I wanted to go, and how many men I wished to take with me. From the eager throng of men who pressed round I selected two of my late companions, and with them to guide me set off to visit the scene of the last human tragedy.

The people of our hills are Hindus and cremate their dead, and when one of their number had been carried off by a man-eater it is incumbent on the relatives to recover some portion of the body for cremation even if it be only a few splinters of bone. In the case of this woman the cremation ceremony was yet to be performed, and as we started out, the relatives requested us to bring back any portion of the body we might find.

From early boyhood I have made a hobby of reading, and interpreting jungle signs. In the present case I had the account of the eye-witnesses who were present when the woman was killed, but eye-witnesses are not always reliable, whereas jungle signs are a true record of all that has transpired. On arrival at the spot a glance at the ground showed me that the tiger could only have approached the tree one way, without being seen, and that was up the ravine. Entering the ravine a hundred yards below the tree, and working up, I found the pugmarks of the tiger in some fine earth that had shifted down between two big rocks; these pugmarks showed the animal to be a tigress, a little past her prime. Further up the ravine, and some ten yards from the tree, the tigress had lain down behind a rock, presumably to wait for the woman to climb down from the tree. The victim had been the first to cut all the leaves she needed, and as she was letting herself down by a branch some two inches in diameter the tigress had crept forward and, standing up on her hind legs, had caught the woman by the foot and pulled her down into the ravine. The branch showed the desperation with which the unfortunate woman had clung to it, for adhering to the rough oak bark where the branch, and eventually the leaves, had slipped through her grasp were strands of skin which had been torn from the palms of her hands and fingers. Where the tigress had killed the woman there were signs of a struggle and a big patch of dried blood; from here the blood trail, now dry but distinctly visible, led across the ravine and up the opposite bank. Following the blood trail from where it left the ravine we found the places in the bushes where the tigress had eaten her kill.

It is a popular belief that man-eaters do not eat the head, hands, and feet of the human victims. This is incorrect. Man-eaters, if not disturbed, eat everything—including the blood-soaked clothes, as I found on one occasion; however, that is another story, and will be told some other time.

On present occasion we found the woman's clothes, and a few pieces of bone which we wrapped up in the clean cloth we

had brought for the purpose. Pitifully little as these remains were, they would suffice for the cremation ceremony which would ensure the ashes of the high-caste women reaching Mother Ganges.

After tea I visited the scene of yet another tragedy. Separated from the main village by the public road was a small holding of a few acres. The owner of this holding had built himself a hut on the hillside just above the road. The man's wife, and the mother of his two children, a boy and a girl aged four and six respectively, was the younger of two sisters. These two sisters were out cutting grass one day on the hill above the hut when the tigress suddenly appeared and carried off the elder sister. For a hundred yards the younger woman ran after the tigress to let her sister go, and take her instead. This incredible act of heroism was witnessed by the people in the main village. After carrying the dead woman for a hundred yards the tigress put her down and turned on her pursuer. With a loud roar it sprang at the brave woman who, turning, raced down the hillside, across the road, and into the village, evidently with the intention of telling the people what they, unknown to her, had already witnessed. The woman's incoherent noises were at the time attributed to loss of breath, fear, and excitement, and it was not until the rescue party that had set out with all speed had returned, unsuccessful, that it was found the woman had lost her power of speech. I was told this tale in the village; and when I climbed the path to the two-roomed hut where the woman was engaged in washing clothes, she had then been dumb for twelve months.

Except for a strained look in her eyes the dumb woman appeared to be quite normal and, when I stopped to speak to her and tell her I had come to try and shoot the tiger that had killed her sister, she put her hands together and stooping down touched my feet, making me feel a wretched impostor. True, I had come with the avowed object of shooting the man-eater, but with an animal that had the reputation of never killing twice in the same locality, never returning to a kill, and whose domain extended over an area of many hundred square miles, the chance

of my accomplishing my object was about as good as finding a needle in two haystacks.

Plans in plenty I had made way back in Naini Tal; one I had already tried and wild horses would not induce me to try it again, and the others—now that I was on the ground—were just as unattractive. Further there was no one I could ask for advice, for this was the first man-eater that had ever been known in Kumaon; and yet something would have to be done. So for the next three days I wandered through the jungle from sunrise to sunset, visiting all the places for miles round where the villagers told me there was a chance of seeing the tigress.

I would like to interrupt my tale here for a few minutes to refute a rumour current throughout the hills that on this, and on several subsequent occasions, I assumed the dress of a hill woman and, going into the jungle, attracted the man-eaters to myself and killed them with either a sickle or an axe. All I have ever done in the matter of alteration of dress has been to borrow a sari and with it draped round me cut grass, or climbed into trees and cut leaves, and in no case has the ruse proved successful; though on two occasions—to my knowledge—man-eaters have stalked the tree I was on, taking cover, on one occasion behind a rock and on the other behind a fallen tree, and giving me no opportunity of shooting them.

To continue. As the tigress now appeared to have left this locality I decided, much to the regret of the people of Pali, to move to Champawat fifteen miles due east of Pali. Making an early start, I breakfasted at Dhunaghat, and completed the journey to Champawat by sunset. The roads in this area were considered very unsafe, and men only moved from village to village or to the bazaars in large parties. After leaving Dhunaghat, my party of eight was added to by men from villages adjoining the road, and we arrived at Champawat thirty strong. Some of the men who joined me had been in a party of twenty men who had visited Champawat two months earlier, and they told me the following very pitiful story.

'The road for a few miles on this side of Champawat runs along the south face of the hill, parallel to, and about fifty yards above the valley. Two months ago a party of twenty of us men were on our way to the bazaar at Champawat, and as we were going along this length of the road at about midday, we were startled by hearing the agonized cries of a human being coming from the valley below. Huddled together on the edge of the road we cowered in fright as these cries drew nearer and nearer, and presently into view came a tiger, carrying a naked woman. The woman's hair was trailing on the ground on one side of the tiger, and her feet on the other—the tiger was holding her by the small of the back—and she was beating her chest and calling alternately on God and man to help her. Fifty yards from, and in clear view of us, the tiger passed with its burden, and when the cries had died away in the distance we continued on our way.'

'And you twenty men did nothing?'

'No, *sahib*, we did nothing for we were afraid, and what can men do when they are afraid? And further, even if we had been able to rescue the woman without angering the tiger and bringing misfortune on ourselves, it would have availed the woman nothing, for she was covered with blood and would of a surety have died of her wounds.'

I subsequently learned that the victim belonged to a village near Champawat, and that she had been carried off by the tiger while collecting dry sticks. Her companions had run back to the village and raised an alarm, and just as a rescue party was starting, the twenty frightened men arrived. As these men knew the direction in which the tiger had gone with its victim they joined the party, and can best carry on the story.

'We were fifty or sixty strong when we set out to rescue the woman, and several of the party were armed with guns. A furlong from where the sticks collected by the woman were lying, and from where she had been carried off, we found her torn clothes. Thereafter the men started beating their drums and firing off their guns, and in this way we proceeded for more than a mile right up to the head of the valley, where we found the woman, who was little more than a girl, lying dead on a great slab of rock. Beyond licking off all the blood and making her body clean the tiger had not touched her, and, there being no woman in our party, we men averted our faces as we wrapped her body in the loincloths which one and another gave, for she looked as she lay on her back as one who sleeps, and would waken in shame when touched.'

With experiences such as these to tell and retell through the long night watches behind fast-shut doors, it is little wonder that the character and outlook on life of people living year after year in a man-eater country should change, and that one coming from the outside should feel that he had stepped right into a world of stark realities and the rule of the tooth and claw, which forced man in the reign of the sabre-toothed tiger to shelter in dark caverns. I was young and unexperienced in those far-off Champawat days, but, even so, the conviction I came to after a brief sojourn in that stricken land, that there is no more terrible thing than to live and have one's being under the shadow of a man-eater, has been strengthened by thirty-two years' subsequent experience.

The Tahsildar of Champawat, to whom I had been given letters of introduction, paid me a visit that night at the Dak Bungalow where I was putting up, and suggested I should move next day to a bungalow a few miles away, in the vicinity of which many human beings had been killed.

Early next morning, accompanied by the Tahsildar, I set out for the bungalow, and while I was having breakfast on the verandah two men arrived with news that a cow had been killed by a tiger in a village ten miles away. The Tahsildar excused himself to attend to some urgent work at Champawat, and said he would return to the bungalow in the evening and stay the night with me. My guides were good walkers, and as the track went downhill most of the way we covered the ten miles in record time. Arrived at the village I was taken to a cattleshed in which I found a week-old calf, killed and partly eaten by a leopard. Not having the time or the inclination to shoot the leopard I rewarded my guides, and retraced my steps to the bungalow. Here I found the Tahsildar had not returned, and as there was still an hour or more of daylight left I went out with the chowkidar of the bungalow to look at a place where he informed me a tiger was in the habit of drinking; this place I found to be the head of the spring which supplied the garden with irrigation water. In the soft earth round the spring were tiger pugmarks several days old, but these tracks were quite different from the pugmarks I had seen, and carefully examined, in the ravine in which the woman from Pali village had been killed.

On returning to the bungalow I found the Tahsildar was back, and as we sat on the verandah I told him of my day's experience. Expressing regret at my having had to go so far on a wild-goose chase, he rose, saying that as he had a long way to go he must start at once. This announcement caused me no little surprise, for twice that day he had said he would stay the night with me. It was not the question of his staying the night that concerned me, but the risk he was taking; however, he was deaf to all my arguments and, as he stepped off the verandah into the dark night, with only one man following him carrying a smoky lantern which gave a mere glimmer of light, to do a walk of four miles in a locality in which men only moved in a large parties in daylight, I took off my hat to a very brave man. Having watched him out of sight I turned and entered the bungalow.

I have a tale to tell of that bungalow but I will not tell it here, for this is a book of jungle stories, and tales 'beyond the laws of nature' do not consort well with such stories.

## II

I spent the following morning in going round the very extensive fruit orchard and tea garden and in having a bath at the spring, and at about midday the Tahsildar, much to my relief, returned safely from Champawat.

I was standing talking to him while looking down a long sloping hill with a village surrounded by cultivated land in the distance, when I saw a man leave the village and start up the hill in our direction. As the man drew nearer I saw he was alternately running and walking, and was quite evidently the bearer of important news. Telling the Tahsildar I would return in a few minutes, I set off at a run down the hill, and when the man saw me coming he sat down to take breath. As soon as I was near enough to hear him he called out, 'Come quickly, *sahib*, the man-eater had just killed a girl.' 'Sit still,' I called back , and turning, ran up to the bungalow. I passed the news on to the Tahsildar while I was getting a rifle and some cartridges, and asked him to follow me down to the village.

The man who had come for me was one of those exasperating individuals whose legs and tongue cannot function at the same time. When he opened his mouth he stopped dead, and when he started to run his mouth closed; so telling him to shut his mouth and lead the way, we ran in silence down the hill.

At the village an excited crowd of men, women, and children awaited us and, as usually happens on these occasions, all started to talk at the same time. One man was vainly trying to quieten the babel. I led him aside and asked him to tell me what had happened. Pointing to some scattered oak trees on a gentle slope a furlong or so from the village, he said a dozen people were collecting dry sticks under the trees when a tiger suddenly appeared and caught one of their number, a girl sixteen or seventeen years of age. The rest of the parties had run back to the village, and as it was known that I was staying at the bungalow, a man had immediately been dispatched to inform me.

The wife of the man I was speaking to had been of the party, and she now pointed out the tree, on the shoulder of the hill, under which the girl had been taken. None of the party had looked back to see if the tiger was carrying away its victim and, if so, in which direction it had gone. Instructing the crowd not to make a noise, and to remain in the village until I returned, I set off in the direction of the tree. The ground here was quite open and it was difficult to conceive how an animal the size of the tiger could have approached twelve people unseen, its presence not detected, until attention had been attracted by the choking sound made by the girl.

The spot where the girl had been killed was marked by a pool of blood and near it, in vivid contrast to the crimson pool, was a broken necklace of brightly coloured blue beads which the girl had been wearing. From this spot the track led up and round the shoulder of the hill.

The track of the tigress was clearly visible. On one side of it were great splashes of blood where the girl's head had hung down, and on the other side the trail of her feet. Half a mile up the hill I found the girl's sari, and on the brow of the hill her skirt. Once again the tigress was carrying a naked woman, but mercifully on this occasion her burden was dead.

On the brow of the hill the track led through a thicket of blackthorn, on the thorns of which long strands of the girl's raven-black hair had caught. Beyond this was a bed of nettles through which the tigress had gone, and I was looking for a way round this obstruction when I heard footsteps behind me. Turning round I saw a man armed with a rifle coming towards me. I asked him why he followed me when I had left instructions at the village that no one was to leave it. He said the Tahsildar had instructed him to accompany me, and that he was afraid to disobey orders. As he appeared determined to carry out his orders, and to argue the point would have meant the loss of valuable time, I told him to remove the heavy pair of boots he was wearing and, when he had hidden them under bush, I advised him to keep close to me, and to keep a sharp lookout behind.

I was wearing a very thin pair of stockings, shorts, and a pair of rubber-soled shoes, and as there appeared to be no way round the nettles I followed the tigress through them—much to my discomfort.

Beyond the nettles the blood trail turned sharply to the left, and went straight down the very steep hill, which was densely clothed with bracken and *ringals*.[1] A hundred yards down, the blood trail led into a narrow and very steep watercourse, down which the tigress had gone with some difficulty, as could be seen from the dislodged stones and earth. I followed this watercourse for five or six hundred yards, my companion getting more and more agitated the further we went. A dozen times he caught my arm and whispered—in a voice full of tears—that he could hear the tiger, either on one side or the other, or behind us. Half-way down the hill we came on a great pinnacle of rock some thirty feet high, and as the man had by now had all the man-eater hunting he could stand, I told him to climb the rock and remain on it until I returned. Very gladly he went up, and when he straddled the top and signalled to me that he was all right I continued on down the watercourse, which after skirting round the rock, went straight down for a hundred yards to where it met a deep ravine coming down from the left. At the junction was a small pool, and as I approached it I saw patches of blood on my side of water.

The tigress had carried the girl straight down on this spot, and my approach had disturbed her at her meal. Splinters of bone were scattered round the deep pugmarks into which discoloured water was slowly seeping, and at the edge of the pool was an object which had puzzled me as I came down the watercourse, and which I now found was part of a human leg. In all the subsequent years I have hunted man-eaters, I have not seen anything as pitiful as that young comely leg—bitten off a little below the knee as clean as though severed by the stroke of an axe—out of which the warm blood was trickling.

While looking at the leg I had forgotten all about the tigress

[1] Hill bamboos.

until I suddenly felt that I was in
a great danger. Hurriedly grounding
the butt of the rifle I put two fingers
on the triggers raising my head as I did
so, and saw a little earth from the fifteen-
foot bank in front of me, come rolling down
the steep side and plop into the pool. I was
new to this game of man-eater hunting or I
should not have exposed myself to an attack in
the way I had done. My prompt action in pointing the
rifle upwards had possibly saved my life, and in stopping her
spring, or in turning to get away, the tigress had dislodged the
earth from the top of the bank.

The bank was too steep for scrambling, and the only way of
getting up was to take it at a run. Going up the watercourse a
short distance I sprinted down, took the pool in my stride, and
got far enough up the other side to grasp a bush and pull myself
on to the bank. A bed of Strobilanthes, the bent stalks of which
were slowly regaining their upright position, showed where, and
how recently, the tigress had passed, and a little further on under
an overhanging rock I found where she had left her kill when
she came to have a look at me.

Her tracks now—as she carried away the girl—led into the
wilderness of rocks, some acres in extent, where the going was
both difficult and dangerous. The cracks and chasms between
the rocks were masked with ferns and blackberry vines, and a
false step, which might easily have resulted in a broken limb,
would have been fatal. Progress under these conditions was of
necessity slow, and the tigress was taking advantage of it to
continue her meal. A dozen times I found where she had rested
and after each of this rests the blood trail became more distinct.

This was her four hundred and thirty-sixth human kill and
she was quite accustomed to being disturbed at her meals by
rescue parties but this, I think, was the first time she had been
followed up so persistently and she now began to show her

resentment by growling. To appreciate a tiger's growl to the full it is necessary to be situated as I then was—rocks all round with dense vegetation between, and the imperative necessity of testing each footstep to avoid falling headlong into unseen chasms and caves.

I cannot expect you who read this at your fireside to appreciate my feelings at the time. The sound of the growling and the expectation of an attack terrified me at the same time as it gave me hope. If the tigress lost her temper sufficiently to launch an attack, it would not only give me an opportunity of accomplishing the object for which I had come, but it would enable me to get even with her for all the pain and suffering she had caused.

The growling, however, was only a gesture, and when she found that instead of shooing me of it was bringing me faster on her heels, she abandoned it.

I had now been on her track for over four hours. Though I had repeatedly seen the undergrowth moving I had not seen so much as a hair of her hide, and a glance at the shadows climbing up the opposite hillside warned me it was time to retrace my steps if I was to reach the village before dark.

The late owner of the severed leg was a Hindu, and some portion of her would be needed for the cremation, so as I passed the pool I dug a hole in the bank and buried the leg where it would be safe from the tigress, and could be found when wanted.

My companion on the rock was very relieved to see me. My long absence, and the growling he had heard, had convinced him that the tigress had secured another kill and his difficulty, as he quite frankly admitted, was how he was going to get back to the village alone.

I thought when we were climbing down the watercourse that I knew of no more dangerous proceeding than walking in front of the nervous man carrying a loaded gun, but I changed my opinion when on walking behind him he slipped and fell, and I saw where the muzzle of his gun—a converted ·450 without a safety catch—was pointing. Since that day—except when accompanied by Ibbotson—I have made it a hard and fast rule to go alone when hunting man-eaters, for if one's companion is unarmed it is difficult to protect him, and if he is armed, it is even more difficult to protect oneself.

Arrived at the crest of the hill, where the man had hidden his boots, sat down to have a smoke and think out my plans for the morrow.

The tigress would finish what was left of the kill during the night, and would certainly lie among the rocks the next day.

On the ground she was on there was very little hope of my being able to stalk her, and if I disturbed her without getting a shot, she would probably leave the locality and I should lose touch with her. A beat therefore was the only thing to do, provided I could raise sufficient men.

I was sitting on the south edge of the great amphitheatre of hills, without a habitation of any kind in sight. A stream entering from the west had fretted its way down, cutting a deep valley right across the amphitheatre. To the east the stream had struck solid rock, and turning north had left the amphitheatre by a narrow gorge.

The hill in front of me, rising to a height of some two thousand feet, was clothed in short grass with a pine tree dotted here and there, and the hill to the east was too precipitous for anything but a *ghooral* to negotiate. If I could collect sufficient men to man the entire length of the ridge from the stream to the precipitous hill, and get them to stir up the tigress, her most natural line of retreat would be through the narrow gorge.

Admittedly a very difficult beat, for the steep hillside facing north, on which I had left the tigress, was densely wooded and roughly three-quarters of a mile long and half-a-mile wide; however, if I could get the beaters to carry out instructions, there was a reasonable chance of my getting a shot.

The Tahsildar was waiting for me at the village. I explained the position to him, and asked him to take immediate steps to collect as many men as he could, and to meet me at the tree where the girl had been killed at ten o'clock the following morning. Promising to do his best, he left for Champawat, while I climbed the hill to the bungalow.

I was up at the crack of dawn next morning, and after a substantial meal told my men to pack up and wait for me at Champawat, and went down to have another look at the ground I intended beating. I could find nothing wrong with the plans I had made, and an hour before my time I was at the spot where I had asked the Tahsildar to meet me.

That he would have a hard time in collecting the men I had no doubt, for the fear of the man-eater had sunk deep into the countryside and more than mild persuasion would be needed to make the men leave the shelter of their homes. At ten o'clock the Tahsildar and one man turned up, and thereafter the men came in twos, and threes and tens, until by midday two hundred and ninety-eight had collected.

The Tahsildar had let it be known that he would turn a blind eye towards all unlicensed firearms, and further that he would provide ammunition where required; and the weapons that were produced that day would have stocked a museum.

When the men were assembled and had received the ammunition they needed, I took them to the brow of the hill where the girl's skirt was lying, and pointing to a pine tree on the opposite hill that had been struck by lightning and stripped of bark, I told them to line themselves up along the ridge and, when they saw me wave a handkerchief from under the pine, those of them who were armed were to fire off their pieces, while the others beat drums, shouted, and rolled down rocks, and that no one was on any account to leave the ridge until I returned and personally collected him. When I was assured that all present had heard and understood my instructions, I set off with the Tahsildar, who said he would be safer with me than with the beaters whose guns would probably burst and cause many casualities.

Making a wide detour I crossed the upper end of the valley,

gained the opposite hill, and made my way down to the blasted pine. From here the hill went steeply down and the Tahsildar, who had on a thin pair of patent leather shoes, said it was impossible for him to go any further. While he was removing his inadequate footgear to ease his blisters, the men on the ridge, thinking I had forgotten to give the prearranged signal, fired off their guns and set up a great shout. I was still a hundred and fifty yards from the gorge, and that I did not break my neck a dozen times in covering this distance was due to my having been brought up on the hills, and being in consequence as sure-footed as a goat.

As I ran down the hill I noticed that there was a patch of green grass near the mouth of the gorge, and as there was no time to look round for a better place, I sat down in the grass, with my back to the hill down which I had just come. The grass was about two feet high and hid half my body and if I kept perfectly still there was a good chance of my not being seen. Facing me was the hill that was being beaten, and the gorge that I hoped the tigress would make for was behind my left shoulder.

Pandemonium had broken loose on the ridge. Added to the fusillade of guns was the wild beating of drums and the shouting of hundreds of men, and when the din was at its worst, I caught sight of the tigress bounding down a grassy slope between two ravines to my right front, and about three hundred yards away. She had only gone a short distance when the Tahsildar from his position under the pine let off both barrels of his shotgun. On hearing the shots the tigress whipped round and went straight back the way she had come and as she disappeared into thick cover I threw up my rifle and sent a despairing bullet after her.

The men on the ridge, hearing the three shots, not unnaturally concluded that the tigress had been killed. They emptied all their guns and gave a final yell, and I was holding my breath and listening for the screams that would herald the tigress's arrival on the ridge, when she suddenly broke cover to my left front and, taking the stream at a bound, came straight for the gorge.

The ·500 modified cordite rifle, sighted at sea level, shot high at this altitude, and when the tigress stopped dead I thought the bullet had gone over her back, and that she had pulled up on finding her retreat cut off; as a matter of fact I had hit her all right, but a little far back. Lowering her head, she half turned towards me, giving me a beautiful shot at the point of her shoulder at a range of less than thirty yards. She flinched at this second shot but continued, with her ears laid flat and bared teeth, to stand her ground, while I sat with rifle to shoulder trying to think what it would be best for me to do when she charged, for the rifle was empty and I had no more cartridges. Three cartridges were all that I had brought with me, for I never thought I should get a chance of firing more than two shots, and the third cartridge was for—an emergency.

Fortunately the wounded animal most unaccountably decided against a charge. Very slowly she turned, crossed the stream to her right, climbed over some fallen rocks, and found a narrow ledge that went diagonally up and across the face of the precipitous hill to where there was a great flat projecting rock. Where this rock joined the cliff a small bush had found root-hold, and going up to it the tigress started to strip its branches. Throwing caution to the winds I shouted to the Tahsildar to bring me his gun. A long reply was shouted back, the only word of which I caught was 'feet'. Laying down my rifle I took the hill at a run, grabbed the gun out of the Tahsildar's hands and raced back.

As I approached the stream the tigress left the bush and came out on the protecting rock towards me. When I was within twenty feet of her I raised the gun and found to my horror that there was a gap of about three-eighths of an inch between the barrels and the breech-block. The gun had not burst when both barrels had been fired, and would probably not burst now, but there was danger of being blinded by a blow back. However, the risk would have to be taken, and, aligning the great blob of a bead that did duty as a sight on the tigress's open mouth, I fired. Maybe I bobbed, or maybe the gun was not capable of throwing the cylindrical bullet accurately for twenty feet; anyway, the missile missed the tigress's mouth and struck her on the right paw, from where I removed it later with my finger-nails. Fortunately she was at her last gasp, and the tap on the foot was sufficient to make her lurch forward. She came to rest with her head projecting over the side of the rock.

From the moment the tigress had broken cover in her attempt to get through the gorge I had forgotten the beaters, until I was suddenly reminded of their existence by hearing a shout, from a short distance up the hill, of 'There it is on the rock! Pull it down and let us hack it to bits.' I could not believe my ears when I heard 'hack it to bits', and yet I had heard a right, for others now had caught sight of the tigress and from all over the hillside the shout was being repeated.

The ledge by which the wounded animal had gained the projecting rock was fortunately on the opposite side from the beaters, and was just wide enough to permit my shuffling along it sideways. As I reached the rock and stepped over the tigress— hoping devoutly she was dead for I had not had time to carry out the usual test of pelting her with stones—the men emerged from the forest and came running across the open, brandishing guns, axes, rusty swords, and spears.

At the rock, which was twelve to fourteen feet in height, their advance was checked, for the outer face had been worn smooth by the stream when in spate and afforded no foothold even for their bare toes. The rage of the crowd on seeing their dread enemy was quite understandable, for there was not a man among them who had not suffered at her hands. One man, who appeared demented and was acting as ringleader, was shouting over and over again as he ran to and fro brandishing a sword, 'This is the *shaitan*[2] that killed my wife and my two sons.' As happens with crowds, the excitement died down as suddenly as it had flared up, and to the credit of the man who had lost his wife and sons be it said

[2]Devil

that he was the first to lay down his weapon. He came near to the rock and said, 'We were mad, *sahib*, when we saw our enemy, but the madness has now passed, and we ask you and the Tahsildar *sahib* to forgive us.' Extracting the unspent cartridge, I laid the gun across the tigress and hung down by my hands and was assisted to the ground. When I showed the men how I had gained the rock the dead animal was very gently lowered and carried to an open spot, where all could crowd round and look at her.

When the tigress had stood on the rock looking down at me I had noticed that there was something wrong with her mouth, and on examining her now I found that the upper and lower canine teeth on the right side of her mouth were broken, the upper one in half, and the lower one right down to the bone. This permanent injury to her teeth—the result of a gunshot wound—had prevented her from killing her natural prey, and had been the cause of her becoming a man-eater.

The men begged me not to skin the tigress there, and asked me to let them have her until nightfall to carry through their villages, saying that if their womenfolk and children did not see her with their own eyes, they would not believe that their dreaded enemy was dead.

Two saplings were now cut and laid one on either side of the tigress, and with *pugrees*, waistbands and loincloths she was carefully and very securely lashed to them. When all was ready the saplings were manned and we moved to the foot of the precipitous hill; the men preferred to take the tigress up this hill, on the far side of which their villages lay, to going up the densely wooded hill which they had just beaten. Two human ropes were made by the simple expedient of the man behind taking a firm grip of the waistband, or other portion of clothing, of the man in front of him. When it was considered that the ropes were long and strong enough to stand the strain, they attached themselves to the saplings, and with men on either side to hold the feet of the bearers and give them a foothold, the procession moved up the hill, looking for all the world like an army of ants carrying a beetle up the face of a wall. Behind the main army was a second and a smaller one—the Tahsildar being carried up. Had the ropes broken at any stage of that thousand-foot climb, the casualties would have been appalling, but the rope did not break. The men gained the crest of the hill and set off eastwards, singing on their triumphal march, while the Tahsildar and I turned west and made for Champawat.

Our way lay along the ridge and once again I stood among the blackthorn bushes on the thorns of which long tresses of the girl's hair had caught, and for the last time looked down into the amphitheatre which had been the scene of our recent exploit.

On the way down, the hill the beaters had found the head of the unfortunate girl, and a thin column of smoke rising straight up into the still air from the mouth of the gorge showed where the relations were performing the last rites of the Champawat man-eater's last victim, on the very spot on which the man-eater had been shot.

After dinner, while I was standing in the courtyard of the *tahsil*, I saw a long procession of pine torches winding its way down the opposite hillside, and presently the chanting of a hill song by a great concourse of men was borne up on the still night air. An hour later, the tigress was laid down at my feet.

It was difficult to skin the animal with so many people crowding round, and to curtail the job I cut the head and paws from the trunk and left them adhering to the skin, to be dealt

with later. A police guard was then mounted over the carcass, and next day, when all the people of the countryside were assembled, the trunk, legs, and tail of the tigress were cut up into small pieces and distributed. These pieces of flesh and bone were required for the lockets which hill children wear around their necks; and the addition of a piece of tiger to the other potent charms is credited with giving the wearer courage, as well as immunity from the attacks of wild animals. The fingers of the girl which the tigress had swallowed whole were sent to me in spirits by the Tahsildar, and were buried by me in the Naini Tal lake close to the Nandadevi temples.

While I had been skinning the tigress the Tahsildar and his staff, assisted by the Headmen and greybeards of the surrounding villages and merchants of the Champawat bazzar, had been busy drawing up a programme for a great feast and dance for the morrow, at which I was to preside. Round about midnight, when the last of the great throng of men had left with shouts of delight at being able to use roads and village paths that the man-eater had closed for four years, I had a final smoke with the Tahsildar, and telling him that I could not stay any longer and that he would have to take my place at the festivities, my men and I set off on our seventy-five mile journey, with two days in hand to do it in.

At sunrise I left my men and, with the tigress's skin strapped to the saddle of my horse, rode on ahead to put in a few hours in cleaning the skin at Dabidhura, where I intended spending the night. When passing the hut on the hill at Pali it occurred to me that it would be some little satisfaction to the dumb woman to know that her sister had been avenged, so leaving the horse to browse—he had been bred near the snowline and could eat anything from oak trees to nettles—I climbed the hill to the hut, and spread out the skin with the head supported on a stone facing the door. The children of the house had been round-eyed spectators of these proceedings and, hearing me talking to them, their mother, who was inside cooking, came to the door.

I am not going to hazard any theories about shock, and counter-shock, for I know nothing of these matters. All I know is that this woman, who was alleged to have been dumb a twelvemonth and who four days previously had made no attempt to answer any questions, was now running backwards and forwards from the hut to the road calling to her husband and the people in the village to come quickly and see what the *sahib* had brought. This sudden return of speech appeared greatly to mystify the children, who could not take their eyes off their mother's face.

I rested in the village while a dish of tea was being prepared for me and told the people who thronged round how the man-eater had been killed. An hour later I continued my journey and for half a mile along my way I could hear the shouts of goodwill of the men of Pali.

I had a very thrilling encounter with a leopard the following morning, which I only mention because it delayed my start from Dabidhura and put an extra strain on my small mount and myself. Fortunately the little pony was as strong on his legs as he was tough inside, and by holding his tail on the up-grades, riding him on the flat, and running behind him on the down-grades, we covered the forty-five miles to Naini Tal between 9 a.m. and 6 p.m.

At a durbar held in Naini Tal a few months later Sir John Hewett, Lieutenant-Governor of the United Provinces, presented the Tahsildar of Champawat with a gun, and the man who accompanied me when I was looking for the girl with a beautiful hunting-knife, for the help they had given me. Both weapons were suitably engraved and will be handed down as heirlooms in the respective families.

# ROBIN

I never saw either of his parents. The Knight of the Broom I purchased him from said he was a spaniel, that his name was Pincha, and that his father was a 'keen gun dog'. This is all I can tell you about his pedigree.

I did not want a pup, and it was quite by accident that I happened to be with a friend when the litter of seven was decanted from a very filthy basket for her inspection. Pincha was the smallest and the thinnest of the litter, and it was quite evident that he had reached the last ditch in his fight for survival. Leaving his little less miserable brothers and sisters, he walked once round me, and then curled himself up between my big feet. When I picked him up and put him inside my coat—it was a bitterly cold morning—he tried to show his gratitude by licking my face, and I tried to show him I was not aware of his appalling stench.

He was rising three months then, and I bought him for fifteen rupees. He·is rising thirteen years now, and all the gold in India would not buy him.

When I got him home and he had made his first acquaintance with a square meal, warm water, and soap, we scrapped his kennel name of Pincha and rechristened him Robin, in memory of a faithful old collie who had saved my young brother, aged four, and myself, aged six, from the attack of an infuriated she-bear.

Robin responded to regular meals as parched land does to rain, and after he had been with us for a few weeks, acting on the principle that a boy's and a pup's training cannot be started too early, I took him out one morning, intending to get a little away from him and fire a shot or two to get him used to the sound of gunfire.

At the lower end of our estate there are some dense thorn bushes, and while I was skirting round them a peafowl got up, and forgetting all about Robin, who was following at heel, I brought the bird fluttering down. It landed in the thorn bushes and Robin dashed in after it. The bushes were too thick and thorny for me to enter them, so I ran round to the far side where beyond the bushes was open ground, and beyond that again heavy tree and grass jungle which I knew the wounded bird would make for. The open ground was flooded with morning sunlight, and if I had been armed with a movie camera I should have had an opportunity of securing a unique picture. The peafowl, an old hen, with neck feathers stuck out at right angles, and one wing broken, was making for the tree jungle, while Robin, with stern to the ground, was hanging on to her tail and being dragged along. Running forward I very foolishly caught the bird by the neck and lifted it clear of the ground, whereon it promptly lashed out with both legs, and sent Robin heels-over-head. In a second he was up and on his feet again, and when I laid the dead bird down, he danced round it making little dabs alternately at its head and tail. The lesson was over for that morning, and as we returned home it would have been difficult to say which of us was the more proud—Robin, at bringing home his first bird, or I, at having picked a winner out of a filthy basket. The shooting season was now drawing to a close, and for the next few days Robin was not given anything larger than quail, doves and an occasional partridge to retrieve.

We spent the summer on the hills, and on our annual migration to the foothills in November, at the end of a long fifteen-mile march as we turned a sharp corner, one of a big troop of *langurs* (*Entellus* monkeys) jumped off the hillside and crossed the road a few inches in front of Robin's nose. Disregarding my whistle, Robin dashed down the khudside after the *langur*, which promptly sought safety in a tree. The ground was open with a few trees here and there, and after going steeply down for thirty or forty yards flattened out for a few yards, before going sharply down into the valley below. On the right-hand side of this flat ground there were a few bushes, with a deep channel scoured out by rainwater running through them.

Robin had hardly entered these bushes when he was out again, and with ears laid back and tail tucked in was running for dear life, with an enormous leopard bounding after him and gaining on him at every bound. I was unarmed and all the assistance I could render was to 'Ho' and 'Har' at the full extent of my lungs. The men carrying M.'s *dandy* joined in lustily, the pandemonium reaching its climax when the hundred or more *langurs* added their alarm-calls in varying keys. For twenty-five or thirty yards the desperate and unequal race continued, and just as the leopard was within reach of Robin, it unaccountably swerved and disappeared into the valley, while Robin circled round a shoulder of the hill and rejoined us on the road. Two very useful lessons Robin learned from his hairbreadth escape, which he never in his afterlife forgot. First, that it was dangerous to chase *langurs*, and second that the alarm-call of a *langur* denoted the presence of a leopard.

Robin resumed his training where it had been interrupted in spring, but it soon became apparent that his early neglect and starvation had affected his heart, for he fainted now after the least exertion.

There is nothing more disappointing for a gun dog than to be left at home when his master goes out, and as bird-shooting was now taboo for Robin, I started taking him with me when I went out after big game. He took to this new form of sport as readily as duck takes to water, and from then on has accompanied me whenever I have been out with a rifle.

The method we employ is to go out early in the morning, pick up the tracks of a leopard or tiger, and follow them. When the pugmarks can be seen, I do the tracking, and when the animal we are after takes to the jungle, Robin does the tracking. In this way we have on occasions followed an animal for miles before coming up with it.

When shooting on foot, it is very much easier to kill an animal outright than when shooting down on it from a *machan*, or from the back of an elephant. For one thing, when wounded animals have to be followed up on foot, chance shots are not indulged in, and for another, the vital parts are more accessible when shooting on the same level as the animal than when shooting down on it. However, even after exercising the greatest care over the shot, I have sometimes only wounded leopards and tigers, who have rampaged round before being quietened by a second or third shot, and only once during all the years that we have shot together has Robin left me in a tight corner. When he rejoined me after his brief absence that day, we decided that the incident was closed and would never be referred to again, but we are older now and possibly less sensitive, anyway Robin—who has exceeded the canine equivalent of three-score-years-and-ten, and who lies at my feet as I write, on a bed he will never again leave—has with a smile from his wise brown eyes and a wag of his small stump of a tail given me permission to go ahead and tell you the story.

We did not see the leopard until it stepped clear of the thick undergrowth and, coming to a stand, looked back over its left shoulder.

He was an outsized male with a beautiful dark glossy coat, the rosettes on his skin standing out like clear-cut designs on a rich velvet ground. I had an unhurried shot with an accurate rifle at his right shoulder, at the shot range of fifteen yards. By how little I missed his heart makes no matter, and while the bullet was kicking up the dust fifty yards away he was high in the air, and, turning a somersault, landed in the thick undergrowth he had a minute before left. For twenty, forty, fifty yards we heard him crashing through the cover, and then the sound ceased as abruptly as it had begun. This sudden cessation of sound could be accounted for in two ways: either the leopard had collapsed and died in his tracks, or fifty yards away he had reached open ground.

We had walked far that day; the sun was near setting and we were still four miles from home. This part of the jungle was not frequented by man, and there was not one chance in a million of anyone passing that way by night, and last, and the best reason of all for leaving the leopard, M. was unarmed and could neither be left alone nor taken along to follow up the wounded animal—so we turned to the north and made for home. There was no need for me to mark the spot, for I had walked through these jungles by day—and often by night—for near on half a century, and could have found my way blindfold to any part of them.

Night had only just given place to day the following morning when Robin—who had not been with us the previous evening—and I arrived at the spot I had fired from. Very warily Robin, who was leading, examined the ground where the leopard had stood, and then raising his head and sniffing the air, he advanced to the edge of the undergrowth where the leopard, in falling, had left great splashes of blood. There was no need for me to examine the blood to determine the position of the wound, for at the short range I had fired at I had seen the bullet strike, and the spurt of dust on the far side was proof that the bullet had gone right through the leopard's body.

It might be necessary later on to follow up the blood trail, but just at present a little rest after our four-mile walk in the dark would do no harm, and might on the other hand prove of great value to us. The sun was near rising, and at that early hour of the morning all the jungle folk were on the move, and it would be advisable to hear what they had to say on the subject of the wounded animal before going further.

Under a nearby tree I found a dry spot to which the saturating dew had not penetrated, and with Robin stretched out at my feet, had finished my cigarette when a *chital* hind, and then a second and a third, started calling some sixty yards to our left front. Robin sat up and slowly turning his head looked at me, and, on catching my eye, as slowly turned back in the direction of the calling deer. He had travelled far along the road of experience since the day he had first heard the alarm-call of a *langur*, and he knew now—as did every bird and animal within hearing—that the *chital* were warning the jungle folk of the presence of a leopard.

From the manner in which the *chital* were calling it was evident that the leopard was in full view of them. A little more patience and they would tell us if he was alive. They had been calling for about five minutes when suddenly, and all together, they called once and again, and then settled down to their regular call; the leopard was alive and had moved, and was now quiet again. All that we needed to know now was the position of the leopard, and this information we could get by stalking the *chital*.

Moving down-wind for fifty yards we entered the thick undergrowth, and started to stalk the deer—not a difficult task, for Robin can move through any jungle as silently as a cat, and long practice has taught me where to place my feet. The *chital* were not visible until we were within a few feet of them. They were standing in the open and looking towards the north in the exact direction, as far as I was able to judge, in which the crashing sound of the evening before had ceased.

Up to this point, the *chital* had been of great help to us; they had told us the leopard was lying out in the open and that it was alive, and they had now given us the direction. It had taken us the best part of an hour to acquire this information, and if the *chital* now caught sight of us and warned the jungle folk of our presence, they would in one second undo the good they had so far done. I was debating whether it would be better to retrace our steps and work down below the calling deer and try to get a shot from behind them, or move them from our vicinity by giving the call of a leopard, when one of the hinds turned her head and looked straight into my face. Next second, with a cry of 'Ware man', they dashed away at top speed. I had only about five yards to cover to reach the open ground, but quick as I was the leopard was quicker, and I was only in time to see his hind quarters and tail disappearing behind some bushes. The *chital* had very effectively spoilt my chance of a shot, and the leopard would now have to be located and marked down all over again— this time by Robin.

I stood on the open ground for some minutes, to give the leopard time to settle down and the scent he had left in his passage to blow past us, and then took Robin due west across the track of the wind, which was blowing from the north. We had gone about sixty or seventy yards when Robin, who was leading, stopped and turned to face into the wind. Robin is mute in the jungles, and has a wonderful control over his nerves. There is one nerve, however, running down the back of his hind legs, which he cannot control when he is looking at a leopard, or when the scent of a leopard is warm and strong. This nerve was now twitching, and agitating the long hair on the upper part of his hind legs.

A very violent cyclonic storm had struck this part of the forest the previous summer, uprooting a number of trees; it was towards one of these fallen trees, forty yards from where we were standing, that Robin was now looking. The branches were towards us, and on either side of the trunk there were light bushes and a few scattered tufts of short grass.

At any other time Robin and I would have made straight for our quarry; but on this occasion a little extra caution was advisable. Not only were we dealing with an animal who when wounded knows no fear, but in addition we were dealing with a leopard who had had fifteen hours in which to nurse his grievance against man, and who could in consequence be counted on to have all his fighting instincts thoroughly aroused.

When leaving home that morning I had picked up the ·275 rifle I had used the previous evening. A good rifle to carry when miles have to be covered, but not the weapon one would select to deal with a wounded leopard; so instead of a direct approach, I picked a line that would take us fifteen yards from, and parallel to, the fallen tree. Step by step, Robin leading, we moved along this line, and had passed the branches and were opposite the trunk when Robin stopped.

Taking the direction from him, I presently saw what had attracted his attention—the tip of the leopard's tail slowly raised, and as slowly lowered—the warning a leopard invariably gives before charging. Pivoting to the right on my heels, I had just got the rifle to my shoulder when the leopard burst through the intervening bushes and sprang at us. My bullet, fired more with the object of deflecting him than with any hope of killing or even hitting him, passed under his belly and went through the fleshy part of his left thigh. The crack of the rifle, more than the wound, had the effect of deflecting the leopard sufficiently to make him pass my right shoulder without touching me, and before I could get in another shot, he disappeared into the bushes beyond.

Robin had not moved from my feet, and together we now

examined the ground the leopard had passed over. Blood we found in plenty, but whether it had come from the old wounds torn open by the leopard's violent exertions, or from my recent shot, it was impossible to say. Anyway it made no difference to Robin, who without a moment's hesitation took up the trail. After going through some very heavy cover we came on knee-high undergrowth, and had proceeded about a couple of hundred yards when I saw the leopard get up in front of us, and before I could get the rifle to bear on him, he disappeared under a lantana bush. This bush with its branches resting on the ground was as big as a cottage tent, and in addition to affording the leopard ideal cover gave him all the advantages for launching his next attack.

Robin and I had come very well out of our morning's adventure and it would have been foolish now, armed as I was, to pursue the leopard further, so without more ado we turned about and made for home.

Next morning we were back on the ground. From a very early hour Robin had been agitating to make a start, and, ignoring all the interesting smells the jungle holds in the morning, would have made me do the four miles at a run had that been possible.

I had armed myself with a 450/400, and was in consequence feeling much happier than I had done the previous day. When we were several hundred yards from the lantana bush, I made Robin slow down and advance cautiously, for it is never safe to assume that wounded animal will be found where it has been left hours previously, as the following regrettable incident shows.

A sportsman of my acquaintance wounded a tiger one afternoon, and followed the blood trail for several miles along a valley. Next morning, accompanied by a number of men, one of whom was carrying his empty rifle and leading the way, he set out intending to take up the tracking where he had left off. His way led over the previous day's blood trail, and while still a mile from the spot where the tiger had been left, the leading man, who incidentally was the local *shikari*, walked on to the wounded tiger and was killed. The rest of the party escaped, some by climbing trees and others by showing a clean pair of heels.

I had marked the exact position of the lantana bush, and now took Robin along a line that would pass a few yards on the lee side of it. Robin knew all that was worth knowing about this method of locating the position of an animal by cutting across the wind, and we had only gone a short distance, and were still a hundred yards from the bush, when he stopped, turned and faced into the wind, and communicated to me that he could smell the leopard. As on the previous day, he was facing a fallen tree which was lying along the edge of, and parallel to, the thick undergrowth through which we had followed the leopard to the lantana bush after he had charged us. On our side of the tree the ground was open, but on the far side there was a dense growth of waist-high basonta bushes. Having signalled to Robin to carry on along our original line, we went past the lantana bush, in which he showed no interest, to a channel washed out by rainwater. Here, removing my coat, I filled it with as many stones as the stitches would hold, and with this improvised sack slung over my shoulder returned to the open ground near the tree.

Resuming my coat, and holding the rifle ready for instant use, I took up a position fifteen yards from the tree and started throwing the stones, first on to the tree and then into the bushes on the far side of it with the object of making the leopard— assuming he was still alive—charge on to the open ground where I could deal with him. When all my ammunition was exhausted I coughed, clapped my hands, and shouted, and neither during the bombardment nor after it did the leopard move or make any sound to indicate that he was alive.

I should now have been justified in walking straight up to the tree and looking on the far side of it, but remembering an old jungle saying, 'It is never safe to assume that a leopard is dead until it he has been skinned,' I set out to circle round the tree, intending to reduce the size of the circle until I could see right under the branches and along the whole length of the trunk. I made the radius of the first circle about twenty-five yards, and had gone two-thirds of the way round when Robin stopped. As I looked down to see what had attracted his attention, there was a succession of deep-throated, angry grunts, and the leopard made straight for us. All I could see was the undergrowth being violenty agitated in a direct line towards us, and I only just had time to swing half right and bring the rifle up, when the head and shoulders of the leopard appeared out of the bushes a few feet away.

The leopard's spring and my shot were simultaneous, and side-stepping to the left and leaning back as far as I could I fired the second barrel from my hip into his side as he passed me.

When a wounded animal, be he leopard or tiger, makes a headlong charge and fails to contact he invariably carries on and does not return to the attack until he is again disturbed.

I had side-stepped to the left to avoid crushing Robin, and when I looked down for him now, he was nowhere to be seen. For the first time in all the years we had hunted together we had parted company in a tight corner, and he was now probably trying to find his way home, with very little chance of being able to avoid the many dangers that lay before him in the intervening four miles of jungle. Added to the natural dangers he would have to face in jungle with which, owing to its remoteness from home, he was not familiar, was the weak condition of his heart. And it was therefore with very great misgivings that I turned about to go in search of him; as I did so, I caught sight of his head projecting from behind a tree trunk at the edge of a small clearing only a hundred yards away. When I raised my hand and beckoned, he disappeared into the undergrowth, but a little later, with drooped eyes and drooping ears, he crept silently to my feet. Laying down the rifle I picked him up in my arms and, for the second time in his life, he licked my face—telling me as he did so, with little throaty sounds, how glad he was to find me unhurt, and how terribly ashamed he was of himself for having parted company from me

Our reactions to the sudden and quite unexpected danger that had confronted us were typical of how a canine and a human being act in an emergency, when the danger that threatens is heard, and not seen. In Robin's case it had impelled him to seek safety in silent and rapid retreat; where as in my case it had the effect of gluing my feet to the ground and making retreat—rapid or otherwise—impossible.

When I had satisfied Robin that he was not to blame for our temporary separation, and his small body had stopped trembling, I put him down and together we walked up to where the leopard, who had put up such a game fight, and had so nearly won the last round, was lying dead.

I have told you the story, and while I have been telling it, Robin—the biggest-hearted and the most faithful friend man ever had, has gone to the Happy Hunting Grounds, where I know I shall find him waiting for me.

# THE CHOWGARH TIGERS

## I

The map of Eastern Kumaon that hangs on the wall before me is marked with a number of crosses, and below each cross is a date. These crosses indicate the locality, and the date, of the officially recorded human victims of the man-eating tiger of Chowgarh. There are sixty-four crosses on the map. I do not claim this as being a correct tally, for the map was posted up by me for two years and during this period all kills were not reported to me; further, victims who were only mauled, and who died subsequently, have not been awarded a cross and a date.

The first cross is dated 15 December 1925, and the last, 21 March 1930. The distance between the extreme crosses, north to south, is fifty miles, and east to west, thirty miles, an area of 1,500 square miles of mountain and vale where the snow lies deep during winter, and the valleys are scorching hot in summer. Over this area the Chowgarh tiger had established a reign of terror. Villages of varying size, some with a population of hundred or more, and others with only a small family or two, are scattered

## HUMAN BEINGS KILLED
## BY THE CHOWGARH MAN-EATER

| Village | Number |
|---|---|
| THALI | 1 |
| DEBGURA | 1 |
| BARHON | 2 |
| CHAMOLI | 6 |
| KAHOR | 1 |
| AM | 2 |
| DALKANIA | 7 |
| LOHAR | 8 |
| AGHAURA | 2 |
| PAHARPANI | 1 |
| PADAMPURI | 2 |
| TANDA | 1 |
| NESORIYA | 1 |
| JHANGAON | 1 |
| KABRAGAON | 1 |
| KALA AGAR | 8 |
| RIKHAKOT | 1 |
| MATELA | 3 |
| KUNDAL | 3 |
| BABYAR | 1 |
| KHANSIUN | 1 |
| GARGARI | 1 |
| HAIRAKHAN | 2 |
| UKHALDHUNGA | 1 |
| PAKHARI | 1 |
| DUNGARI | 2 |
| GALNI | 3 |
| **TOTAL** | **64** |

## ANNUAL TOTALS

|  |  |
|---|---|
| 1926 | 15 KILLED |
| 1927 | 9 KILLED |
| 1928 | 14 KILLED |
| 1929 | 17 KILLED |
| 1930 | 9 KILLED |
| **TOTAL** | **64** |

throughout the area. Footpaths, beaten hard by bare feet, connect the villages. Some of these paths pass through thick forests, and when a man-eater renders their passage dangerous, inter-village communication is carried on by shouting. Standing on a commanding point, maybe a big rock or the roof of a house, a man cooees to attract the attention of the people in a neighbouring village, and when the cooee is answered, the message is shouted across in a high-pitched voice. From village to village the message is tossed, and is broadcast throughout large areas in an incredibly short space of time.

It was at a District Conference in February 1929 that I found myself committed to have a try for this tiger. There were at that time three man-eaters in the Kumaon division, and as the Chowgarh tiger had done most damage I promised to go in pursuit of it first.

The map with the crosses and date, furnished to me by the Government, showed that the man-eater was most active in the villages on the north and east face of the Kala Agar ridge. This ridge, some forty miles in length, rises to a height of 8,500 feet and is thickly wooded along the crest. A forest road runs along the north face of the ridge, in some places passing for miles through dense forest of oak and rhododendron, and in others forming a boundary between the forest and cultivated lands. In one place the road forms a loop, and in this loop is situated the Kala Agar Forest Bungalow. This Bungalow was my objective, and after a four days' march, culminating in a stiff climb of 4,000 feet, I arrived at it one evening in April 1929. The last human victim in this area was a young man of twenty-two, who had been killed while out grazing cattle, and while I was having breakfast, the morning after my arrival, the grandmother of the young man came to see me.

She informed me that the man-eater had, without any provocation, killed the only relative she had in the world. After giving me her grandson's history from the day he was born, and extolling his virtues, she pressed me to accept her three milch

buffaloes to use as a bait for the tiger,
saying that if I killed the tiger with
the help of her buffaloes, she would
have the satisfaction of feeling that she
had assisted in avenging her grandson.
These full-grown animals were of no
use to me, but knowing that refusal
to accept them would give offence, I
thanked the old lady and assured her
I would draw on her for bait as soon
as I had used up the four young male
buffaloes I had brought with me from

Naini Tal. The Headmen of the nearby villages had now assembled,
and from them I learned that the tiger had last been seen ten
days previously in a village twenty miles away, on the eastern slope
of the ridge, where it had killed and eaten a man and his wife.

A trail ten days old was not worth following up, and after a
long discussion with the Headmen, I decided to make for Dalkania
village on the eastern side of the ridge. Dalkania is ten miles
from Kala Agar, and about the same distance from the village
where the man and his wife had been killed.

From the number of crosses Dalkania and the villages adjoining
it had earned, it appeared that the tiger had its headquarters in
the vicinity of these villages.

After breakfast next morning I left Kala Agar and followed
the forest road, which I informed would take me to the end of
the ridge, where I should have to leave the road and take a path
two miles downhill to Dalkania. This road, running right to the
end of the ridge through dense forest was very little used, and,
examining it for tracks as I went along, I arrived at the point
where the path took off at about 2 p.m. Here I met a number
of men from Dalkania. They had heard—via the cooee method
of communication—of my intention of camping at their village
and had come up to the ridge to inform me that the tiger had
that morning attacked a party of women, while they had been

cutting their crops in a village ten miles to the north of Dalkania.

The men carrying my camp equipment had done eight miles and were quite willing to carry on, but on learning from the villagers that the path of this village ten miles away was very rough and ran through dense forest, I decided to send my men with the villagers to Dalkania, and visit the scene of tiger's attack alone. My servant immediately set about preparing a substantial meal for me, and at 3 p.m., having fortified myself, I set out on my ten-mile walk. Ten miles under favourable conditions is comfortable two-and-a-half hours' walk, but here the conditions were anything but favourable. The trace running along the east face of the hill wound in and out through deep ravines and was bordered alternately by rocks, dense undergrowth, and trees; and when every obstruction capable of concealing sudden death, in the form of a hungry man-eater, had to be approached with caution, progress was of necessity slow. I was still several miles from my objective when the declining day warned me it was time to call a halt.

In any other area, sleeping under the stars on a bed of dry leaves would have ensured a restful night, but here, to sleep on the ground would have been to court death in a very unpleasant form. Long practice in selecting a suitable tree, and the ability to dispose myself comfortably in it, has made sleeping up aloft a simple matter. On this occasion I selected an oak tree, and, with the rifle tied securely to a branch, had been asleep for some hours when I was awakened by the rustling of several animals under the tree. The sound moved on, and presently I heard the scraping of claws on bark and realized that a family of bears were climbing some karphal[1] trees I had noticed growing a little way down the hill side. Bears are very quarrelsome when feeding, and sleep was impossible until they had eaten their fill and moved on.

[1]*Karphal* is found on our hills at an elevation of 6,000 feet. The tree grows to a height of about forty feet and produces a small red and very sweet berry, which is greatly fancied by both human beings and bears.

The sun had been up a couple of hours when I arrived at the village, which consisted of two huts and a cattle-shed, in a clearing of five acres surrounded by forest. The small community was in a state of terror and was overjoyed to see me. The wheatfield, a few yards from the huts, where the tiger, with belly to ground, had been detected only just in time, stalking the three women cutting the crop, was eagerly pointed out to me. The man who had seen the tiger, and given the alarm, told me that the tiger had retreated into the jungle, where it had been joined by a second tiger, and that the two animals had gone down the hill side into the valley below. The occupants of the two huts had no sleep, for the tigers, baulked of their prey, had called at short intervals throughout the night, and had only ceased calling a little before my arrival. This statement, that there were two tigers, confirmed the reports I had already received that the man-eater was accompanied by a full-grown cub.

Our hill folks are very hospitable, and when the villagers learned that I spent the night in the jungle, and that my camp was at Dalkania, they offered to prepare a meal for me. This I knew would strain the resources of the small community, so I asked for a dish of tea, but as there was no tea in the village I was given a drink of fresh milk sweetened to excess with jaggery, a very satisfying and not unpleasant drink—when one gets used to it. At the request of my hosts I mounted guard while the remaining portion of the wheat crop was cut; and at midday, taking the good wishes of the people with me, I went down into the valley in the direction in which the tigers had been heard calling.

The valley, starting from the watershed of the three rivers Ladhya, Nandhour and Eastern Goula, runs south-west for twenty miles and is densely wooded. Tracking was impossible, and my only hope of seeing the tigers was to attract them to myself, or helped by the jungle folk to stalk them.

To those of you who may be inclined to indulge in the sport of man-eater hunting on foot, it will be of interest to know that the birds and animals of the jungle, and the four winds of heaven, play a very important part in this form of sport. This is not the place to give the name of the jungle folk on whose alarm-calls the sportsman depends, to a great extent, for his safety and knowledge of his quarry's movements; for in a country in which a walk up or downhill of three or four miles might mean a difference in altitude of as much as a thousand feet, the variation in fauna, in a well-stocked area, is considerable. The wind, however, at all altitudes, remains a constant factor, and a few words relevant to its importance in connexion with man-eater hunting on foot will not be out of place.

Tigers do not know that human beings have no sense of smell, and when a tiger becomes a man-eater it treats human beings exactly as it treats wild animals, that is, it approaches its victims up-wind, or lies up in wait for them down-wind.

The significance of this will be apparent when it is realized that while the sportsman is trying to spot the tiger, the tiger is in all probability trying to stalk the sportsman, or is lying up in wait for him. This contest, owing to the tiger's height, colouring, and ability to move without making a sound, would be very unequal were it not for the wind-factor operating in favour of the sportsman.

In all cases where killing is done by stalking or stealth, the victim is approached from behind. This being so, it would be suicidal for the sportsman to enter the dense jungle in which he had every reason to believe a man-eater was lurking, unless he was capable of making full use of the currents of air. For example, assuming that the sportsman has to proceed, owing to the nature of the ground, in the direction from which the wind is blowing, the danger would lie behind him, where he would be least able to deal with it, but by frequently tracking across the wind he could keep the danger alternately to right and left of him. In print this scheme may not appear very attractive, but in practice it works; and, short of walking backwards, I do not know of a better or safer method of going up-wind through dense cover in which a hungry man-eater is lurking.

By evening I had reached the upper end of the valley, without having seen the tigers and without having received any indication from bird or animal of their presence in the jungle. The only habitation then in sight was a cattle-shed, high up on the north side of the valley.

I was careful in the selection of a tree on this second night, and was rewarded by an undisturbed night's rest. Not long after dark the tigers called, and a few minutes later two shots from a muzzle-loader came echoing down the valley, followed by a lot of shouting from the graziers at the cattle station. Thereafter the night was silent.

By the afternoon of the following day I had explored every bit of the valley, and I was making my way up a grassy slope intent on rejoining my men at Dalkania when I heard a long-drawn-out cooee from the direction of the cattle-shed. The cooee was repeated once and again, and on my sending back an answering call I saw a man climb on a projecting rock, and from this vantage point he shouted across the valley to ask if I was the *sahib* who had come from Naini Tal to shoot the man-eater. On my telling him I was that *sahib*, he informed me that his cattle had stampeded out of a ravine on my side of the valley at about midday, and that when he counted them on arrival at the cattle station he found that one—a white cow—was missing.

He suspected that the cow had been killed by the tigers he had heard calling the previous night, half a mile to the west of where I was standing. Thanking him for his information, I set off to investigate the ravine. I had gone but a short distance along the edge of the ravine when I came on the tracks of the stampeding cattle, and following these tracks back I had no difficult in finding the spot where the cow had been killed. After killing the cow the tigers had taken it down the steep hillside into the ravine. An approach along the drag was not advisable, so

going down into the valley I made a wide detour, and approached the spot where I expected the kill to be from the other side of the ravine. This side of the ravine was less steep than the side down which the kill had been taken, and was deep in young bracken—ideal ground for stalking over. Step by step, and as silently as a shadow, I made my way through the bracken, which reached above my waist, and when I was some thirty yards from the bed of the ravine a movement in front of me caught my eye. A white leg was suddenly thrust up into the air and violently agitated, and the next moment there was a deep-throated growl— the tigers were on the kill and were having a difference of opinion over some toothful morsel.

For several minutes I stood perfectly still; the leg continued to be agitated, but the growl was not repeated. A nearer approach was not advisable, for even if I succeeded in covering the thirty yards without being seen, and managed to kill one of the tigers, the other, as likely as not, would blunder into me, and the ground I was on would give me no chance of defending myself. Twenty yards to my left front, and about the same distance from the tigers, there was an outcrop of rock, some ten to fifteen feet high. If I could reach this rock without being seen, I should in all probability get an easy shot at the tigers. Dropping on hands and knees, and pushing the rifle before me, I crawled through the bracken to the shelter of the rocks, paused a minute to regain my breath and make quite sure the rifle was loaded, and then climbed the rock. When my eyes were level with the top, I looked over, and saw the two tigers.

One was eating at the hind quarters of the cow, while the other was lying nearby licking its paws. Both tigers appeared to be about the same size, but the one that was licking its paws was several shades lighter than the other, and concluding that her light colouring was due to age and that she was the old man-eater, I aligned the sights very carefully on her, and fired. At my shot she reared up and fell backwards, while the other bounded down the ravine and was out of sight before I could press the second trigger. The tiger I had shot did not move again, and after pelting it with stones to make sure it was dead, I approached and met with a great disappointment: for a glance at close quarters showed me I had make a mistake and shot the cub—a mistake that during the ensuing twelve months cost the district fifteen lives and incidentally nearly cost me my own life.

Disappointment was to a certain extent mitigated by the thought that this young tigress, even if she had not actually killed any human beings herself, had probably assisted her old mother to kill (this assumption I later found to be correct), and in any case, having been nurtured on human flesh she could—to salve my feelings—be classified as a potential man-eater.

Skinning a tiger with assistance on open ground and with the requisite appliances is an easy job, but here the job was anything but easy, for I was alone, surrounded by thick cover, and my only appliance was a penknife; and though there was no actual danger to be apprehended from the man-eater, for tigers never kill in excess of their requirements, there was the uneasy feeling in the back of my mind that the tiger had returned and was watching my every movement.

The sun was near setting before the arduous task was completed, and as I should have to spend yet another night in the jungles I decided to remain where I was. The tigress was a very old animal, as I could see from her pugmarks, and having lived all her life in a district in which there are nearly as many fire-arms as men to use them, had nothing to learn about men and their ways. Even so, there was just a chance that she might return to the kill some time during the night, and remain in the vicinity until light came in the morning.

My selection of a tree was of necessity limited, and the one I spent that night in proved, by morning, to be the most uncomfortable tree I have ever spent twelve hours in. The tigress called at intervals throughout the night, and as morning drew near the calling became fainter and fainter, and eventually died away on the ridge above me.

Cramped, and stiff, and hungry—I had been without food for sixty hours—and with my clothes clinging to me—it had rained for an hour during the night—I descended from the tree when objects were clearly visible, and, after tying the tiger's skin up in a coat, set off for Dalkania.

I have never weighed a tiger's skin when green, and if the skin, plus the head and paws, which I carried for fifteen miles that day weighed 40 pounds at the start, I would have taken my oath it weighed 200 pounds before I reached my destination.

In a courtyard, flagged with great slabs of blue slate, and common to a dozen houses, I found my men in conference with a hundred or more villagers. My approach, along a yard-wide lane between two houses, had not been observed, and the welcome I received when, bedraggled and covered with blood, I staggered into the circle of squatting men will live in my memory as long as memory lasts.

My 40-lb. tent had been pitched in a field of stubble a hundred yards from the village, and I had hardly reached it before tea

was laid out for me on a table improvised
out of a couple of suitcases and planks
borrowed from the village. I was
told later by the villagers that
my men, who had been
with me for years and
had accompanied me on
several similar expeditions,
refusing to believe that
the man-eater had claimed me as a victim, had kept a
kettle on the boil night and day in anticipation of my return,
and, further, had stoutly opposed the Headmen of Dalkania and
the adjoining villages sending a report to Almora and Naini Tal
that I was missing.

A hot bath, taken of necessity in the open and in full view
of the village—I was too dirty and too tired to care who saw
me—was followed by an ample dinner, and I was thinking of
turning in for the night when a flash of lightning succeeded by
a loud peal of thunder heralded the approach of a storm. Tent-
pegs are of little use in a field, so long stakes were hurriedly
procured and securely driven into the ground, and to these stakes
the tent-ropes were tied. For further safety all the available ropes
in camp were criss-crossed over the tent and lashed to the stakes.
The storm of wind and rain lasted an hour and was one of the
worst the little tent had ever weathered. Several of the guy-ropes
were torn from the canvas, but the stakes and criss-cross ropes
held. Most of my things were soaked through, and a little stream
several inches deep was running from end to end of the tent;
my bed, however, was comparatively dry, and by 10 o'clock my
men were safely lodged behind locked doors in the house the
villagers had placed at their disposal, while I, with a loaded rifle
for company, settled down to a sleep which lasted for twelve hours.

The following day was occupied in drying my kit and in
cleaning and pegging out the tiger's skin. While these operations
were in progress the villagers, who had taken a holiday from their

field work, crowded round to hear my experiences and to tell me theirs. Every man present had lost one or more relatives, and several bore tooth and claw marks, inflicted by the man-eater, which they will carry to their graves. My regret at having lost an opportunity of killing the man-eater was not endorsed by the assembled men. True, there had originally been only one man-eater; but, of recent months, rescue parties who had gone out to recover the remains of human victims had found two tigers on the kill, and only a fortnight previously a man and his wife had been killed simultaneously, which was proof sufficient for them that both tigers were established man-eaters.

My tent was on a spur of the hill, and commanded an extensive view. Immediately below me was the valley of the Nandhour river, with a hill, devoid of any cultivation, rising to a height of 9,000 feet on the far side. As I sat on the edge of the terraced fields that evening with a pair of good binoculars in my hand and the Government map spread out beside me, the villagers pointed out the exact positions where twenty human beings had been killed during the past three years. These kills were more or less evenly distributed over an area of forty square miles.

The forests in this area were open to grazing, and on the cattle-paths leading to them I decided to tie up my four young buffaloes.

During the following ten days no news was received of the tigress, and I spent the time in visiting the buffaloes in the morning, searching the forests in the day, and tying out the buffaloes in the evening. On the eleventh day my hopes were raised by the report that a cow had been killed on a ravine on the hill above my tent. A visit to the kill, however, satisfied me the cow had been killed by an old leopard, whose pugmarks I had repeatedly seen. The villagers complained that the leopard had for several years been taking heavy toll of their cattle and goats, so I decided to sit up for him. A shallow cave close to the dead cow gave me the cover I needed. I had not been long in the cave when I caught sight of the leopard coming down the opposite side of the ravine, and I was raising my rifle for a shot when I heard a very agitated voice from the direction of the village calling to me.

There could be but one reason for this urgent call, and grabbing up my hat I dashed out of the cave, much to the consternation of the leopard, who first flattened himself out on the ground, and then with an angry woof went bounding back the way he had come, while I scrambled up my side of the ravine; and, arriving at the top, shouted to the man that I was coming, and set off at top speed to join him.

The man had run all the way uphill from the village, and when he regained his breath he informed me that a women had just been killed by the man-eater, about half a mile on the far side of the village. As we ran down the hillside I saw a crowd of people collected in the courtyard already alluded to. Once again my approach through the narrow lane was not observed, and looking over the heads of the assembled men, I saw a girl sitting on the ground.

The upper part of her clothing had been torn off her young body, and with head thrown back and hands resting on the ground behind to support her, she sat without sound or movement, other than the heaving up and down of her breast, in the hollow of which the blood, that was flowing down her face and neck, was collecting in a sticky congealed mass.

My presence was soon detected and a way made for me to approach the girl. While I was examining her wounds, a score of people, all talking at the same time, informed me that the attack on the girl had been made on comparatively open ground in full view of a number of people including the girl's husband; that alarmed at their combined shouts the tiger had left the girl and gone off in the direction of the forest; that leaving the girl for dead where she had fallen, her companions had run back to the village to inform me; that subsequently the girl had regained consciousness and returned to the village; that she would without doubt die of her injuries in a few minutes; and that they would then carry her back to the scene of the attack, and I could sit up over the corpse and shoot the tiger.

While this information was being imparted to me the girl's eyes never left my face and followed my every movement with the liquid pleading gaze of a wounded and frightened animal. Room to move unhampered, quiet to collect my wits, and clean air for the girl to breathe were necessary, and I am afraid the methods I employed to gain them were not as gentle as they might have been. When the last of the men had left in a hurry, I set the women, who up to now had remained in the background, to warming water and to tearing my shirt, which was comparatively clean and dry, into bandages, while one girl, who appeared to be on the point of getting hysterics, was bundled off to scour the village for a pair of scissors. The water and bandages were ready before the girl I had sent for the scissors returned with the only pair, she said, the village could produce. They had been found in the house of a tailor, long since dead, and had been used by the widow for digging up potatoes. The rusty blades, some eight inches long, could not be made to meet at any point, and after a vain attempt I decided to leave the thick coils of blood-caked hair alone.

The major wounds consisted of two claw cuts, one starting between the eyes and extending right over the head and down to the nape of the neck, leaving the scalp hanging in two halves, and the other, starting near the first, running across the forehead up to the right ear. In addition to these ugly gaping wounds there were a number of deep scratches on the right breast, right shoulder and neck, and one deep cut on the back of the right hand, evidently inflicted when the girl had put up her hand in a vain attempt to shield her head.

A doctor friend whom I had once taken out tiger-shooting on foot had, on our return after an exciting morning, presented me with a two-ounce bottle of yellow fluid which he advised me to carry whenever I went out shooting. I had carried the bottle in the inner pocket of my shooting jacket for over a year and a portion of the fluid had evaporated; but the bottle was still three-parts full, and after I had washed the girl's head and body I knocked the neck off the bottle and poured the contents, to the last drop, into the wounds. This done I bandaged the head, to try to keep the scalp in position, and then picked up the girl and carried her to her home—a single room combining living quarters, a kitchen and a nursery—with the women following behind.

Slung from a rafter near the door was an open basket, the occupant of which was now clamouring to be fed. This was a complication with which I could not deal, so I left the solution of it to the assembled women. Ten days later, when on the eve of my departure I visited the girl for the last time, I found her sitting on the doorstep of her home with the baby asleep in her lap.

Her wounds, except for a sore at the nape of her neck where the tiger's claws had sunk deepest into the flesh, were all healed, and when parting her great wealth of raven-black hair to show me where the scalp had made a perfect join, she said, with a smile, that she was very glad her young sister had—quite by mistake—borrowed the wrong pair of scissors from the tailor's widow (for a shorn head here is the sign of widowhood). If these lines should ever be read by my friend, the doctor, I should like him to know that the little bottle of yellow fluid he so thoughtfully provided for me, saved the life of a very brave young mother.

While I had been attending to the girl my men had procured a goat. Following back the blood trail made by the girl I found the spot where the attack had taken place, and tying the goat to a bush I climbed into a stunted oak, the only tree in the vicinity, and prepared for an all-night vigil. Sleep, even in snatches, was not possible for my seat was only a few feet from the ground, and the tigress was still without her dinner. However, I neither saw nor heard anything throughout the night.

On examining the ground in the morning—I had not had time to do this the previous evening—I found that the tigress, after attacking the girl, had gone up the valley for half a mile to where a cattle track crossed the Nandhour river. This track it had followed for two miles, to its junction with the forest road on the ridge above Dalkania. Here on the hard ground I lost the tracks.

For two days the people in all the surrounding villages kept as close to their habitations as the want of sanitary conveniences permitted, and then on the third day news was brought to me by tour runners that the man-eater had claimed a victim at Lohali, a village five miles to the south of Dalkania. The runners stated that the distance by the forest road was ten miles, but only five by a short cut by which they proposed taking me back. My preparations were soon made, and a little after midday I set off with my four guides.

A very stiff climb of two miles brought us to the crest of the long ridge south of Dalkania and in view of the valley three miles below, where the 'kill' was reported to have taken place. My guides could give me no particulars. They lived in a small village a mile on the near side of Lohali, and at 10 a.m. a message had come to them—in the manner already described—that a woman of Lohali had been killed by the man-eater, and they were instructed to convey this information to me at Dalkania.

The top of the hill on which we were standing was bare of trees, and, while I regained my breath and had a smoke, my companions pointed out the landmarks. Close to where we were resting, and under the shelter of a great rock, there was a small ruined hut, with a circular thorn enclosure nearby. Questioned about this hut, the men told me the following story. Four years previously a Bhutia (a man from across the border), who had all the winter been sending packages of *gur*, salt, and other commodities from the bazaars at the foot-hills into the interior of the district, had built the hut with the object of resting and fattening his flock of goats through the summer and rains, and getting them fit for the next winter's work. After a few weeks the goats wandered down the hill and damaged my informants' crops, and when they came up to lodge a protest, they found the hut empty, and the fierce sheep-dog these men invariably keep with them to guard their camps at night, chained to an iron stake and dead. Foul play was suspected, and next day men were collected from adjoining villages and a search organized. Pointing to an oak tree scored by lightning and distant some four hundred yards, my informants said that under it the remains of the man—his skull and a few splinters of bone—and his clothes had been found. This was the Chowgarh man-eater's first human victim.

There was no way of descending the precipitous hill from where we were sitting, and the men informed me we should have to proceed half a mile along the ridge to where we should find a very steep and rough track which would take us straight down, past their village, to Lohali, which we could see in the valley below. We had covered about half the distance we had to go along the ridge, when all at once, and without being able to ascribe any reason for it, I felt we were being followed. Arguing with myself against this feeling was of no avail; there was only one man-eater in all this area and she had procured a kill three miles away which she was not likely to leave. However, the uneasy feeling persisted, and as we were now at the widest part of the grassy ridge I made the men sit down, instructing them not to move until I returned and myself set out on a tour of investigation. Retracing my steps to where we had first come out on the ridge, I entered the jungle and carefully worked round the open ground and back to where the men were sitting. No alarm-call of animal or bird indicated that a tiger was anywhere in the vicinity, but from there on I made the four men walk in front of me, while I brought up the rear, with thumb on safety-catch and a constant lookout behind.

When we arrived at the little village my companions had started from, they asked for permission to leave me. I was very glad of this request, for I had a mile of dense scrub jungle to go through, and though the feeling that I was being followed had long since left me, I felt safer and more comfortable with only my own life to guard. A little below the outlying terraced fields, and where the dense scrub started, there was a crystal-clear spring of water, from which the village drew its water-supply. Here in the soft wet ground I found the fresh pugmarks of the man-eater.

These pugmarks, coming from the direction of the village I was making for, coupled with the uneasy feeling I had experienced on the ridge above, convinced me that something had gone wrong with the 'kill' and that my quest would be fruitless. As I emerged from the scrub jungle I came in view of Lohali, which consisted of five or six small houses. Near the door of one of these houses a group of people were collected.

My approach over the steep open ground and narrow terraced fields was observed, and a few men detached themselves from the group near the door and advanced to meet me. One of the number, on old man, bent down to touch my feet, and with tears streaming down his cheeks implored me to save the life of his daughter. His story was as short as it was tragic. His daughter, who was a widow and the only relative he had in the world, had gone out at about ten o'clock to collect dry sticks with which to cook their midday meal. A small stream flows through the valley, and on the far side of the stream from the village the hill goes steeply up. On the lower slope of this hill there are a few terraced fields. At the edge of the lowest field, and distant about 150 yards from the home, the woman had started to collect sticks. A little later, some women who were washing their clothes in the stream heard a scream, and on looking up saw the woman and a tiger disappearing together into the dense thorn bushes, which extended from the edge of the field right down to the stream. Dashing back to the village, the women raised an alarm. The frightened villagers made no attempt at a rescue, and a message for help was shouted to a village higher up the valley, from where it was tossed back to the village from which the four men had set out to find me. Half an hour after the message had been sent, the wounded woman crawled home. Her story was that she had seen the tiger just as it was about to spring on her, and as there was no time to run, she had jumped down the almost perpendicular hillside and while she was in the air the tiger had caught her and they had gone down the hill together. She remembered nothing further until she regained consciousness and found herself near the stream; and being unable to call for help, she had crawled back to the village on her hands and knees.

We had reached the door of the house while this tale was being told. Making the people stand back from the door—the only opening in the four walls of the room—I drew the blood-stained sheet off the woman, whose pitiful condition I am not going to attempt to describe. Had I been a qualified doctor, armed with modern appliances, instead of just a mere man with a little permanganate of potash in his pocket, I do not think it would have been possible to have saved the woman's life; for the deep tooth and claw wounds in her face, neck, and other parts of her body had, in that hot unventilated room, already turned septic. Mercifully she was only semi-conscious. The old father had followed me into the room, and, more for his satisfaction than for any good I thought it would do, I washed the caked blood from the woman's head and body, and cleaned out the wounds as best I could with my handkerchief and a strong solution of permanganate.

It was now too late to think of returning to my camp, and a place would have to be found in which to pass the night. A little way up the stream, and not far from where the women had been washing their clothes, there was a giant *pipal* tree, with a foot-high masonry platform round it used by the villagers for religious ceremonies.

I undressed on the platform and bathed in the stream; and when the wind had carried out the functions of a towel, dressed again, put my back to the tree and, laying the loaded rifle by my side, prepared to see the night out. Admittedly it was an unsuitable place in which to spend the night, but any place was preferable to the village, and that dark room, with its hot fetid atmosphere and swarm of buzzing flies, where a woman in torment fought desperately for breath.

During the night the wailing of women announced that the sufferer's troubles were over, and when I passed through the village at day break preparations for the funeral were well advanced.

From the experience of this unfortunate woman, and that of the girl at Dalkania, it was now evident that the old tigress had depended, to a very great extent, on her cub to kill the human beings she attacked. Usually only one out of every hundred people attacked by man-eating tigers escapes, but in the case of this man-eater it was apparent that more people would be mauled than killed outright, and as the nearest hospital was fifty miles away, when I returned to Naini Tal I appealed to Government to send a supply of disinfectants and dressings to all the headmen of villages in the area in which the man-eater was operating. On my subsequent visit I was glad to learn that the request had been complied with, and that the disinfectants had saved the lives of a number of people.

I stayed a Dalkania for another week and announced on a Saturday that I would leave for home the following Monday. I had now been in the man-eater's domain for close on a month, and the constant strain of sleeping in an open tent, and of walking endless miles during the day with the prospect of every step being the last, was beginning to tell on my nerves. The villagers received my announcement with consternation, and only desisted from trying to make me change my decision when I promised them I would return at the first opportunity.

After breakfast on Sunday morning the Headman of Dalkania paid me a visit and requested me to shoot them some game before I left. The request was gladly acceded to, and half an hour later, accompanied by four villagers and one of my own men, and armed with a 275 rifle and a clip of cartridges, I set off for the hill on the far side of the Nandhour river, on the

upper slopes of which I had, from my camp, frequently seen *ghooral* feeding.

One of the villagers accompanying me was a tall gaunt man with a terribly disfigured face. He had been a constant visitor to my camp, and finding in me a good listener had told and retold his encounter with the man-eater so often that I could, without effort, repeat the whole story in my sleep. The encounter had taken place four years previously and is best told in his own words.

'Do you see that pine tree, *sahib*, at the bottom of the grassy slope on the shoulder of the hill? Yes, the pine tree with a big white rock to the east of it. Well, it was at the upper edge of the grassy slope that the man-eater attacked me. The grassy slope is as perpendicular as the wall of a house, and none but a hillman could find foothold on it. My son, who was eight years of age at the time, and I had cut grass on that slope on the day of my misfortune, carrying the grass up in armfuls to the belt of trees where the ground is level.

'I was stooping down at the very edge of the slope, tying the grass into a big bundle, when the tiger sprang at me and buried its teeth, one under my right eye, one in my chin and the other two here at the back of my neck. The tiger's mouth struck me with a great blow and I fell over on my back, while the tiger lay on top of me chest to chest, with its stomach between my legs. When falling backwards I had flung out my arms and my right hand had come in contact with an oak sapling. As my fingers grasped the sapling, an idea came to me. My legs were free, and if I could draw them up and insert my feet under and against the tiger's belly, I might be able to push the tiger off, and run away. The pain, as the tiger crushed all the bones on the right side of my face, was terrible; but I did not lose consciousness, for you see, *sahib*, at that time I was a young man, and in all the hills there was no one to compare with me in strength. Very slowly, so as not to anger the tiger, I drew my legs up on either side of it, and gently inserted my bare feet against its belly. Then placing my left hand against its chest and pushing and kicking upwards with all my might, I lifted the tiger right off the ground and, we being on the very edge of the perpendicular hillside, the tiger went crashing down and belike would have taken me with him, had my hold on the sapling not been a good one.

'My son had been too frightened to run away, and when the tiger had gone, I took his loincloth from him and wrapped it round my head, and holding his hand I walked back to the village. Arrived at my home I told my wife to call all my friends together, for I wished to see their faces before I died. When my friends were assembled and saw my condition, they wanted to put me on a *charpoy* and carry me fifty miles to the Almora hospital, but this I would not consent to; for my suffering was great, and being sure that my time had come I wanted to die where I had been born, and where I had lived all my life. Water was brought, for I was thirsty and my head was on fire, but when it was poured into my mouth, it all flowed out through the holes in my neck. Thereafter, for a period beyond measure, there was great confusion in my mind, and much pain in my head and in my neck, and while I waited and longed for death to end my sufferings, my wounds healed of themselves, and I became well.

'And now, *sahib*, I am as you see me, old and thin, and with white hair, and a face that no man can look on without repulsion. My enemy lives and continues to claim victims but do not be deceived into thinking it is a tiger, for it is no tiger but an evil spirit, who, when it craves for human flesh and blood, takes on for a little while the semblance of a tiger. But they say you are a *sadhu*, *sahib*, and the spirits that guard *sadhus* are more powerful than this evil spirit, as is proved by the fact that you spent three days and three nights alone in the jungle, and came out—as your men said you would—alive and unhurt.'

Looking at the great frame of the man, it was easy to picture him as having been a veritable giant. And a giant in strength he must have been, for no man, unless he had been endowed with strength far above the average, could have lifted the tigress into the air, torn its hold from the side of his head, carrying away, as it did, half his face with it, and hurled it down the precipitous hill.

My gaunt friend constituted himself our guide, and with a beautifully polished axe, with a long tapering handle, over his shoulder, led us by devious steep paths to the valley below. Fording the Nandhour river, we crossed several wide terraced fields, now out of cultivation for fear of the man-eater, and on reaching the foot of the hill started, what proved to be a very stiff climb, through forest, to the grass slopes above. Gaunt my friend may have been, but he lacked nothing in wind, and tough as I was it was only by calling frequent halts—to admire the view—that I was able to keep up with him.

Emerging from the tree forest, we went diagonally across the grassy slope, in the direction of a rock cliff that extended upwards for a thousand feet or more. It was on this cliff, sprinkled over with tufts of short grass, that I had seen *ghooral* feeding from my tent. We had covered a few hundred yards when one of these small mountain-goats started up out of a ravine, and at my shot crumpled up and slipped back out of sight. Alarmed by the report of the rifles, another *ghooral*, that had evidently been lying asleep at the foot of the cliff, sprang to his feet and went up the rock face, as only he or his big brother the tahr could have done.

As he climbed upwards, I lay down and, putting the sight to 200 yards, waited for him to stop. This he presently did, coming out on a projecting rock to look down on us. At my shot he staggered, regained his footing, and very slowly continued his climb. At the second shot he fell, hung for a second or two on a narrow ledge, and then fell through space to the grassy slope from whence he had started. Striking the ground he rolled over and over, passing within a hundred yards of us, and eventually came to rest on a cattle track a hundred and fifty yards below.

I have only once, in all the three years I have been shooting, witnessed a similar sight to the one we saw during the next few minutes, and on that occasion the marauder was a leopard.

The *ghooral* had hardly come to rest when a big Himalayan bear came lumbering out of a ravine on the side of the grassy slope and, with never a pause or backward look, came at a fast trot along the cattle track. On reaching the dead goat he sat down and took it into his lap, and as he started nosing the goat, I fired. Maybe I hurried over my shot, or allowed too much for refraction; anyway the bullet went low and struck the bear in the stomach instead of in the chest. To the six of us who were intently watching, it appeared that the bear took the smack of the bullet as an assault from the *ghooral*, for, rearing up, he flung the animal from him and came galloping along the track, emitting angry grunts. As he passed a hundred yards below us I fired my fifth and last cartridge, the bullet, as I found later, going through the fleshy part of his hind quarters.

While the man retrieved the two *ghooral* I descended to examine the blood trail. The blood on the track showed the bear to be hard hit, but even so there was danger in following it up with an empty rifle, for bears are bad tempered at the best of times, and are very ugly customers to deal with when wounded.

When the men rejoined me a short council of war was held. Camp was three and a half miles away, and as it was now 2 p.m. it would not be possible to fetch more ammunition, track down and kill the bear, and get back home by dark; so it was unanimously decided that we should follow up the wounded animal and try to finish it off with stones and the axe.

The hill was steep and fairly free of undergrowth, and by keeping above the bear there was a sporting chance of our being able to accomplish our task without serious mishap. We accordingly set off, I leading the way, followed by three men, the rear being brought up by two men each with a *ghooral* strapped to his back. Arrived at the spot where I had fired my last shot, additional blood on the track greatly encouraged us. Two hundred yards further on, the blood trail led down into a deep ravine. Here we divided up our force, two men crossing to the far side, the owner of the axe and I remaining on the near side, with the men carrying the *ghooral* following in our rear. On the word being given we started to advance down the hill. In the bed of the ravine, and fifty feet below us, was a dense patch of stunted bamboo, and when a stone was thrown into this thicket, the bear got up with a scream of rage; and six men, putting their best foot foremost, went straight up the hill. I was not trained to this form of exercise, and on looking back to see if the bear was gaining in us, I saw, much to my relief, that he was going as hard downhill as we were going uphill. A shout to my companions, a rapid change of direction, and we were off in a full cry and rapidly gaining on our quarry. A few well-aimed shots had been registered, followed by delighted shouts from the marksmen, and angry grunts from the bear, when at a sharp bend in the ravine, which necessitated a cautious advance, we lost touch with the bear. To have followed the blood trail would have been easy, but here the ravine was full of big rocks, behind any of which the bear might have been lurking, so while the encumbered men sat down for a rest, a cast was made on either side of the ravine. While my companion went forward to look down into the ravine, I went to the right to prospect a rocky cliff that went sheer down for some two hundred feet. Holding on to a tree for support, I leaned over and saw the bear lying on a narrow ledge forty feet immediately below me. I picked up a stone, about thirty pounds in weight, and, again advancing to the edge and in imminent danger of going over myself, I raised the stone above my head with both hands and hurled it.

The stone struck the ledge a few inches from the bear's head, and scrambling to his feet he disappeared from sight, to reappear a minute later on the side of the hill. Once again the hunt was on. The ground was here more open and less encumbered with rocks, and the four of us who were running light had no difficulty in keeping up with him. For a mile or more we ran him at top speed, until we eventually cleared the forest and emerged on to the terraced fields. Rainwater had cut several deep and narrow channels across the fields, and in one of these channels the bear took cover.

The man with the distorted face was the only armed member of the party and he was unanimously elected executioner. Nothing loth, he cautiously approached the bear and, swinging his beautifully polished axe aloft, brought the square head down on the bear's skull. The result was as alarming as it was unexpected. The axe-head rebounded off the bear's skull as though it had been struck on a block of rubber, and with a scream of rage the animal reared up on his hind legs. Fortunately he did not follow up his advantage, for we were bunched together, and in trying to run got in each other's way.

The bear did not appear to like this open ground, and after going a short way down the channel again took cover. It was now my turn with the axe. The bear, however, having once been struck resented my approach, and it was only after a great deal of manoeuvring that I eventually got within striking distance. It has been my ambition when a boy to be a lumber-man in Canada, and I had attained sufficient proficiency with an axe to split a match-stick. I had no fear, therefore, as the owner had, of the axe glancing of and getting damaged on the stones, and the moment

I got within reach I buried the entire blade in the bear's skull.

Himalayan bearskins are very greatly prized by our hill folk, and the owner of the axe was a very proud and envied man when I told him he could have the skin in addition to a double share of the *ghooral* meat. Leaving the men, whose numbers were being rapidly augmented by new arrivals from the village, to skin and divide up the bag, I climbed up to the village and paid, as already related, a last visit to the injured girl. The day had been a strenuous one, and if the man-eater had paid me a visit that night she would have 'caught me napping'.

On the road I had taken when coming to Dalkania there was several long stiff climbs up treeless hills, and when I mentioned the discomforts of this road to the villagers they had suggested that I should go back via Haira Khan. This route would necessitate only one climb to the ridge above the village, from where it was downhill all the way to Ranibagh, whence I could complete the journey to Naini Tal by car.

I had warned my men overnight to prepare for an early start, and a little before sunrise, leaving them to pack up and follow me, I said good-bye to my friends at Dalkania, and started on the two-mile climb to the forest road on the ridge above. The footpath I took was not the one by which my men, and later I, had arrived to Dalkania, but was one the villagers used when going to, and returning from, the bazaars in the foot-hills.

The path wound in and out of deep ravines, through thick oak and pine forests and dense undergrowth. There had been no news of the tigress for a week. This absence of news made me all the more careful, and an hour after leaving camp I arrived without mishap at an open glade near the top of the hill, within a hundred yards of the forest road.

The glade was pear-shaped, roughly a hundred yards long and fifty yards wide, with a stagnant pool of rainwater in the centre of it. *Sambhar* and other game used this pool as a drinking place and to wallow and, curious to see the tracks round it, I left the path, which skirted the left-hand side of the glade and passed close under a cliff of rock which extended up to the road. As I approached the pool I saw the pugmarks of the tigress in the soft earth at the edge of the water. She had approached the pool from the same direction as I had, and, evidently disturbed by me, had crossed the water and gone into the dense tree and scrub jungle on the right-hand side of the glade. A great chance lost, for had I kept as careful a lookout in front as I had behind I should have seen her before she saw me. However, though I had missed a chance, the advantages were now all on my side and distinctly in my favour.

The tigress had seen me, or she would not have crossed the pool and hurried for shelter, as her tracks showed she had done. Having seen me she had also seen that I was alone, and watching me from cover as she undoubtedly was, she would assume I was going to the pool to drink as she had done. My movements up to this point had been quite natural, and if I could continue to make her think I was unaware of her presence, she would possibly give me a second chance. Stooping down and keeping a very sharp lookout from under my hat, I coughed several times, splashed the water about, and then, moving very slowly and gathering dry sticks on the way, I went to the foot of the steep rock. Here I built a small fire, and resting my back against the rock, lit a cigarette. By the time the cigarette had been smoked the fire had burnt out. I then lay down, and pillowing my head on my left arm placed the rifle on the ground with my finger on the trigger.

The rock above me was too steep for any animal to find foothold on. I had therefore only my front to guard, and as the heavy cover nowhere approached to within less than twenty yards of my position I was quite safe. I had all this time neither seen nor heard anything; nevertheless, I was convinced that the tigress was watching me. The rim of my hat, while effectually shading my eyes, did not obstruct my vision and inch by inch I scanned every bit of the jungle with in my range of view. There was not a breath of wind blowing, and not a leaf or a blade of grass stirred. My men, whom I had instructed to keep close together and sing from the time they left camp until they joined me on the forest road, were not due for an hour and a half, and during this time it was more than likely that the tigress would break cover and try to stalk, or rush, me.

There are occasions when time drags, and others when it flies. My left arm, on which my head was pillowed, had long since ceased to prick and had gone dead, but even so the singing of the men in the valley below reached me all too soon. The voices grew louder, and presently I caught sight of the men as they rounded a sharp bend. It was possibly at this bend that the tigress had seen me as she turned round to retrace her steps after having her drink. Another failure, and the last chance on this trip gone.

After my men had rested we climbed up to the road, and set off on what proved to be a very long twenty-mile march to the Forest Rest House at Haira Khan. After going a couple of hundred yards over open ground, the road entered very thick forest, and here I made the men walk in front while I brought up the rear. We had gone about two miles in this order, when on turning a corner I saw a man sitting on the road, herding buffaloes. It was now time to call a halt for breakfast, so I asked the man where we could get the water. He pointed down the hill straight in front of him, and said there was a spring down there from which his village, which was just round the shoulder of the hill, drew its water-supply. There was, however, no necessity for us to go down the hill for water, for if we continued a little further we should find a good spring on the road.

His village was at the upper end of the valley in which the women of Lohali had been killed the previous week, and he told me that nothing had been heard of the man-eater since, and added that the animal was possibly now at the other end of the district. I disabused his mind on this point by telling him about a fresh pugmarks I had seen at the pool, and advised him very strongly to collect his buffaloes and return to the village. His buffaloes, some ten in number, were straggling up towards the road and he said he would leave as soon they had grazed up to where he was sitting. Handing him a cigarette, I left him with a final warning. What occurred after I left was related to me by the man of the village, when I paid the district a second visit some months later.

When the man eventually got home that day he told the assembled villagers of our meeting, and my warning and said that after he had watched me go round a bend in the road a hundred yards away, he started to light the cigarette I had given him. A wind was blowing, and to protect the flame of the match he bend forward, and while in this position he was seized from behind by the right shoulder and pulled backwards. His first thought was of the party who had just left him, but unfortunately, his cry for help was not heard by them. Help, however, was near at hand, for as soon as the buffaloes heard his cry, mingled with the growl of the tigress, they charged on to the road and drove the tigress off. His shoulder and arms were broken, and with great difficulty he managed to climb on the back of one of his brave rescuers, and followed by the rest of the head, reached his home. The villagers tied up his wounds as best they could and carried him thirty miles, non-stop to the Haldwani hospital, where he died shortly after admission.

When Atropos who snips the threads of life misses one thread she cuts another, and we who do not know why one thread is missed and another cut, call it Fate, *Kismet*, or what we will.

For a month I had lived in an open tent, a hundred yards from the nearest human being, and from dawn to dusk had wandered through the jungles, and on several occasions had disguised myself as a woman and cut grass in places where no local inhabitant dared to go. During this period the man-eater had quite possibly, missed many opportunities of adding me to her bag and now, when making a final effort, she had quite by chance encountered this unfortunate man and claimed him as a victim.

## II

The following February I returned to Dalkania. A number of human beings had been killed, and many more wounded, over a wide area since my departure from the district the previous summer, and as the whereabouts of the tigress was not known and the chances in one place were as good as in another, I decided to return and camp on the ground with which I was now familiar.

On my arrival at Dalkania I was told that a cow had been killed the previous evening, on the hill on which the bear hunt had taken place. The men who had been herding the cattle at the time were positive that the animal they had seen killing the cow was a tiger. The kill was lying near some bushes at the edge of a deserted field, and was clearly visible from the spot where my tent was being put up. Vultures were circling over the kill, and looking through my field-glasses I saw several of these birds perched on a tree, to the left of the kill. From the fact that the kill was lying out in the open, and the  vultures had not descended on it, I concluded (a) that the cow had been killed by a leopard, and (b) that the leopard was lying up close to the kill.

The ground below the field on which the cow was lying was very steep and overgrown with dense brushwood. The man-eater was still at large, and an approach over this ground was therefore inadvisable.

To the right was a grassy slope, but the ground here was too open to admit of my approaching the kill without being seen. A deep heavily wooded ravine, starting from near the crest of the hill, ran right down to the Nandhour river, passing within a short distance of the kill. The tree on which the vultures were perched was growing on the edge of this ravine. I decided on this ravine as my line of approach. While I had been planning out the stalk with the assistance of the villagers, who knew every foot of the ground, my men had prepared tea for me. The day was now on the decline but by going hard I should just have time to visit the kill and return to camp before nightfall.

Before setting off I instructed my men to be on the lookout. If, after hearing a shot, they saw me on the open ground near the kill, three or four of them were immediately to leave camp, and, keeping to the open ground, to join me. On the other hand if I did not fire, and failed to return by morning, a search party was to be organized.

The ravine was overgrown with raspberry bushes and strewn with great rocks, and as the wind was blowing downhill, my progress was slow. After a stiff climb I eventually reached the tree on which the vultures were perched, only to find that the kill was not visible from this spot. The deserted field, which through my field-glasses had appeared to be quite straight, I found to be crescent-shaped, ten yards across at its widest part and tapering to a point at both ends. The outer edge was bordered with dense undergrowth, and the hill fell steeply away from the inner edge. Only two-thirds of the field was visible from where I was standing, and in order to see the remaining one-third, on which the kill was lying, it would be necessary either to make a wide detour and approach from the far side or climb the tree on which the vultures were perched.

I decided on the latter course. The cow, as far as I could judge, was about twenty yards from the tree, and it was quite possible that the animal that had killed her was even less than that distance from me. To climb the tree without disturbing the killer would have been an impossible feat, and would not have been attempted had it not been for the vultures. There were by now some twenty of these birds on the tree and their number was being added to by new arrivals, and as the accommodation on the upper branches was limited there was much flapping of wings and quarrelling. The tree was leaning outwards away from the hill, and about ten feet from the ground a great limb projected out over the steep hillside. Hampered with the rifle I had great difficulty in reaching this limb. Waiting until a fresh quarrel had broken out among the vultures, I stepped out along the branch— a difficult balancing feat where a slip or false step would have resulted in a fall of a hundred or more feet on to the rocks below—reached a fork, and sat down.

The kill, from which only a few pounds of flesh had been eaten, was now in full view. I had been in position about ten minutes, and was finding my perch none too comfortable, when two vultures, who had been circling round and were uncertain of their reception on the tree, alighted on the field a short distance from the cow. They had hardly come to rest when they were on the wing again, and at the same moment the bushes on my side of the kill were gently agitated and out into the open stepped a fine male leopard.

Those who have never seen a leopard under favourable conditions in his natural surroundings can have no conception of the grace of movement, and beauty of colouring, of this the most graceful and the most beautiful of all animals in our Indian jungles. Nor are his attractions limited to outward appearances, for, pound for pound, his strength is second to none, and in courage he lacks nothing. To class such an animal as VERMIN, as is done in some parts of India, is a crime which only those could perpetrate whose knowledge of the leopard is limited to the miserable, underfed, and mangy specimens seen in captivity.

But beautiful as the specimen was that stood before me, his life was forfeit, for he had taken to cattle killing, and I had promised the people of Dalkania and other villages on my last visit that I would rid them of this their minor enemy, if opportunity offered. The opportunity had now come, and I do not think the leopard heard the shot that killed him.

Of the many incomprehensible things one meets with in life, the hardest to assign any reason for is the way in which misfortune dogs an individual, or a family. Take as an example the case of the owner of the cow over which I had shot the leopard. He was a boy, eight years of age, and an only child. Two years previously his mother, while out cutting grass for the cow, had been killed and eaten by the man-eater, and twelve months later his father had suffered a like fate. The few pots and pans the family possessed had been sold to pay off the small debt left by the father, and the son started life as the owner of one cow; and this particular cow the leopard had selected, out of a herd of two or three hundred head of village cattle, and killed. (I am afraid my attempt to repair a heartbreak was not very successful in this case, for though the new cow, a red one, was an animal of parts, it did not make up to the boy for the loss of his lifelong white companion.)

My young buffaloes had been well cared for by the man in whose charge I had left them, and the day after my arrival I started tying them out, though I had little hope of the tigress accepting them as bait.

Five miles down the Nandhour valley nestles a little village at the foot of a great cliff of rock, some thousand or more feet high. The man-eater had, during the past few months, killed four people on the outskirts of this village. Shortly after I shot the leopard, a deputation came from this village to request me to move my camp from Dalkania to a site that had been selected for me near their village. I was told that the tiger had frequently been seen on the cliff above the village and that it appeared to have its home in one of the many caves in the cliff face. That very morning, I was informed, some women out cutting grass had seen the tiger, and the villagers were now in a state of terror, and too frightened to leave their homes. Promising the deputation I would do all I could to help them, I made a very early start next morning, climbed the hill opposite the village, and scanned the cliff for an hour or more through my field-glasses. I then crossed the valley, and by way of a very deep ravine climbed the cliff above the village. Here the going was very difficult and not at all to my liking, for added to the danger of a fall, which would have resulted in a broken neck, was the danger of an attack on ground on which it would be impossible to defend oneself.

By 2 p.m. I had seen as much of the rock cliff as I shall ever want to see again, and was making my way up the valley towards my camp and breakfast, when on looking back before starting the stiff climb to Dalkania I saw two men running towards me from the direction in which I had just come. On joining me the men informed me that a tiger had just killed a bullock in the deep ravine up which I had gone earlier in the day. Telling one of the men to go on up to my camp and instruct my servant to send tea and some food, I turned round and, accompanied by the other man, retraced my steps down the valley.

The ravine where the bullock had been killed was about two hundred feet deep and one hundred feet wide. As we approached it I saw a number of vultures rising, and when we arrived at the kill I found the vultures had cleaned it out, leaving only the skin and bones. The spot where the remains of the bullock were lying was only a hundred yards from the village but there was no way up the steep bank, so my guide took me a quarter of a mile down the ravine, to where a cattle track crossed it. This track, after gaining the high ground, would in and out through dense scrub jungle before it finally fetched up at the village. On arrival at the village I told the Headman that the vultures had ruined the kill, and asked him to provide me with a young buffalo and a short length of stout rope; while these were being procured, two of my men arrived from Dalkania with the food I had sent for.

The sun was near setting when I re-entered the ravine, followed by several men leading a vigorous young male buffalo which the Headman had purchased for me from an adjoining village. Fifty yards from where the bullock had been killed, one end of a pine tree washed down from the hill above had been buried deep in the bed of the ravine. After tying the buf-buffalo very securely to the exposed end of the pine, the men returned to the village. There were no trees in the vicinity, and the only possible place for a sit-up was a narrow ledge on the village side of the ravine. With great difficulty I climbed to this ledge, which was about two feet wide by five feet long, and twenty feet above the bed of the ravine. From a little below the ledge the rock shelved inwards, forming a deep recess that was not visible from the ledge. The ledge canted downwards at an uncomfortable angle, and when I had taken my seat on it, I had my back towards the direction from which I expected the tiger to come, while the tethered buffalo was to my left front, and distant about thirty yards from me.

The sun had set when the buffalo, who had been lying down, scrambled to his feet and faced up the ravine, and a moment later a stone came rolling down. It would not have been possible for me to have fired in the direction from which the sound had come, so to avoid detection I sat perfectly still. After some time the buffalo gradually turned to the left until he was facing in my direction. This showed that whatever he was frightened of—and I could see he was frightened—was in the recess below me. Presently the head of a tiger appeared directly under me. A head-shot at a tiger is only justified in an emergency, and any movement on my part might have betrayed my presence. For a long minute or two the head remained perfectly still, and then, with a quick dash forward, and one great bound, the tiger was on the buffalo. The buffalo, as I have stated, was facing the tiger, and to avoid a frontal attack with the possibility of injury from the buffalo's horns, the tiger's dash carried him to the left of the buffalo, and he made his attack at right angles. There was no fumbling for tooth-hold, no struggle, and no sound beyond the impact of the two heavy bodies, after which the buffalo lay quite still with the tiger lying partly over it and holding it by the throat. It is generally believed that tigers kill by delivering a smashing blow on the neck. This is incorrect. Tigers kill with their teeth.

The right side of the tiger was towards me and, taking careful aim with the ·275 I had armed myself with when leaving camp that morning, I fired. Relinquishing its hold on the buffalo, the tiger, without making a sound, turned and bounded off up the ravine and out of sight. Clearly a miss, for which I was unable to assign any reason. If the tiger had not seen me or the flash of the rifle there was a possibility that it would return; so recharging the rifle I sat on.

The buffalo, after the tiger left him, lay without movement, and the conviction grew on me that I had shot him instead of the tiger. Ten, fifteen minutes had dragged by, when the tiger's head for a second time appeared from the recess below me. Again there was a long pause, and then, very slowly, the tiger emerged, walked up to the buffalo and stood looking down at it. With the whole length of the back as a target I was going to make no mistake the second time. Very carefully the sights were aligned, and the trigger slowly pressed; but instead of the tiger falling dead as I expected it to, it sprang to the left and went tearing up a little ravine, dislodging stones as it went up the steep hillside.

Two shots fired in comparatively good light at a range of thirty yards, and heard by anxious villagers for miles round; and all I should have to show for them would be, certainly one, and quite possibly two, bullet holes in a dead buffalo. Clearly my eyesight was failing, or in climbing the rock I had knocked the foresight out or alignment. But on focusing my eyes on small objects I found there was nothing wrong with my eyesight, and a glance along the barrel showed that the sights were all right, so the only reason I could assign for having missed the tiger twice was bad shooting.

There was no chance of the tiger returning a third time; and even if it did return, there was nothing to be gained by risking the possibility of only wounding it in bad light when I had not been able to kill it while the light had been comparatively good.

Under these circumstances there was no object in my remaining any longer on the ledge.

My clothes were still damp from my exertions earlier in the day, a cold wind was blowing and promised to get colder, my shorts were of thin khaki and the rock was hard and cold, and a hot cup of tea awaited me in the village. Good as these reasons were, there was a better and a more convincing reason for my remaining where I was—the man-eater. It was now quite dark. A quarter-of-mile walk, along a boulder-strewn ravine and a winding path through dense undergrowth, lay between me and the village. Beyond the suspicions of the villagers that the tiger they had seen the previous day—and that I had quite evidently just fired at—was the man-eater, I had no definite knowledge of the man-eater's whereabouts; and though at that moment she might have been fifty miles away, she might also have been watching me from a distance of fifty yards, so, uncomfortable as my perch was, prudence dictated that I should remain where I was. As the long hours dragged by, the conviction grew on me that man-eater shooting, by night, was not a pastime that appealed to me, and that if this animal could not be shot during daylight hours she would have to be left to die of old age. This conviction was strengthened, when, cold and stiff, I started to climb down as soon as there was sufficient light to shoot by, and slipping on the dew-drenched rock completed the descent with my feet in the air. Fortunately I landed on a bed of sand, without doing myself or the rifle any injury.

Early as it was I found the village astir, and I was quickly in the middle of a small crowd. In reply to the eager questions from all sides, I was only able to say that I had been firing at an imaginary tiger with blank ammunition.

A pot of tea drunk while sitting near a roaring fire did much to restore warmth to my inner and outer man, and then, accompanied by most of the men and all the boys of the village, I went to where a rock jutted out over the ravine and directly above my overnight exploit. To the assembled throng I explained how the tiger had appeared from the recess under me and had bounded on to the buffalo, and how after I fired it had dashed off in *that* direction; and as I pointed up the ravine there was an excited shout of 'Look, *sahib*, there's the tiger lying dead!' My eyes were strained with an all-night vigil, but even after looking away and back again there was no denying the fact the tiger was lying there, dead. To the very natural question of why I had fired a second shot after a period of twenty or thirty minutes, I said that the tiger had appeared a second time from exactly the same place, and that I had fired at it while it was standing near the buffalo and that it had gone up *that* side ravine—and there were renewed shouts, in which the women and girls who had now come up joined, of 'Look, *sahib*, there is another tiger lying dead!' Both tigers appeared to be about the same size and both were lying sixty yards from where I had fired.

Questioned on the subject of this second tiger, the villagers said that when the four human beings had been killed, and also on the previous day when the bullock had been killed, only one tiger had been seen. The mating season for tigers is an elastic one extending from November to April, and the man-eater—if either of two tigers lying within view was the man-eater—had evidently provided herself with a mate.

A way into the ravine, down the steep rock face, was found some two hundred yards below where I had sat up, and, followed by the entire population of the village, I went past the dead buffalo to where the first tiger was lying. As I approached it hopes rose high, for she was an old tigress. Handing the rifle to the nearest man I got down on my knees to examine her feet. On that day when the tigress had tried to stalk the women cutting wheat she had left some beautiful pugmarks on the edge of the field. They were the first pugmarks I had seen of the man-eater, and I had examined them very carefully. They showed the tigress to be a very old animal, whose feet had splayed out with age.

The pads of the forefeet were heavily rutted, one deep rut running right across the pad of the right forefoot, and the toes were elongated to a length I had never before seen in a tiger. With these distinctive feet it would have been easy to pick the man-eater out of a hundred dead tigers. The animal before me was, I found to my great regret, not the man-eater. When I conveyed this information to the assembled throng of people there was a murmur of strong dissent from all sides. It was asserted that I myself, on my previous visit, had declared the man-eater to be an old tigress, and such an animal I had now shot a few yards from where, only a short time previously, four of their number had been killed. Against this convincing evidence, of what value was the evidence of the feet, for the feet of all tigers were alike!

The second tiger could, under the circumstances, only be a male, and while I made preparations to skin the tigress, I sent a party of men to fetch him. The side ravine was steep and narrow, and after a great deal of shouting and laughter the second tiger— a fine male—was laid down alongside the tigress.

The skinning of those two tigers that had been dead fourteen hours, with the sun beating down on my back and an evergrowing crowd pressing round, was one of the most unpleasant tasks I have ever undertaken. By early afternoon the job was completed, and with the skins neatly tied up for my men to carry I was ready to start on my five-mile walk back to camp.

During the morning Headmen and others had come in from adjoining villages, and before leaving I assured them that the Chowgarh man-eater was not dead and warned them that the slackening of precautions would give the tigress the opportunity she was waiting for. Had my warning been heeded, the man-eater would not have claimed as many victims as she did during the succeeding months.

There was no further news of the man-eater, and after a stay of a few weeks at Dalkania, I left to keep an appointment with the district officials in the terai.

## III

In March 1930, Vivian, our District Commissioner, was touring through the man-eater's domain, and on the 22nd of the month I received an urgent request from him to go to Kala Agar, where he said he would await my arrival. It is roughly fifty miles from Naini Tal to Kala Agar, and two days after receipt of Vivian's letter I arrived in time for breakfast at the Kala Agar Forest Bungalow, where he and Mrs Vivian were staying.

Over breakfast the Vivians told me they had arrived at the bungalow on the afternoon of 21st, and while they were having tea on the verandah, one of six women who were cutting grass in the compound of the bungalow had been killed and carried off by the man-eater. Rifles were hurriedly seized and, accompanied by some of his staff, Vivian followed up the 'drag' and found the dead woman tucked away under a bush at the foot of an oak tree. On examining the ground later, I found that on the approach of Vivian's party the tigress had gone off down the hill, and throughout the subsequent proceedings had remained in a thicket of raspberry bushes, fifty yards from the kill. A *machan* was put up in the oak tree for Vivian, and two others in trees near the forest road which passed thirty yards above the kill, for members of his staff. The *machan*s were occupied as soon as they were ready and the party sat up the whole night, without, however, seeing anything of the tigress.

Next morning the body of the woman was removed for cremation, and a young buffalo was tied up on the forest road about half a mile from the bungalow, and killed by the tigress the same night. The following evening the Vivians sat up over the buffalo. There was no moon, and just as daylight was fading out and nearby objects becoming indistinct, they first heard, and then saw an animal coming up to the kill, which in the uncertain light they mistook for a bear; but for this unfortunate mistake their very sporting effort would have resulted in their bagging the man-eater for both the Vivians are good rifle shots.

On the 25th the Vivians left Kala Agar, and during the course of the day my four buffaloes arrived from Dalkania. As the tigress now appeared to be inclined to accept this form of bait I tied them up at intervals of a few hundred yards along the forest road. For three nights in succession the tigress passed within a few feet of the buffaloes without touching them, but on the fourth night the buffalo nearest the bungalow was killed. On examining the kill in the morning I was disappointed to find that the buffalo had been killed by a pair of leopards I had heard calling the previous night above the bungalow. I did not like the idea of firing in this locality, for fear of driving away the tigress, but it was quite evident that if I did not shoot the leopards they would kill my three remaining buffaloes, so I stalked them while they were sunning themselves on some big rocks above the kill, and shot both of them.

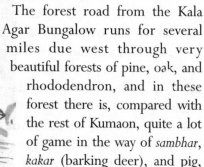

The forest road from the Kala Agar Bungalow runs for several miles due west through very beautiful forests of pine, oak, and rhododendron, and in these forest there is, compared with the rest of Kumaon, quite a lot of game in the way of *sambhar*, *kakar* (barking deer), and pig, in addition to a great wealth of bird life. On two occasions I suspected the tigress of having killed *sambhar* in this forest, and though on both occasions I found the blood-stained spot where the animal had been killed, I failed to find either of the kills.

For the next fourteen days I spent all the daylight hours either on the forest road, on which no one but myself ever set foot, or in the jungle, and only twice during that period did I get near the tigress. On the first occasion I had been down to visit an isolated village, on the south face of Kala Agar ridge, that had been abandoned the previous year owing to the depredations of the man-eater, and on the way back had taken a cattle track that went over the ridge and down the far side to the forest road, when, approaching a pile of rocks, I suddenly felt there was danger ahead. The distance from the ridge to the forest road was roughly three hundred yards. The track, after leaving the ridge, went steeply down for a few yards and then turned to the right and ran diagonally across the hill for a hundred yards; the pile of rocks was about midway on the right-hand side of this length of the track. Beyond the rocks a hairpin bend carried the track to the left, and a hundred yards further on, another sharp bend took it down to its junction with the forest road.

I had been along this track many times, and this was the first occasion on which I hesitated to pass the rocks. To avoid them I should either have had to go several hundred yards through dense undergrowth, or make a wide detour round and above them; the former would have subjected me to very great danger, and there was no time for the latter, for the sun was near setting and I had still two miles to go. So, whether I liked it or not, there was nothing for it but to face the rocks. The wind was blowing up the hills so I was able to ignore the thick cover on the left of the track, and concentrate all my attention on the rocks to my right. A hundred feet would see me clear of the danger zone, and this distance I covered foot by foot, walking sideways with my face to the rocks and the rifle to my shoulder; a strange mode of progression, had there been any to see it.

Thirty yards beyond the rocks was an open glade, starting from the right-hand side of the track and extending up the hill for fifty or sixty yards, and screened from the rocks by a fringe of bushes. In this glade a *kakar* was grazing. I saw her before she saw me, and watched her out of the corner of my eye. On catching sight of me she threw up her head, and as I was not looking in her direction and was moving slowly on she stood stock still, as these animals have a habit of doing when they are under the impression that they have not been seen. On arrival at the hairpin bend I looked over my shoulder and saw that the *kakar* had lowered her head, and was once more cropping the grass.

I had walked a short distance along the track after passing the bend when the *kakar* went dashing up the hill, barking hysterically. In a few quick strides I was back at the bend, and was just in time to see a movement in the bushes on the lower side of the track. That the *kakar* had seen the tigress was quite evident, and the only place where she could have seen her was on the track. The movement I had seen might have been caused by the passage of a bird, on the other hand it might have been caused by the tigress; anyway, a little investigation was necessary before proceeding further on my way.

A trickle of water seeping out from under the rocks had damped the red clay of which the track was composed, making an ideal surface for the impression of tracks. In this damp clay I had left footprints, and over these footprints I now found the splayed-out pugmarks of the tigress where she had jumped down from the rocks and followed me, until the *kakar* had seen her and given its alarm-call, whereupon the tigress had left the track and entered the bushes where I had seen the movement. The tigress was undoubtedly familiar with every foot of the ground, and not having had an opportunity of killing me at the rocks— and her chance of bagging me at the first hairpin bend having been spoilt by the *kakar*—she was probably now making her way through the dense under-growth to try to intercept me at the second bend.

Further progress along the track was now not advisable, so I followed the *kakar* up the glade, and turning to the left worked my way down, over open ground, to the forest road below. Had there been sufficient daylight I believe I could, that evening, have turned the tables on the tigress, for the conditions, after she left the shelter of the rocks, were all in my favour. I knew the ground as well as she did, and while she had no reason to suspect my intention towards her, I had the advantage of knowing, very clearly, her intentions towards me. However, though the conditions were in my favour, I was unable to take advantage of them owing to the lateness of the evening.

I have made mention elsewhere of the sense that warns us of impending danger, and will not labour the subject further beyond stating that this sense is a very real one and that I do not know, and therefore cannot explain, what brings it into operation. On this occasion I had neither heard nor seen the tigress, nor had I received any indication from bird or beast of her presence and yet I knew, without any shadow of doubt, that she was lying up for me among the rocks. I had been out for many hours that day and had covered many miles of jungle with unflagging caution, but without one moment's unease, and then, on cresting the ridge, and coming in sight of the rocks, I knew they held danger for me, and this knowledge was confirmed a few minutes later by the kakar's warning call to the jungle folk, and by my finding the man-eater's pugmarks superimposed on my footprints.

## IV

To those of my readers who have had the patience to accompany me so far in my narrative, I should like to give a clear and a detailed account of my first—and last—meeting with the tigress.

The meeting took place in the early afternoon of the 11th of April 1930, nineteen days after my arrival at Kala Agar.

I had gone out that day at 2 p.m. with the intention of tying up my three buffaloes at selected places along the forest road, when at a point a mile from the bungalow, where the road crosses a ridge and goes from the north to the west face of the Kala Agar range, I came on a large party of men who had been out collecting firewood. In the party was an old man who, pointing down the hill to a thicket of young oak trees some five hundred yards from where we were standing, said it was in that thicket where the man-eater, a month previously, had killed his only son, a lad eighteen years of age. I had not heard the father's version of the killing of his son, so, while we sat on the edge of the road smoking, he told his story, pointing out the spot where the lad had been killed, and where all that was left of him had been found the following day. The old man blamed the twenty-five men who had been out collecting firewood on that day for the death of his son, saying, very bitterly, that they had run away and left him to be killed by the tiger. Some of the men sitting near me had been in that party of twenty-five and they hotly repudiated responsibility for the lad's death, accusing him of having been responsible for the stampede by screaming out that he had heard the tiger growling and telling everyone to run for their lives. This did not satisfy the old man. He shook his head and said, 'You are grown men and he was only a boy, and you ran away and left him to be killed.' I was sorry for having asked the questions that had led to this heated discussion, and more to placate the old man than for any good it would do, I said I would tie up one of my buffaloes near the spot where he said his son had been killed. So, handing two of the buffaloes over to the party to take back to the bungalow, I set off followed by two of my men leading the remaining buffalo.

A footpath, taking off close to where we had been sitting, went down the hill to the valley below and zigzagged up the opposite pine-clad slope to join the forest road two miles further on. The path passed close to an open patch of ground which bordered the oak thicket in which the lad had been killed. On this patch of ground, which was about thirty yards square, there was a solitary pine sapling. This I cut down. I tied the buffalo to the stump, set one man to cutting a supply of grass for it, and sent the other man, Madho Singh, who served in the Garhwalis during the Great War and is now serving in the United Provinces Civil Pioneer Force, up an oak tree with instructions to strike a dry branch with the head of his axe and call at the top of his voice as hill people do when cutting leaves for their cattle. I then took up a position on a rock, about four feet high, on the lower edge of the open ground. Beyond the rock the hill fell steeply away to the valley below and was densely clothed with tree and scrub jungle.

The man on the ground had made several trips with the grass he had cut, and Madho Singh on the tree was alternately shouting and singing lustily, while I stood on the rock smoking, with the rifle in the hollow of my left arm, when, all at once, I became aware that the man-eater had arrived. Beckoning urgently to the man on the ground to come to me, I whistled to attract Madho Singh's attention and signalled to him to remain quiet. The ground on three sides was comparatively open. Madho Singh on the tree was to my left front, the man cutting grass had been in front of me, while the buffalo—now showing signs of uneasiness—was to my right front. In this area the tigress could not have approached without my seeing her; and as she *had* approached, there was only one place where she could now be, and that was behind and immediately below me.

When taking up my position I had noticed that the further side of the rock was steep and smooth, that it extended down the hill for eight or ten feet, and that the lower portion of it was masked by thick undergrowth and young pine saplings. It would have been a little difficult, but quite possible, for the tigress to have climbed the rock, and I relied for my safety on hearing her in the undergrowth should she make the attempt.

I have no doubt that the tigress, attracted, as I had intended she should be, by the noise Madho Singh was making, had come to the rock, and that it was while she was looking up at me and planning her next move that I had become aware of her presence. My change of front, coupled with the silence of the men, may have made her suspicious; anyway, after a lapse of a few minutes, I heard a dry twig snap a little way down the hill; thereafter the feeling of unease left me, and the tension relaxed. An opportunity lost; but there was still a very good chance of my getting a shot, for she would undoubtedly return before long, and when she found us gone would probably content herself with killing the buffalo. There were still four or five hours of daylight, and by crossing the valley and going up the opposite slope I should be able to overlook the whole of the hillside on which the buffalo was tethered. The shot, if I did get one, would be a long one of from two to three hundred yards, but the ˙275 rifle I was carrying was accurate, and even if I only wounded the tigress I should have a blood trail to follow, which would be better than feeling about for her in hundreds of square miles of jungle, as I had been doing these many months.

The men were a difficulty. To have sent them back to the bungalow alone would have been nothing short of murder, so of necessity I kept them with me.

Tying the buffalo to the stump in such a manner as to make it impossible for the tigress to carry it away, I left the open ground and rejoined the path to carry out the plan I have outlined, of trying to get a shot from the opposite hill.

About a hundred yards along the path I came to a ravine. On the far side of this the path entered very heavy undergrowth, and as it was inadvisable to go into thick cover with two men following me, I decided to take to the ravine, follow it down to its junction with the valley, work up the valley and pick up the path on the far side of the undergrowth.

The ravine was about ten yards wide and four or five feet deep, and as I stepped down into it a nightjar fluttered off a rock on which I had put my hand. On looking at the spot from which the bird had risen, I saw two eggs. These eggs, straw-colored, with rich brown markings, were of a most unusual shape, one being long and very pointed, while the other was as round as a marble; and as my collection lacked nightjar eggs I decided to add this odd clutch to it. I had no receptacle of any kind in which to carry the eggs, so cupping my left hand I placed the eggs in it and packed them round with a little moss.

As I went down the ravine the banks became higher, and sixty yards from where I had entered it I came on a deep drop of some twelve to fourteen feet. The water that rushes down all these hill ravines in the rains had worn the rock as smooth as glass, and as it was too steep to offer a foothold I handed the rifle to the men and, sitting on the edge, proceeded to slide down. My feet had hardly touched the sandy bottom when the two men, with a flying leap, landed one on either side of me, and thrusting the rifle into my hand asked in a very agitated manner if I had heard the tiger. As a matter of fact I had heard nothing, possibly due to the scraping of my clothes on the rocks, and when questioned, the men said that what they had heard was a deep-throated growl from somewhere close at hand, but exactly from which direction the sound had come, they were unable to say. Tigers do not betray their presence by growling when looking for their dinner and the only, and very unsatisfactory, explanation I can offer is that the tigress followed us after we left the open ground, and on seeing that we were going down the ravine had gone ahead and taken up a position where the ravine narrowed to half its width; and that when she was on the point of springing out on me, I had disappeared out of sight down the slide and she had involuntarily given vent to her disappointment with a low growl. Not a satisfactory reason, unless one assumes—without any reason—that she had selected me for her dinner, and therefore had no interest in the two men.

Where the three of us now stood in a bunch we had the smooth steep rock behind us, to our right a wall of rock slightly leaning over the ravine and fifteen feet high, and to our left a tumbled bank of big rocks thirty or forty feet high. The sandy bed of the ravine, on which we were standing, was roughly forty feet long and ten feet wide. At the lower end of this sandy bed a great pine tree had fallen across, damming the ravine, and the collection of the sand was due to this dam. The wall of overhanging rock came to an end twelve or fifteen feet from the fallen tree, and as I approached the end of the rock, my feet making no sound on the sand, I very fortunately noticed that the sandy bed continued round to the back of the rock.

This rock about which I have said so much I can best describe as a giant school slate, two feet thick as its lower end, and standing up—not quite perpendicularly—on one of its long sides.

As I stepped clear of the giant slate, I looked behind me over right shoulder and—looked straight into the tigress's face.

I would like you to have a clear picture of the situation.

The sandy bed behind the rock was quite flat. To the right of it was the smooth slate fifteen feet high and leaning slightly outwards, to the left of it was a scoured-out steep bank also some fifteen feet high overhung by a dense tangle of thorn bushes, while at the far end was a slide similar to, but a little higher than, the one I had glissaded down. The sandy bed, enclosed by the these three natural walls, was about twenty feet long and half as wide, and lying on it, with her fore-paws stretched out and her hind legs well tucked under her, was the tigress. Her head which was raised a few inches off her paws, was eight feet (measured later) from me, and on her face was a smile, similar to that one sees on the face of a dog welcoming his master home after a long absence.

Two thoughts flashed through my mind, one, that it was up to me to make the first move, and the other, that the move would have to be made in such a manner as not to alarm the tigress or make her nervous.

The rifle was in my right hand held diagonally across my chest, with the safety-catch off, and in order to get it to bear on the tigress the muzzle would have to be swung round three-quarters of a circle.

The movement of swinging round the rifle, with one hand, was begun very slowly, and hardly perceptibly, and when a quarter of a circle had been made, the stock came in contact with my right side. It was now necessary to extend my arm, and as the stock cleared my side, the swing was very slowly continued. My arm was now at full stretch and the weight of the rifle was beginning to tell. Only a little further now for the muzzle to go, and the tigress—who had not once taken her eyes off mine—was still looking up at me, with the pleased expression still on her face.

How long it took the rifle to make the three-quarter circle, I am not in a position to say. To me, looking into the tigress's eyes and unable therefore to follow the movement of the barrel, it appeared that my arms was paralysed, and that the swing would never be completed. However, the movement was completed at last, and as soon as the rifle was pointing at the tigress's body, I pressed the trigger.

I heard the report, exaggerated in that restricted space and felt the jar of the recoil, and but for these tangible proofs that the rifle had gone off, I might, for all the immediate result the shot produced, have been in the grip of one of those awful nightmares in which triggers are vainly pulled of rifles that refused to be discharged at the critical moment.

For a perceptible fraction of time the tigress remained perfectly still, and then, very slowly, her head sank on to her outstretched paws, while at the same time a jet of blood issued from the bullet-hole. The bullet had injured her spine and shattered the upper portion of her heart.

The two men who were following a few yards behind me, and who were separated from the tigress by the thickness of the rock came to a halt when they saw me stop and turn my head. They knew instinctively that I had seen the tigress and judged from my behaviour that she was close at hand, and Madho Singh said afterwards that he wanted to call out and tell me to drop the eggs and get both hands on the rifle. When I had fired my shot and lowered the point of the rifle on to my toes, Madho Singh, at a sign, came forward to relieve me of it, for very suddenly my legs appeared to be unable to support me, so I made for the fallen tree and sat down. Even before looking at the pads of her feet I knew it was the Chowgarh tigress I had sent to the Happy Hunting Grounds, and that the shears that had assisted her to cut the threads of sixty-four human lives—

the people of the district put the number at twice that figure—had, while the game was in her hands, turned, and cut the thread of her own life.

Three things, each of which would appear to you to have been to my disadvantage, were actually in my favour. These were (a) the eggs in my left hand (b) the light rifle I was carrying, and (c) the tiger being a man-eater. If I had not had the eggs in my hand I should have had both hands on the rifle, and when I looked back and saw the tiger at such close quarters I should instinctively have tried to swing round to face her, and the spring that was arrested by my lack of movement would inevitably have been launched. Again, if the rifle had not been a light one it would not have been possible for me to have moved it in the way it was imperative I should move it, and then discharge it at the full extent of my arm, And lastly, if the tiger had been just an ordinary tiger, and not a man-eater, it would, on finding itself cornered, have made for the opening and wiped me out of the way; and to be wiped out of the way by a tiger usually has fatal results.

While the men made a detour and went up the hill to free the buffalo and secure the rope, which was needed for another and more pleasant purpose, I climbed over the rocks and went up the ravine to restore the eggs to their rightful owner. I plead guilty of being as superstitious as my brother sportsmen. For three long periods, extending over a whole year, I had tried—and tried hard—to get a shot at the tigress, and had failed; and now within a few minutes of having picked up the eggs my luck had changed.

The eggs, which all this time had remain safely in the hollow of my left hand, were still warm when I replaced them in the little depression in the rock that did duty as a nest, when I again passed that way half an hour later, they had vanished under the brooding mother whose colouring so exactly matched the mottled rock that it was difficult for me, who knew the exact spot where the nest was situated, to distinguish her from her surroundings.

The buffalo, who after months of care was now so tame that it followed like a dog, came scrambling down the hill in the wake of the men, nosed the tigress and lay down on the sand to chew the cud of contentment, while we lashed the tigress to the stout pole the men had cut.

I had tried to get Madho Singh to return to the bungalow for help, but this he would not hear of doing. With no one would he and his companion share the honour of carrying in the man-eater, and if I would lend a hand the task, he said, with frequent halts for rest, would not be too difficult. We were three hefty men—two accustomed from childhood to carry heavy loads—and all three hardened by a life of exposure; but even so, the task we set ourselves was a herculean one.

The path down which we had come was too narrow and too winding for the long pole to which the tigress was lashed, so, with frequent halts to regain breath and readjust pads to prevent the pole biting too deep into shoulder muscles, we went straight up the hill through a tangle of raspberry and briar bushes, on the thorns of which we left a portion of our clothing and an amount of skin which made bathing for many days a painful operation.

The sun was still shining on the surrounding hills when three dishevelled and very happy men, followed by a buffalo, carried the tigress to the Kala Agar Forest Bungalow, and from that evening to this day no human being has been killed—or wounded—over the hundreds of square miles of mountain and vale over which the Chowgarh tigress, for a period of five years, held sway.

I have added one more cross and date to the map of Eastern Kumaon that hangs on the wall before me—the cross and the date the man-eater earned. The cross is two miles west of Kala Agar, and the date under it is 11 April 1930.

The tigress's claws were broken, and bushed out, and one of her canine teeth was broken, and her front teeth were worn down to the bone. It was these defects that had made her a man-eater and were the cause of her not being able to kill outright—and by her own efforts—a large proportion of the human beings she had attacked since the day she had been deprived of the assistance of the cub I had, on my first visit shot by mistake.

# THE BACHELOR OF POWALGARH

## I

**T**hree miles from our winter home, and in the heart of the forest there is an open glade some four hundred yards long and half as wide, grassed with emerald-green and surrounded by big trees interlaced with cane creepers. It was in this glade, which for beauty has no equal, that I first saw the tiger who was known throughout the United Provinces as 'The Bachelor of Powalgarh', who from 1920 to 1930 was the most sought-after big-game trophy in the province.

The sun had just risen one winter's morning when I crested the high ground overlooking the glade. On the far side, a score of red jungle fowl were scratching among the dead leaves bordering a crystal-clear stream, and scattered over the emerald-green grass, now sparkling with dew, fifty or more *chital* were feeding. Sitting on a tree stump and smoking, I had been looking at this scene for sometime when the hind nearest to me raised her head, turned in my direction and called; and a moment later the Bachelor stepped into the open, from the thick bushes below

me. For a long minute he stood with head held high surveying the scene, and then with slow unhurried steps started to cross the glade. In his rich winter coat, which the newly risen sun was lighting up, he was a magnificent sight as, with head turning now to the right and now to the left, he walked down the wide lane the deer had made for him. At the stream he lay down and quenched his thirst, then sprang across and, as he entered the dense tree jungle beyond, called three times in acknowledgement of the homage the jungle folk had paid him, for from the time he had entered the glade every *chital* had called, every jungle fowl had cackled, and every one of a troupe of monkeys on the trees had chattered.

The Bachelor was far afield that morning, for his home was in a ravine six miles away. Living in an area in which the majority of tigers are bagged with the aid of elephants, he had chosen his home wisely. The ravine, running into the foot-hills, was half a mile long, with steep hills on either side raising to a height of a thousand feet. At the upper end of the ravine there was a waterfall some twenty feet high, and at the lower end, where the water had cut through red clay, it narrowed to four feet. Any sportsman, therefore, who wished to try conclusions with the Bachelor, while he was at home, would of a necessity have to do so on foot. It was this secure retreat, and Government rules prohibiting night shooting that had enabled the Bachelor to retain possession of his much sought-after skin.

In spite of the many and repeated attempts that had been made to bag him with the aid of buffalo bait, the Bachelor had never been fired at, though on two occasions, to my knowledge, he had only escaped death by the skin of his teeth. On the first occasion, after a perfect beat, a guy rope by which the *machan* was suspended interfered with the movement of Fred Anderson's rifle at the critical moment, and the second occasion the Bachelor arrived at the *machan* before the beat started and found Huish Edye filling his pipe. On both these occasions he had been viewed at a range of only a few feet, and while Anderson described him as being as big as a Shetland pony, Edye said he was as big as a donkey.

The winter following these and other unsuccessful attempts, I took Wyndham, our Commissioner, who knows more about tigers than any other man in India, to a fire track skirting the upper end of the ravine in which the Bachelor lived, to show him the fresh pugmarks of the tiger which I had found on the fire track that morning. Wyndham was accompanied by two of his most experienced shikaris, and after the three of them had carefully measured and examined the pugmarks, Wyndham said that in his opinion the tiger was ten feet between pegs, and while one *shikari* said he was 10' 5'' over curves, the other said he was 10' 6'' or a little more. All three agreed that they had never seen the pugmarks of a bigger tiger.

In 1930 the Forest Department started extensive fellings in the area surrounding the Bachelor's home and annoyed at the disturbance he changed his quarters; this I learnt from two sportsmen who had taken out a shooting pass with the object of hunting down the tiger. Shooting passes are only issued for fifteen days of each month, and throughout that winter, shooting party after shooting party failed to make contact with the tiger.

Towards the end of the winter an old *dak* runner, who passes our gate every morning and evening on his seven-mile run through the forest to a hill village, came to me one evening and reported that on his way out that morning he had seen the biggest pugmarks of a tiger that he had seen during the thirty years of his service. The tiger, he said, had come from the west and after proceeding along the road for two hundred yards had gone east, taking a path that started from near an almond tree. This tree was about two miles from our home, and was a well-known landmark. The path the tiger had taken runs through very heavy jungle for half a mile before crossing a wide watercourse, and then joins a cattle track which skirts the foot of the hills before entering a deep and well-wooded valley; a favourite haunt of tigers.

Early next morning, with Robin at my heels, I set out to prospect, my objective being the point where the cattle track entered the valley, for at this point the tracks of all the animals entering or leaving the valley are to be found. From the time we started Robin appeared to know that we had a special job at hand and he paid not the least attention to the jungle fowl we disturbed, the *kakar* that let us get quite close to it, and the two *sambhar* that stood and belled at us. Where the cattle track entered the valley the ground was hard and stony, and when we reached this spot Robin put down his head and very carefully smelt the stones, and on receiving a signal from me to carry on he turned and started down the track, keeping a yard ahead of me; I could tell from his behaviour that he was on the scent of a tiger, and that the scent was hot. A hundred yards further down, where the track flattens out and run along the foot of the hill, the ground is soft; here I saw the pugmarks of a tiger, and a glance at them satisfied me we were on the heels of the Bachelor and that he was only a minute or two ahead of us.

Beyond the soft ground the track runs for three hundred yards over stones, before going steeply down onto an open plain. If the tiger kept to the track we should probably see him on this open ground. We had gone another fifty yards when Robin stopped and, after running his nose up and down a blade of grass on the left of the track, turned and entered the grass which was here about two feet high. On the far side of the grass there was a patch of clerodendron, about forty yards wide. This plant grows in dense patches to a height of five feet, and has widely spread leaves and a big head of flowers not unlike horse-chestnut. It is greatly fancied by tiger, *sambhar* and pig because of the shade it gives. When Robin reached the clerodendron he stopped and backed towards me, thus telling me that he could not see into the bushes ahead and wished to be carried. Lifting him up, I put his hind legs into my left-hand pocket, and when he had hooked his forefeet over my left arm, he was safe and secure, and I had both hands free for the rifle. On these occasions Robin was always in deadly earnest, and no matter what he saw, or how our quarry behaved before or after fired at, he never moved and spoilt my shot, or impeded my view. Proceeding very slowly, we had gone half-way through the clerodendron when I saw the bushes directly in front of us swaying. Waiting until the tiger had cleared the bushes. I went forward expecting to see him in the more or less open jungle, but he was nowhere in sight, and when I put Robin down he turned to the left and indicated that the tiger had gone into a deep and narrow ravine nearby. This ravine ran to the foot of an isolated hill on which there were caves frequented by tigers, and as I was not armed to deal with a tiger at close quarters, and further, as it was time for breakfast, Robin and I turned and made for home.

After breakfast I returned alone, armed with heavy ·450 rifle, and as I approached the hill, which in the days of long ago had been used by the local inhabitants as a rallying point against the Gurkha invaders, I heard the boom of a big buffalo bell, and a man shouting. These sounds were coming from the top of the hills, which is flat, and about half an acre in extent, so I climbed up and saw a man on a tree, striking a dead branch with the head of his axe and shouting, while at the foot of the tree a number of buffaloes were collected. When he saw me the man called out, saying I had just arrived in time to save him and his buffaloes from a *shaitan* of a tiger, the size of a camel, that had been threatening them for hours. From his story I gathered that he had arrived on the hill shortly after Robin and I had left for home, and that as he started to cut bamboo leaves for his buffaloes he saw a tiger coming towards him. He shouted to drive the tiger away, as he had done on many previous occasions with other tigers, but instead of going away this one had started to growl. He took to his heels, followed by his buffaloes, and climbed up the nearest tree. The tiger, paying no heed to his shouts, had then set to pacing round and round, while the buffaloes kept their heads towards it. Probably the tiger had heard me coming, for it had left only a moment before I had arrived. The man was an old friend, who before his quarrel with the Headman of his village had done a considerable amount of poaching in these jungles with the Headman's gun. He now begged me to conduct both himself and his cattle safely out of the jungle; so telling him to lead on, I followed behind to see that there were no stragglers. At first the buffaloes were disinclined to break up their close formation, but after a little persuasion we got them to start, and we had gone half-way across the open plain I have alluded to when the tiger called in the jungle to our right. The man quickened his pace, and I urged on the buffaloes, for a mile of very thick jungle lay between us and the wide, open watercourse beyond which lay my friend's village and safety for his buffaloes.

I have earned the reputation of being keener on photographing animals than on killing them, and before I left my friend he begged me to put aside photography for this once, and kill the tiger, which he said was big enough to eat a buffalo a day, and ruin him in twenty-five days. I promised to do my best and turned to retrace my steps to the open plain, to meet with an experience every detail of which has burnt itself deep into my memory.

On reaching the plain I sat down to wait for the tiger to disclose his whereabouts, or for the jungle folk to tell me where he was. It was then about 3 p.m., and as the sun was warm and comforting, I put my head down on my drawn up knees and had been dozing a few minutes when I was awakened by the tiger calling; thereafter he continued to call at short intervals. Between the plain and the hills there is a belt, some half a mile wide, of the densest scrub jungle for a hundred miles round, and I located the tiger as being on the hills on the far side of the scrub—about three-quarters of a mile from me—and from the way he was calling it was evident he was in search of a mate.

Starting from the upper left-hand corner of the plain, and close to where I was sitting, an old cart track, used some years previously for extracting timber, ran in an almost direct line to where the tiger was calling. This track would take me in the direction of the calling animal, but on the hills was high grass, and without Robin to help me there would be little chance of my seeing him. So instead of my going to look for the tiger, I decided he should come and look for me. I was too far away for him to hear me, so I sprinted up the cart track for a few hundred yards, laid down my rifle, climbed to the top of a high tree and called three times. I was immediately answered by the tiger. After climbing down, I ran back, calling as I went, and arrived on the plain without having found a suitable place in which to sit and await the tiger. Something would have to be done and done in a hurry, for the tiger was rapidly coming nearer, so, after rejecting a little hollow which I found to be full of black stinking water, I lay down flat in the open, twenty yards from where the track entered the scrub. From this point I had a clear view up the track for fifty yards, to where a bush, leaning over it, impeded my further view. If the tiger came down the track, as I expected him

to, I decided to fire at him as soon as he cleared the obstruction.

After opening the rifle to make quite sure it was loaded, I threw off the safety-catch, and with elbows comfortably resting on the soft ground waited for the tiger to appear. I had not called since I came out on the plain, so to give him direction I now gave a low call, which he immediately answered from a distance of a hundred yards. If he came on at his usual pace, I judged he would clear the obstruction in thirty seconds. I counted this number very slowly, and went on counting up to eighty, when out of the corner of my eye I saw a movement to my right front, where the bushes approached to within ten yards of me. Turning my eyes in that direction I saw a great head projecting above the bushes, which here were four feet high. The tiger was only a foot or two inside the bushes, but all I could see of him was his head. As I very slowly swung the point of the rifle round and ran my eyes along the sights I noticed that his head was not quite square on to me, and as I was firing up and he was looking down, I aimed an inch below his right eye, pressed the trigger, and for the next half-hour nearly died of fright.

Instead of dropping dead as I expected him to, the tiger went straight up into the air above the bushes for his full length, falling backwards onto a tree a foot thick which had been blown down in a storm and was still green. With unbelievable fury he attacked this tree and tore it to bits, emitting as he did so roar upon roar, and what was even worse, a dreadful blood-curdling sound as though he was savaging his worst enemy. The branches of the tree tossed about as though struck by a tornado, while the bushes on my side shook and bulged out, and every moment I expected to have him on top of me, for he had been looking at me when I fired, and knew where I was.

Too frightened even to recharge the rifle for fear the slight movement and sound should attract the attention of the tiger, I lay and sweated for half an hour with my finger on the left trigger. At last the branches of the tree and the bushes ceased waving about, and the roaring became less frequent, and eventually, to my great relief, ceased. For another half-hour I lay perfectly still, with arms cramped by the weight of the heavy rifle, and then started to pull myself backwards with my toes. After progressing for thirty yards in this manner I got to my feet, and, crouching low, made for the welcome shelter of the nearest tree. Here I remained for some minutes, and as all was now silent I turned and made for home.

## II

Next morning, I returned accompanied by one of my men, an expert tree-climber. I had noticed the previous evening that there was a tree growing on the edge of the open ground, and about forty yards from where the tiger had fallen. We approached this tree very cautiously, and I stood behind it while the man climbed to the top. After a long and a careful scrutiny he looked down and shook his head, and when he rejoined me on the ground he told me that the bushes over a big area had been flattened down, but that the tiger was not in sight.

I sent him back to his perch on the tree with instructions to keep a sharp lookout and warn me if he saw any movement in the bushes, and went forward to have a look at the spot where the tiger had raged. He had raged to some purpose, for, in addition to tearing branches and great strips of wood off the tree, he had torn up several bushes by the roots, and bitten down others. Blood in profusion was sprinkled everywhere, and on the ground were two congealed pools, near one of which was lying a bit of bone two inches square, which I found on examination to be part of the tiger's skull.

No blood trail led away from this spot and this, combined with the two pools of blood, was proof that the tiger was still here when I left and that the precautions I had taken the previous evening had been very necessary, for when I started on my 'get-away' I was only ten yards from the most dangerous animal in the world—a freshly wounded tiger. On circling round the spot I found a small smear of blood here and there on leaves that had brushed against his face. Noting that these indications of the tiger's passage led in a direct line to a giant *semul* tree[1] two hundred yards away, I went back and climbed the tree my man was on in order to get a bird's-eye view of the ground I should have to go over, for I had a very uneasy feeling that I should find him alive: a tiger shot in the head can live for days and can even recover from the wound. True, this tiger had a bit of his skull missing, and as I had never dealt with an animal in his condition before, I did not know whether he was likely to live for a few hours or days, or live on to die of old age. For this reason I decided to treat him as an ordinary wounded tiger, and not to take any avoidable risks when following him up.

From my elevated position on the tree I saw that, a little to the left of the line to the *semul* tree, there were two trees, the nearer one thirty yards from where the blood was, and the other fifty yards further on. Leaving my man on the tree, I climbed down, picked up my rifle and a shot-gun and bag of a hundred cartridges, and very cautiously approached the nearer tree and climbed up it to a height of thirty feet, pulling the rifle and gun, which I had tied to one end of a strong cord, up after me. After fixing the rifle in a fork of the tree where it would be handy if needed, I started to spray the bushes with small shot, yard by yard up to the foot of the second tree. I did this with the object of locating the tiger, assuming he was alive and in that area, for a wounded tiger, on hearing a shot fired close to him, or on being struck by a pellet, will either growl or charge. Receiving no indication of the tiger's presence I went to the second tree, and sprayed the bushes to within a few yards of the *semul* tree, firing the last shot at the tree itself. After this last shot I thought I heard a low growl,

[1]*Bombax malabaricum*, the silk cotton tree.

but it was not repeated and I put it down to my imagination. My bag of cartridges was now empty, so after recovering my man I called it a day, and went home.

When I returned next morning I found my friend the buffalo man feeding his buffaloes on the plain. He appeared to be very much relieved to see me, and the reason for this I learnt later. The grass was still wet with dew, but we found a dry spot and there sat down to have a smoke and relate our experiences. My friend, as I have already told you, had done a lot of poaching, and having spent all his life in tiger-infested jungles tending his buffaloes, or shooting, his jungle knowledge was considerable.

After I had left him that day at the wide, open water course, he had crossed to the far side and had sat down to listen for sounds coming from the direction in which I had gone. He had heard two tigers calling; he had heard my shot followed by the continuous roaring of a tiger, and very naturally concluded I had wounded one of the tigers and that it had killed me. On his return next morning to the same spot, he had been greatly mystified by hearing a hundred shots fired, and this morning, not being able to contain his curiosity any longer, he had come to see what had happened. Attracted by the smell of blood, his buffaloes had shown him where the tiger had fallen, and he had seen the patches of dry blood and had found the bit of bone. No animal in his opinion could possibly live for more than a few hours after having a bit of its skull blown away, and so sure was he that the tiger was dead that he offered to take his buffaloes into the jungle and find it for me. I had heard of this method of recovering tigers with the help of buffaloes but had never tried it myself, and after my friend had agreed to accepting compensation for any damage to his cattle I accepted his offer.

Rounding up the buffaloes, twenty-five in number, and keeping to the line I had sprinkled with shot the previous day, we made for the *semul* tree, followed by the buffaloes. Our progress was slow, for not only had we to move the chin-high bushes with our hands to see where to put our feet, but we also had frequently to check a very natural tendency on the part of the buffaloes to stray. As we approached the *semul* tree, where the bushes were lighter, I saw a little hollow filled with dead leaves that had been pressed flat and on which were several patches of blood, some dry, others in the process of congealing, and one quite fresh; and when I put my hand to the ground I found it was warm. Incredible as it may appear, the tiger had lain in this hollow the previous day while I had expended a hundred cartridges, and had only moved off when he saw us and the buffaloes approaching. The buffaloes had now found the blood and were pawing up the ground and snorting, and as the prospect of being caught between a charging tiger and angry buffaloes did not appeal to me, I took hold of my friend's arm, turned him round and made for the open plain, followed by the buffaloes. When we were back on safe ground I told the man to go home, and said I would return next day and deal with the tiger alone.

The path through the jungles that I had taken each day when coming from and going home ran for some distance over soft ground, and on this soft ground, on this fourth day, I saw the pugmarks of a big male tiger. By following these pugmarks I found the tiger had entered the dense brushwood a hundred yards to the right of the *semul* tree. Here was an unexpected complication, for if I now saw a tiger in this jungle I should not know—unless I got a very close look at it—whether it was the wounded or the unwounded one. However, this contingency would have to be dealt with when met, and in the meantime worrying would not help, so I entered the bushes and made for the hollow at the foot of the *semul* tree.

There was no blood trail to follow so I zigzagged through the bushes, into which it was impossible to see further than a few inches, for an hour or more, until I came to a ten-foot-wide dry watercourse. Before stepping down into this watercourse I looked up it, and saw the left hind leg and tail of a tiger. The tiger was standing perfectly still with its body and head hidden by a tree, and only this one leg visible. I raised the rifle to my shoulder, and then lowered it. To have broken the leg would have been easy, for the tiger was only ten yards away, and it would have been the right thing to do if its owner was the wounded animal; but there were two tigers in this area, and to have broken the leg of the wrong one would have doubled my difficulties, which were already considerable. Presently the leg was withdrawn and I heard the tiger moving away, and going to the spot where he had been standing I found a few drops of blood—too late now to regret not having broken that leg.

A quarter of a mile further on there was a little stream, and it was possible that the tiger, now recovering from his wound, was making for this stream. With the object of intercepting him or failing that, waiting for him at the water, I took a game path which I knew went to the stream and had proceeded along it for some distance when a *sambhar* belled to my left, and went dashing off through the jungle. It was evident now that I was abreast of the tiger, and I had only taken a few more steps when I heard the loud crack of a dry stick breaking as though some heavy animal had fallen on it; the sound had come from a distance of fifty yards and from the exact spot where the *sambhar* had belled. The *sambhar* had in unmistakable tones warned the jungle folk of the presence of a tiger, and the stick therefore could only have been broken by the same animal; so getting down on my hands and knees I started to crawl in the direction from which the sound had come.

The bushes here were from six to eight feet high, with dense foliage on the upper branches and

very few leaves on the stems, so that I could see through them
for a distance of ten to fifteen feet. I had covered thirty yards,
hoping fervently that if the tiger charged he would come from
in front (for in no other direction could I have fired), when I
caught sight of something red on which the sun, drifting through
the upper leaves, was shining; it might only be a bunch of dead
leaves; on the other hand, it might be the tiger. I could get a
better view of this object from two yards to the right, so lowering
my head until my chin touched the ground. I crawled this
distance with belly to ground, and on raising my head saw the
tiger in front of me. He was crouching down looking at me,
with the sun shining on his left shoulder, and on receiving my
two bullets he rolled over on his side without making a sound.

As I stood over him and ran my eyes over his magnificent
proportions, it was not necessary to examine the pads of his feet
to know that before me lay the Bachelor of Powalgarh.

The entry of the bullet fired four days previously was hidden
by a wrinkle of skin, and at the back of his head was a big hole
which, surprisingly, was perfectly clean and healthy.

The report of my rifle was, I knew, being listened for; so I
hurried home to relieve anxiety, and while I related the last chapter
of the hunt and drank a pot of tea, my men were collecting.

Accompanied by my sister and Robin and a carrying party
of twenty men, I returned to where the tiger was lying, and before
he was roped to a pole my sister and I measured him from nose
to tip of tail, and from tip of tail to nose. At home we again
measured him to make quite sure we had made no mistake the
first time. These measurements are valueless, for there were no
independent witnesses present to certify them. They are however
interesting as showing the accuracy with which experienced
woodsmen can judge the length of a tiger from his pugmarks.
Wyndham, you will remember, said the tiger was ten feet between
pegs, which would give roughly 10'6" over curves; and while
one *shikari* said was 10'5.09" over curves, the other said he was

10'6" or a little more. Shot seven years after these estimates were made, my sister and I measured the tiger as being 10'7" over curves.

I have told the story at some length, as I feel sure that those who hunted the tiger between 1920 and 1930 will be interested to know how the Bachelor of Powalgarh met his end.

# THE MOHAN MAN-EATER

## I

Eighteen miles from our summer home in the Himalayas
there is a long ridge running east and west, some 9,000 feet in
height. On the upper slopes of the eastern end of this ridge, there
is a luxuriant growth of oat grass; below this grass the hill falls
steeply away in a series of rock cliffs to the Kosi river below.

One day a party of women and girls from the village on the
north face of the ridge were cutting the oat grass, when a tiger
suddenly appeared in their midst. In the stampede that followed,
an elderly woman lost her footing, rolled down the steep slope,
and disappeared over the cliff. The tiger, evidently alarmed by
the screams of the women, vanished as mysteriously as it had
appeared, and when the women had reassembled and recovered
from their fright, they went down the grassy slope and, looking
over the cliff, saw their companion lying on a narrow ledge some
distance below them.

The woman said she was badly injured—it was found later
that she had broken a leg and fractured several ribs—and that

she could not move. Ways and means of a rescue were discussed, and it was finally decided that it was a job for men; and as no one appeared to be willing to remain at the spot, they informed the injured woman that they were going back to the village for help. The woman begged not to be left alone, however, and at her entreaty a girl, sixteen years of age, volunteered to stay with her. So, while the rest of the party set off for the village, the girl made her way down to the right, where a rift in the cliff enabled her to get a foothold on the ledge.

This ledge only extended half-way across the face of the cliff and ended, a few yards from where the woman was lying, in a shallow depression. Fearing that she might fall off the ledge and be killed on the rocks hundreds of feet below, the woman asked the girl to move her to this depression, and this difficult and dangerous feat the girl successfully accomplished. There was only room for one in the depression, so that the girl squatted, as only an Indian can squat, on the ledge facing the woman.

The village was four miles away, and once, and once again, the two on the ledge speculated as to the length of time it would take their companions to get back to the village; what men they were likely to find in the village at that time of day; how long it would take to explain what had happened, and finally, how long it would take the rescue party to arrive.

Conversation had been carried on in whispers for fear that the tiger might be lurking in the vicinity and hear them and then, suddenly, the woman gave a gasp and the girl, seeing the look of horror on her face and the direction in which she was looking, turned her head and over her shoulder saw the tiger, stepping out of the rift in the cliff onto the ledge.

Few of us, I imagine, have escaped that worst of all nightmares in which, while our limbs and vocal cords are paralysed with fear, some terrible beast in a monstrous form approaches to destroy us; the nightmare from which, sweating fear in every pore, we waken with a cry of thankfulness to Heaven that it was only a dream. There was no such happy awakening from the nightmare of that unfortunate girl, and little imagination is needed to picture the scene. A rock cliff with a narrow ledge running partly across it and ending in a little depression in which an injured woman is lying; a young girl frozen with terror, squatting on the ledge, and a tiger slowly creeping towards her; retreat in every direction cut off, and no help at hand.

Mothi Singh, an old friend of mine, was in the village visiting a sick daughter when the women arrived, and he headed the rescue party. When this party went down the grassy slope and looked over the cliff, they saw the woman lying in a swoon, and on the ledge they saw splashes of blood.

The injured woman was carried back to the village, and when she had been revived and had told her story, Mothi Singh set out on his eighteen-mile walk to me. He was an old man well over sixty, but he scouted the suggestion that he was tired and needed a rest, so we set off together to make investigations. But there was nothing that I could do, for twenty-four hours had elapsed and all that the tiger had left of the brave young girl, who had volunteered to stay with her injured companion, were a few bits of bone and her torn and blood-stained clothes.

This was the first human being killed by the tiger which later received recognition in the Government records as 'The Mohan Man-eater'.

After killing the girl, the tiger went down the Kosi valley for the winter, killing on its way—among other people—two men of the Public Works Department, and the daughter-in-law of our member of the Legislative Council. As summer approached, it returned to the scene of its first kill, and for several years thereafter its beat extended up and down the Kosi valley from Kakrighat to Gargia—a distance of roughly forty miles—until it finally took up its quarters on the hill above Mohan, in the vicinity of a village called Kartkanoula.

At the District Conference, to which reference has been made in a previous story, the three man-eating tigers operating at that time in the Kumaon Division were classed, as follows, in their order of importance:

1st—Chowgarh, Naini Tal District.
2nd—Mohan, Almora District.
3rd—Kanda, Garhwal District.

After the Chowgarh tiger had been accounted for, I was reminded by Baines, Deputy Commissioner, Almora, that only a part of my promise made at the conference had been fulfilled, and that the Mohan tiger was next on the list. The tiger, he stated, was becoming more active and a greater menace every day, and had during the previous week killed three human beings, residents of Kartkanoula village. It was to this village Baines now suggested I should go.

While I had been engaged with the Chowgarh tiger, Baines had persuaded some sportsmen to go to Kartkanoula, but though they had sat up over human and animal kills, they had failed to make contact with the man-eater and had returned to their depot at Ranikhet. Baines informed me I should now have the ground to myself—a very necessary precaution, for nerves wear thin when hunting man-eaters, and accidents are apt to result when two or more parties are hunting the same animal.

## II

It was on a blistering hot day in May that I, my two servants, and the six Garhwalis I had brought with me from Naini Tal alighted from the 1 p.m. train at Ramnagar and set off on our twenty-four-mile foot journey to Kartkanoula. Our first stage was only seven miles, but it was evening before we arrived at Gargia. I had left home in a hurry on receiving Baines' letter, and had not had time to ask for permission to occupy the Gargia Forest Bungalow, so I slept out in the open.

On the far side of the Kosi river at Gargia there is a cliff several hundred feet high, and while I was trying to get sleep I heard what I thought were stones falling off the cliff on the rocks below. The sound was exactly the same as would be made by bringing two stones violently together. After some time this sound worried me, as sounds will on a hot night, and as the moon was up and the light good enough to avoid stepping on snakes, I left my camp bed and set out to make investigations. I found that the sound was being made by a colony of frogs in a marsh by the side of the road. I have heard land, water and tree-frogs making strange sounds in different parts of the world, but I have never heard anything so strange as the sound made by the frogs at Gargia in the month of May.

After a very early start next morning, we did the twelve miles to Mohan before the sun got hot, and while my men were cooking their food and my servants were preparing my breakfast, the chowkidar of the bungalow, two Forest Guards, and several men from the Mohan bazaar, entertained me with stories of the man-eater, the most recent of which concerned the exploits of a fisherman who had been fishing in the Kosi river. One of the Forest Guards claimed to be the proud hero of this exploit, and he described very graphically how he had been out one day with the fisherman and, on turning a bend in the river, they had come face to face with the man-eater; and how the fisherman had thrown away his rod and had grabbed the rifle off his—the Forest Guard's—shoulder; and how they had run for their lives with the tiger close on their heels. 'Did you look back?' I asked. 'No, *sahib*,' said he, pitying my ignorance. 'How could a man who was running for his life from a man-eater look back?'; and how the fisherman, who was leading by a head, in a thick patch of grass had fallen over a sleeping bear, after which there had been great confusion and shouting and everyone, including the bear, had run in different directions and the fisherman had got lost; and how after a long time the fisherman had eventually found his way back to the bungalow and had said a lot to him—the Forest Guard—on the subject of having run away with his rifle and left him empty-handed to deal with a man-eating tiger and an angry bear.

The Forest Guard ended up his recital by saying that the fisherman had left Mohan the following day saying that he had hurt his leg when he fell over the bear, and that anyway there were no fish to be caught in the Kosi river.

By midday we were ready to continue our journey, and, with many warnings from the small crowd that had collected to see us off, to keep a sharp lookout for the man-eater while going through the dense forest that lay ahead of us, we set out on our four-thousand-foot climb to Kartkanoula.

Our progress was slow, for my men were carrying heavy loads and the track was excessively steep, and the heat terrific. There had been some trouble in the upper villages a short time previously, necessitating the dispatch from Naini Tal of a small police force, and I had been advised to take everything I needed for myself and my men with me, as owing to the unsettled conditions it would not be possible to get any stores locally. This was the reason for the heavy loads my men were carrying.

After many halts we reached the edge of the cultivated land in the late afternoon, and as there was now no further danger to be apprehended for my men from the man-eater, I left them and set out alone for the Foresters' Hut which is visible from Mohan, and which had been pointed out to me by the Forest Guards as the best place for my stay while at Kartkanoula.

The hut is on the ridge of the high hill overlooking Mohan, and as I approached it along the level stretch of road running across the face of the hill, in turning a corner in a ravine where there is some dense undergrowth, I came upon a woman filling an earthenware pitcher from a little trickle of water flowing down a wooden trough. Apprehending that my approach on rubber-soled shoes would frighten her, I coughed to attract her attention, noticed that she started violently as I did so, and a few yards beyond her, stopped to light a cigarette. A minute or two later I asked, without turning my head, if it was safe for anyone to be in this lonely spot, and after a little hesitation the woman answered that it was not safe, but that water had to be fetched and as there was no one in the home to accompany her, she had come alone. Was there no man? Yes, there was a man, but he was in the fields ploughing, and in any case it was the duty of women to fetch water. How long would it take to fill the pitcher? Only a little longer. The woman had got over her fright and shyness, and I was now subjected to a close cross-examination. Was I a policeman? No. Was I a Forest Officer? No. Then who was I? Just a man. Why had I come? To try and help the people of Kartkanoula. In what way? By shooting the man-eater. Where had I heard about the man-eater? Why had I come alone? Where were my men? How many were there? How long would I stay? And so on.

The pitcher was not declared full until the woman had satisfied her curiosity, and as she walked behind me, she pointed to one of several ridges running down the south face of the hill, and pointing out a big tree growing on a grassy slope said that three days previously the man-eater had killed a woman under it; this tree I noted, with interest, was only two or three hundred yards from my objective—the Foresters' Hut. We had now come to a footpath running up the hill, and as she took it, the woman said the village from which she had come was just round the shoulder of the hill, and added that she was now quite safe.

Those of you who know the women of India will realize that I had accomplished a lot, especially when it is remembered that

there had recently been trouble in this area with the police. So far from alarming the woman and thereby earning the hostility of the entire countryside, I had, by standing by while she filled her pitcher and answering a few questions, gained a friend who would in the shortest time possible acquaint the whole population of the village with my arrival; that I was not an officer of any kind, and that the sole purpose of my visit was to try to rid them of the man-eater.

## III

The Foresters' Hut was on a little knoll some twenty yards to the left of the road, and as the door was only fastened with a chain, I opened it and walked inside. The room was about ten feet square and quite clean, but had a mouldy disused smell; I learnt later that the hut had not been occupied since the advent of the man-eater in that area eighteen months previously. On either side of the main room there were two narrow slips of rooms, one used as a kitchen, and the other as a fuel store. The hut would make a nice safe shelter for my men, and having opened the back door to let a current of air blow through the room, I went outside and selected a spot between the hut and the road for my 40-lb. tent. There was no furniture of any kind in the hut, so I sat down on a rock near the road to await the arrival of my men.

The ridge at this point was about fifty yards wide, and as the hut was on the south edge of the ridge, and the village on the north face of the hill, the latter was not visible from the former. I had been sitting on the rock for about ten minutes when a head appeared over the crest from the direction of the village, followed by a second and a third. My friend, the water-carrier had not been slow in informing the village of my arrival.

When strangers meet in India and wish to glean information on any particular subject from each other, it is customary to refrain from broaching the subject that has brought them together—whether accidentally or of set purpose—until the very last moment, and to fill up the interval by finding out everything concerning each other's domestic and private affairs; as for instance, whether married, and if so, the number and sex of children and their ages; if not married, why not; occupation and amount of pay, and so on. Questions that would in any other part of the world earn one a thick ear, are in India—and especially in our hills—asked so artlessly and universally that no one who has lived among the people dreams of taking offence at them.

In my conversation with the woman I had answered many of the set questions, and the ones of a domestic nature which it is not permissible for a woman to ask of a man, were being put to me when my men arrived. They had filled a kettle at the little spring, and in an incredibly short time dry sticks were collected, a fire lit, the kettle boiled, and tea and biscuits produced. As I opened a tin of condensed milk I heard the men asking my servants why condensed milk was being used instead of fresh milk, and receiving the answer that there was no fresh milk; and further that, as it had been apprehended that owing to some previous trouble in this area no fresh milk would be available, a large supply of tinned milk had been brought. The men appeared to be very distressed on hearing this and after a whispered conversation one of them, who I learnt later was the Headman of Kartkanoula, addressed me and said it was an insult to them to have brought tinned milk, when all the resources of the village were at my disposal. I admitted my mistake, which I said was due to my being a stranger to that locality, and told the Headman that if he had any milk to spare, I would gladly purchase a small quantity for my daily requirement, but that beyond the milk, I wanted for nothing.

My loads had now been unstrapped, while more men had arrived from the village, and when I told my servants where I wanted them to pitch my tent there was a horrified exclamation from the assembled villagers. Live in a tent—indeed! Was I ignorant of the fact that there was a man-eating tiger in this area and that it used this road regularly every night? If I doubted their word, let me come and see the claw marks on the doors of the houses where the road ran through the upper end of the village. Moreover, if the tiger did not eat me in the tent it would certainly eat my men in the hut, if I was not there to protect them. This last statement made my men prick up their ears and add their entreaties to the advice of the villagers, so eventually I agreed to stay in the main room, while my two servants occupied the kitchen, and the six Garhwalis the fuel store.

The subject of the man-eater having been introduced, it was now possible for me to pursue it without admitting that it was the one subject I had wished to introduce from the moment the first man had put his head over the ridge. The path leading down to the tree where the tiger had claimed its last victim was pointed out to me, and the time of day, and the circumstances under which the woman had been killed, explained. The road along which the tiger came every night, I was informed, ran eastward to Baital Ghat with a branch down to Mohan, and westward to Chaknakl on the Ramganga river. The road going west, after running through the upper part of the village and through cultivated land for half a mile, turned south along the face of the hill, and on rejoining the ridge on which the hut was, followed the ridge right down to Chaknakl. This portion of the road between Kartkanoula and Chaknakl, some six miles long, was considered to be very dangerous, and had not been used since the advent of the man-eater; I subsequently found that after leaving the cultivated land, the road entered, dense tree and scrub jungle, which extended right down to the river.

The main cultivation of Kartkanoula village is on the north face of the hill, and beyond this cultivated land there are several small ridges, with deep ravines between. On the nearest of these ridges, and distant about a thousand yards from the Foresters' Hut, there a big pine tree. Near this tree, some ten days previously, the tiger had killed, partly eaten, and left a woman, and as the three sportsmen who were staying in a forest bungalow four miles away were unable to climb the pine tree, the villagers had put up three *machan*s in three separate trees, at distances varying from one hundred to one hundred and fifty yards from the kill, and the *machan*s had been occupied by the sportsmen and their servants a little before sunset. There was a young moon at the time, and after it had set, the villagers heard a number of shots being fired, and when they questioned the servants next morning, the servants said they did not know what had been fired at for they themselves had not seen anything. Two days later a cow had been killed over which the sportsmen had sat, and again, as on the previous occasion, shots had been fired after the moon had set. It is these admittedly sporting but unsuccessful attempt to bag man-eaters that makes them so wary, and the more difficult to shoot the longer they live.

The villagers gave me one very interesting item of news in connexion with the tiger. They said they always knew when it had come into the village by the low moaning sound it made. On questioning them closely, I learnt that at times the sound was continuous as the tiger passed between the houses, while at other times the sound stopped for sometimes short and other times long periods.

From this information I concluded (a) that the tiger was suffering from a wound, (b) that the wound was of such a nature that the tiger only felt it when in motion, and that therefore, (c) the wound was in one of its legs. I was assured that the tiger had not been wounded by any local *shikari*, or by any of the sportsmen from Ranikhet who had sat up for it; however this was of little importance, for the tiger had been a man-eater for years, and the wound that I believed it was suffering from, might have been the original cause of its becoming a man-eater. A very interesting point and one that could only be cleared up by examining the tiger—after it was dead.

The men were curious to know why I was so interested in the sound made by the tiger, and when I told them that it indicated the animal had a wound in one of its legs and that the wound had been caused either by a bullet, or porcupine quills, they disagreed with my reasoning and said that on the occasions they had seen the tiger it appeared to be in sound condition, and further, that the ease with which it killed and carried off its victims was proof that it was not crippled in any way. However, what I told them was remembered and later earned me the reputation of being gifted with second sight.

IV

When passing through Ramnagar, I had asked the Tahsildar to purchase two young male buffaloes for me and to send them to Mohan, where my men would take them over.

I told the villagers I intended tying up one of the buffaloes near the tree where three days previously the woman had been killed and the other on the road to the Chaknakl, and they said they could think of no better sites, but that they would talk the matter over among themselves, and let me know in the morning if they had any other suggestions to make. Night was now drawing in, and before leaving the Headman promised to send word to all the adjoining villages in the morning to let them know of my arrival, the reason for my coming, and to impress on them the urgency of letting me know without loss of time of any kills, or attacks by the tiger in their areas.

The musty smell in the room had much decreased though it was still noticeable. However, I paid no attention to it, and after a bath and dinner put two stones against the doors—there being no other way of keeping them shut—and being bone-tried after my day's exertions went to bed and to sleep. I am a light sleeper, and two or three hours later I awoke on hearing an animal moving about in the jungle. It came right up to the back door. Getting hold of a rifle and a torch, I moved the stone aside with my foot and heard an animal moving off as I opened the door—it might from the sound it was making have been the tiger, but it might also have been a leopard or a porcupine. However, the jungle was too thick for me to see what it was. Back in the room and with the stone once more in position, I noticed I had developed a sore throat, which I attributed to having sat in the wind after the hot walk up from Mohan; but when my servant pushed the door open and brought in my early morning cup of tea, I found I was suffering from an attack of laryngitis, possibly due to my having slept in a long-disused hut, the roof of which was swarming with bats. My servant informed me that he and his companion had escaped infection, but that the six Garhwalis in the fuel store were all suffering from the same complaint as I was. My stock of medicine consisted of a two-ounce bottle of iodine and a few tablets of quinine, and on rummaging in my gun-case I found a small paper pocket of permanganate which my sister had provided for me on a previous occasion. The packet was soaked through with gun oil, but the crystals were still soluble, and I put a liberal quantity of the crystals into a tin of hot water, together with some iodine. The resulting gargle was very potent, and while it blackened our teeth, it did much to relieve the soreness in our throats.

After an early breakfast I sent four men down to Mohan to bring up the two buffaloes, and myself set off to prospect the ground where the woman had been killed. From the directions I had received overnight, I had no difficulty in finding the spot where the tiger had attacked and killed the woman, as she was tying the grass she had cut into the bundle. The grass, and the rope she was using, were lying just as they had been left, as were also two bundles of grass left by her companions when they had run off in fright to the village. The men had told me that the body of the woman had not been found, but from the fact that three perfectly good lengths of rope and the dead woman's sickle had been left in the jungle, I am inclined to think that no attempt had been made to find her.

The woman had been killed at the upper end of a small landslide, and the tiger had taken her down the slide and into a thick patch of undergrowth. Here the tiger had waited, possibly to give the women time to get out of sight, and had then crossed the ridge visible from the hut, after which it had gone with its kill straight down the hill for a mile or more into, dense tree and scrub jungle. The tracks were now four days old, and there was nothing to be gained by following them further, I turned back to the hut.

The climb back to the ridge was a very steep one, and when I reached the hut at about midday I found an array of pots and pans of various shapes and sizes on the verandah, all containing milk. In contrast to the famine of the day before, there was now abundance, sufficient milk in fact for me to have bathed in. My servants informed me they had protested to no effect and that each man had said, as he deposited his vessel on the verandah, that he would take good care that I used no more condensed milk while I remained in their midst.

I did not expect the man to return from Mohan with the buffaloes before nightfall, so after lunch I set out to have a look at the road to Chaknakl.

From the hut the hill sloped gradually upwards to a height of about five hundred feet, and was roughly triangular in shape. The road, after running through cultivated land for half a mile, turned sharply to the left, went across a steep rocky hill until it regained the ridge, and then turned to the right and followed the ridge down to Chaknakl. The road was level for a short distance after coming out on the ridge, and then went steeply down, the gradient in places being eased by hairpin bends.

I had the whole afternoon before me, and examined about three miles of the road very carefully. When a tiger uses a road regularly it invariably leaves signs of its passage by making scratch marks on the side of the road. These scratch marks, made for the same purpose as similar marks made by domestic cats and all other members of the cat family, are of very great interest to the sportsman, for they provide him with the following very useful information, (1) whether the animal that has made the mark is a male or a female, (2) the direction in which it was travelling, (3) the length of time that has elapsed since it passed, (4) the direction and approximate distance of its headquarters, (5) the nature of its kills, and finally (6) whether the animal has recently had a meal of human flesh. The value of this easily-acquired information to one who is hunting a man-eater on strange ground will be easily understood. Tigers also leave their pugmarks on the roads they use and these pugmarks can provide one with quite a lot of useful information, as for instance the direction and speed at which the animal was travelling, its sex and age, whether all four limbs are sound, and if not sound, which particular limb is defective.

The road I was on had through long disuse got overgrown with short stiff grass and was therefore not, except in one or two damp places, a good medium on which to leave pugmarks. One of these damp places was within a few yards of where the road came out on the ridge, and just below this spot there was a green and very stagnant pool of water; a regular drinking place for *sambhar*.

I found several scratch marks just round the corner where the road turned to the left after leaving the cultivated ground, the most recent of which was three days old. Two hundred yards from these scratch marks the road, for a third of its width, ran under an overhanging rock. This rock was ten feet high and at the top of it there was a flat piece of ground two or three yards wide, which was only visible from the road when approaching the rock from the village side. On the ridge I found more scratch marks, but I did not find any pugmarks until I got to the first hairpin bend. Here, in cutting across the bend, the tiger had left its trace where it had jumped down onto the same soft earth. The tracks, which were a day old, were a little distorted, but even so it was possible to see that they had been made by a big, old, male tiger.

When one is moving in an area in which

a man-eating tiger is operating, progress is of necessity very slow, for every obstruction in one's line of walk, be it a bush, a tree, a rock, or an inequality in the ground capable of concealing death, has to be cautiously approached, while at the same time, if a wind is not blowing—and there was no wind that evening—a careful and constant lookout has to be maintained behind and on either side. Further, there was much of interest to be looked at, for it was the month of May, when orchids at this elevation— 4,000 to 5,000 feet—are at their best, and I have never seen a greater variety or a greater wealth of bloom than the forests on that hill had to show. The beautiful white butterfly orchids were in greatest profusion, and every second tree of any size appeared to have decked itself out with them.

It was here that I first saw a bird that Prater of the Bombay Natural History Society later very kindly identified for me as the Mountain Crag Martin, a bird of a uniform ash colour, with a slight tinge of pink on its breast, and in size a little smaller than a Rosy Pastor. These birds had their broods with them, and while the young ones—four to a brood—sat in a row on a dry twig at the top of a high tree, the parent birds kept darting away— often to a distance of two or three hundred yards—to catch insects. The speed at which they flew was amazing, and I am quite sure there is nothing in feathers in north India, not excluding our winter visitor the great Tibetan Swallow, that these Martins could not make rings round. Another thing about these birds that was very interesting was their wonderful eyesight. On occasion they would fly in a dead straight line for several hundred yards before turning and coming back. It was not possible, at the speed they were going, that they were chasing insects on these long flights, and as after each flight they invariably thrust some minute object into one of the gaping mouths, I believed they were able to see insects at a range at which they would not have been visible to the human eye through the most powerful field-glasses.

Safeguarding my neck, looking out for tracks, enjoying nature generally, and listening to all the jungle sounds—a *sambhar* a mile away down the hillside in the direction of Mohan was warning the jungle folk of the presence of a tiger, and a *kakar* and a *langur* on the road to Chaknakl were warning other jungle folk of the presence of a leopard—time passed quickly, and I found myself back at the over hanging rock as the sun was setting. As I approached this rock, I marked it as being quite the most dangerous spot in all the ground I had so far gone over. A tiger lying on the grass-covered bit of ground above the rock would only have to wait until anyone going either up or down the road was under, or had passed it, to have them at his mercy—a very dangerous spot indeed, and one that needed remembering.

When I got back to the hut I found the two buffaloes had arrived, but it was too late to do anything with them that evening.

My servants had kept a fire going most of the day in the hut, the air of which was now sweet and clean, but even so I was not going to risk sleeping in a closed room again; so I made them cut two thorn bushes and wedge them firmly into the doorways before going to bed. There was no movement in the jungle near the back door that night, and after a sound sleep I woke in the morning with my throat very much better.

I spent most of the morning talking to the village people and listening to the tales they had to tell of the man-eater and the attempts that had been made to shoot it, and after lunch I tied up one buffalo on the small ridge the tiger had crossed when carrying away the woman, and the other at the hairpin bend where I had seen the pugmarks.

Next morning I found both buffaloes sleeping peacefully after having eaten most of the big feed of grass I had provided them with. I had tied bells round the necks of both animals, and the absence of any sound from these bells as I approached each buffalo gave me two disappointments for, as I have said, I found both of them asleep. That evening I changed the position of the second buffalo from the hairpin bend to where the road came out on the ridge, close to the pool of stagnant water.

The methods most generally employed in tiger shooting can

briefly be described as (a) sitting up, and (b) beating, and young male buffaloes are used as bait in both cases. The procedure followed is to select the area most convenient for a sit up, or for a beat, and to tie the bait out in the late evening using a rope which the bait cannot, but which the tiger can, break; and when the bait is taken to either sit up over the kill on a *machan* in a tree, or beat the cover into which the kill has been taken.

In the present case neither of these methods was feasible. My throat, though very much better, was still sore and it would not have been possible for me to have sat up for any length of time without coughing, and a beat over that vast area of heavily wooded and broken ground would have been hopeless even if I had been able to muster a thousand men, so I decided to stalk the tiger, and to this end carefully sited my two buffaloes and tied them to stout saplings with four one inch-thick hemp ropes, and left them out in the jungle for the whole twenty-four hours.

I now stalked the buffaloes in turn each morning as soon as there was sufficient light to shoot by, and again in the evening, for tigers, be they, man-eaters or not, kill as readily in the day as they do at night in areas in which they are not disturbed, and during the day, while I waited for news from the outlying villages, nursed my throat, and rested, my six Garhwalis fed and watered the buffaloes.

On the fourth evening when I was returning at sunset after visiting the buffalo on the ridge, as I came round a bend in the road thirty yards from the overhanging rock, I suddenly, and for the first time since my arrival at Kartkanoula, felt I was in danger, and that the danger that threatened me was on the rock in front of me. For five minutes I stood perfectly still with my eyes fixed on the upper edge of the rock, watching for movement. At that short range the flicker of an eyelid would have caught my eyes, but there was not even this small movement; and after going forward ten paces, I again stood watching for several minutes. The fact that I had seen no movement did not in any way reassure me—the man-eater was on the rock, of that I was sure; and the question was, what was I going to do about it? The hill, as I have already told you, was very steep, had great rocks jutting out of it, and was overgrown with long grass and tree and scrub jungle. Bad as the going was, had it been earlier in the day I would have gone back and worked round and above the tiger to try to get a shot at him, but with only half an hour of daylight left, and the best part of a mile still to go, it would have been madness to have left the road. So, slipping up the safety-catch and putting the rifle to my shoulder, I started to pass the rock.

The road here was about eight feet wide, and going to the extreme outer edge I started walking crab-fashion, feeling each step with my feet before putting my weight down to keep from stepping off into space. Progress was slow and difficult, but as I drew level with the overhanging rock and then began to pass it, hope rose high that the tiger would remain where he was, until I reached that part of the road from which the flat bit of ground above the rock, on which he was lying, was visible. The tiger, however, having failed to catch me off my guard was taking no chances, and I had just got clear of the rock when I heard a low muttered growl above me, and a little later first a *kakar* went off barking to the right, and then two *sambhar* hind started belling near the crest of the triangular hill.

The tiger had got away with a sound skin, but for that matter, so had I, so there was no occasion for regrets, and from the place on the hill where the *sambhar* was, I felt sure he would hear the bell I had hung round the neck of the buffalo that was tied on the ridge near the stagnant pool.

When I reached the cultivated land I found a group of men waiting for me. They had heard the *kakar* and *sambhar* and were very disappointed that I had not seen the tiger, but cheered up when I told them I had great hopes for the morrow.

## V

During the night a dust-storm came on, followed by heavy rain, and I found to my discomfort that the roof of the hut was very

porous. However, I eventually found a spot where it was leaking less than in others, dragged my camp bed to it and continued my sleep. It was brilliantly clear morning when I awoke; the rain had washed the heat haze and dust out of the atmosphere, and every leaf and blade of grass was glistering in the newly risen sun.

Hitherto I had visited the nearer buffalo first, but this morning I had an urge to reverse the daily procedure, and after instructing my men to wait until the sun was well up and then go to feed and water the nearer buffalo, I set off with high hopes down the Chaknakl road; having first cleaned and oiled my 450/400 rifle— a very efficient weapon, and a good and faithful friend of many years' standing.

The overhanging rock that I had passed with such trouble the previous evening did not give me a moment's uneasiness now and after passing it I started looking for tracks, for the rain had softened the surface of the road. I saw nothing however until I came to the damp place on the road, which, as I have said, was on the near side of the ridge and close to the pool where the buffalo was tied. Here in the soft earth I found the pugmarks of the tiger, made before the storm had come on, and going in the direction of the ridge. Close to this spot there is a rock about three feet high, on the *khud* side of the road. On the previous occasions that I had stalked down the road, I had found that by standing on this rock I could look over a hump in the road and see the buffalo where it was tied forty yards away. When I now climbed on to the rock and slowly raised my head, I found that the buffalo had gone. This discovery was as disconcerting as it was inexplicable. To prevent the tiger from carrying the buffalo away to some distant part of the jungle, where the only method of getting a shot would have been by sitting up on the ground or in a tree—a hopeless proceeding with my throat in the condition it was in—I had used four thicknesses of strong one-inch-thick hemp rope, and even so the tiger had got away with the kill.

I was wearing the thinnest of rubber-soled shoes, and very silently I approached the sapling to which the buffalo had been tied and examined the ground. The buffalo had been killed before the storm, but had been carried away after the rain had stopped, without any portion of it having been eaten. Three of the ropes I had twisted together had been gnawed through, and the fourth had been broken. Tigers do not usually gnaw through ropes; however, this one had done so, and had carried off the kill down the hill facing Mohan. My plans had been badly upset, but very fortunately the rain had come to my assistance. The thick carpet of dead leaves which the day before had been as dry as tinder were now wet and pliable, and provided I made no mistakes, the pains the tiger had been to in getting away with the kill might yet prove his undoing.

When entering a jungle in which rapid shooting might at any moment become necessary, I never feel happy until I have reassured myself that my rifle is loaded. To pull a trigger in an emergency and wake up in the Happy Hunting Grounds—or elsewhere—because one had omitted to load a weapon, would be one of those acts of carelessness for which no excuse could be found; so though I knew I had loaded my rifle before I came to the overhanging rock, I now opened it and extracted the cartridges. I changed one that was discoloured and dented, and after moving the safety-catch up and down several times to make sure it was working smoothly—I have never carried a cocked weapon—I set off to follow the drag.

This word 'drag', when it is used to describe the mark left on the ground by a tiger when it is moving its kill from one place to another, is misleading, for a tiger when taking its kill any distance (I have seen a tiger carry a full-grown cow for four miles) does not drag it, it carries it; and if the kill is too heavy to be carried, it is left. The drag is distinct or faint according to the size of the animal that is being carried, and the manner in which it is being held. For instance, assuming the kill is a *sambhar* and the tiger is holding it by the neck, the hind quarters will trail on the ground leaving a distinct drag mark. On the other hand, if the *sambhar* is being held by the middle of the back, there may be a faint drag mark, or there may be none at all.

In the present case the tiger was carrying the buffalo by the neck, and the hind quarters trailing on the ground were leaving a drag mark it was easy to follow. For a hundred yards the tiger went diagonally across the face of the hill until he came to a steep clay bank. In attempting to cross this bank he had slipped and relinquished his hold of the kill, which had rolled down the hill for thirty or forty yards until it had fetched up against a tree. On recovering the kill the tiger picked it up by the back, and from now on only one leg occasionally touched the ground, leaving a faint drag mark, which nevertheless, owing to the hillside being carpeted with bracken, was not very difficult to follow. In his fall the tiger had lost direction, and he now appeared to be undecided where to take the kill. First he went a couple of hundred yards to the right, then a hundred yards straight down the hill through a dense patch of *ringals*. After forcing his way with considerable difficulty through the *ringals*, he turned to the left and went diagonally across the hill for a few hundred yards until he came to a great rock, to the right of which he skirted. This rock was flush with the ground on the approach side, and rising gently for twenty feet, appeared to project out over a hollow or dell of considerable extent. If there was a cave or recess under the projection, it would be a very likely place for the tiger to have taken his kill to, so leaving the drag I stepped on to the rock and moved forward very slowly, examining every yard of ground below, and on either side of me, as it came into view. On reaching the end of the projection and looking over, I was disappointed to find that the hill came up steeply to meet the rock, and that there was no cave or recess under it as I had expected there would be.

As the point of the rock offered a good view of the dell and of the surrounding jungle—and was comparatively safe from an attack from the man-eater—I sat down; and as I did so, I caught sight of a red and white object in a dense patch of short undergrowth, forty or fifty yards directly below me. When one is looking for a tiger in a dense jungle, everything red that catches the eye is immediately taken for the tiger, and here, not only could I see the red of the tiger, but I could also see his stripes. For a long minute I watched the object intently, and then, as the face you are told to look for in a freak picture suddenly resolves itself, I saw that the object I was looking at was the kill, and not the tiger; the red was blood where he had recently been eating, and the stripes were the ribs from which he had torn away the skin. I was thankful for having held my fire for that long minute, for in a somewhat similar case a friend of mine ruined his chance of bagging a very fine tiger by putting two bullets into a kill over which he had intended sitting; fortunately he was a good shot, and the two men whom he had sent out in advance to find the kill and put up a *machan* over it, and who were, at the time he fired, standing near the kill screened by a bush, escaped injury.

When a tiger that has not been disturbed leaves his kill out in the open, it can be assumed that he is lying up close at hand to guard the kill from vultures and other scavengers, and the fact that I could not see the tiger did not mean that he was not lying somewhere close by in the dense undergrowth.

Tigers are troubled by flies and do not lie long in one position, so I decided to remain where I was and watch for movement; but hardly had I come to this decision, when I felt an irritation in my throat. I had not quite recovered from my attack of laryngitis and the irritation grew rapidly worse until it became imperative for me to cough. The usual methods one employs on these occasions, whether in church or the jungle, such as holding the breath and swallowing hard, gave no relief until it became a case of cough, or burst; and in desperation I tried to relieve my throat by giving the alarm-call of the *langur*. Sounds are difficult to translate into words and for those of you who are not acquainted with our jungles I would try to describe this alarm-call, which can be heard for half a mile, as *khok*, *khok*, *khok*, repeated again and again at short intervals, and ending up with *khokorror*. All *langurs* do not call at tigers, but the ones in our hills certainly do, and as this tiger had probably heard the call every day of his life, it was the one sound I could make to which he would not pay the slightest attention. My rendering of the call in this emergency did not sound very convincing, but it had the desired effect of removing the irritation from my throat.

For half an hour thereafter I continued to sit on the rock, watching for movement and listening for news from the jungle folk, and when I had satisfied myself that the tiger was not anywhere within my range of vision, I got off the rock, and, moving with the utmost caution, went down to the kill.

VI

I regret I am not able to tell you what weight of flesh a full-grown tiger can consume at a meal, but you will have some idea of his capacity when I tell you he can eat a *sambhar* in two days, and a buffalo in three, leaving possibly a small snack for the fourth day.

The buffalo I had tied up was not full-grown but he was by no means a small animal, and the tiger had eaten approximately half of him. With a meal of that dimension inside of him I felt sure he had not gone far, and as the ground was still wet, and would remain so for another hour or two, I decided to find out in what direction he had gone, and if possible, stalk him.

There was a confusion of tracks near the kill but by going round in widening circles I found the tracks the tiger had made when leaving. Soft-footed animals are a little more difficult to track than hard-footed ones, yet after long years of experience tracking needs as little effort as a gun dog exerts when following a scent. As silently and as slowly as a shadow I took up the track, knowing that the tiger would be close at hand. When I had gone a hundred yards I came on a flat bit of ground, twenty feet square, and carpeted with that variety of short soft grass that has highly scented roots; on this grass the tiger had lain, the imprint of his body being clearly visible.

As I was looking at the imprint and guessing at the size of the animal that had made it, I saw some of the blades of grass that had been crushed down, spring erect. This indicated that the tiger had been gone only a minute or so.

You will have some idea of the layout when I tell you that the tiger had brought the kill down from the north, and on leaving it had gone west, and that the rock on which I had sat, the kill, and the spot where I was now standing, formed the points of a triangle, one side of which was forty yards, and the other two sides a hundred yards long.

My first thought on seeing the grass spring erect was that the tiger had seen me and moved off, but this I soon found was not likely, for neither the rock nor the kill was visible from the grass plot, and that he had not seen me and moved after I had taken up his track I was quite certain. Why then had he left his comfortable bed and gone away? The sun shining on the back of my neck provided the answer. It was now nine o'clock of an unpleasantly hot May morning, and a glance at the sun and the tree-tops over which it had come showed that it had been shining on the grass for ten minutes. The tiger had evidently found it too hot, and gone away a few minutes before my arrival to look for a shady spot.

I have told you that the grass plot was twenty feet square. On the far side to that from which I had approached, there was a fallen tree, lying north and south. This tree was about four feet in diameter, and as it was lying along the edge of the grass plot in the middle of which I was standing, it was ten feet away from me. The root end of the tree was resting on the hillside, which here went up steeply and was overgrown with brushwood, and the branch end (which had been snapped off when the tree had fallen) was projecting out over the hillside. Beyond the tree the hill appeared to be more or less perpendicular, and running across the face of it was a narrow ledge of rock, which disappeared into the dense jungle thirty yards further on.

If my surmise, that the sun had been the cause of the tiger changing his position, was correct, there was no more suitable place than the lee of the tree for him to have taken shelter in, and the only way of satisfying myself on this point was to walk up to the tree—and look over. Here a picture seen long years ago in *Punch* flashed into memory. The picture was of a lone sportsman who had gone out to hunt lions and who on glancing up, on to the rock he was passing, looked straight into the grinning face of the most enormous lion in Africa. Underneath the picture was written, 'When you go out looking for a lion, be quite sure that you want to see him'. True, there would be this small difference, that whereas my friend in Africa looked up—into the lion's face, I would look down—into the tiger's; otherwise the two cases—assuming that the tiger *was* on the far side of the tree—would be very similar.

Slipping my feet forward an inch at a time on the soft grass, I now started to approach the tree, and had covered about half the distance that separated me from it when I caught sight of a black-and-yellow object about three inches long on the rocky ledge, which I now saw was a well-used game path. For a long minute I stared at this motionless object, until I was convinced that it was the tip of the tiger's tail. If the tail was pointing away from me the head must obviously be towards me, and as the ledge was only some two feet wide, the tiger could only be crouching down and waiting to spring the moment my head appeared over the bole of the tree. The tip of the tail was twenty feet from me, and allowing eight feet for the tiger's length while crouching, his head would be twelve feet away. But I should have to approach much nearer before I should be able to see enough of his body to get in a crippling shot, and a crippling shot it would have to be if I wanted to leave on my feet. And now, for the first time in my life, I regretted my habit of carrying an uncocked rifle. The safety-catch of my 450/400 makes a very distinct click when thrown off, and to make any sound now would either bring the tiger right on top of me, or send him straight down the steep hillside without any possibility of my getting in a shot.

Inch by inch I again started to creep forward, until the whole of the tail, and after it the hind quarters, came into view. When I saw the hind quarters, I could have shouted with delight, for they showed that the tiger was not crouching and ready to spring, but was lying down. As there was only room for his body on the two-foot-wide ledge, he had stretched his hind legs out and was resting them on the upper branches of an oak sapling growing up the face of the almost perpendicular hillside. Another foot forward and his belly came into view, and from the regular way in which it was heaving up and down I knew that he was asleep. Less slowly now I moved forward, until his shoulder, and then his whole length, was exposed to my view. The back of his head was resting on the edge of the grass plot, which extended for three or four feet beyond the fallen tree; his eyes were fast shut, and his nose was pointing to heaven.

Aligning the sights of the rifle on his forehead I pressed the trigger and, while maintaining a steady pressure on it, pushed up the safety-catch. I had no idea how this reversal of the usual method of discharging a rifle would work, but it did work; and when the heavy bullet at that short range crashed into his forehead not so much as a quiver went through his body. His tail remained stretched straight out; his hind legs continued to rest on the upper branches of the sapling; and his nose still pointed to heaven. Nor did his position change in the slightest when I sent a second, and quite unnecessary, bullet to follow the first. The only change noticeable was that his stomach had stopped heaving up and down, and that blood was trickling down his forehead from two surprisingly small holes.

I do not know how the close proximity of a tiger reacts on others, but me it always leaves with a breathless feeling—due possibly as much to fear as to excitement—and a desire for a little rest. I sat down on the fallen tree and lit the cigarette I had denied myself from the day my throat had got bad, and allowed my thoughts to wander. Any task well accomplished gives satisfaction, and the one just completed was no exception. The reason for my presence at that spot was the destruction of the man-eater, and from the time I had left the road two hours previously right up to the moment I pushed up the safety-catch everything—including the *langur* call—had worked smoothly and without a single fault.

In this there was great satisfaction, the kind of satisfaction I imagine an author must feel when he writes FINIS to the plot that, stage by stage, has unfolded itself just as he desired it to. In my case, however, the finish had not been satisfactory, for I had killed the animal, that was lying five feet from me, in his sleep.

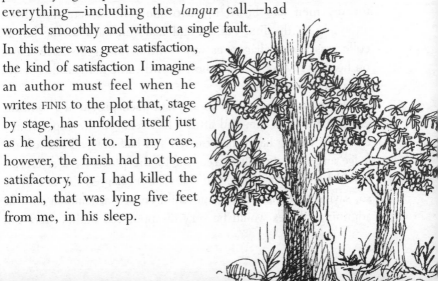

My personal feelings in the matter are, I know, of little interest to others, but it occurs to me that possibly you also might think it was not cricket, and in that case I should like to put the arguments before you that I used on myself, in the hope that you will find them more satisfactory than I did. These arguments were (a) the tiger was a man-eater that was better dead than alive, (b) therefore it made no difference whether he was awake or asleep when killed, and (c) that had I walked away when I saw his belly heaving up and down I should have been morally responsible for the deaths of all the human beings he killed thereafter. All good and sound arguments, you will admit, for my having acted as I did; but the regret remains that through fear of the consequences to myself, or fear of losing the only chance I might ever get, or possibly a combination of the two, I did not awaken the sleeping animal and give him a sporting chance.

The tiger was dead, and if my trophy was to be saved from falling into the valley below and ruined, it was advisable to get him off the ledge with as little delay as possible. Leaning the rifle, for which I had no further use, against the fallen tree, I climbed up to the road and, once round the corner near the cultivated land, I cupped my hands and sent a cooee echoing over the hills and valleys. I had no occasion to repeat the call, for my men had heard my two shots when returning from attending to the first buffalo and had run back to the hut to collect as many villagers as were within calling distance. Now, on hearing my cooee, the whole crowd came helterskelter down the road to meet me.

When stout ropes and an axe had been procured I took the crowd back with me, and after I had secured the ropes round the tiger, willing hands half carried and half dragged him off the ledge and over the fallen tree, on to the plot of grass. Here I would have skinned him, but the villagers begged me not to do so, saying that the women and children of Kartkanoula and the adjoining villages would be very disappointed if they were not given an opportunity of seeing the tiger with their own eyes and satisfying themselves that the man-eater, in fear of whom they had lived for so many years, and who had established a reign of terror over the whole district, was really and truly dead.

While a couple of saplings to assist in carrying the tiger back to the hut were being felled, I saw some of the men passing their hands over the tiger's limbs, and knew they were satisfying themselves that their assertion that the tiger had not been suffering from any old, or crippling, wounds was correct. At the hut the tiger was placed in the shade of a wide-spreading tree and the villagers informed that it was at their disposal up to two o'clock— longer I could not give them, for it was a very hot day and there was fear of the hair slipping, and the skin being ruined.

I myself had not looked closely at the tiger, but at 2 p.m., when I laid him on his back to start the skinning, I noticed that most of the hair from the inner side of his left foreleg was missing, and that there were a number of small punctures in the skin, from which yellow fluid was exuding. I did not draw attention to these punctures, and left the skinning of the leg, which was considerably thinner than the right leg, to the last. When the skin had been removed from the rest of the animal, I made a long cut from the chest to the pad of the festering left leg, and as I removed the skin, drew out of the flesh, one after another, porcupine quills which the men standing round eagerly seized as souvenirs; the longest of these quills was about five inches, and their total number was between twenty-five and thirty. The flesh under the skin, from the tiger's chest to the pad of his foot, was soapy, and of a dark yellow colour; cause enough to have made

the poor beast moan when he walked, and quite sufficient reason for his having become—and having remained—a man-eater, for porcupine quills do not dissolve no matter how long they are embedded in flesh.

I have extracted, possibly, a couple of hundred porcupine quills from the man-eating tigers I have shot. Many of these quills have been over nine inches in length and as thick as pencils. The majority were embedded in hard muscles, a few were wedged firmly between bones, and all were broken off short under the skin.

Unquestionably the tigers acquired the quills when killing porcupines for food, but the question arises—to which I regret I am unable to give any satisfactory answer—why animals with the intelligence, and the agility, of tigers, should have been so careless as to drive quills deep into themselves, or so slow in their movements as to permit porcupines—whose only method of defending themselves is walking backwards—to do so; and further, why the quills should have been broken off short, for porcupine quills are not brittle.

Leopards are just as partial to porcupines as our hill tigers are, but they do not get quills stuck in them, for they kill porcupines—as I have seen—by catching them by the head; and why tigers do not employ the same safe and obvious method of killing as leopards employ, and so avoid injury to themselves is a mystery to me.

And now I have done telling you the story of the second of the three man-eating tigers mentioned at that District Conference of long ago and, when opportunity offers, I will tell you how the third tiger, the Kanda man-eater, died.

# THE FISH OF MY DREAMS

**F**ishing for *mahseer* in a well-stocked submontane river is, in my opinion, the most fascinating of all field sports. Our environments, even though we may not be continuously conscious of them, nevertheless play a very important part in the sum total of our enjoyment of any form of outdoor sport. I am convinced that the killing of the fish of one's dreams in uncongenial surroundings would afford an angler as little pleasure as the winning of the Davis Cup would to a tennis player if the contest were staged in the Sahara.

The river I have recently been fishing in flows, for some forty miles of its length, through a beautifully wooded valley, well stocked with game and teeming with bird life. I had the curiosity to count the various kinds of animals and birds seen in one day, and by the evening of that day my count showed, among animals, *sambhar*, *chital*, *kakar*, *ghooral*, pig, *langur* and red monkeys; and among birds seventy-five varieties including peafowl, red jungle fowl, *kalege* pheasants, black partridge, and bush quail.

In addition to these I saw a school of five otter in the river, several small mugger, and a python. The python was lying on the surface of a big still pool, with only the top of its flat head and eyes projecting above the gin-clear water. The subject was one I had long wished to photograph, and in order to do this it was necessary to cross the river above the pool and climb the opposite hillside; but fortunately I had been seen by those projecting eyes, and as I cautiously stepped backwards, the reptile, which appeared to be about eighteen feet long, submerged, to retire to its subterranean home among the piled-up boulders at the head of the pool.

In some places the valley through which the river flows, is so narrow that a stone can be tossed with ease from one side to the other, and other places it widens out to a mile or more. In these open spaces grow amaltas with their two-feet-long sprays of golden bloom, *karaunda* and box bushes with their white star-shaped flowers. The combined scent from these flowers fills the air, throbbing with the spring songs of a multitude of birds, with the most delicate and pleasing of perfumes. In these surroundings angling for *mahseer* might well be described as the sport fit for kings. My object in visiting this sportsman's paradise was not, however, to kill *mahseer*, but to try to secure a daylight picture of a tiger, and it was only when light conditions were unfavourable that I laid aside my movie camera for a rod.

I had been out from dawn one day, trying, hour after hour, to get a picture of a tigress and her two cubs. The tigress was a young animal, nervous as all young mothers are, and as often as I stalked her, she retired with the cubs into heavy cover. There is a limit to the disturbance a tigress, be she young or old, will suffer when accompanied by cubs, and when the limit on this occasion had been reached I altered my tactics and tried sitting up in trees over open glades, and lying in high grass near a stagnant pool in which she and her family were accustomed to drink, but with no better success.

When the declining sun was beginning to cast shadows over the open places I was watching, I gave up the attempt, and

added the day to the several hundred days I had already spent in trying to get a picture of a tiger in its natural surroundings. The two men I had brought from camp had passed the day in the shade of a tree on the far side of the river. I instructed them to return to camp by way of the forest track, and, exchanging my camera for a rod, set off along the river, intent on catching a fish for my dinner.

The fashion in rods and tackle has altered, in recent years, as much as the fashion in ladies' dress. Gone, one often wonders where, are the 18-foot greenheart rods with their unbreakable accompaniments, and gone the muscles to wield them, and their place has been taken by light one-handed fly rods.

I was armed with an 11-foot tournament trout rod, a reel containing 50 yards of casting line and 200 yards of fine silk backing, a medium gut cast, and a one-inch home-made brass spoon.

When one has unlimited undisturbed water to fish one is apt to be over-critical. A pool is discarded because the approach to it is over rough ground, or a run is rejected because of a suspected snag. On this occasion, half a mile had been traversed before a final selection was made: a welter of white water cascading over rocks at the head of a deep oily run 80 yards long, and at the end of the run a deep still pool 200 yards long and 70 yards wide. Here was the place to catch the fish for my dinner.

Standing just clear of the white water I flicked the spoon into the run, pulling a few yards of line off the reel as I did so, and as I raised the rod to allow the line to run through the rings the spoon was taken by a fish, near the bank, and close to where I was standing. By great good luck the remaining portion of the slack line tightened on the drum of the reel and did not foul the butt of the rod or handle of the reel, as so often happens.

In a flash the fish was off downstream, the good well-oiled reel singing a paean of joy as the line was stripped off it. The 50 yards of casting line followed by 100 yards of backing were gone, leaving in their passage burned furrows in the fingers of my left hand, when all at once the mad rush ceased as abruptly as it had begun, and the line went dead.

The speculations one makes on these occasions chased each other through my mind, accompanied by a little strong language to ease my feelings. The hold had been good without question. The cast, made up a few days previously from short lengths of gut procured from the Pilot Gut Coy., had been carefully tied and tested. Suspicion centred on the split ring: possibly, cracked on a stone on some previous occasion, it had now given way.

Sixty yards of the line are back on the reel, when the slack line is seen to curve to the left, and a moment later is cutting a strong furrow upstream—the fish is still on, and is heading for the white water. Established here, pulling alternately from upstream, at right angles and downstream fails to dislodge him. Time drags on, and the conviction grows that the fish has gone, leaving the line hung up on a snag. Once again and just as hope is being abandoned the line goes slack, and then tightens a moment later, as the fish for the second time goes madly downstream.

And now he appears to have made up his mind to leave this reach of the river for the rapids below the pool. In one strong steady run he reaches the tail of the pool. Here, where the water fans out and shallows, he hesitates, and finally returns to the pool. A little later he shows on the surface for the first time, and if not for the fact that the taut line runs direct from the point of the rod to the indistinctly seen object on the far side of the pool, it would be impossible to believe that the owner of that great triangular fin, projecting five inches out of the water, had taken a fly spoon a yard or two from my feet.

Back in the depths of the pool, he was drawn inch by inch into slack water. To land a big fish single-handed on a trout rod is not an easy accomplishment. Four times he was stranded with a portion of his great shoulders out of water, and four times at my very cautious approach he lashed out, and, returning to the pool, had to be fought back inch by inch. At the fifth attempt, with the butt of the rod held at the crook of my thumb and reversed, rings upwards to avoid the handle of the reel coming into contact with him, he permits me to place one hand and then the other against his sides and very gently propel him through the shallow water up on to dry land.

A fish I had set out to catch, and a fish I had caught, but he would take no part in my dinner that night, for between me and camp lay three and a half miles of rough ground, half of which would have to be covered in the dark.

When sending away my 11-lb camera, I had retained the cotton cord I use for drawing it up after me when I sit in trees. One end of this cord was passed through the gills of the fish and out at his mouth, and securely tied in a loop. The other end was made fast to the branch of a tree. When the cord was paid out the fish lay snugly against a great slab of rock, in comparatively still water. Otter were the only danger, and to scare them off I made a flag of my handkerchief, and fixed the end of the improvised flagstaff in the bed of the river a little below the fish.

The sun was gilding the mountain tops next morning when I was back at the pool, and found the fish lying just where I had left it the previous evening. Having unfastened the cord from the branch, I wound it round my hand as I descended the slab of rock towards the fish. Alarmed at my approach, or feeling the vibration of the cord, the fish suddenly galvanized into life, and with a mighty splash dashed upstream. Caught at a disadvantage, I had no time to brace my feet on the sloping and slippery rock, but was jerked headlong into the pool.

I have a great distaste for going over my depth in these submontane rivers, for the thought of being encircled by a hungry python is very repugnant to me, and I am glad there were no witnesses to the manner in which I floundered out of that pool. I had just scrambled out on the far side, with the fish still attached to my right hand, when the men I had instructed to follow me arrived. Handing the fish over to them to take down to our camp on the bank of the river, I went on ahead to change and get my camera ready.

I had no means of weighing the fish and at a rough guess both the men and I put it at 50 lb.

The weight of the fish is immaterial, for weights are soon forgotten. Not so forgotten are the surroundings in which the sport is indulged in. The steel blue of the fern-fringed pool where the water rests a little before cascading over rock and shingle to draw breath again in another pool more beautiful than the one just left—the flash of the gaily coloured kingfisher as he breaks the surface of the water, shedding a shower of diamonds from his wings as he rises with a chirp of delight, a silver minnow held firmly in his vermilion bill—the belling of the *sambhar* and the clear tuneful call of the *chital* apprising the jungle folk that the tiger, whose pugmarks show wet on the sand where a few minutes before he crossed the river, is out in search of his dinner. These are things that will not be forgotten and will live in my memory, the lodestone to draw me back to that beautiful valley, as yet unspoiled by the hand of man.

# THE KANDA MAN-EATER

**H**owever little faith we have in the superstitions we share with others—thirteen at a table, the passing of wine at dinner, walking under a ladder, and so on—our own private superstitions, though a source of amusement to our friends, are very real to us.

I do not know if sportsmen are more superstitious than the rest of mankind, but I do know that they take their superstitions very seriously. One of my friends invariably takes five cartridges, never more and never less, when he goes out after big game, and another as invariably takes seven cartridges. Another, who incidentally was the best-known big-game sportsman in northern India, never started the winter shooting season without first killing a *mahseer*. My own private superstition concerns snakes. When after man-eaters I have a deep-rooted conviction, that, however much I may try, all my efforts will be unavailing until I have first killed a snake.

During the hottest days of one May, I had from dawn to dark climbed innumerable miles up and down incredibly steep hills,

and through thick thorn bushes that had left my hands and knees a mass of ugly scratches, in search of a very wary man-eater. I returned on that fifteenth evening, dog-tired, to the two-roomed Forest Bungalow I was staying at to find a deputation of villagers waiting for me with the very welcome news that the man-eater, a tiger, had been seen that day on the outskirts of their village. It was too late to do anything that night, so the deputation were provided with lanterns and sent home with strict injunctions that no one was to leave the village the following day.

The village was situated at the extreme end of the ridge on which the bungalow was, and because of its isolated position and the thick forest that surrounded it, had suffered more from the depredations of the tiger than any other village in the district. The most recent victims were two women and a man.

I had made one complete circle of the village the following morning and had done the greater part of a second circle, a quarter of a mile below the first, when after negotiating a difficult scree of shale I came upon a little *nullah* made by the rush of rainwater down the steep hillside. A glance up and down the *nullah* satisfied me that the tiger was not in it, and then a movement just in front of me, and about twenty-five feet away, caught my eye. At this spot there was a small pool of water the size of a bath-tub, and on the far side of it was a snake that had evidently been drinking. The lifting of the snake's head had caught my eye and it was not until the head had been raised some two or three feet from the ground and the hood expanded that I realized it was a hamadryad. It was the most beautiful snake I had ever seen. The throat, as it faced me, was a deep orange red shading to golden yellow where the body met the ground. The back, olive green, was banded by ivory-coloured chevrons, and some four feet of its length from the tip of its tail upwards was shiny black, with white chevrons. In length the snake was between thirteen and fourteen feet.

One hears many tales about hamadryads, their aggressiveness when disturbed, and the speed at which they can travel. If, as it seemed about to do, the snake attacked, up or down hill I should be at a disadvantage, but across the shale scree I felt that I could hold my own. A shot at the expanded hood, the size of a small plate, would have ended the tension, but the rifle in my hands was a heavy one and I had no intention of disturbing the tiger that had showed up after so many days of weary waiting and toil. After an interminably long minute, during which time the only movement was the flicking in and out of a long and quivering forked tongue, the snake closed his hood, lowered his head to the ground and, turning, made off up the opposite slope. Without taking my eyes off him I groped with my hand on the hillside and picked up a stone that filled my hand as comfortably as a cricket ball. The snake had just reached a sharp ridge of hard clay when the stone, launched with the utmost energy I was capable of, struck it on the back of the head. The blow would have killed any other snake outright but the only, and very alarming, effect it had on the hamadryad was to make it whip round and come straight towards me. A second and a larger stone fortunately caught it on the neck when it had covered half the distance between us, and after that the rest was easy. With a great feeling of satisfaction I completed the second circle round the village, and through it proved as fruitless as the first, I was elated at having killed the snake. Now, for the first time in many days, I had a feeling that my search for the man-eater would be successful.

The following day I again searched the forest surrounding the village, and towards evening found the fresh pugmarks of the tiger at the edge of a ploughed field overlooking the village. The occupants of the village, numbering about a hundred, were by now thoroughly alarmed, and leaving them with the assurance that I would return early next day I set out on my lonely four-mile walk back to the Forest Bungalow.

To walk with safety through forests or along deserted roads in an area in which a man-eater is operating, calls for the utmost caution and the strict observance of many rules. It is only when the hunter has repeatedly been the hunted that the senses can be attuned to the required pitch, and those rules be strictly adhered to, the breaking of which would provide the man-eater with an easy victim.

The reader may ask, 'Why a lonely walk?', when I probably had men and to spare with me in camp. My answer to this very natural question would be: first, because one is apt to get careless and rely too much on one's companions, and second, because in a mix-up with a tiger one has a better chance when one is alone.

The next morning, as I approached the village, I saw an eager throng of men waiting for me, and when within earshot I was greeted with the gratifying news that a buffalo had been killed during the night. The animal had been killed in the village, and after being dragged some distance along the ridge had been taken down into a narrow, deep, and very heavily wooded valley on the north face of the hill.

A very careful reconnaissance from a projecting rock on the ridge satisfied me that an approach down the steep hill, along the line of the drag, would not be advisable, and that the only thing to do was to make a wide detour, enter the valley from the lower end and work up to the spot where I expected to find the kill.

This manoeuvre was successfully accomplished, and by midday I had arrived at the spot—marked from above—where the valley flattened out for a hundred yards before going straight up three hundred yards to the ridge above. It was at the upper end of this flat bit of ground that I expected to find the kill, and with luck, the tiger. The long and difficult climb up the valley through dense thickets of thorn bush and stunted bamboo had brought out a bath of sweat, and as it was not advisable to take on a job where quick firing might be necessary with sweaty hands, I sat down for a much needed rest and for a smoke.

The ground in front of me was strewn with large smooth boulders among which a tiny stream meandered, forming wherever possible small crystal-clear pools. Shod with the thinnest of rubber-soled shoes, the going over these boulders was ideal for my purpose, and when I had cooled and dried I set off to stalk the kill in the hope of finding the tiger lying asleep near it. When three-quarters of the ground had been covered I caught sight of the kill tucked away under a bank of ferns, and about twenty-five yards away from where the hill went steeply up to the ridge. The tiger was not in sight, and, very cautiously drawing level with the kill I took up my position on a flat boulder to scan every inch of ground visible.

The premonition of impending danger is too well known and established a fact to need any comment. For three or four minutes I had stood perfectly still with no thought of danger and then all at once I became aware that the tiger was looking at me at a very short range. The same sense that had conveyed the feeling of impending danger to me had evidently operated in the same way on the tiger and

awakened him from his sleep. To my left front were some dense bushes, growing on a bit of flat ground. On these bushes, distant fifteen to twenty feet from me, and about the same distance from the kill, my interest centred. Presently the bushes were gently stirred and the next second I caught sight of the tiger going at full speed up the steep hillside. Before I could get the rifle to bear on him he disappeared behind a creeper-covered tree, and it was not until he had covered about sixty yards that I again saw him, as he was springing up the face of a rock. At my shot he fell backwards and came roaring down the hill, bringing an avalanche of stones with him. A broken back, I concluded; and just as I was wondering how best to deal with him when he should arrive all-of-a-heap at my feet, the roaring ceased, and the next minute, as much to my relief as to my disappointment, I saw him going full out, and apparently unwounded, across the side of the hill. The momentary glimpses I caught of him offered no shot worth taking, and with a crash through some dry bamboos he disappeared round the shoulder of the hill into the next valley.

I subsequently found that my bullet, fired at an angle of seventy-five degrees, had hit the tiger on the left elbow and chipped out a section from that bone which some cynical humorist has named the 'funny bone'. Carrying on, the bullet had struck the rock and, splashing back, had delivered a smashing blow on the point of the jaw. Neither wound, however painful it may have been, was fatal, and the only result of my following up the very light blood trail into the next valley was to be growled at from a dense thorn thicket, to enter which would have been suicidal.

My shot had been heard in the village and an expectant crowd were waiting for me on the ridge. They were even more disappointed, if that were possible, than I was at the failure of my carefully planned and as carefully executed stalk.

On visiting the kill the following morning, I was very pleased and not a little surprised to find that the tiger had returned to it during the night and taken a light meal. The only way now of getting a second shot was to sit up over the kill; and here a difficulty presented itself. There were no suitable trees within convenient distance of the kill, and the very unpleasant experience I had on a former occasion had effectively cured me of sitting at night on the ground for a man-eater. While still undecided where to sit I heard the tiger call, some distance down the valley up which I had climbed the previous day. The calling of the tiger offered me a very welcome chance of shooting it in the most pleasant way it is possible of bringing one of these animals to bag. The conditions under which a tiger can be called up are (a) when rampaging through the forest in search of a mate and (b) when rampaging, wounded. It goes without saying that the sportsman must be able to call sufficiently well to deceive the tiger, and that the call must come from a spot to which the tiger will quite naturally come—a dense thicket, or a patch of heavy grass—and that the sportsman must be prepared to take his shot at a very close range. I am quite certain that many sportsmen will be sceptical of a statement I have made that a lightly wounded tiger will come to a call. I would ask all such to reserve their judgement until they have tried to experiment for themselves. On the present occasion, however, though the tiger answered me, call for call, for upwards of an hour, he refused to come any nearer, and I attributed my failure to the fact that I was calling from the spot where the previous day the tiger had met with an unfortunate experience.

The tree I finally selected was growing on the very edge of a perpendicular bank and had a convenient branch about eight feet from the ground. When sitting on this branch I should be thirty feet from, and directly above, the boulder-strewn ravine up which I expected the tiger to come. The question of the tree settled, I returned to the ridge where I had instructed my men to meet me with breakfast.

By four o'clock in the evening I was comfortably seated on the branch and prepared for a long and hard sit-up. Before leaving my men I had instructed them to cooee to me from the ridge at sunrise next morning. If I answered with the call of a leopard they were to sit tight, but if they received no answer, they were to form two parties with as many villagers as they could collect and come down on either side of the valley, shouting and throwing stones.

I have acquired the habit of sleeping in any position on a tree, and as I was tired the evening did not pass unpleasantly. As the setting sun was gilding the hilltops above me I was roused to full consciousness by the alarm-call of a *langur*. I soon located the monkey, sitting in a tree-top on the far side of the valley, and as it was looking in my direction I concluded it had mistaken me for a leopard. The alarm-call was repeated at short intervals, and finally ceased as darkness came on.

Hour after hour I strained my eyes and ears, and was suddenly startled by a stone rolling down the hillside and striking my tree. The stone was followed by the stealthy padding of a heavy, soft-footed animal, unmistakably the tiger. At first I comforted myself with the thought that his coming in this direction, instead of up the valley, was accidental, but this thought was soon dispelled when he started to emit low deep growls from immediately behind me. Quite evidently he had come into the valley while I was having breakfast, and, taking up a position on the hill, where the monkey had later seen him, had watched me climbing into the tree. Here was a situation I had not counted on and one that needed careful handling. The branch that had provided a comfortable seat while daylight lasted, admitted of little change of position in the dark. I could, of course, have fired off my rifle into the air, but the terrible results I have seen following an attempt to drive away a tiger at very close quarters by discharging a gun dissuaded me from taking this action. Further, even if the tiger had not attacked, the discharge of the rifle (a 450/400) so near him would probably have made him leave the locality and all my toil would have gone for nothing.

I knew the tiger would not spring for that would have carried him straight down a drop of thirty feet on to the rocks below. But there was no need for him to spring, for by standing on his hind legs he could easily reach me. Lifting the rifle off my lap and reversing it, I pushed the barrel between my left arm and side, depressing the muzzle and slipping up the safety-catch as I did so. This movement was greeted by a deeper growl than any that had preceded it. If the tiger now reached up for me he would in all probability come in contact with the rifle, round the triggers of which my fingers were crooked, and even if I failed to kill him the confusion following on my shot would give me a sporting chance of climbing higher into the tree. Time dragged by on leaden feet, and, eventually, tiring of prowling about the hillside and growling, the tiger sprang across a little ravine on my left and a few minutes later I heard the welcome sound of a bone being cracked at the kill. At last I was able to relax in my uncomfortable position and the only sounds I heard for the rest of the night came from the direction of the kill.

The sun had been up but a few minutes and the valley was still in deep shadow when my men cooeed from the ridge, and almost immediately afterwards I caught sight of the tiger making off at a fast canter up, and across, the hill on my left. In the uncertain light and with my nightlong-strained eyes the shot was a very difficult one, but I took it, and had the satisfaction of seeing the bullet going home. Turning with a great roar, he came straight for my tree, and as he was in the act of springing the second bullet, with great good fortune, crashed into his chest. Diverted in his spring by the impact of the heavy bullet, the tiger struck the tree just short of me, and ricochetting off it went headlong into the valley below, where his fall was broken by one of the small pools already alluded to. He foundered out of the water, leaving it dyed red with his blood, and went lumbering down the valley and out of sight.

Fifteen hours on the hard branch had cramped every muscle in my body, and it was not until I had swarmed down the tree, staining my clothes in the great gouts of blood the tiger had left on it, and had massaged my stiff limbs, that I was able to follow him. He had gone but a short distance, and I found him lying dead at the foot of a rock in another pool of water.

Contrary to my orders the men, collected on the ridge, hearing my shot and the tiger's roar followed by a second shot, came in a body down the hill. Arrived at the bloodstained tree, at the foot of which my soft hat was lying, they not unnaturally concluded I had been carried off by the tiger. Hearing their shouts of alarm I called out to them, and again with a gasp of dismay when they saw my blood-stained clothes. Reassured that I was not injured and that the blood on my clothes was not mine, a moment later they were crowding round the tiger. A stout sapling was soon cut and lashed to him with creepers, and the tiger, with no little difficulty and a great deal of shouting, was carried up the steep hill to the village.

In remote areas in which long-established man-eaters are operating, many gallant acts of heroism are performed, which the local inhabitants accept as everyday occurrences and the outside world has no means of hearing about. I should like to put on record one such act concerning the Kanada man-eater's last human victim. I arrived on the scene shortly after the occurrence, and from details supplied by the villagers and from a careful examination of the ground, which had not been disturbed in the interval; I am able to present you with a story which I believe to be correct in every detail.

In the village near which I shot the Kanda man-eater lived an elderly man and his only son. The father had served in the army during the 1914–18 war and it was his ambition to get his son enlisted in the Royal Garhwal Rifles—not as simple a job in the 'piping days of peace', when vacancies were few and applicants many, as it is today. Shortly after the lad's eighteenth birthday a party of men passed through the village on their way to the bazaar at Lansdowne. The lad joined this party and immediately on arrival at Lansdowne presented himself at the Recruiting Office. As his father had taught him to salute with military precision and how to conduct himself in the presence of a Recruiting Officer, he was accepted without any hesitation, and, after enrolment, was given leave to deposit his few personal possessions at home before starting his army training.

He arrived back home at about midday, after an absence of five days, and was told by the friends who thronged round him to hear his news that his father was away ploughing their small holding at the extreme end of the village and would not return before nightfall. (The field that was being ploughed was the same one on which I had seen the pugmarks of the man-eater the day I killed the hamadryad.)

One of the lad's jobs had been to provide fodder for their cattle, and after he had partaken of the midday meal in a neighbour's house he set out with a party of twenty men to collect leaves.

The village, as I have told you, is situated on a ridge, and is surrounded by forests. Two women had already been killed by the man-eater while cutting grass in these forests, and for several months the cattle had been kept alive on leaves cut from the trees surrounding the village. Each day the men had to go further afield to get their requirements, and on this particular day the party of twenty-one, after crossing the cultivated land, went for a quarter of a mile down a very steep rocky hill to the head of the valley which runs east for eight miles, through dense forest, to where it meets the Ramganga river opposite the Dhikala Forest Bungalow.

Copy of Petition

Sent to the Author by the People of Garhwal

The Promise mentioned on Page 125, was made after receiving this petition

From    The Public of Patty Painaun, Bungi and Bickla Badalpur District Garhwal

To      Captain J. E. Carbitt, Esq., I.A.R.O., Kaladhungi Distt. Naini Tal

Respected Sir,

We all the public (of the above 3 Patties) most humbly and respectfully beg to lay the following few lines for your kind consideration and doing needful.

That in this vicinity a tiger has turned out man-eater since December last. Up to this date he has killed 5 men and wounded 2. So we the public are in a great distress. By the fear of this tiger we cannot watch our wheat crop at night so the deers have nearly ruined it. We cannot go in the forest for fodder grass nor we can enter our cattles in the forest to graze so many of our cattle are to die. Under the circumstances we are nearly to be ruined. The Forest Officials are doing every possible arrangement to kill this tiger but there is no hope of any success. 2 *shikari* gentlemen also tried to shoot it but unfortunately they could not get it. Our kind District Magistrate has notified Rs. 150 reward for killing this tiger, so every one is trying to kill it but no success. We have heard that your kind self have killed many man-eater tigers and leopards. For this you have earned a good name specially in Kumaon revenue Division. The famous man-eater leopard of Nagpur has been shoot by you. This it the voice of all the public here that this tiger also will be killed only by you. So we the public venture to request that you very kindly take trouble to come to this place and shoot this tiger (our enemy) and save the public from this calamity. For this act of kindness we the public will be highly obliged and will pray for your long life and prosperity. Hope you will surely consider on our condition and take trouble to come here for saving us from this calamity. The route to this place is as follows Ramnagar to Sultan, Sultan to Lahachaur, Lahachaur to Kanda. If your honour kindly informs us the date of your arrival at Ramnagar we will send our men and cart to Ramnagar to meet you and accompany you.

We beg to remain
Sir
Your most sincerely
Signed Govind Singh

Dated Jharat
Negi
The 18th February 1933                                    Headman Village Jharat

*followed by 40 signatures and 4 thumb impressions of*
*inhabitants of Painaun, Bungi and Bickla Badalpur Patties.*

Address
The Govind Singh Negi
Village Jharat Patty
Painaun P. O.
Badialgaon Dist., Garhwal, U.P.

At the head of the valley the ground is more or less flat and overgrown with big trees. Here the men separated, each climbing into a tree of his choice, and after cutting the quantity of leaves required they tied them into bundles with rope brought for the purpose, and returned to the village in twos and threes.

Either when the party of men were coming down the hill, talking at the top of their voices to keep up their courage and scare away the man-eater, or when they were on the trees shouting to each other, the tiger, who was lying up in a dense patch of cover half a mile down the valley, heard them. Leaving the cover, in which it had four days previously killed and eaten a *sambhar* hind, the tiger crossed a stream and by way of a cattle track that runs the entire length of the valley hurried up in the direction of the men. (The speed at which a tiger has travelled over any ground on which he has left signs of his passage can be easily determined from the relative position of his fore and hind pugmarks.)

The lad of my story had selected a Bauhinea tree from which to cut leaves for his cattle. This tree was about twenty yards above the cattle track, and the upper branches were leaning out over a small ravine in which there were two rocks. From a bend in the cattle track the tiger saw the lad on the tree, and after lying down and watching him for some time it left the track and concealed itself behind a fallen silk cotton tree some thirty yards from the ravine. When the lad had cut all the leaves he needed, he descended from the tree and collected them in a heap, preparatory to tying them into a bundle. While doing this on the open flat ground he was comparatively safe, but unfortunately he had noticed that two of the branches he had cut had fallen into the ravine between the two big rocks, and he sealed his fate by stepping down into the ravine to recover them. As soon as he was out of sight the tiger left the shelter of the fallen tree and crept forward to the edge of the ravine, and as the lad was stooping down to pick up the branches, it sprang on him and killed him. Whether the killing took place while the other men were still on the trees, or after they had left, it was not possible for me to determine.

The father of the lad returned to the village at sunset and was greeted with the very gratifying news that his son had been accepted for the army, and that he had returned from Lansdowne on short leave. Asking where the lad was, he was told that he had gone out earlier in the day to get fodder, and surprise was expressed that the father had not found him at home. After bedding down the bullocks the father went from house to house to find his son. All the men who had been out that day were questioned in turn, and all had the same tale to tell—that they had separated at the head of the valley, and no one could remember having seen the lad after that.

Crossing the terraced cultivated land the father went to the edge of the steep hill, and called, and called again, to his son, but received no answer.

Night was by now setting in. The man returned to his home and lit a small smoke-dimmed lantern, and as he passed through the village he horrified his neighbours by telling them, in reply to their questions, that he was going to look for his son. He was asked if he had forgotten the man-eater and answered that it was because of the man-eater that he was so anxious to find his son, for it was possible he had fallen off a tree and injured himself and, for fear of attracting the man-eater, had not answered to his call.

He did not ask anyone to accompany him, and no one offered to do so, and for the whole of that night he searched up and down that valley in which no one had dared to set foot since the advent of the man-eater. Four times during the night—as I saw from his footprints—when going along the cattle track he had passed within ten feet of where the tiger was lying eating his son.

Weary and heartsick he climbed a little way up the rocky hill as light was coming, and sat down for a rest. From this raised position he could see into the ravine. At sunrise he saw a glint of blood on the two big rocks, and hurrying down to the spot he found all that the tiger had left of his son. These remains he collected and took back to his home, and when a suitable shroud had been procured, his friends helped him to carry the remains to the burning ghat on the banks of the Mandal river.

I do not think it would be correct to assume that acts such as these are performed by individuals who lack imagination and who therefore do not realize the grave risks they run. The people of our hills, in addition to being very sensitive to their environments, are very superstitious, and every hilltop, valley, and gorge is credited with possessing a spirit in one form or another, all of the evil and malignant kind most to be feared during the hours of darkness. A man brought up in these surroundings, and menaced for over a year by a man-eater, who, unarmed and alone, from sunset to sunrise, could walk through dense forests which his imagination peopled with evil spirits, and in which he had every reason to believe a man-eater was lurking, was in my opinion possessed of a quality and a degree of courage that is given to few. All the more do I give him credit for his act of heroism for not being conscious that he had done anything unusual, or worthy of notice. When at my request he sat down near the man-eater to enable me to take a photograph he looked up at me and said, in a quiet and collected voice, 'I am content now, *sahib*, for you have avenged my son.'

This was the last of the three man-eaters that I had promised the District Officials of Kumaon, and later the people of Garhwal, that I would do my best to rid them of.

# THE PIPAL PANI TIGER

**B**eyond the fact that he was born in a ravine running deep into the foot-hills and was one of a family of three, I know nothing of his early history.

He was about a year old when, attracted by the calling of a *chital* hind early one November morning, I found his pugmarks in the sandy bed of the little stream known locally as Pipal Pani. I thought at first that he had strayed from his mother's care, but, as week succeeded week and his single tracks showed on the game paths of the forest, I came to the conclusion that the near approach of the breeding season was an all-sufficient reason for his being alone. Jealously guarded one day, protected at the cost of the parent life if necessary, and set adrift the next, is the lot of all jungle folk; nature's method of preventing inbreeding.

The winter he lived on peafowl, *kakar*, small pig and an occasional *chital* hind, making his home in a prostrate giant of the forest felled for no apparent reason, and hollowed out by times and porcupines. Here he brought most of his kills, basking,

when the days were cold, on the smooth bole of the tree, where many a leopard had basked before him.

It was not until January was well advanced that I saw the cub at close quarters. I was out one evening without any definite object on view, when I saw a crow rise from the ground and wipe its beak as it lit on the branch of tree. Crows, vultures, and magpies always interest me in the jungle, and many are the kills I have found both in India and in Africa with the help of the these birds. On the present occasion the crow led me to the scene of an overnight tragedy. A *chital* had been killed and partly eaten and, attracted to the spot probably as I had been, a party of men passing along the road, distant some fifty yards, had cut up and removed the remains. All that was left of the *chital* were a few splinters of bone and a little congealed blood off which the crow had lately made his meal. The absence of thick cover and the proximity of the road convinced me that the animal responsible for the kill had not witnessed the removal and that it would return in due course; so I decided to sit up, and myself as comfortable in a plum tree as the thorns permitted.

I make no apology to you, my reader, if you differ with me on the ethics of the much-debated subject of sitting up over kills. Some of my most pleasant *shikar* memories centre round the hour or two before sunset that I have spent in tree over a natural kill, ranging from the time when, armed with a muzzle-loader whipped round with brass wire to prevent the cracked barrel from bursting, I sat over a *langur* killed by a leopard, to a few days ago, when with the most modern rifle across my knees, I watched a tigress and her two full-grown cubs eat up the *sambhar* stag they had killed, and counted myself no poorer for not having secured a trophy.

True, on the present occasion there is no kill below me, but for the reason given, that will not affect any chance of shot; scent to interest the jungle folk there is in plenty in the bloodsoaked ground, as witness the old grey-whiskered boar who has been quietly rooting along for the past ten minutes, and who suddenly stiffens to attention as he comes into the line of the blood-tainted wind. His snout held high, and worked as only a pig can work that member, tells him more than I was able to glean from the ground which showed no tracks; his method of approach, a short excursion to the right and back into the wind, and then a short to the left and again back into the wind, each manoeuvre bringing him a few yards nearer, indicates the *chital* was killed by a tiger. Making sure once and again that nothing worth eating has been left, he finally trots off and disappears from view.

Two *chital*, both with horns in velvet, now appear and from the fact that they are coming down-wind, and making straight for the blood-soaked spot, it is evident they were witnesses to the overnight tragedy. Alternately snuffing the ground, or standing rigid with every muscle tensed for instant flight, they satisfy their curiosity and return the way they came.

Curiosity is not a human monopoly: many an animal's life is cut short by indulging in it. A dog leaves the verandah to bark at a shadow, a deer leaves the herd to investigate a tuft of grass that no wind agitated, and the waiting leopard is provided with a meal.

The sun is nearing the winter line when a movement to the right front attracts attention. An animal has crossed an opening between two bushes at the far end of a wedge of scrub that terminates thirty yards from my tree. Presently the bushes at my end part, and out into the open, with never a look to right or left, steps the cub. Straight up to the spot where his kills had been he goes, his look of expectancy giving place to one of disappointment as he realizes that his *chital*, killed, possibly, after house of patient stalking, is gone. The splinters of bone and congealed blood are rejected, and his interest centres on a tree stump lately used as a butcher's block, to which some shreds of flesh are adhering. I was not the only one who carried fire-arms in these jungles and, if the cub was to grow into a tiger, it was necessary he should be taught the danger of carelessly approaching kills in daylight. A scatter-gun and dust-shot would have served my purpose better, but the rifle will have to do this time; and, as he raises his head to smell the stump, my bullet crashes into the hard wood an inch from his nose. Only once in the years that followed did the cub forget that lesson.

The following winter I saw him several times. His ears did not look so big now and he had changed his baby hair for a coat of rich tawny red with well-defined stripes. The hollow tree had been given up to its rightful owners, a pair of leopards, new quarter found in a thick belt of scrub skirting the foot-hills, and young *sambhar* added to his menu.

On my annual descent from the hills next winter, the familiar pugmarks no longer showed on the game paths and at the drinking places, and for severals weeks I thought the cub had abandoned his old haunts and gone further afield. Then one morning his absence was explained for, side by side with his tracks, were the smaller and more elongated tracks of the mate he had gone to find. I only once saw the tiger, for the cub was a tiger now, together. I had been out before dawn to try to bag a *sarao* that lived in the foot-hills, and returning along a fire track my attention was arrested by a vulture, perched on the dead limb of a *sal* tree.

The bird had his back towards me and was facing a short stretch of scrub with dense jungle beyond. Dew was still heavy on the ground, and without a sound I reached the tree and peered

round. One antler of a dead *sambhar*, for no living deer would lie
in that position, projected above the low bushes. A convenient
moss-covered rock afforded my rubbershod feet silent and safe
hold, and as I drew myself erect, the *sambhar* came into full view.
The hind quarters had been eaten away and, lying on either side
of the kill, were the pair, the tiger being on the far side with
only his hind legs showing. Both tigers were asleep. Ten feet
straight in front, to avoid a dead branch, and thirty feet to the
left would give me a shot at the tiger's neck, but in planning the
stalk I had forgotten the silent spectator. Where I stood I was
invisible to him, but before the ten feet had been covered I came
into view and, alarmed at my near proximity, he flapped off his
perch, omitting as he did so to notice a thin creeper dependent
from a branch above him against which he collided, and came
ignominiously to ground. The tigress was up and away in an
instant, clearing at a bound the kill and her mate, the tiger
not being slow to follow; a possible shot, but too risky with
thick jungle ahead where a wounded animal would have all the
advantages. To those who have never tried it, I can recommend
the stalking of leopards and tigers on their kills as a most pleasant
form of sport. Great care should however be taken over the shot,
for if the animal is not killed outright, or anchored, trouble is
bound to follow.

A week later the tiger resumed his bachelor existence. A change
had now come over his nature. Hitherto he had not objected
to my visiting his kills but, after his mate left, at the first drag I
followed up I was given very clearly to understand that no liberties
would in future be permitted. The angry growl of a tiger at close
quarters, than which there is no more terrifying sound in the
jungles, has to be heard to be appreciated.

Early in March the tiger killed his first full-grown buffalo. I
was near the foot-hills one evening when the agonized bellowing
of a buffalo, mingled with the angry roar of a tiger, rang through
the forest. I located the sound as coming from a ravine about six
hundred yards away. The going was bad, mostly over loose rocks

and through thorn bushes and when I crawled up a steep bluff commanding a view of the ravine the buffalo's struggles were over, and the tiger nowhere to be seen. For an hour I lay with finger on trigger without seeing anything of the tiger. At dawn next morning I again crawled up the bluff, to find the buffalo lying just as I had left her. The soft ground, torn up by hoof and claw, testified to the desperate nature of the struggle and it was not until the buffalo had been hamstrung that the tiger had finally succeeded in pulling her down, in a fight which had lasted from ten to fifteen minutes. The tiger's tracks led across the ravine and, on following them up, I found a long smear of blood on a rock, and, a hundred yards further on, another smear on a fallen tree. The wound inflicted by the buffalo's horns was in the tiger's head and sufficiently severe to make the tiger lose all interest in the kill, for he never returned to it.

Three years later the tiger, disregarding the lesson received when a cub (his excuse may have been that it was the close season for tigers), incautiously returned to a kill, over which a zamindar and some of his tenants were sitting at night, and received a bullet in the shoulder which fractured the bone. No attempt was made to follow him up, and thirty-six hours later, his shoulder covered with a swarm of flies, he limped through the compound of the Inspection Bungalow, crossed a bridge flanked on the far side by a double row of tenanted houses, the occupants of which stood at their doors to watch him pass, entered the gate of a walled-in compound and took possession of a vacant godown. Twenty-four hours later, possibly alarmed by the number of people who had collected from neighbouring villages to see him, he left the compound the way he had entered it, passed our gate, and made his way to the lower end of our village. A bullock belonging to one of our tenants had died the previous night and had been dragged into some bushes at the edge of the village; this the tiger found, and here he remained a few days, quenching his thirst at an irrigation furrow.

When we came down from the hills two months later the

tiger was lying on small animals (calves, sheep, goats, etc.) that he was able to catch on the outskirts of the village. By March his wound had healed, leaving his right foot turned inwards. Returning to the forest where he had been wounded, he levied heavy toll on the village cattle, taking, for safety's sake, but one meal off each and in this way killing five times as many as he would ordinarily have done. The zamindar who had wounded him and who had a herd of some four hundred head of cows and buffaloes was the chief sufferer.

In the succeeding years he gained as much in size as in reputation, and many were the attempts made by sportsmen, and others, to bag him.

One November evening, a villager, armed with a single-barrel muzzle-loading gun, set out to try to bag a pig, selecting for his ground *machan* an isolated bush growing in a twenty-yard-wide *rowkah* (dry watercourse) running down the centre of some broken ground. This ground was rectangular, flanked on the long sides by cultivated land and on the short sides by a road, and by a ten-foot canal that formed the boundary between our cultivation and the forest. In front of the man was a four-foot-high bank with a cattle track running along the upper edge; behind him a patch of dense scrub. At 8 p.m. an animal appeared on the track and, taking what aim he could, he fired. On receiving that shot the animal fell off the bank, and passed within a few feet of the man, grunting as it entered the scrub behind. Casting aside his blanket, the man ran to his hut two hundred yards away. Neighbours soon collected and, on hearing the man's account, came to the conclusion that a pig had been hard hit. It would be a pity, they said, to leave the pig for hyenas and jackals to eat, so a lantern was lit and as a party of six bold spirits set out to retrieve the bag, one of my tenants (who declined to join the expedition, and who confessed to me later that he had no stomach for looking for wounded pig in dense scrub in the dark) suggested that the gun should be loaded and taken.

His suggestion was accepted and, as a liberal charge of powder was being rammed home, the wooden ramrod jammed and broke inside the barrel. A trivial accident which undoubtedly saved the lives of six men. The broken rod was eventually and after great trouble extracted, the gun loaded, and the party set off.

Arrived at the spot where the animal had entered the bushes, a careful search was made and, on blood being found, every effort to find the 'pig' was made; it was not until the whole area had been combed out that the quest for that night was finally abandoned. Early next morning the search was resumed, with the addition of my informant of weak stomach, who was a better woodsman than his companions and who, examining the ground under a bush where there was a lot of blood, collected and brought some blood-stained hairs to me which I recognized as tiger's hairs. A brother sportsman was with me for the day and together we went to have a look at the ground.

The reconstruction of jungle events from signs on the ground has always held great interest for me. True, one's deductions are sometimes wrong, but they are also sometimes right. In the present instance I was right in placing the wound in the inner forearm of the right foreleg, but was wrong in assuming the leg had been broken and that the tiger was a young animal and a stranger to the locality.

There was no blood beyond the point where the hairs had been found and, as tracking on the hard ground was impossible, I crossed the canal to where the cattle track ran through a bed of sand. Here from the pugmarks I found that the wounded animal was not a young tiger as I had assumed, but my old friend the Pipal Pani tiger who, when taking a short cut through the village, had in the dark been mistaken for a pig.

Once before when badly wounded he had passed through the settlement without harming man or beast, but he was older now, and if driven by pain and hunger might do considerable damage. A disconcerting prospect, for the locality was thickly populated, and I was due to leave within the week, to keep an engagement that could not be put off.

For three days I searched every bit of the jungle between the canal and the foot-hills, an area of about four square miles, without finding any trace of the tiger. On the fourth afternoon, as I was setting out to continue the search, I met an old woman and her son hurriedly leaving the jungle. From them I learnt that the tiger was calling near the foot-hills and that all the cattle in the jungle had stampeded. When out with a rifle I invariably go alone; it is safer in a mix-up, and one can get through the jungle more silently. However, I stretched a point on this occasion, and let the boy accompany me since he was very keen on showing me where he had heard the tiger.

Arrived at the foot-hills, the boy pointed to a dense bit of cover, bounded on the far side by the fire-track to which I have already referred, and on the near side by the Pipal Pani stream. Running parallel to and about a hundred yards from the stream was a shallow depression some twenty feet wide, more or less open on my side and fringed with bushes on the side nearer the stream. A well-used path crossed the depression at right angles. Twenty yards from the path, and on the open side of the depression, was a small tree. If the tiger came down the path he would in all likelihood stand for a shot on clearing the bushes. Here I decided to take my stand and, putting the boy into the tree with his feet on a level with my head and instructing him to signal with his toes if from his raised position he saw the tiger before I did, I put my back to the tree and called.

You, who have spent as many years in the jungle as I have, need no description of the call of a tigress in search of a mate, and to you less fortunate ones I can only say that the call, to acquire which necessitates close observation and the liberal use of throat salve, cannot be described in words.

To my great relief, for I had crawled through the jungle for three days with finger on trigger, I was immediately answered from a distance of about five hundred yards, and for half an hour thereafter—it may have been less and certainly appeared more—the call was tossed back and forth. On the one side the urgent summons of the king and on the other, the subdued and coaxing answer of his handmaiden. Twice the boy signalled, but

I had as yet seen nothing of the tiger, and it was not until the setting sun was flooding the forest with golden light that he suddenly appeared, coming down the path at a fast walk with never a pause as he cleared the bushes. When half-way across the depression, and just as I was raising the rifle, he turned to the right and came straight towards me.

This manoeuvre, unforeseen when selecting my stand, brought him nearer than I had intended he should come and, moreover, presented me with a head shot which at that short range I was not prepared to take. Resorting to an old device, learned long years ago and successfully used on similar occasions, the tiger was brought to a stand without being alarmed. With one paw poised, he slowly raised his head, exposing as he did so his chest and throat. After the impact of the heavy bullet, he struggled to his feet and tore blindly through the forest, coming down with a crash within a few yards of where, attracted by the calling of a *chital* hind one November morning, I had first seen his pugmarks.

It was only then that I found he had been shot under a misapprehension, for the wound which I feared might make him dangerous proved on examination to be almost healed and caused by a pellet of lead having severed a small vein in his right forearm.

Pleasure at having secured a magnificent trophy—he measured 10'3" over curves and his winter coat was in perfect condition—was not unmixed with regret, for never again would the jungle folk and I listen with bated breath to his deep-throated call resounding through the foothills, and never again would his familiar pugmarks show on the game paths that he and I had trodden for fifteen years.

# THE THAK MAN-EATER

## I

Peace had reigned in the Ladhya valley for many months when in September 1938 a report was received in Naini Tal that a girl, twelve years of age, had been killed by a tiger at Kot Kindri village. The report which reached me through Donald Stewart of the Forest Department gave no details, and it was not until I visited the village some weeks later that I was able to get particulars of the tragedy. It appeared that, about noon one day, this girl was picking up windfalls from a mango tree close to and in full view of the village, when a tiger suddenly appeared. Before the men working nearby were able to render any assistance, it carried her off. No attempt was made to follow up the tiger, and as all signs of drag and blood trail had been obliterated and washed away long before I arrived on the scene, I was unable to find the place where the tiger had taken the body.

Kot Kindri is about four miles south-west of Chuka, and three miles due west of Thak. It was in the valley between Kot Kindri

and Thak that the Chuka man-eater had been shot the previous April.

During the summer of 1938 the Forest Department had marked all the trees in this area for felling, and it was feared that if the man-eater was not accounted for before November—when the felling of the forest was due to start—the contractors would not be able to secure labour, and would repudiate their contracts. It was in this connexion that Donald Stewart had written to me shortly after the girl had been killed, but when in compliance with his request I promised to go to Kot Kindri, I must confess that it was more in the interests of the local inhabitants than in the interest of the contractors that I gave my promise.

My most direct route to Kot Kindri was to go by rail to Tanakpur, and from there by foot via Kaldhunga and Chuka. This route, however, though it would save me a hundred miles of walking, would necessitate my passing through the most deadly malaria belt in northern India, and to avoid it I decided to go through the hills to Mornaula, and from there along the abandoned Sherring road to its termination of the ridge above Kot Kindri.

While my preparations for this long trek were still under way a second report reached Naini Tal of a kill at Sem, a small village on the left bank of the Ladhya and distant about half a mile from Chuka.

The victim on this occasion was an elderly woman, the mother of the Headman of Sem. This unfortunate woman had been killed while cutting brushwood on a steep bank between two terraced fields. She had started work at the further end of the fifty-yard-long bank, and had cut the brushwood to within a yard of her hut when the tiger sprang on her from the field above. So sudden and unexpected was the attack that the woman only had time to scream once before the tiger killed her, and taking her up the twelve-foot-high bank crossed the upper field and disappeared with her into the dense jungle beyond. Her son, a lad some twenty years of age, was at the time working in a paddy field a few yards away and witnessed the whole occurrence, but was too frightened to try to render any assistance. In response to the lad's urgent summons the Patwari arrived at Sem two days later, accompanied by eighty men he had collected. Following up in the direction the tiger had gone, he found the woman's clothes and a few small bits of bone. This kill had taken place at 2 p.m. on a bright sunny day, and the tiger had eaten its victim only sixty yards from the hut where it had killed her.

On receipt of this second report, Ibbotson, Deputy Commissioner of the three Districts of Almora, Naini Tal and Garhwal, and I held a council of war, the upshot of which was that Ibbotson, who was on the point of setting out to settle a land dispute at Askot on the border of Tibet, changed his tour programme and, instead of going via Bagashwar, decided to accompany me to Sem, and from there go on to Askot.

The route I had selected entailed a considerable amount of hill-climbing so we eventually decided to go up the Nandhour valley, cross the watershed between the Nandhour and Ladhya, and follow the latter river down to Sem. The Ibbotsons accordingly left Naini Tal on 12th October, and the following day I joined them at Chaurgallia.

Going up the Nandhour and fishing as we went—our best day's catch on light trout rods was a hundred and twenty fish— we arrived on the fifth day at Durga Pepal. Here we left the river, and after a very stiff climb camped for the night on the watershed. Making an early start next morning we pitched our tents that night on the left bank of the Ladhya, twelve miles from Chalti.

The monsoon had given over early, which was very fortunate for us, for owing to the rock cliffs that run sheer down into the valley the river has to be crossed every quarter of a mile or so. At one of these fords my cook, who stands five feet in his boots, was washed away and only saved from a watery grave by the prompt assistance of the man who was carrying our lunch basket.

On the tenth day after leaving Chaurgallia we made camp on a deserted field at Sem, two hundred yards from the hut where the woman had been killed, and a hundred yards from the junction of the Ladhya and Sarda rivers.

Gill Waddell, of the Police, whom we met on our way down the Ladhya, had camped for several days at Sem and had tied out a buffalo that MacDonald of the Forest Department had very kindly placed at our disposal, and though the tiger had visited Sem several times during Waddell's stay, it had not killed the buffalo.

The day following our arrival at Sem, while Ibbotson was interviewing Patwaris, Forest Guards, and Headmen of the surrounding villages, I went out to look for pugmarks. Between our camp and the junction, and also on both banks of the Ladhya, there were long stretches of sand. On this sand I found the tracks of a tigress, and of a young male tiger—possibly one of the cubs I had seen in April. The tigress had crossed and recrossed the Ladhya a number of times during the last few days, and the previous night had walked along the strip of sand in front of our tents. It was this tigress the villagers suspected of being the man-eater, and as she had visited Sem repeatedly since the day the Headman's mother had been killed, they were probably correct.

An examination of the pugmarks of the tigress showed her as being an average-sized animal, in the prime of life. Why she had become a man-eater would have to be determined later, but one of the reasons might have been that she had assisted to eat the victims of the Chuka tiger when they were together the previous mating season, and having acquired a taste for human flesh and no longer having a mate to provide her with it, had now turned a man-eater herself. This was only a surmise, and proved later to be incorrect.

Before leaving Naini Tal I had written to the Tahsildar of Tanakpur and asked him to purchase four young male buffaloes for me, and to send them to Sem. One of these buffaloes died on the road, the other three arrived on the 24th, and we tied them out the same evening together with the one MacDonald had given us. On going out to visit these animals next morning, I found the people of Chuka in a great state of excitement. The fields round the village had been recently ploughed, and the tigress the previous night had passed close to three families who were sleeping out on the fields with their cattle; fortunately in each case the cattle had seen the tigress and warned the sleepers of her approach. After leaving the cultivated land the tigress had gone up the track in the direction of Kot Kindri, and had passed close to two of our buffaloes without touching either of them.

The Patwari, Forest Guards, and villagers had told us on our arrival at Sem that it would be a waste of time tying out our young buffaloes, as they were convinced the man-eater would not kill them. The reason they gave was that this method of trying to shoot the man-eater had been tried by others without success, and that in any case if the tigress wanted to eat buffaloes there were many grazing in the jungles for her to choose from. In spite of this advice however we continued to tie out our buffaloes, and for the next two nights the tigress passed close to one or more of them, without touching them.

On the morning of the 27th, just as we were finishing breakfast, a party of men led by Tewari, the brother of the Headman of Thak, arrived in camp and reported that a man from their village was missing. They stated that this man had left the village at about noon the previous day, telling his wife before leaving that he was going to see that his cattle did not stray beyond the village boundary, and as he had not returned they feared he had been killed by the man-eater.

Our preparations were soon made, and at ten o'clock the Ibbotsons and I set off for Thak, accompanied by Tewari and the men he had brought with him. The distance was only about two miles but the climb was considerable, and as we did not want to lose more time than we could possibly help, we arrived at the outskirts of the village out of breath, and in a lather of sweat.

As we approached the village over the scrub-covered flat bit of ground which I have reason to refer to later, we heard a woman crying. The wailing of an Indian woman mourning her dead is unmistakable, and on emerging from the jungle we came on the mourner—the wife of the missing man—and some ten or fifteen men, who were waiting for us on the edge of the cultivated land. These people informed us that from their houses above they had seen some white object, which looked like part of the missing man's clothing, in a field over grown with scrub thirty yards from where we were now standing. Ibbotson, Tewari, and I set off to investigate the white object, while Mrs Ibbotson took the woman and the rest of the men up to the village.

The field, which had been out of cultivation for some years, was covered with a dense growth of scrub not unlike chrysanthemum, and it was not until we were standing right over the white object that Tewari recognized it as the loincloth of the missing man. Near it was the man's cap. A struggle had taken place at this spot, but there was no blood. The absence of blood where the attack had taken place and for some considerable distance along the drag could be accounted for by the tigress having retained her first hold, for no blood would flow in such a case until the hold had been changed.

Thirty yards on the hill above us there was a clump of bushes roofed over with creepers. This spot would have to be looked at before following up the drag, for it was not advisable to have the tigress behind us. In the soft earth under the bushes we found the pugmarks of the tigress, and where she had lain before going forward to attack the man.

Returning to our starting point we agreed on the following plan of action. Our primary object was to try to stalk the tigress and shoot her on kill: to achieve this end I was to follow the trail and at the same time keep a lookout in front, with Tewari— who was unarmed—a yard behind me keeping a sharp lookout to right and left, and Ibbotson a yard behind Tewari to safeguard us against an attack from the rear. In the event of either Ibbotson or I seeing so much as a hair of the tigress, we were to risk a shot.

Cattle had grazed over this area the previous day, disturbing the ground, and as there was no blood and the only indication of the tigress's passage was an occasional turned-up leaf or crushed blade of grass, progress was slow. After carrying the man for two hundred yards the tigress had killed and left him. She had returned and carried him off several hours later, when the people of Thak had heard several *sambhar* calling in this direction. The reason why the tigress did not carry the man away after she had killed him was possibly because the cattle had witnessed the attack on him, and had driven her away.

A big pool of blood had formed where the man had been lying, and as the blood from the wound in his throat had stopped flowing by the time the tigress had picked him up again, and further, as she was now holding him by the small of the back, whereas she had previously held him by the neck tracking became even more difficult. The tigress kept to the contour of the hill, and as the undergrowth here was very dense and visibility only extended to a few yards, our advance was slowed down. In two hours we covered half a mile, and reached a ridge beyond which

lay the valley in which, six months
previously, we had tracked down
and killed the Chuka man-eater.
On this ridge was a great slab of
rock, which sloped upwards and
away from the direction in which
we had come. The tigress's tracks
went down to the right of the
rock and I felt sure she was lying up
under the over-hanging portion of it,
or in the close vicinity.

Both Ibbotson and I had on light rubber-
soled shoes—Tewari was bare-footed—and we had reached the
rock without making a sound. Signing to my two companions
to stand still and keep a careful watch all round, I got a foothold
on the rock, and inch by inch went forward. Beyond the rock
was a short stretch of flat ground, and as more of this ground
came into view, I felt certain my suspicion that the tigress was
lying under the projection was correct. I had still a foot or two
to go before I could look over, when I saw a movement to my
left front. A golden-rod that had been pressed down had sprung
erect, and a second later there was a slight movement in the
bushes beyond, and a monkey in a tree on the far side of the
bushes started calling.

The tigress had chosen the spot for her after-dinner sleep
with great care, but unfortunately for us she was not asleep; and
when she saw the top of my head—I had removed my hat—
appearing over the rock, she had risen and, taking a step sideways,
had disappeared under a tangle of blackberry bushes. Had she
been lying anywhere but where she was she could not have got
away, no matter how quickly she had moved, without my getting
a shot at her. Our so-carefully-carried-out stalk had failed at the
very last moment, and there was nothing to be done now but
to find the kill, and see if there was sufficient of it left for us to
sit up over. To have followed her into the blackberry thicket would

have been useless, and would also have reduced our chances of getting a shot at her later.

The tigress had eaten her meal close to where she had been lying and as this spot was open to the sky and to the keen eyes of vultures she had removed the kill to a place of safety where it would not be visible from the air. Tracking now was easy, for there was a blood trail to follow. The trail led over a ridge of great rocks and fifty yards beyond these rocks we found the kill.

I am not going to harrow your feelings by attempting to describe that poor torn and mangled thing; stripped of every stitch of clothing and atom of dignity, which only a few hours previously had been a Man, the father of two children and the breadwinner of the wailing woman who was facing—without any illusions—the fate of a widow of India. I have seen many similar sights, each more terrible than the one preceding it, in the thirty-two years I have been hunting man-eaters, and on each occasion I have felt that it would have been better to have left the victim to the slayer than recover a mangled mass of flesh to be a nightmare ever after to those who saw it. And yet the cry of blood for blood, and the burning desire to rid a countryside of a menace than which there is none more terrible, is irresistible; and then there is always the hope, no matter how absurd one knows it to be, that the victim by some miracle may still be alive and in need of succour.

The chance of shooting—over a kill—an animal that has in all probability become a man-eater through a wound received over a kill, is very remote, and each succeeding failure, no matter what its cause, tends to make the animal more cautious, until it reaches a state when it either abandons its kill after one meal or approaches it as silently and as slowly as a shadow, scanning every leaf and twig with the certainty of discovering its would-be slayer, no matter how carefully he may be concealed or how silent and motionless he may be; a one-in-a-million chance of getting a shot, and yet, who is there among us who would not take it?

The thicket into which the tigress had retired was roughly

forty yards square, and she could not leave it without the monkey seeing her and warning us, so we sat down back to back, to have a smoke and listen if the jungle had anything further to tell us while we considered our next move.

To make a *machan* it was necessary to return to the village, and during our absence the tigress was almost certain to carry away the kill. It had been difficult when she was carrying a whole human being to track her, but now, when her burden was considerably lighter and she had been disturbed, she would probably go for miles and we might never find her kill again, so it was necessary for one of us to remain on the spot, while the other two went back to the village for ropes.

Ibbotson, with his usual disregard for danger, elected to go back, and while he and Tewari went down the hill to avoid the difficult ground we had recently come over, I stepped up on to a small tree close to the kill. Four feet above ground the tree divided in two, and by leaning on one half and putting my feet against the other, I was able to maintain a precarious seat which was high enough off the ground to enable me to see the tigress if she approached the kill, and also high enough, if she had any designs on me, to see her before she got to within striking distance.

Ibbotson had been gone fifteen or twenty minutes when I heard a rock tilt forward, and then back. The rock was evidently very delicately poised, and when the tigress had put her weight on it and felt it tilt forward she had removed her foot and let the rock fall back into place. The sound had come from about twenty yards to my left front, the only direction in which it would have been possible for me to have fired without being knocked out of the tree.

Minutes passed, each pulling my hopes down a little lower from the heights to which they had soared, and then, when tension on my nerves and the weight of the heavy rifle were becoming unbearable, I heard a stick snap at the upper end of the thicket. Here was an example of how a tiger can move through the jungle. From the sound she had made I knew her exact position, had kept my eyes fixed on the spot, and yet she had come, seen me, stayed some time watching me, and then gone away without my having seen a leaf or a blade of grass move.

When tension on nerves is suddenly relaxed, cramped and aching muscles call loudly for ease, and though in this case it only meant the lowering of the rifle on to my knees to take the strain off my shoulders and arms, the movement, small though it was, sent a comforting feeling through the whole of my body. No further sound came from the tigress, and an hour or two later I heard Ibbotson returning.

Of all the men I have been on *shikar* with, Ibbotson is by far and away the best, for not only has he the heart of a lion, but he thinks of everything, and with it all is the most unselfish man that carries a gun. He had gone to fetch a rope and he returned with rugs, cushions, more hot tea than even I could drink, and an ample launch; and while I sat—on the windward side of the kill—to refresh myself, Ibbotson put a man in a tree forty yards away to distract the tigress's attention, and climbed into a tree overlooking the kill to make a rope *machan*.

When the *machan* was ready Ibbotson moved the kill a few feet—a very unpleasant job—and tied it securely to the foot of a sapling to prevent the tigress carrying it away, for the moon was on the wane and the first two hours of the night at this heavily wooded spot would be pitch dark. After a final smoke I climbed on to the *machan*, and when I had made myself comfortable Ibbotson recovered the man who was making a diversion and set off in the direction of Thak to pick up Mrs Ibbotson and return to camp at Sem.

The retreating party were out of sight but were not yet out of sound when I heard a heavy body brushing against leaves, and at the same moment the monkey, which had been silent all this time and which I could now see sitting in a tree on the far side of blackberry thicket, started calling. Here was more luck than I hoped for, and our ruse of putting a man up a tree to cause a diversion appeared to be working as successfully as it had done on a previous occasion. A tense minute passed, a second, and a third, and then from the ridge where I had climbed on to the big slab of rock a *kakar* came dashing down towards me, barking hysterically. The tigress was not coming to the kill but had gone off after Ibbotson. I was now in a fever of anxiety, for it was quite evident that she had abandoned her kill and gone to try to secure another victim.

Before leaving, Ibbotson had promised to take every precaution but on hearing the *kakar* barking on my side of the ridge he would naturally assume the tigress was moving in the vicinity of the kill, and if he relaxed his precautions the tigress would get her chance. Ten very uneasy minutes for me passed, and then I heard a second *kakar* barking in the direction of Thak; the tigress was still following, but the ground there was more open, and there was less fear of her attacking the party. The danger to the Ibbotsons was, however, not over by any means for they had to go through two miles of very heavy jungle to reach camp; and if they stayed at Thak until sundown listening for my shot, which I feared they would do and which as a matter of fact they did do, they would run a very grave risk on the way down. Ibbotson fortunately realized the danger and kept his party close together, and though the tigress followed them the whole way—as her pugmarks the following morning showed—they got back to camp safely.

The calling of *kakar* and *sambhar* enabled me to follow the movements of the tigress. An hour after sunset she was down at the bottom of the valley two miles away. She had the whole night before her, and though there was only one chance in a million of her returning to the kill I determined not to lose that chance. Wrapping a rug round me, for it was a bitterly cold night, I made myself comfortable in a position in which I could remain for hours without movement.

I had taken my seat on the *machan* at 4 p.m., and at 10 p.m. I heard two animals coming down the hill towards me. It was too dark under the trees to see them, but when they got to the lee of the kill I knew they were porcupines. Rattling their quills, and making the peculiar booming noise that only a porcupine can make, they approached the kill and, after walking round it several times, continued on their way. An hour later, and when the moon had been up some time, I heard an animal in the valley below. It was moving from east to west, and when it came into the wind blowing downhill from the kill it made a long pause, and then came cautiously up the hill. While it was still some distance away I heard it snuffing the air, and knew it to be a bear. The smell of blood was attracting him, but mingled with it was the less welcome smell of a human being, and taking no chances he was very carefully stalking the kill. His nose, the keenest of any animal's in the jungle, had apprised him while he was still in the valley that the kill was the property of a tiger. This to a Himalayan bear who fears nothing, and who will, as I have on several occasions seen, drive a tiger away from its kill, was no deterrent, but what was, and what was causing him uneasiness, was the smell of a human being mingled with the smell of blood and tiger.

On reaching the flat ground the bear sat down on his haunches a few yards from the kill, and when he had satisfied himself that the hated human smell held no danger for him he stood erect and turning his head sent a long-drawn-out cry, which I interpreted as a call to a mate, echoing down into the valley.

Then without any further hesitation he walked boldly up to the kill, and as he nosed it I aligned the sights of my rifle on him. I know of only one instance of a Himalayan bear eating a human being; on that occasion a woman cutting grass had fallen down a cliff and been killed, and a bear finding the mangled body had carried it away and had eaten it. This bear, however, on whose shoulder my sights were aligned, appeared to draw the line at human flesh, and after looking at and smelling the kill continued his interrupted course to the west. When the sounds of his retreat died away in the distance the jungle settled down to silence until interrupted, a little after sunrise, by Ibbotson's very welcome arrival.

With Ibbotson came the brother and other relatives of the dead man, who very reverently wrapped the remains in a clean white cloth and, lying it on a cradle made of two saplings and rope which Ibbotson provided, set off for the burning ghat on the banks of the Sarda, repeating under their breath as they went the Hindu hymn of praise 'Ram nam sat hai' with its refrain, 'Satya bol gat hai'.

Fourteen hours in the cold had not been without its effect on me, but after partaking of the hot drink and food Ibbotson had brought I felt none the worse for my long vigil.

## II

After following the Ibbotsons down to Chuka on the evening of the 27th the tigress, some time during the night, crossed the Ladhya in the scrub jungle at the back of our camp. Through this scrub ran a path that had been regularly used by the villagers of the Ladhya valley until the advent of the man-eater had rendered its passage unsafe. On the 28th the two mail-runners who carried Ibbotson's dak on its first stage to Tanakpur got delayed in camp and to save time took, or more correctly started to take, a short cut through this scrub. Very fortunately the leading man was on the alert and saw the tigress as she crept through the scrub and lay down near the path ahead of them.

Ibbotson and I had just got back from Thak when these two men dashed into camp, and taking our rifles we hurried off to investigate. We found the pugmarks of the tigress where she had come out on the path and followed the men for a short distance, but we did not see her though in one place where the scrub was very dense we saw a movement and heard an animal moving off.

On the morning of the 29th, a party of men came down from Thak to report that one of their bullocks had not returned to the cattle-shed the previous night, and on a search being made where it had last been seen a little blood had been found. At 2 p.m. the Ibbotsons and I were at this spot, and a glance at the ground satisfied us that the bullock had been killed and carried away by tiger. After a hasty lunch Ibbotson and I, with two men following carrying ropes for a *machan*, set out along the drag. It went diagonally across the face of the hill for a hundred yards and then straight down into the ravine in which I had fired at and missed the big tiger in April. A few hundred yards down this ravine the bullock which was an enormous animal, had got fixed between two rocks and, not being able to move it, the tigress had eaten a meal off its hind quarters and left it.

The pugmarks of the tigress, owing to the great weight she was carrying, were splayed out and it was not possible to say whether she was the man-eater or not; but as every tigress in this area was suspect I decided to sit up over the kill. There was only one tree within reasonable distance of the kill, and as the men climbed into it to make a *machan* the tigress started calling in the valley below. Very hurriedly a few strands of rope were tied between two branches, and while Ibbotson stood on guard with his rifle I climbed the tree and took my seat on what, during the next fourteen hours, proved to be the most uncomfortable as well as the most dangerous *machan* I have sat on. The tree was leaning away from the hill, and from the three uneven strands of rope I was sitting on there was a drop of over a hundred feet into the rocky ravine below.

The tigress called several times as I was getting into the tree and continued to call at longer intervals late into the evening, and the last call coming from a ridge half a mile away. It was now quite evident that the tigress had been lying up close to the kill and had seen the men climbing into the tree. Knowing from past experience what this meant, she had duly expressed resentment at being disturbed and then gone away, for though

I sat on the three strands of rope until Ibbotson returned next morning I did not see or hear anything throughout the night.

Vultures were not likely to find the kill, for the ravine was deep and overshadowed by trees, and as the bullock was large enough to provide tigress with several meals we decided not to sit up over it again where it was now lying, hoping the tigress would remove it to a place more convenient and where we should have a better chance of getting a shot. In this however we were disappointed, for the tigress did not again return to the kill.

Two nights later the buffalo we had tied out behind our camp at Sem was killed, and through a little want of observation on my part a great opportunity of bagging the man-eater was lost.

The men who brought in the news of this kill reported that the rope securing the animal had been broken, and that the kill had been carried away up the ravine at the lower end of which it had been tied. This was the same ravine in which MacDonald and I had chased a tigress in April, and as on that occasion she had taken her kill some distance up the ravine I now very foolishly concluded she had done the same with this kill.

After breakfast Ibbotson and I went out to find the kill and see what prospect there was for an evening sit-up.

The ravine in which the buffalo had been killed was about fifty yards wide and ran deep into the foot-hills. For two hundred yards the ravine was straight and then bent round to the left. Just beyond the bend, and on the left-hand side of it, there was a dense patch of young saplings backed by a hundred-foot ridge on which thick grass was growing. In the ravine, and close to the saplings, there was a small pool of water. I had been up the ravine several times in April and had failed to mark the patch of saplings as being a likely place for a tiger to lie up in, and did not take the precautions I should have taken when rounding the bend, with the result that the tigress who was drinking at the pool saw us first. There was only one safe line of retreat for her and she took it. This was straight up the steep hill, over the ridge, and into the *sal* forest beyond.

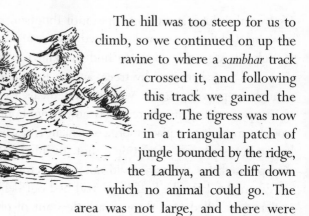

The hill was too steep for us to climb, so we continued on up the ravine to where a *sambhar* track crossed it, and following this track we gained the ridge. The tigress was now in a triangular patch of jungle bounded by the ridge, the Ladhya, and a cliff down which no animal could go. The area was not large, and there were several deer in it which from time to time advised us of the position of the tigress, but unfortunately the ground was cut up by a number of deep and narrow rainwater channels in which we eventually lost touch with her.

We had not yet seen the kill, so we re-entered the ravine by the *sambhar* track and found the kill hidden among the saplings. These saplings were from six inches to a foot in girth, and were not strong enough to support a *machan*, so we had to abandon the idea of a *machan*. With the help of a crowbar a rock could possibly have been prised from the face of the hill and a place made in which to sit, but this was not advisable when dealing with a man-eater.

Reluctant to give up the chance of a shot we considered the possibility of concealing ourselves in the grass near the kill, in the hope that the tigress would return before dark and that we should see her before she saw us. There were two objections to this plan: (a) if we did not get a shot and the tigress saw us near her kill she might abandon it as she had done her other two kills, and (b) between the kill and camp there was very heavy scrub jungle, and if we tried to go through this jungle in the dark the tigress would have us at her mercy. So very reluctantly we decided to leave the kill to the tigress for that night, and hope for the best on the morrow.

On our return next morning we found that the tigress had

carried away the kill. For three hundred yards she had gone up the bed of the ravine, stepping from rock to rock, and leaving no drag marks. At this spot—three hundred yards from where she had picked up the kill—we were at sea, for though there was a number of tracks on a wet patch of ground, none of them had been made while she was carrying the kill. Eventually, after casting round in circles, we found where she had left the ravine and gone up the hill on the left.

This hill up which the tigress had taken her kill was overgrown with ferns and golden-rod and tracking was not difficult, but the going was, for the hill was very steep and in places a detour had to be made and the track picked up further on. After a stiff climb of a thousand feet we came to a small plateau, bordered on the left by a cliff a mile wide. On the side of the plateau nearest the cliff the ground was seamed and cracked, and in these cracks a dense growth of *sal*, two to six feet in height, had sprung up. The tigress had taken her kill into this dense cover and it was not until we actually trod on it that we were aware of its position.

As we stopped to look at all that remained of the buffalo there was a low growl to our right. With rifles raised we waited for a minute and then, hearing a movement in the undergrowth a little beyond where the growl had come from, we pushed our way through the young *sal* for ten yards and come on a small clearing, where the tigress had made herself a bed on some soft grass. On the far side of this grass the hill sloped upwards for twenty yards to another plateau, and it was from this slope that the sound we had heard had come. Proceeding up the slope as silently as possible we had just reached the flat ground, which was about fifty yards wide, when the tigress left the far side and went down into the ravine, disturbing some *kalege* pheasants and a *kakar* as she did so. To have followed her would have been useless, so we went back to the kill and, as there was still a good meal on it, we selected two trees to sit in, and returned to camp.

After an early lunch we went back to the kill and, hampered by our rifles, climbed with some difficulty into the trees we had selected. We sat up for five hours without seeing or hearing anything. At dusk we climbed down from our trees, and stumbling over the cracked and uneven ground eventually reached the ravine when it was quite dark. Both of us had an uneasy feeling that we were being followed, but by keeping close together we reached camp without incident at 9 p.m.

The Ibbotsons had now stayed at Sem as long as it was possible for them to do so, and early next morning they set out on their twelve days' walk to keep their appointment at Askot. Before leaving, Ibbotson extracted a promise from me that I would not follow up any kills alone, or further endanger my life by prolonging my stay at Sem for more than a day or two.

After the departure of the Ibbotsons and their fifty men, the camp, which was surrounded by dense scrub, was reduced to my two servants and myself—my coolies were living in a room in the Headman's house—so throughout the day I set all hands to collecting driftwood, of which there was an inexhaustible supply at the junction, to keep a fire going all night. The fire would not scare away the tigress but it would enable us to see her if she prowled round our tents at night, and anyway the nights were setting in cold and there was ample excuse, if one were needed, for keeping a big fire going all night.

Towards evening, when my men were safely back in camp, I took a rifle and went up the Ladhya to see if the tigress had crossed the river. I found several tracks in the sand, but no fresh ones, and at dusk I returned, convinced that the tigress was still on our side of the river. An hour later, when it was quite dark, a *kakar* started barking close to our tents and barked persistently for half an hour.

My men had taken over the job of tying out the buffaloes, a task which Ibbotson's men had hitherto performed, and next morning I accompanied them when they went out to bring in the buffaloes. Though we covered several miles I did not find any trace of the tigress. After breakfast I took a rod and went down to the junction, and had one of the best day's fishing I have ever had. The junction was full of big fish, and though my light tackle was broken frequently, I killed sufficient *mahseer* to feed the camp.

Again, as on the previous evening, I crossed the Ladhya, with the intention of taking up a position on a rock overlooking the open ground on the right bank of the river and watching for the tigress to cross. As I got away from the roar of the water at the junction, I heard a *sambhar* and a monkey calling on the hill to my left, and as I neared the rock I came on the fresh tracks of the tigress. Following them back I found the stones still wet where she had forded the river. A few minutes' delay in camp to dry my fishing line and have a cup of tea cost a man his life, several thousand men weeks of anxiety, and myself many days of strain, for though I stayed at Sem for another three days I did not get another chance of shooting the tigress.

On the morning of the 7th, as I was breaking camp and preparing to start on my twenty mile walk to Tanakpur, a big contingent of men from all the surrounding villages arrived, and begged me not to leave them to the tender mercies of the maneater. Giving them what advice it was possible to give people situated as they were, I promised to return as soon as it was possible for me to do so.

I caught the train at Tanakpur next morning and arrived back in Naini Tal on 9 November, having been away nearly a month.

### III

I left Sem on the 7th of November and on the 12th the tigress killed a man at Thak. I received news of this kill through the Divisional Forest Officer, Haldwani, shortly after we had moved down to our winter home at the foot of the hills, and by doing forced marches I arrived at Chuka a little after sunrise on the 24th.

It had been my intention to breakfast at Chuka and then go

on to Thak and make that village my headquarters, but the Headman of Thak, whom I found installed at Chuka, informed me that every man, woman, and child had left Thak immediately after the man had been killed on the 12th, and added that if I carried out my intention of camping at Thak I might be able to safeguard my own life, but it would not be possible to safeguard the lives of my men. This was quite reasonable, and while waiting for my men to arrive, the Headman helped me to select a site for my camp at Chuka where my men would be reasonably safe and I should have some privacy from the thousands of men who were now arriving to fell the forest.

On receipt of the Divisional Forest Officer's telegram acquainting me of the kill, I had telegraphed to the Tahsildar at Tanakpur to send three young male buffaloes to Chuka. My request had been promptly complied with and the three animals had arrived the previous evening.

After breakfast I took one of the buffaloes and set out for Thak, intending to tie it up on the spot where the man had been killed on the 12th. The Headman had given me a very graphic account of the events of that date, for he himself had nearly fallen a victim to the tigress. It appeared that towards the afternoon, accompanied by his granddaughter, a girl ten years of age, he had gone to dig up ginger tubers in field some sixty yards from his house. This field is about half an acre in extent and is surrounded on three sides by jungle and being on the slope of a fairly steep hill it is it is visible from the Headman's house. After the old man and his granddaughter had been at work for some time his wife, who was husking rice in the courtyard of the house, called out in a very agitated voice and asked him if he was deaf that he could not hear the pheasants and other birds that were chattering in the jungle above him. Fortunately for him, he acted promptly. Dropping his hoe, he grabbed the child's hand and together they ran back to the house, urged on by the woman who said she could now see a red animal in the bushes at the upper end of the field. Half an hour later

the tigress killed a man who was looping branches off a tree in a field three hundred yards from the Headman's house.

From the description I had received from the Headman I had no difficulty in locating the tree. It was a small gnarled tree growing out of a three-foot-high bank between two terraced fields, and had been lopped year after year for cattle fodder. The man who had been killed was standing on the trunk holding one branch and cutting another, when the tigress came up from behind, tore his hold from the branch and, after killing him, carried him away into the dense brushwood bordering the fields.

Thak village was a gift from the Chand Rajas, who ruled Kumaon for many hundreds of years before the Gurkha occupation, to the forefathers of the present owners in return for their services at the Purnagiri temples. (The promise made by the Chand Rajas that the lands of Thak and two other villages would remain rent-free for all time has been honoured by the British Government for a hundred years.) From a collection of grass huts the village has in the course of time grown into a very prosperous settlements with masonry houses roofed with slate tiles, for not only is the land very fertile, but the revenue from the temples is considerable.

Like all other villages in Kumaon, Thak during its hundreds of years of existence has passed through many vicissitudes, but never before in its long history had it been deserted as it now was. On my previous visits I had found it a hive of industry, but when I went up to it this afternoon, taking the young buffalo with me, silence reigned over it. Every one of the hundred or more inhabitants had fled taking their livestock with them—the only animal I saw in the village was a cat, which gave me a warm welcome; so hurried had the evacuation been that many of the doors of the houses had been left wide open. On every path in the village, in the courtyards of the houses and in the dust before all the doors, I found the tigress's pugmarks. The open doorways were a menace, for the path as it wound through the village passed close to them, and in any of the houses the tigress might have been lurking.

On the hill thirty yards above the village were several cattle shelters, and in the vicinity of these shelter I saw more *kalege* pheasants, red jungle fowl, and white-capped babblers than I have ever before seen, and from the confiding way in which they permitted me to walk among them it is quite evident that the people of Thak have a religious prejudice against the taking of life.

From the terraced fields above the cattle shelters a bird's-eye view of the village is obtained, and it was not difficult, from the description the Headman had given me, to locate the tree where the tigress had secured her last victim. In the soft earth under the tree there were signs of a struggle and a few clots of dried blood. From here the tigress had carried her kill a hundred yards over a ploughed field, through a stout hedge, and into the dense brushwood beyond. The footprints from the village, and back the way they had come, showed that the entire population of the village had visited the scene of the kill, but from the tree to the hedge there was only one track, the track the tigress had made when carrying away her victim. No attempt had been made to follow her up and recover the body.

Scraping away a little earth from under the tree I exposed a root and to this root I tied my buffalo, bedding it down with a liberal supply of straw taken from a nearby haystack.

The village, which is on the north face of the hill, was now in shadow, and if I was to get back to camp before dark it was time for me to make a start. Skirting round the village to avoid the menace of the open doorways, I joined the path below the houses.

This path after it leaves the village passes under a giant mango tree from the roots of which issues a cold spring of clear water. After running along a groove cut in a massive slab of rock, this water falls into a rough masonry trough, from where it spreads onto the surrounding ground, rendering it soft and slushy. I had drunk at the spring on my way up, leaving my foot-prints in this slushy ground, and on approaching the spring now for a second drink, I found the tigress's pugmarks superimposed on my footprints. After quenching her thirst the tigress had avoided the path and had gained the village by climbing a steep bank overgrown with strobilanthes and nettles, and taking up a position in the shelter of one of the houses had possibly watched me while I was tying up the buffalo, expecting me to return the way I had gone; it was fortunate for me that I had noted the danger of passing those open doorways a second time, and had taken the longer way round.

When coming up from Chuka I had taken every precaution to guard against a sudden attack, and it was well that I had done so, for I now found from her pugmarks that the tigress had followed me all the way up from my camp, and next morning when I went back to Thak I found she had followed me from where I had joined the path below the houses, right down to the cultivated land at Chuka.

Reading with the illumination I had brought with me was not possible, so after dinner that night, while sitting near a fire which was as welcome for its warmth as it was for the feeling of security it gave me, I reviewed the whole situation and tried to think out some plan by which it would be possible to circumvent the tigress.

When leaving home on the 22nd I had promised that I would return in ten days, and that this would be my last expedition after man-eaters. Years of exposure and strain and long absences from home—extending as in the case of the Chowgarh tigress and the Rudraprayag leopard to several months on end—were beginning to tell as much on my constitution as on the nerves of those at home, and if by the 30th of November I had not succeeded in killing this man-eater, others would have to be found who were willing to take on the task.

It was now the night of the 24th, so I had six clear days before me. Judging from the behaviour of the tigress that evening, she appeared to be anxious to secure another human victim, and it should not therefore be difficult for me, in the time at my disposal, to get in touch with her. There were several methods by which this could be accomplished, and each would be tried in turn. The method that offers the greatest chance of success of shooting a tiger in the hills is to sit up in a tree over a kill, and if during that night the tigress did not kill the buffalo I had tied up at Thak, I would the following night, and every night thereafter, tie up the other two buffaloes in places I had already selected, and failing to secure a human kill it was just possible that the tigress might kill one of my buffaloes, as she had done on a previous occasion when the Ibbotsons and I were camped at Sem in April. After making up the fire with logs that would burn all night, I turned in, and went to sleep listening to a *kakar* barking in the scrub jungle behind my tent.

While breakfast was being prepared the following morning, I picked up a rifle and went out to look for tracks on the stretch of sand on the right bank of the river, between Chuka and Sem. The path, after leaving the cultivated land, runs for a short distance through scrub jungle, and here I found the tracks of a big male leopard, possibly the same animal that had alarmed the *kakar* the previous night. A small male tiger had crossed and recrossed the Ladhya many times during the past week, and in the same period the man-eater had crossed only once, coming from the direction of Sem. A big bear had traversed the sand a little before my arrival, and when I got back to camp the timber contractors complained that while distributing work that morning they had run into a bear which had taken up a very threatening attitude, in consequence of which their labour had refused to work in the area in which the bear had been seen.

Several thousand men—the contractors put the figure at five thousand—had now concentrated at Chuka and Kumaya Chak to fell and saw up the timber and carry it down to the motor road that was being constructed, and all the time this considerable labour force was working they shouted at the tops of their voices to keep up their courage. The noise in the valley resulting from axe and saw, the crashing of giant trees down the steep hillside, the breaking of rocks with sledge hammers, and combined with it all the shouting of thousands of men, can better be imagined than described. That there were many frequent alarms in this nervous community was only natural, and during the next few days I covered much ground and lost much valuable time in investigating false rumours of attacks and kills by the man-eater, for the dread of the tigress was not confined to the Ladhya valley but extended right down the Sarda through Kaldhunga to the gorge, an area of roughly fifty square miles in which an additional ten thousand men were working.

That a single animal should terrorize a labour force of these dimensions in addition to the residents of the surrounding villages and the hundreds of men who were bringing foodstuffs for the labourers or passing through the valley with hill produce in the way of oranges (purchasable at twelve annas a hundred), walnuts, and chillies to the market at Tanakpur, is incredible, and would be unbelievable were it not for the historical, and nearly parallel, case of the man-eater of Tsavo, where a pair of lions, operating only at night, held up work for long periods on the Uganda Railway.

To return to my story. Breakfast disposed of on the morning of the 25th, I took a second buffalo and set out for Thak. The path, after leaving the cultivated land at Chuka, skirts along the foot of the hill for about half a mile before it divides. One arm goes straight up a ridge to Thak and the other, after continuing along the foot of the hill for another half-mile, zigzags up through Kumaya Chak to Kot Kindri.

At the divide I found the pugmarks of the tigress and followed them all the way back to Thak. The fact that she had come down the hill after me the previous evening was proof that she had not killed the buffalo. This, though very disappointing, was not at all unusual; for tigers will on occasions visit an animal that is tied up for several nights in succession before they finally kill it, for tigers do not kill unless they are hungry.

Leaving the second buffalo at the mango tree, where there was an abundance of green grass, I skirted round the houses and found No. 1 buffalo sleeping peacefully after a big feed and a disturbed night. The tigress, coming from the direction of the village as her pugmarks showed, had approached to within a few feet of the buffalo, and had then gone back the way she had come. Taking the buffalo down to the spring I let it graze for an hour or two, and then took it back and tied it up at the same spot where it had been the previous night.

The second buffalo I tied up fifty yards from the mango tree and at the spot where the wailing woman and villagers had met us the day the Ibbotsons and I had gone up to investigate the human kill. Here a ravine a few feet deep crossed the path, on one side of which there was a dry stump, and on the other an almond tree in which a *machan* could be made. I tied the second buffalo to the stump, and bedded it down with sufficient hay to keep it going for several days. There was nothing more to be done at Thak so I returned to camp and, taking the third buffalo, crossed the Ladhya and tied it up behind Sem, in the ravine where the tigress had killed one of our buffaloes in April.

At my request the Tahsildar of Tanakpur had selected three of the fattest young male buffaloes he could find. All three were now tied up in places frequented by the tigress, and as I set out to visit them on the morning of the 26th I had great hopes that one of them had been killed and that I should get an opportunity of shooting the tigress over it. Starting with the one across the Ladhya, I visited all in turn and found that the tigress had not touched any of them. Again, as on the previous morning, I found her tracks on that path leading to Thak, but on this occasion there was a double set of pugmarks, one coming down and the other going back. On both her journeys the tigress had kept to the path and had passed within a few feet of the buffalo that was tied to the stump, fifty yards from the mango tree.

On my return to Chuka a deputation of Thak villagers led by the Headman came to my tent and requested me to accompany them to the village to enable them to replenish their supply of foodstuffs, so at midday, followed by the Headman and his tenants, and by four of my own men carrying ropes for a *machan* and food for me, I returned to Thak and mounted guard while the men hurriedly collected the provisions they needed.

After watering and feeding the two buffaloes, I retied No. 2 to the stump and took No. 1 half a mile down the hill and tied it to a sapling on the side of the path. I then took the villagers back to Chuka and returned a few hundred yards up the hill for a scratch meal while my men were making the *machan*.

It was now quite evident that the tigress had no fancy for my fat buffaloes, and as in three days I had seen her tracks five times on the path leading to Thak, I decided to sit up over the path and try to get a shot at her that way. To give me warning of the tigress's approach I tied a goat with a bell round its neck on the path, and at 4 p.m. I climbed into the tree. I told my men to return at 8 a.m. the following morning, and began my watch.

At sunset a cold wind started blowing and while I was attempting to pull a coat over my shoulders the ropes on one side of the *machan* slipped, rendering my seat very uncomfortable. An hour later a storm came on, and though it did not rain for long it wet me to the skin, greatly adding to my discomfort. During the sixteen hours I sat in the tree I did not see or hear anything. The men turned up at 8 a.m. I returned to camp for a hot bath and a good meal, and then, accompanied by six of my men, set out for Thak.

The overnight rain had washed all the tracks off the path, and two hundred yards above the tree I had sat in I found the fresh pugmarks of the tigress, where she had come out of the jungle and gone up the path in the direction of Thak. Very cautiously I stalked the first buffalo, only to find it lying asleep on the path; the tigress had skirted round it, rejoined the path a few yards further on, and continued up the hill. Following on her tracks I approached the second buffalo, and as I got near the place where it had been tied, two blue Himalayan magpies rose off the ground and went screaming down the hill.

The presence of these birds indicated (a) that the buffalo was dead, (b) that it had been partly eaten and not carried away, and (c) that the tigress was not in the close vicinity.

On arrival at the stump to which it had been tied I saw that the buffalo had been dragged off the path and partly eaten, and on examining the animal I found that it had not been led by the tigress but that it had in all probability died of snake-bite (there were many hamadryads in the surrounding jungles), and that, finding it lying dead on the path, the tigress had eaten a meal of it and had then tried to drag it away. When she found she could not break the rope, she had partly covered the kill over with dry leaves and brushwood and continued on her way up to Thak.

Tigers as a rule are not carrion eaters but they do on occasions eat animals they themselves have not killed. For instance, on one occasion I left the carcass of a leopard on a fire track and, when I returned next morning to recover a knife I had forgotten,

I found that a tiger had removed the carcass to a distance of a hundred yards had eaten two-thirds of it.

On my way up from Chuka I had dismantled the *machan* I had sat on the previous night, and while two of my men climbed into the almond tree to make a seat for me—the tree was not big enough for a *machan*—the other four went to the spring to fill a kettle and boil some water for tea. By 4 p.m. I had partaken of a light meal of biscuits and tea which would have to keep me going until next day, and refusing the men's request to be permitted to stay the night in one of the houses in Thak, I sent them back to camp. There was a certain amount of risk in doing this, but it was nothing compared to the risk they would run if they spent the night in Thak.

My seat on the tree consisted of several strands of rope tied between two upright branches, with a couple of strands lower down for my feet to rest on. When I had settled down comfortably I pulled the branches round me and secured them in position with a thin cord, leaving a small opening to see and fire through. My 'hide' was soon tested, for shortly after the men had gone the two magpies returned, and attracted others, and nine of them fed on the kill until dusk. The presence of the birds enabled me to get some sleep, for they would have given me warning of the tigress's approach, and with their departure my all-night vigil started.

There was still sufficient daylight to shoot by when the moon, a day off the full, rose over the Nepal hills behind me and flooded the hillside with brilliant light. The rain of the previous night had cleared the atmosphere of dust and smoke and, after the moon had been up a few minutes, the light was so good that I was able to see a *sambhar* and her young one feeding in a field of wheat a hundred and fifty yards away.

The dead buffalo was directly in front and about twenty yards away, and the path along which I expected the tigress to come was two or three yards nearer, so I should have an easy shot at a range at which it would be impossible to miss the tigress—provided she came; and there was no reason why she should not do so.

The moon had been up two hours, and the *sambhar* had approached to within fifty yards of my tree, when a *kakar* started barking on the hill just above the village. The *kakar* had been barking for some minutes when suddenly a scream which I can only very inadequately describe as 'Ar-Ar-Arr' dying away on a long-drawn-out note, came from the direction of the village. So sudden and so unexpected had the scream been that I involuntarily stood up with the intention of slipping down from the tree and dashing up to the village, for the thought flashed through my mind that the man-eater was killing one of my men. Then in a second flash of thought I remembered I had counted them one by one as they had passed my tree, and that I had watched them out of sight on their way back to camp to see if they were obeying my instructions to keep close together.

The scream had been the despairing cry of a human being in mortal agony, and reason questioned how such a sound could have come from a deserted village. It was not a thing of my imagination, for the *kakar* had heard it and had abruptly stopped barking, and the *sambhar* had dashed away across the fields closely followed by her young one. Two days previously, when I had escorted the men to the village, I had remarked that they appeared to be very confident to leave their property behind doors that were not even shut or latched, and the Headman had answered that even if their village remained untenanted for years their property would be quite safe, for they were priests of Purnagiri and no one would dream of robbing them; he added that as long as the tigress lived she was a better guard of their property—if guard were needed—than any hundred men could be, for no one in all that countryside would dare to approach the village for

any purpose, through the dense forests that surrounded it, unless escorted by me as they had been.

The screams were not repeated, and as there appeared to be nothing that I could do I settled down again on my rope seat. At 10 p.m. a *kakar* that was feeding on the young wheat crop at the lower end of the fields dashed away barking, and a minute later the tigress called twice. She had now left the village and was on the move, and even if she did not fancy having another meal off the buffalo there was every hope of her coming along the path which she had used twice every day for the past few days. With finger on trigger and eyes straining on the path I sat hour after hour until daylight succeeded moonlight, and when the sun had been up an hour, my men returned. Very thoughtfully they had brought a bundle of dry wood with them, and in a surprisingly short time I was sitting down to a hot cup of tea. The tigress may have been lurking in the bushes close to us, or she may have been miles away, for after she had called at 10 p.m. the jungles had been silent.

When I got back to camp I found a number of men sitting near my tent. Some of these men had come to inquire what luck I had the previous night, and others had come to tell me that the tigress had called from midnight to a little before sunrise at the foot of the hill, and that all the labourers engaged in the forests and on the new export road were too frightened to go to work. I had already heard about the tigress from my men, who had informed me that, together with the thousands of men who were camped round Chuka, they had sat up all night to keep big fires going.

Among the men collected near my tent was the Headman of Thak, and when the others had gone I questioned him about the kill at Thak on the 12th of the month when he so narrowly escaped falling a victim to the man-eater.

Once again the Headman told me in great detail how he had gone to his fields to dig ginger, taking his grandchild with him, and how on hearing his wife calling he had caught the child's hand and run back to the house—where his wife had said a word or two to him about not keeping his ears open and thereby endangering his own and the child's life—and how a few minutes later the tigress had killed a man while he was cutting leaves off a tree in a field above his house.

All this part of the story I had heard before, and I now asked him if he had actually seen the tigress killing the man. His answer was, no; and he added that the tree was not visible from where he had been standing. I then asked him how he knew the man had been killed, and he said, because he had heard him. In reply to further questions he said the man had not called for help but had cried out; and when asked if he had cried out once he said, 'No, three times', and then at my request he gave an imitation of the man's cry. It was the same—but a very modified rendering—as the screams I had heard the previous night.

I then told him what I had heard and asked him if it was possible for anyone to have arrived at the village accidentally, and his answer was an emphatic negative. There were only two paths leading to Thak, and every man, woman, and child in the village through which these two paths passed knew that Thak was deserted and the reason for its being so. It was known throughout the district that it was dangerous to go near Thak in daylight, and it was therefore quite impossible for anyone to have been in the village at eight o'clock the previous night.

When asked if he could give any explanation for screams having come from a village in which there could not—according to him—have been any human beings, his answer was that he could not. And as I could do no better than the Headman it were best to assume that neither the *kakar*, the *sambhar*, nor I heard those very real screams—the screams of a human being in mortal agony.

IV

When all my visitors, including the Headman, had gone, and I was having breakfast, my servant informed me that the Headman of Sem had come to the camp the previous evening and had left word for me that his wife, while cutting grass near the hut where his mother had been killed, had come on a blood trail, and that he would wait for me near the ford over the Ladhya in the morning. So after breakfast I set out to investigate this trail.

While I was fording the river I saw four men hurrying towards me, and as soon as I was on dry land they told me that when they were coming down the hill above Sem they had heard a tiger calling across the valley on the hill between Chuka and Thak. The noise of the water had prevented my hearing the call. I told the men that I was on my way to Sem and would return to Chuka shortly, and left them.

The Headman was waiting for me near his house, and his wife took me to where she had seen the blood trail the previous day. The trail, after continuing along a field for a short distance, crossed some big rocks, on one of which I found the hairs of a *kakar*. A little further on I found the pugmarks of a big male leopard, and while I was looking at them I heard a tiger call. Telling my companions to sit down and remain quiet, I listened, in order to locate the tiger. Presently I heard the call again, and thereafter it was repeated at intervals of about two minutes.

It was the tigress calling and I located her as being five hundred yards below Thak and in the deep ravine which, starting from the spring under the mango tree, runs parallel to the path and crosses it at its junction with the Kumaya Chak path.

Telling the Headman that the leopard would have to wait to be shot at a more convenient time, I set off as hard as I could go for camp, picking up at the ford the four men who were waiting for my company to Chuka.

On reaching camp I found a crowd of men round my tent, most of them sawyers from Delhi, but including the petty contractors, agents, clerks, timekeepers, and gangmen of the financier who had taken up the timber and road construction contracts in the Ladhya valley. These men had come to see me in connexion with my stay at Chuka. They informed me that many of the hillmen carrying timber and working on the road

had left for their homes that morning and that if I left Chuka
on 1st December, as they had heard I intended doing, the entire
labour force, including themselves, would leave on the same day;
for already they were too frightened to eat or sleep, and no one
would dare to remain in the valley after I had gone. It was
then the morning of 29th November and I told the men that I
still had two days and two nights and that much could happen in
that time, but that in any case it would not be possible for me
to prolong my stay beyond the morning of the 1st.

The tigress had by now stopped calling, and when my servant
had put together something for me to eat I set out for Thak
intending, if the tigress called again and I could locate her position,
to try to stalk her; and if she did not call again, to sit up over
the buffalo. I found her tracks on the path and saw where she
had entered the ravine, and though I stopped repeatedly on my
way up to Thak and listened I did not hear her again. So a little
before sunset I ate the biscuits and drank the bottle of tea I had
brought with me, and then climbed into the almond tree and
took my seat on the few strands of rope that had to serve me as
a *machan*. On this occasion the magpies were absent, so I was
unable to get the hour or two's sleep the birds had enabled me
to get the previous evening.

If a tiger fails to return to its kill the first night it does not
necessarily mean that the kill has been abandoned. I have on
occasions seen a tiger returned on the tenth night and eat what
could no longer be described as flesh. On the present occasion,
however, I was not sitting over a kill, but over an animal that the
tigress had found dead and off which she had made a small meal,
and had she not been a man-eater I would not have considered
the chance of her returning the second night good enough to
justify spending a whole night in a tree when she had not taken
sufficient interest in the dead buffalo to return to it the first
night. It was therefore with very little hope of getting a shot that
I spent was not as long as it had been the previous night, my
discomfort was very much greater, for the ropes I was sitting on

cut into me, and a cold wind that started blowing shortly after moonrise and continued throughout the night chilled me to the bone. On this second night I heard no jungle or other the sounds nor did the *sambhar* and her young one come out to feed on the fields. As daylight was succeeding moonlight I thought I heard a tiger call in the distance, but could not be sure of the sound or of its direction.

When I got back to camp my servant had a cup of tea and a hot bath ready for me, but before I could indulge in the latter—my 40-Ib. tent was not big enough for me to bathe in—I had to get rid of the excited throng of people who were clamouring to tell me their experiences of the night before. It appeared that shortly after moonrise the tigress had started calling close to Chuka, and after calling at intervals for a couple of hours had gone off in the direction of the labour camps at Kumaya Chak The men in these camps hearing her coming started shouting to try to drive her away, but so far from having this effect the shouting only infuriated her the more and she demonstrated in front of the camps until she had cowed the men into silence. Having accomplished this she spent the rest of the night between the labour camps and Chuka, daring all and sundry to shout at her. Towards morning she had gone away in the direction of Thak, and my informants were surprised and very disappointed that I had not met her.

This was my last day of man-eater hunting, and though I was badly in need of rest and sleep, I decided to spend what was left of it in one last attempt to get in touch with the tigress.

The people, not only of Chuka and Sem but of all the surrounding villages, and especially the men from Talla Des where some years previously I had shot three man-eaters, were very anxious that I should try sitting up over a live goat, for, said they, 'All hill tigers eat goats, and as you have had no luck with buffaloes, why not try a goat?' More to humour them than with any hope of getting a shot, I consented to spend this last day in sitting up over the two goats I had already purchased for this purpose.

I was convinced that no matter where the tigress wandered to at night her headquarters were at Thak, so at midday, taking the two goats, and accompanied by four of my men, I set out for Thak.

The path from Chuka to Thak, as I have already mentioned, runs up a very steep ridge. A quarter of a mile on this side of Thak the path leaves the ridge, and crosses a more or less flat bit of ground which extends right up to the mango tree. For its whole length across this flat ground the path passes through dense brushwood, and is crossed by two narrow ravines which run east and join the main ravine. Midway between these two ravines, and a hundred yards from the tree I had sat in the previous two nights, there is a giant almond tree; this tree had been my objective when I left camp. The path passes right under the tree and I thought that if I climbed half-way up not only should I be able to see the two goats, one of which I intended tying at the edge of the main ravine and the other at the foot of the hill to the right, but I should also be able to see the dead buffalo. As all three of these points were at some distance from the tree, I armed myself with an accurate ·275 rifle, in addition to the 450/400 rifle which I took for an emergency.

I found the climb up from Chuka on this last day very trying, and I had just reached the spot where the path leaves the ridge for the flat ground, when the tigress called about a hundred and fifty yards to my left. The ground here was covered with dense undergrowth and trees interlaced with creepers, and was cut up by narrow and deep ravines, and strewn over with enormous boulders—a very unsuitable place in which to stalk a man-eater. However, before deciding on what action I should take it was necessary to know whether the tigress was lying down, as she very well might be, for it was then 1 p.m., or whether she was on the move and if so in what direction. So making the men sit down behind me I listened, and presently the call was repeated; she had moved some fifty yards, and appeared to be going up the main ravine in the direction of Thak.

This was very encouraging, for the tree I had selected to sit in was only fifty yards from the ravine. After enjoining silence on the men and telling them to keep close behind me, we hurried along the path. We had about two hundred yards to go to reach the tree and had covered half the distance when, as we approached a spot where the path was bordered on both sides by dense brushwood, a covey of *kalege* pheasants rose out of the brushwood and went screaming away. I knelt down and covered the path for a few minutes, but as nothing happened we went cautiously forward and reached the tree without further incident. As quickly and as silently as possible one goat was tied at the edge of the ravine, while the other was tied at the foot of the hill to the right; then I took the man to the edge of the cultivated land and told them to stay in the upper verandah of the Headman's house until I fetched them, and ran back to the tree. I climbed to a height of forty feet, and pulled the rifle up after me with a cord I had brought for the purpose. Not only were the two goats visible from my seat, one at a range of seventy and the other at a range of sixty yards, but I could also see part of the buffalo, and as the ·275 rifle was accurate I felt sure I could kill the tigress if she showed up anywhere on the ground I was overlooking.

The two goats had lived together ever since I had purchased them on my previous visit, and, being separated now, were calling lustily to each other. Under normal conditions a goat can be heard at a distance of four yards, but here the conditions were not normal, for the goats were tied on the side of a hill down which a strong wind was blowing, and even if the tigress had moved after I had heard her, it was impossible for her not to hear them. If she was hungry, as I had every reason to believe she was, there was a very good chance of my getting a shot.

After I had been on the tree for ten minutes a *kakar* barked near the spot the pheasants has risen from. For a minute or two my hopes rose sky-high and then dropped back to earth, for the *kakar* barked only three times and ended on a note of enquiry; evidently there was a snake in the scrub which neither he nor the pheasants liked the look of.

My seat was not comfortable and the sun was pleasingly warm, so for the next three hours I remained in the tree without any discomfort. At 4 p.m. the sun went down behind the high hill above Thak and thereafter the wind became unbearably cold. For an hour I stood the discomfort, and then decided to give up, for the cold had brought on an attack of ague, and if the tigress came now it would not be possible for me to hit her. I retied the cord to the rifle and let it down, climbed down myself and walked to the edge of the cultivated land to call up my men.

V

There are few people, I imagine, who have not experienced that feeling of depression that follows failure to accomplish anything they have set out to do. The road back to the camp after a strenuous day when the *chukor* (hill partridge) bag is full is only a step compared with the same road which one plods over, mile after weary mile, when the bag is empty, and if this feeling of depression has ever assailed you at the end of a single day, and when the quarry has only been *chukor*, you will have some idea of the depth of my depression that evening when, after calling up my men and untying the goats, I set off on my two-mile walk to camp, for my effort had been not of a single day or my quarry a few birds, nor did my failure concern only myself.

Excluding the time spent on the journeys from and to home, I had been on the heels of the man-eater from 23rd October to 7th November, and again from 24th to 30th November, and it is only those of you who have walked in fear of having the teeth of a tiger meet in your throat who will have any idea of the effect on one's nerves of days and weeks of such anticipation.

Then again my quarry was a man-eater, and my failure to shoot it would very gravely affect anyone who was working in, or whose homes were in that area. Already work in the forests had been stopped, and the entire population of the largest village in the district had abandoned their homes. Bad as the conditions were they would undoubtedly get worse if the man-eater was not killed, for the entire labour force could not afford to stop work indefinitely, nor could the population of surrounding villages afford to abandon their homes and their cultivation as the more prosperous people of Thak had been able to do.

The tigress had long since lost her natural fear of human beings as was abundantly evident from her having carried away a girl picking up mangoes in a field close to where several men were working, killing a woman near the door of her house, dragging a man off a tree in the heart of a village, and, the previous night, cowing a few thousand men into silence. And here was I, who knew full well what the presence of a man-eater meant to the permanent and to the temporary inhabitants and to all the people who passed through the district on their way to the markets at the foot-hills or the temples at Punagiri, plodding down to camp on what I had promised others would be my last day of man-eater hunting; reason enough for a depression of soul which I felt would remain with me for the rest of my days. Gladly at that movement would I have bartered the success that had attended thirty-two years of man-eater hunting for one unhurried shot at the tigress.

I have told you of some of the attempts I made during this period of seven days and nights to get a shot at the tigress, but these were by no means the only attempts I made. I knew that I was being watched and followed, and every time I went through the two miles of jungle between my camp and Thak I tried every trick I have learnt in a lifetime spent in the jungles to outwit the tigress. Bitter though my disappointment was, I felt that my failure was not in any way due to anything I had done or left undone.

VI

My men when they rejoined me said that, an hour after the *kakar* had barked, they had heard the tigress calling a long way off but were not sure of the direction. Quite evidently the tigress had a little interest in goats as she had in buffaloes, but even so it was unusual for her to have moved at that time of day from a locality in which she was thoroughly at home, unless she had been attracted away by some sound which neither I nor my men had heard; however that may have been, it was quite evident that she had gone, and as there was nothing further that I could do I set of on my weary tramp to camp.

The path, as I have already mentioned, joins the ridge that runs down to Chuka a quarter of a mile from Thak, and when I now got to this spot where the ridge is only a few feet wide and from where a view is obtained of the two great ravines that run down to the Ladhya river, I heard the tigress call once and again across the valley on my left. She was a little above and to the left of Kumaya Chak, and a few hundred yards below the Kot Kindri ridge on which the men working in that area had built themselves grass shelters.

Here was an opportunity, admittedly forlorn and unquestionably desperate, of getting a shot; still it was an opportunity and the last I should ever have, and the question was, whether or not I was justified in taking it.

When I got down from the tree I had one hour in which to get back to camp before dark. Calling up the men, hearing what they had to say, collecting the goats and walking to the ridge had taken about thirty minutes, and judging from the position of the sun which was now casting a red glow on the peaks of the Nepal hills, I calculated I had roughly half an hour's daylight in hand. This time factor, or perhaps it would be more correct to say light factor, was all-important, for if I took the opportunity that offered, on it would depend the lives of five men.

The tigress was a mile away and the intervening ground was densely wooded, strewn over with great rocks and cut up by a

number of deep *nullahs,* but she could cover the distance well
within the half-hour—if she wanted to. The question I had to
decide was, whether or not I should try to call her up. If I called
and she heard me, and came while it was still daylight and gave
me a shot, all would be well; on the other hand, if she came and
did not give me a shot some of us would not reach camp, for we
had nearly two miles to go and the path the whole way ran
through heavy jungle, and was bordered in some places by big
rocks, and in others by dense brushwood. It was useless to consult
the men, for none of them had ever been in a jungle before
coming on this trip, so the decision would have to be mine.

I decided to try to call up the tigress.

Handing my rifle over to one of the men I waited until the
tigress called again and, cupping my hands round my mouth and
filling my lungs to their utmost limit, sent and answering call
over the valley. Back came her call and thereafter, for several
minutes, call answered call. She would come, had in fact already
started, and if she arrived while there was light to shoot by, all
the advantages would be on my side, for I had the selecting of
the ground on which it would best suit me to meet her. November
is the mating season for tigers and it was evident that for the
past forty-eight hours she had been rampaging through the jungles
in search of a mate, and that now, in hearing what she thought
was a tiger answering her mating call, she would lose no time in
joining him.

Four hundred yards down the ridge the path runs for fifty
yards across a flat bit of ground. At the far right-hand side of
this flat ground the path skirts a big rock and then drops steeply,
and continues in a series of hairpin bends, down to the next
bend. It was at this rock I decided to meet the tigress, and on
my way to it I called several times to let her know I was changing
my position, and also to keep in touch with her.

I want you now to have a clear picture of the ground in your
mind, to enable you to follow the subsequent events. Imagine
then a rectangular piece of ground forty yards wide and eighty

yards long, ending in a more or less perpendicular rock face. The path coming down from Thak runs on to this ground at its short or south end, and after continuing down the centre for twenty-five yards bends to the right and leaves the rectangle on its long or east side. At the point where the path leaves the flat ground there is a rock about four feet high. From a little beyond where the path bends to the right, a ridge of rock, three or four feet high, rises and extends to the north side of the rectangle, where the ground falls away in a perpendicular rock face. On the near or path side of this low ridge there is a dense line of bushes approaching to within ten feet of the four-foot-high rock I have mentioned. The rest of the rectangle is grown over with trees, scattered bushes, and short grasses.

It was my intention to lie on the path by the side of the rock and shoot the tigress as she approached me, but when I tried this position I found it would not be possible for me to see her until she was within two or three yards, and further, that she could get at me either round the rock or through the scattered

bushes on my left without my seeing her at all. Projecting out of the rock, from the side opposite to that from which I expected the tigress to approach, there was a narrow ledge. By sitting sideways I found I could get a little of my bottom on the ledge, and by putting my left hand flat on the top of the rounded rock and stretching out my right leg to its full extent and touching the ground with my toes, retain my position on it. The men and goats I placed immediately behind, and ten to twelve feet below me.

The stage was now set for the reception of the tigress, who while these preparations were being made had approached to within three hundred yards. Sending out one final call to give her direction, I looked round to see if my men were all right.

The spectacle these men presented would under other circumstances have been ludicrous, but was here tragic. Sitting in a tight little circle with the knees drawn up and their heads together, with the goats burrowing in under them, they had that look of intense expectancy on their screwed-up features that one sees on the faces of spectators waiting to hear a big gun go off. From the time we had first heard the tigress from the ridge, neither the men nor the goats had made a sound, beyond one suppressed cough. They were probably by now frozen with fear— as well they might be—and even if they were I take my hat off to those four men who had the courage to do what I, had I been in their shoes, would not have dreamt of doing. For seven days they had been hearing the most exaggerated and blood-curdling tales of this fearsome beast that had kept them awake the past two nights, and now, while darkness was coming on, and sitting unarmed in a position where they could see nothing, they were listening to the man-eater drawing nearer and nearer; greater courage, and greater faith, it is not possible to conceive.

The fact that I could not hold my rifle a D.B. 450/400, with my left hand (which I was using to retain my precarious seat on the ledge) was causing me some uneasiness, for apart from the fear of the rifle slipping on the rounded top of the rock—I had folded my handkerchief and placed the rifle on it to try to prevent this—I did know what would be the effect of the recoil of a high velocity rifle fired in this position. The rifle was pointing along the path, in which there was a hump, and it was my intention to fire into the tigress's face immediately it appeared over this hump, which was twenty feet from the rock.

The tigress however did not keep to the contour of the hill, which would have brought her out on the path a little beyond the hump, but crossed a deep ravine and came straight towards where she had heard my last call, at an angle which I can best describe as one o'clock. This manoeuver put the low ridge of rock, over which I could not see, between us. She had located the direction of my last call with great accuracy, but had misjudged the distance, and not finding her prospective mate at the spot she had expected him to be, she was now working herself up into a perfect fury, and you will have some idea of what the fury of a tigress in her condition can be when I tell you that not many miles from my home a tigress on one occasion closed a public road for a whole week, attacking everything that attempted to go along it, including a string of camels, until she was finally joined by a mate.

I know of no sound more liable to fret one's nerves than the calling of an unseen tiger at close range. What effect this appalling sound was having on my men I frightened to think, and if they had gone screaming down the hill I should not have been at all surprised, for even though I had the heel of a good rifle to my shoulder and the stock against my cheek I felt like screaming myself.

But even more frightening than this continuous calling was the fading out of the light. Another few seconds, ten or fifteen at the most, and it would be too dark to see my sights, and we should then be at the mercy of a man-eater, plus a tigress wanting a mate. Something would have to be done, and done in a hurry if we were not to be massacred, and the only thing I could think of was to call.

The tigress was now so close that I could hear the intake of her breath each time before she called, and as she again filled her lungs, I did the same with mine, and we called simultaneously. The effect was startlingly instantaneous. Without a second's hesitation she came tramping with quick steps through the dead leaves, over the low ridge and into the bushes a little to my right front, and just as I was expecting her to walk right on the top of me she stopped, and the next moment the full blast of her deep-throated call struck me in the face and would have carried the hat off my head had I been wearing one. A second's pause, then again quick steps; a glimpse of her as she passed between two bushes, and then she stepped right out into the open, and, looking into my face, stopped dead.

By great and unexpected good luck the half-dozen steps the tigress took to her right front carried her almost to the exact spot at which my rifle was pointing. Had she continued in the direction in which she was coming before her last call, my story— if written—would have had a different ending, for it would have been as impossible to slew the rifle on the rounded top of the rock as it would have been to lift and fire it with one hand.

Owing to the nearness of the tigress, and the fading light, all that I could see of her was her head. My first bullet caught her under the right eye and the second, fired more by accident than with intent, took her in the throat and she came to rest with her nose against the rock. The recoil from the right barrel loosened my hold on the rock and knocked me off the ledge, and the recoil from the left barrel, fired while I was in the air, brought the rifle up in violent contact with my jaw and sent me head over heels right on top of the men for, not knowing but what the tigress was going to land on them next, they caught me as I fell and saved me from injury and my rifle from being broken.

When I had freed myself from the tangle of the human and goat legs I look the ·275 rifle from the man who was holding it, rammed a clip of cartridges into the magazine and sent a stream of five bullets singing over the valley and across the valley and across the Sarda into Nepal. Two shots, to the thousands of men in the valley and in the surrounding villages who were anxiously listening for the sound of my rifle, might mean anything, but two shots followed by five more, spaced at regular intervals of five seconds, could only be interpreted as conveying one message, and that was that the man-eater was dead.

I had not spoken to my men from the time we had first heard the tigress from the ridge. On my telling them now that she was dead and that there was no longer any reason for us to be afraid, they did not appear to be able to take in what I was saying, so I told them to go up and have a look while I found and lit a cigarette. Very cautiously they climbed up to the rock, but went no further for, as I have told you, the tigress was touching the other side of it. Late in camp that night while sitting round a camp-fire, and relating their experiences to relays of eager listeners, their narrative invariably ended up with, 'and then the tiger whose roaring had turned our livers into water hit the *sahib* on the head and knocked him down on top of us, and if you don't believe us, go and look at his face'. A mirror is superfluous in camp and even if I had one it could not have made the swelling on my jaw, which put me on milk diet for several days, look as large and as painful as it felt.

By the time a sapling had been felled and the tigress lashed to it, lights were begining to show in the Ladhya valley and in all the surrounding camps and villages. The four men were very anxious to have the honour of carrying the tigress to camp, but the task was beyond them; so I left them and set off for help.

In my three visits to Chuka during the past eight months I had been along this path many times by day and always with a loaded rifle in my hands, and now I was stumbling down in the dark, unarmed, my only anxiety being to avoid a fall. If the greatest happiness one can experience is the sudden cessation of great pain, then the second greatest happiness is undoubtedly the sudden cessation of great fear. One short hour previously it would have taken wild elephants to have dragged from their homes and camps the men who now, singing and shouting, were converging from every direction, singly and in groups, on the path leading to Thak. Some of the men of this rapidly growing crowd went up the path to help carry in the tigress, while other accompanied me on my way to camp, and would have carried me had I permitted them. Progress was slow, for frequent halts had to be made to allow each group of new arrivals to express their gratitude in their own particular way. This gave the party carrying the tigress time to catch us up, and we entered the village together. I will not attempt to describe the welcome my men and I received, or the scenes I witnessed at Chuka that night, for having lived the greater part of my life in the jungles I have not the ability to paint word-pictures.

A hayrick was dismantled and the tigress laid on it, and an enormous bonfire made from driftwood close at hand to light up the scene and for warmth, for the night was dark and cold with a north wind blowing. Round about midnight my servant, assisted by the Headman of Thak and Kunwar Singh, near whose house I was camped, persuaded the crowd to return to their respective villages and labour camps, telling them they would have ample opportunity of feasting their eyes on the tigress the following day. Before leaving himself, the Headman of Thak told me he would send word in the morning to the people of Thak to return to their village. This he did, and two days later the entire population returned to their homes, and have lived in peace ever since.

After my midnight dinner I sent for Kunwar Singh and told him that in order to reach home on the promised date I should have to start in a few hours, and that he would have to explain to the people in the morning why I had gone. This he promised to do, and I then started to skin the tigress. Skinning a tiger with a pocket-knife is a long job, but it gives one an opportunity of examining the animal that one would otherwise not get, and in the case of man-eater enables one to ascertain, more or less accurately, the reason for the animal having become a man-eater.

The tigress was a comparatively young animal and in the perfect condition one would expect her to be at the beginning of the mating season. Her dark winter coat was without a blemish, and in spite of her having so persistently refused the meals I had provided for her she was encased in fat. She had two old gun-shot wounds, neither of which showed on her skin. The one in her left shoulder, caused by several pellets of homemade buckshot, had become septic, and when healing the skin, over quite a large surface, had adhered permanently to the flesh. To what extent this wound had incapacitated her it would have been difficult to say, but it had evidently taken a very long time to heal, and could quite reasonably have been the cause of her having become a man-eater. The second wound, which was in her right shoulder, had also been caused by a charge of buckshot, but had healed without becoming septic. These two wounds received over kills in the days before she had become a man-eater were quite sufficient reason for her not having returned to the human and other kills I had sat over.

After having skinned the tigress I bathed and dressed, and though my face was swollen and painful and I had twenty miles of rough going before me, I left Chuka walking on air, while the thousands of men in and around the valley were peacefully sleeping.

I have come to the end of the jungle stories I set out to tell you and I have also come near the end of my man-eater hunting career.

I have had a long spell and count myself fortunate in having walked out on my own feet and not been carried out on a cradle in the manner and condition of the man of Thak.

There have been occasions when life has hung by a thread and others when a light purse and disease resulting from exposure and strain have made the going difficult, but for all these occasions I am amply rewarded if my hunting has resulted in saving one human life.

# JUST TIGERS

I think that all sportsmen who have had the opportunity of indulging in the twin sports of shooting tigers with a camera and shooting them with a rifle will agree with me that the difference between these two forms of sport is as great, if not greater, than the taking of a trout on light tackle in a snow-fed mountain stream, and the killing of a fish on a fixed rod on the sun-baked bank of a tank.

Apart from the difference in cost between shooting with a camera and shooting with a rifle, and the beneficial effect it has on our rapidly decreasing stock of tigers, the taking of a good photograph gives far more pleasure to the sportsman than the acquisition of a trophy; and further, while the photograph is of interest to all lovers of wild life, the trophy is only of interest to the individual who acquired it. As an illustration, I would instance Fred Champion. Had Champion shot his tigers with a rifle instead of with a camera his trophies would long since have lost their hair and been consigned to the dustbin, whereas the records made by his camera are a constant source of pleasure to him, and are of interest to sportsmen in all parts of the world.

It was looking at the photographs in Champion's book *With a Camera in Tiger-Land* that first gave me the idea of taking photographs of tigers. Champion's photographs were taken with a still camera by flashlight and I decided to go one better and try to take tiger pictures with a ciné-camera by daylight. The gift by a very generous friend of a Bell and Howell 16-mm camera put just the weapon I needed into my hands, and the 'Freedom of the Forests' which I enjoy enabled me to roam at large over a very wide field. For ten years I stalked through many hundreds of miles of tiger country, at times being seen off by tigers that resented my approaching their kills, and at other times being shooed out of the jungle by tigresses that objected to my going near their cubs. During this period I learnt a little about the habits and ways of tigers, and though I saw tigers on, possibly, two hundred occasions I did not succeed in getting one satisfactory picture. I exposed films on many occasions, but the results were disappointing owing either to overexposure, underexposure, obstruction of grass or leaves or cobwebs on the lens; and in one case owing to the emulsion on the film having been melted while being processed.

Finally in 1938 I decided to devote the whole winter to making one last effort to get a good picture. Having learnt by experience that it was not possible to get a haphazard picture of a tiger, my first consideration was to find a suitable site, and I eventually selected an open ravine fifty yards wide, with a tiny stream flowing down the centre of it, and flanked on either side by dense tree and scrub jungle. To deaden the sound of my camera when taking pictures at close range I blocked the stream in several places, making miniature waterfalls a few inches high. I then cast round for my tigers, and having located seven, in three widely separated areas, started to draw them a few yards at a time to my jungle studio. This was a long and a difficult job, with many set-backs and disappointments, for the area in which I was operating is heavily shot over, and it was only be keeping my tigers out of sight that I eventually got them to the exact spot where I wanted them. One of the tigers for some reason unknown to me left the day after her arrival, but not before I had taken a picture of her; the other six I kept together and I exposed a thousand feet of film on them. Unfortunately it was one of the wettest winters we have ever had and several hundred feet of the film were ruined through moisture on the lens, underexposure, and packing of the film inside the camera due to hurried and careless threading. But, even so, I have got approximately six hundred feet of film of which I am inordinately proud, for it is a living record of six full grown tigers—four males, two of which are over ten feet, and two females, one of which is a white tigress—filmed in daylight, at ranges varying from ten to sixty feet.

The whole proceeding from start to finish took four and a half months, and during the countless hours I lay near the tiny stream and my miniature waterfalls, not one of the tigers ever saw me.

The stalking to within a few feet of six tigers in daylight would have been an impossible feat, so they were stalked in the very early hours of the morning, before night had gone and daylight come—the heavy winter dew making this possible—and were filmed as light, and opportunity, offered.

# THE TEMPLE TIGER AND MORE
# MAN-EATERS OF KUMAON

# CONTENTS

# THE TEMPLE TIGER

1

**IT IS NOT POSSIBLE FOR** those who have never lived in the upper reaches of the Himalayas to have any conception of the stranglehold that superstition has on the people who inhabit that sparsely populated region. The dividing line between the superstitions of simple uneducated people who live on high mountains, and the beliefs of sophisticated educated people who live at lesser heights, is so faint that it is difficult to determine where the one ends and the other begins. If therefore you are tempted to laugh at the credulity of the actors in the tale I am going to tell, I would ask you to pause for a moment and try to define the difference between superstition as exemplified in my tale, and your beliefs in the faith you have been brought up in.

Shortly after the Kaiser's war, Robert Bellairs and I were on a shooting trip in the interiors of Kumaon and we camped one September evening at the foot of Trisul, where we were informed that 800 goats were sacrificed each year to the demon of Trisul. With us we had fifteen of the keenest and the most cheerful hillmen I have ever been associated with on a *shikar*. One of these men, Bala Singh, a Garhwali, had been with me for years and had accompanied me on many expeditions. It was his pride and pleasure when on *shikar* to select and carry the heaviest of my loads and, striding at the head of the other men, enliven the march with snatches of song. Around the camp-fire at night the men always sang part-songs before going to sleep, and during that first night, at the foot of Trisul, the singing lasted longer than usual and was accompanied by clapping of hands, shouting, and the beating of tin cans.

It had been our intention to camp at this spot and explore the country around for *baral* and *thar*, and we were very surprised as we sat down to breakfast next morning to see our men making preparations to strike camp. On asking for an explanation we were told that the site we had camped on was not suitable: that it was damp; that the drinking water was bad; that fuel was difficult to get; and, finally, that there was a better site two miles away.

I had six Garhwalis to carry my luggage and I noticed that it was being made up into five head-loads, and that Bala Singh was sitting apart near the camp-fire with a blanket over his head and shoulders. After breakfast I walked over to him, and noted as I did so that all the other men had stopped work and were watching me very intently. Bala Singh saw me coming and made no attempt to greet me, which was very unusual, and to all my questions he returned the one answer—that he was not ill. That day we did our two-mile march in silence, Bala Singh bringing up the rear and moving like a man who was walking in his sleep, or who was under the influence of drugs.

It was now quite apparent that whatever had happened to Bala Singh was affecting the other fourteen men, for they were performing their duties without their usual cheerfulness, and all of them had a strained and frightened look on their faces. While the 40-lb tent Robert and I shared was being erected, I took my Garhwali servant Mothi Singh—who had been with me for twenty-five years—aside and demanded to be told what was wrong with Bala Singh. After a lot of hedging and evasive answers I eventually got Mothi Singh's story, which, when it came, was short and direct. 'While we were sitting round the camp-fire last night and singing,' Mothi Singh said, the 'demon of Trisul entered Bala Singh's mouth and he swallowed him'. Mothi Singh went on to say that they had shouted and beaten tin cans to try to drive the demon out of Bala Singh, but that they had not succeeded in doing so, and that now nothing could be done about it.

Bala Singh was sitting apart, with the blanket still draped over his head. He was out of earshot of the other men, so, going over to him, I asked him to tell me what had happened the previous night. For a long minute Bala Singh looked up at me with eyes full of distress, and then in a hopeless tone of voice he said: 'Of what use is it, Sahib, for me to tell you what happened last night, for you will not believe me.' 'Have I ever,' I asked, 'disbelieved you?' 'No,' he said, 'no, you have never disbelieved me, but this is a matter that you will not understand.' 'Whether I understand it or not,' I said, 'I want you to tell me exactly what happened.' After a long silence Bala Singh said: 'Very well, Sahib, I will tell you what happened. You know that in our hill-songs it is customary for one man to sing the verse, and for all the other men present to join in the chorus. Well, while I was singing a verse of one of our songs last night the demon of Trisul jumped into my mouth, and though I tried to eject him, he slipped down my throat into my stomach. The other men saw my struggle with the demon, for the fire was burning brightly, and they tried to drive him away by shouting and beating tin cans; but,' he added with a sob, 'the demon would not go.' 'Where is the demon now?' I asked. Placing his hand on the pit of his stomach, Bala Singh answered with great conviction, 'He is here, Sahib, here; I can feel him moving about.'

Robert had spent the day prospecting the ground to the west of our camp and had shot a *thar*, of which he had seen several. After dinner we sat long into the night reviewing the situation. We had planned for, and looked forward to, this shoot for many months. It had taken Robert seven days' and me ten days' hard walking to reach our shooting ground, and on the night of our arrival Bala Singh had swallowed the demon of Trisul. What our personal opinions were on this subject did not matter, but what did matter was that every man in camp was convinced that Bala Singh had a demon in his stomach, and they were frightened of him and were shunning his company. To carry on a month's shoot under these conditions was not possible, and Robert very reluctantly agreed with me that the only thing to be done was for me to return to Naini Tal with Bala Singh, while he carried on with the shoot alone. So next morning I packed up my things, and after an early breakfast with Robert, set off on my ten-day walk back to Naini Tal.

Bala Singh, a perfect specimen of a man of about thirty years of age, had left Naini Tal full of the joy of life; now he returned silent, with a strained look in his eyes, and with the appearance of one who had lost all interest in life. My sisters, one of whom had been a medical missionary, did all they could for him. Friends from far and near came to visit him, but he just sat at the door of his house, never speaking unless spoken to. The civil surgeon of Naini Tal, Colonel Cooke, a man of great experience and a close friend of the family, came to visit Bala Singh at my request. His verdict after a long and painstaking examination was that Bala Singh was in perfect physical condition, and that he could ascribe no reason for the man's apparent depression.

A few days later I had a brainwave. There was in Naini Tal at that time a very eminent Indian doctor and I thought if I could get him to examine Bala Singh and, after he had done so, tell him about the demon and persuade him to assure Bala Singh that there was no demon in his stomach, he would be able to cure him of his trouble, for in addition to being a Hindu, the doctor was himself a hillman. My brainwave, however, did not work out as I had hoped and anticipated, for as soon as he saw the sick man the doctor appeared to get suspicious and when in reply to some shrewd questions he learnt from Bala Singh that the demon of Trisul was in his stomach, he stepped away from him hurriedly and turning to me said, 'I am sorry you sent for me, for I can do nothing for this man.'

There were two men from Bala Singh's village in Naini Tal. Next day I sent for them. They knew what was wrong with Bala Singh for they had come to see him several times, and at my request they agreed to take him home. Provided with funds the three men started on their eight-day journey next morning. Three weeks later the two men returned and made their report to me.

Bala Singh had accomplished the journey without any trouble. On the night of his arrival home, and while his relatives and friends were gathered around him, he had suddenly announced to the assembly that the demon wanted to be released to return to Trisul, and that the only way this could be accomplished was for him to die. 'So,' my informants concluded, 'Bala Singh just lay down and died, and next morning we assisted at his cremation.'

Superstition, I am convinced, is a mental complaint similar to measles in that it attacks an individual or a community while leaving others immune. I therefore do not claim any credit for not contracting, while living on the upper reaches of the Himalayas, the virulent type of superstition that Bala Singh died of. But though I claim I am not superstitious, I can give no explanation for the experience I met with at the bungalow while hunting the Champawat tiger and the scream I heard coming from the deserted Thak village. Nor can I give any explanation for my repeated failures while engaged in one of the most interesting tiger hunts I have ever indulged in, which I shall now relate.

2

No one who has visited Dabidhura is ever likely to forget the view that is to be obtained from the Rest House built near the summit of 'God's Mountain' by one who, quite evidently, was a lover of scenery. From the veranda of the little three-roomed house, the hill falls steeply away to the valley of the Panar river. Beyond this valley, the hills rise ridge upon ridge until they merge into the eternal snows which, until the advent of aircraft, formed an impenetrable barrier between India and her hungry northern neighbours.

A bridle-road running from Naini Tal, the administrative headquarters of Kumaon, to Loharghat, an outlying subdivision on her eastern border, passes through Dabidhura, and a branch of this road connects Dabidhura with Almora. I was hunting the Panar man-eating leopard—about which I shall tell you later—in the vicinity of this latter road when I was informed by a road overseer, on his way to Almora, that the leopard had killed a man at Dabidhura. So to Dabidhura I went.

The western approach to Dabidhura is up one of the steepest roads in Kumaon. The object the man who designed this road had in view was to get to the top by the shortest route possible, and this he accomplished by dispensing with hairpin bends and running his road straight up the face of the eight-thousand-foot mountain. After panting up this road on a hot afternoon in April, I was sitting on the veranda of the Rest House drinking gallons of tea and feasting my eyes on the breathtaking view, when the priest of Dabidhura came to see me. When two years previously I had been hunting the Champawat man-eater, I had made friends with this frail old man, who officiated at the little temple nestling in the shadow of the great rock that had made Dabidhura a place of pilgrimage, and for whose presence in that unusual place I shall hazard no guess. When passing the temple a few minutes earlier I had made the customary offering which had been acknowledged by a nod by the old priest who was at his devotions. These devotions finished, the priest crossed the road that runs between the temple and the Rest House and accepting a cigarette sat down on the floor of the veranda with his back against the wall for a comfortable chat. He was a friendly old man with plenty of time on his hands, and as I had done all the walking I wanted to that day, we sat long into the evening chatting and smoking.

From the priest I learnt that I had been misinformed by the road overseer about the man alleged to have been killed at Dabidhura the previous night by the man-eater. The alleged victim, a herdsman on his way from Almora to a village south of Dabidhura, had been the priest's guest the previous night. After the evening meal the herdsman had elected, against the priest's advice, to sleep on the *chabutra* (platform) of the temple. Round about midnight, when the rock was casting a shadow over the temple, the man-eater crept up and, seizing the man's ankles, attempted to drag him off the platform. Awakening with a yell, the man grabbed a smouldering bit of wood from the nearby fire, and beat off the leopard. His yell brought the priest and several other men to his rescue and the combined force drove the animal away. The man's wounds were not serious, and after they had received rough-and-ready treatment at the hands of the *bania*, whose shop was near the temple the herdsman continued his journey.

On the evidence of the priest I decided to remain at Dabidhura. The temple and the *bania*'s shop were daily visited by men from the surrounding villages. These men would spread the news of my arrival and—knowing where I was to be found—I would immediately be informed of any kills of human beings, or of animals, that might take place in the area.

As the old priest got up to leave me that evening I asked him if it would be possible for me to get some shooting in the locality, for my men had been without meat for many days and there was none to be purchased at Dabidhura. 'Yes,' he answered, 'there is the temple tiger.' On my assuring him that I had no desire to shoot his tiger he rejoined with a laugh, 'I have no objection, Sahib, to your *trying* to shoot this tiger, but neither you nor anyone else will ever succeed in *killing* it.' And that is how I came to hear of the Dabidhura temple tiger, which provided me with one of the most interesting *shikar* experiences I have ever had.

3

The morning following my arrival at Dabidhura I went down the Loharghat road to see if I could find any trace of the man-eater, or learn anything about it in the village adjoining the road, for the leopard was alleged to have gone in that direction after its attack on the man at the temple. On my return to the Rest House for a late lunch I found a man in conversation with my servant. This man informed me he had learnt from the priest that I wanted to do some shooting and he said he could show me a *jarao*—the hillman's name for *sambhar*—with horns as big as the branches of an oak tree. Hill *sambhar* do on occasions grow very fine horns—one had been shot in Kumaon some time previously with horns measuring forty-seven inches—and as a big animal would not only provide my men with meat but would also provide a meat ration for all at Dabidhura, I told the man I would accompany him after lunch.

Some months previously I had been to Calcutta on a short visit, and one morning walked into Manton's, the gunmaker's shop. On a glass showcase near the door was a rifle. I was looking at the weapon when the manager, who was an old friend of mine, came up. He informed me that the rifle, a .275 by Westley Richards, was a new model which the makers were anxious to introduce on the Indian market for hill shooting. The rifle was a beauty and the manager had little difficulty in persuading me to buy it on the understanding that if it did not suit me I would be at liberty to return it. So when I set out with my village friend that evening to shoot his *jarao* with horns as big as the branches of an oak tree, I was carrying my brand-new rifle.

To the south of Dabidhura the hill is less steep than it is to the north and we had proceeded in this direction through oak and scrub jungle for about two miles when we came to a grassy knoll with an extensive view of the valley below. Pointing to a small patch of grass—surrounded by dense jungle—on the left-hand side of the valley, my guide informed me that the *jarao* came out to graze on this patch of grass morning and evening. He further informed me that there was a footpath on the right-hand side of the valley which he used when on his way to or from Dabidhura, and that it was from this path he was accustomed to seeing the *jarao*. The rifle I was carrying was sighted to five hundred yards and guaranteed to be dead accurate, and as the distance between the path and the *jarao*'s feeding ground appeared to be only about three hundred yards, I decided to go down the path and wait for a shot.

While we had been talking I had noticed some vultures circling to our left front. On drawing my companion's attention to them he informed me there was a small village in a fold of the hill in that direction and suggested that the vultures were possibly interested in some domestic animal that had died in the village. However, he said we would soon know what had attracted the birds, for our way lay through the village. The 'village' consisted of a single grass hut, a cattle shed, and an acre or so of terraced fields from which the crops had recently been cut. In one of these fields, separated from the hut and cattle shed by a ten-foot wide rainwater channel, vultures were tearing the last shreds of flesh from the skeleton of some large animal. A man walked out of the hut as we approached and, after greeting us, asked where I had come from and when I had arrived. On my telling him that I had come from Naini Tal to try to shoot the man-eating leopard and that I had arrived at Dabidhura the previous day, he expressed great regret at not having known of my arrival. 'For you could then,' he said, 'have shot the tiger that killed my cow.' He went on to tell me that he had tethered his fifteen head of cattle in the field, on which the vultures were pulling about the skeleton, the previous night, to fertilize it, and that during the night a tiger had come and killed one of the cows. He had no firearms and as there was no within reach to whom he could appeal to shoot the tiger, he had gone to a village where a man lived who had the contract for collecting hides and skins in that area. This man had removed the hide of the cow two hours before my arrival, and the vultures had then carried out their function. When I asked the man whether he had known that there was a tiger in the locality and, if so, why he had tethered his cattle out in the open at night, he surprised me by saying there had always been a tiger on the Dabidhura hill, but that up to the previous night it had never molested cattle.

As I moved away from the hut the man asked me where I was going and when I told him I was going to try to shoot the *jarao* on the far side of the valley, he begged me to leave the *jarao* alone for the present and to shoot the tiger. 'My holding is small and the land poor, as you can see,' he said, 'and if the tiger kills my cows, on which I depend for a living, my family and I will starve.'

While we had been talking, a woman had come up the hill with a *gharra* of water on her head, followed a little later by a girl carrying a bundle of green grass and a boy carrying a bundle of dry sticks: four people living on an acre or so of poor land and a few pints of milk—for hill cattle give little milk—sold to

the *bania* at Dabidhura. Little wonder, then, that the man was so anxious for me to shoot the tiger.

The vultures had destroyed the kill. This did not matter, however, for there was no heavy cover near the field where the tiger could have lain up and seen the vultures at their work, so he would be almost certain to return, for he had not been disturbed at his feed the previous night. My guide was also keen on my trying to shoot the tiger in preference to his *jarao*, so, telling the two men to sit down, I set off to try to find out in which direction the tiger had gone, for there were no trees on which I could sit near the field, and it was my intention to intercept the tiger on its way back. The hill was criss-crossed with cattle paths but the ground was too hard to show pug marks, and after circling round the village twice I eventually tried the rainwater channel. Here on the soft damp ground I found the pug marks of a big male tiger. These pug-marks showed that the tiger had gone up the channel after his feed, so it was reasonable to assume that he would return the same way. Growing out of the bank, on the same side of the channel as the hut and about thirty yards from it, was a gnarled and stunted oak tree smothered by a wild rose creeper. Laying down the rifle, I stepped from the bank on to the tree, which was leaning out over the channel, and found there was a reasonably comfortable seat on the top of the creeper.

Rejoining the two men at the hut I told them I was going back to the Rest House for my heavy rifle, a double-barrelled .500 express using modified cordite. My guide very sportingly offered to save me this trouble, so after instructing him I sat down with the villager at the door of his hut and listened to the tales he had to tell of a poor but undaunted man's fight against nature and wild animals, to keep a grass roof above his head. When I asked him why he did not leave this isolated place and try to make a living elsewhere, he said simply, 'This is my home.'

The sun was near setting when I saw two men coming down the hill towards the hut. Neither of them had a rifle, but Bala

Singh—one of the best men who ever stepped out of Garhwal, and of whose tragic death some years later I have already told you—was carrying a lantern. On reaching me Bala Singh said he had not brought my heavy rifle because the cartridges for it were locked up in my suitcase and I had forgotten to send the key. Well, the tiger would have to be shot with my new rifle, and it could not have a better christening.

Before taking my seat on the tree I told the owner of the hut that my success would depend on his keeping his two children, a girl of eight and a boy of six, quiet, and that his wife would have to defer cooking the evening meal until I had shot the tiger, or until I decided the tiger was not coming. My instructions to Bala Singh were to keep the inmates of the hut quiet, light the lantern when I whistled, and then await my further orders.

The vesper songs of the multitude of birds in the valley were hushed as the red glow from the setting sun died off the hills. Twilight deepened and a horned owl hooted on the hill above me. There would be a short period of semi-darkness before the moon rose. The time had now come, and the inmates of the hut were as silent as the dead. I was gripping the rifle and straining my eyes on the ground under me when the tiger, who had avoided passing under my tree, arrived at his kill and was angry at what he found. In a low muttering voice he cursed the vultures who, though they had departed two hours earlier, had left their musky smell on the ground they had fouled. For two, three, possibly four minutes he continued to mutter to himself, and then there was silence. The light was getting stronger. Another few minutes and the moon rose over the brow of the hill, flooding my world with light. The bones picked clean by the vultures were showing white in the moonlight, and nowhere was the tiger to be seen. Moistening my lips, which excitement had dried, I gave a low whistle. Bala Singh was on the alert and I heard him ask the owner of the hut for a light from the fire. Through the crevices of the grass hut I saw a glimmer of light, which grew stronger as the lantern was lit. The light moved across the hut and Bala Singh pulled open the door and stood on the threshold awaiting my further orders. With the exception of that one low whistle, I had made no sound or movement from the time I had taken my seat on the tree. And now, when I looked down, there was the tiger standing below me, in brilliant moonlight, looking over his right shoulder at Bala Singh. The distance between the muzzle of my rifle and the tiger's head was about five feet, and the thought flashed through my mind that the cordite would probably singe his hair. The ivory foresight of my rifle was on the exact spot of the tiger's heart—where I knew my bullet would kill him instantaneously—when I gently pressed the trigger. The trigger gave under the pressure, and nothing happened.

Heavens! How incredibly careless I had been. I distinctly remembered having put a clip of five cartridges in the magazine when I took my seat on the tree, but quite evidently when I pushed the bolt home it had failed to convey a cartridge from the magazine into the chamber, and this I had omitted to observe. Had the rifle been old and worn it might still have been possible to rectify my mistake. But the rifle was new and as I raised the lever to draw back the bolt there was a loud metallic click, and in one bound the tiger was up the bank and out of sight. Turning my head to see how Bala Singh had reacted, I saw him step back into the hut and close the door.

There was now no longer any need for silence and as Bala Singh came up at my call, to help me off the tree, I drew back the bolt of the rifle with the object of unloading the magazine and, as I did so, I noticed that the extractor at the end of the bolt held a cartridge. So the rifle had been loaded after all and the safety-catch off. Why then had the rifle not fired when I pulled the trigger? Too late, I knew the reason. One of the recommendations stressed by Manton's manager when showing me the rifle was that it had a double pull off. Never having handled a rifle with this so-called improvement, I did not know it was necessary, after the initial pull had taken up the slack, to pull the trigger a second time to release the striker. When I explained the reason for my failure to Bala Singh, he blamed himself, 'for', said he, 'if I had brought your heavy rifle *and* the suitcase this would not have happened'. I was inclined to agree with him at the time, but as the days went by I was not so sure that even with the heavy rifle I would have been able to kill the tiger that evening.

4

Another long walk next morning, to try to get news of the man-eater, and when I returned to the Rest House I was greeted by a very agitated man who informed me that the tiger had just killed one of his cows. He had been grazing his cattle on the far side of the valley from where I sat the previous evening, when a tiger appeared and killed a red cow that had calved a few days previously. 'And now,' he said, 'the heifer calf will die, for none of my other cows are in milk.'

Luck had been with the tiger the previous evening but his luck could not last indefinitely, and for the killing of this cow he would have to die, for cattle are scarce in the hills and the loss of a milch cow to a poor man was a serious matter. The man had no anxiety about the rest of his small herd, which had stampeded back to his village, so he was willing to wait while I had a meal. At 1 p.m. we set out, the man leading, I on his heels, and two of my men following with material for making a *machan*.

From an open patch of ground on the hillside my guide pointed out the lay of the land. His cattle had been grazing on a short stretch of grass a quarter of a mile below the ridge, when the tiger, coming up from the direction of the valley, had killed his cow. The rest of the herd had stampeded up the hill and over the ridge to his village, which was on the far side. Our shortest way was across the valley and up the other side, but I did not want to risk disturbing the tiger, so we skirted round the head of the valley to approach from above the spot where the cow had been killed. Between the ridge over which the cattle had stampeded and the spot where they had been grazing, was more or less open tree jungle. The tracks of the running animals had bitten deep into the soft loamy earth, and it was easy to follow these tracks back to where they had started. Here there was a big pool of blood with a drag-mark leading away from it. The drag led across the hill for 200 yards to a deep and well-wooded ravine with a trickle of water in it. Up this ravine the tiger had taken his kill.

The cow had been killed at about 10 a.m. on open ground, and the tiger's first anxiety would have been to remove it to some secluded spot where it would be hidden from prying eyes. So he had dragged it up the ravine and, after depositing it in a place he knew of, he had, as his pug-marks showed, gone down the ravine into the valley below. In an area in which human beings and cattle are moving about, it is unwise to predict where a tiger will be lying up, for the slightest disturbance may make him change his position. So, though the pug-marks led down the ravine, the three men and I very cautiously followed the drag up the ravine.

Two hundred yards below the ridge along which we had come, rainwater had scooped out a big hole in the hillside. Here the ravine started. The hole, which at the upper end had a sheer drop into it of fifteen feet, had been made many years previously and was now partly overgrown with oak and ash saplings ten to twelve feet tall. Between these saplings and the fifteen-foot drop was a small open space on which the tiger had deposited his kill. I could sympathize with the owner of the cow when he told me with tears in his eyes that the fine animal that lay dead before us had been bred by him and that it was a special favourite. No portion of the animal had been touched, the tiger having evidently brought it here to eat at his leisure.

A place had now to be found in which to sit. There were several big oak trees on either side of the ravine, but none overlooked the kill and all of them were unclimbable. Thirty yards below the kill and on the left-hand side of the ravine was a small stout holly tree. The branches were growing out at right angles to the trunk, and six feet above ground there was a strong enough branch for me to sit on and another on which to rest my feet. The three men protested strongly against my sitting so close to the ground. However, there was no other suitable place for me to sit, so the holly tree it would have to be. Before sending the men away I instructed them to go to the hut where I had been the previous evening, and to wait there until I called to them, or until I joined them. The distance across the valley was about half a mile and though the men would not be able to see either me or the kill, I was able to see the hut through the leaves of the holly tree.

The men left me at 4 p.m. and I settled down on the holly branch for what I anticipated would be a long wait, for the hill faced west and the tiger would probably not be on the move much before sundown. To the left my field of vision—through the holly leaves—extended down the ravine for fifty yards. In front I had a clear view into the ravine, which was about ten feet deep and twenty feet wide, and of the hill facing me on which there were outcrops of rock but no trees. To the right I had a clear view up to the ridge but I could not see the kill, which was hidden by the thick growth of saplings. Behind me was a dense thicket of *ringals* which extended down to the level of my tree and further helped to mask the kill. The tiger after depositing his kill in the hole, made by rainwater, had gone down the ravine and it was reasonable to assume that when he returned he would come by the same route. So I concentrated all my attention on the ravine, intending to shoot the tiger when he was at right angles to me. That I could kill him at that short range I had no doubt whatsoever and to make quite sure of getting in a second shot, if it was necessary, I cocked both hammers of my rifle.

There were *sambhar*, *kakar*, and *langur* in the jungle and a great number of pheasants, magpies, babblers, thrushes, and jays, all of which call on seeing a member of the cat family, so I thought I would receive ample warning of the tiger's coming. But here I was wrong, for without having heard a single alarm call, I suddenly heard the tiger at his kill. After going down the ravine, possibly for a drink, the tiger had skirted round the thicket of *ringals* and approached his kill without passing me. This did not worry me unduly for tigers are restless at a kill in daylight, and I felt sure that sooner or later the tiger would show up on the open ground in front of me. He had been eating for about fifteen minutes, tearing off great chunks of flesh, when I caught sight of a bear coming along the crest of the hill from left to right. He was a great big Himalayan black bear, and was strolling along as though it did not matter to him how long he took to get from here to there. Suddenly he stopped, turned facing downhill, and lay flat. After a minute or two he raised his head, snuffed the wind, and again lay flat. The wind, as always in daylight in the hills, was blowing uphill and the bear had got the scent of flesh and blood, mingled with the scent of tiger. I was a little to the right of the kill, so he had not got my scent. Presently he got to his feet and, with the bent legs and body held close to the ground, started to stalk the tiger.

It was a revelation to me in animal stalking to see that bear coming down the hill. He had

possibly two hundred yards to go and though he was not built for stalking, as tigers and leopards are, he covered the distance as smoothly as a snake and as silently as a shadow. The nearer he got the more cautious he became. I could see the lip of the fifteen-foot drop into the hole, and when the bear got to within a few feet of this spot he drew himself along with belly to ground. Waiting until the tiger was eating with great gusto, the bear very slowly projected his head over the lip of the hole and looked down, and then as slowly drew his head back. Excitement with me had now reached the stage when the whole of my body was trembling, and my mouth and throat were dry.

On two occasions I have seen Himalayan bears walk off with tigers' kills. On both occasions the tigers were not present. And on two occasions I have seen bears walk up to feeding leopards and, after shooing them off, carry the kills away. But on this occasion the tiger—and a big male at that—was present at his kill and, further, he was not an animal to be shooed away like a leopard. At the back of my mind was the thought that surely this bear would not be so foolish as to try to dispossess the king of the jungle of his kill. But that was just what the bear appeared to intend doing, and his opportunity came when the tiger was cracking a bone. Whether the bear had been waiting for this moment I do not know; anyway, while the tiger was crunching the bone, the bear drew himself to the edge and, gathering his feet under him, launched himself into the hole with a mighty scream. The object of the scream I imagine was to intimidate the tiger, but so far from having this effect it appeared to infuriate him, for the bear's mighty scream was answered by an even mightier roar from the tiger.

Fights in the wild are very rare and this is only the second case I know of different species of animals fighting for the sake of fighting and not for the purpose of one using the other as food. I did not see the fight, for the reasons I have given, but I heard every detail of it. Waged in a hollow of restricted area the sound was terrifying and I was thankful that the fight was a straight one between two contestants who were capable of defending themselves, and not a three-cornered one in which I was involved. Time stands still when every drop of blood racing through a rapidly beating heart is tingling with excitement. The fight may have lasted three minutes, or it may have lasted longer. Anyway, when the tiger considered he had administered sufficient chastisement he broke off the engagement and came along the open ground in front of me at a fast gallop, closely followed by the still screaming bear. Just as I was aligning the sights of my rifle on the tiger's left shoulder he turned sharp to the left and leaping the twenty-foot-wide ravine, landed at my feet. While he was still in the air I depressed the muzzle of the rifle and fired, as I thought, straight into his back. My shot was greeted with an angry grunt as the tiger crashed into the *ringals* behind me. For a few yards he carried on and then there was silence; shot through the heart and died in his tracks, I thought.

A .500 modified cordite rifle fired anywhere makes a considerable noise, but here, in the ravine, it sounded like a cannon. The detonation, however, had not the least effect on the maddened bear. Following close on the heels of the tiger he did not attempt to leap the ravine, as the tiger had done. Storming down one bank he came up the other straight towards me. I had no wish to shoot an animal that had the courage to drive a tiger off his kill, but to have let that screaming fury come any nearer would have been madness, so, when he was a few feet from me, I put the bullet of the left barrel into his broad forehead. Slowly he slid down the bank on his stomach, until his haunches met the opposite bank.

Where a moment earlier the jungle had resounded with angry strife and the detonations of a heavy rifle, there was now silence,

and when my heart had resumed its normal beat, my thoughts turned to a soothing smoke. Laying the rifle across my knees I put both hands into my pockets to feel for cigarette case and matches. At that moment I caught sight of a movement on my right and, turning my head, saw the tiger unhurriedly cantering along on the open ground over which he had galloped a minute or two earlier and looking not at me, but at his dead enemy.

I know that in relating these events as they occurred, sportsmen will accuse me of rank bad shooting and gross carelessness. I have no defence to make against the accusation of bad shooting, but I do not plead guilty to carelessness. When I fired, as I thought, into the tiger's back, I was convinced I was delivering a fatal wound, and the angry response followed by the mad rush and sudden cessation of sound were ample justification for thinking the tiger had died in his tracks. My second shot had killed the bear outright so there was no necessity—while I was still on the tree—to reload the rifle before laying it across my knees.

Surprise at seeing the tiger alive and unhurt lost me a second or two, and thereafter I acted quickly. The rifle was of the under-lever model; the lever being held in position by two lugs on the trigger guard. This made the rapid loading of the rifle difficult, and, further, the spare cartridges were in my trousers pocket; easy to get at when standing up, but not so easy when sitting on a thin branch. Whether the tiger knew the bear was dead, or whether he was just keeping an eye on it to avoid a flank attack, I do not know. Anyway, he carried on across the face of the steep hill at a slow canter and had reached a spot forty yards away—which I can best describe as eleven o'clock— and was passing a great slab of rock when, with only one barrel loaded, I put up the rifle and fired. At my shot he reared up, fell over sideways, made a bad landing, scrambled to his feet, and cantered on round the shoulder of the hill with his tail in the air. The nickel-cased soft-nosed bullet with steel base had struck the rock a few inches from the tiger's face and the blow-back had thrown him off his balance but had done him no harm.

After a quiet smoke I stepped down from the holly tree and went to have a look at the bear, who, I found, was even bigger than I had at first thought. His self-sought fight with the tiger had been a very real one, for blood from a number of deep cuts was seeping through the thick fur on his neck and in several places his scalp was torn right down to the bone. These wounds in themselves would have mattered little to a tough animal like a bear, but what did matter and what had annoyed him was the injury to his nose. All males resent being struck on the nose, and not only had the bear been struck on that tender spot but insult had been added to injury by his nose being torn in half. Reason enough for him to have chased the tiger with murder in his eyes, and for him to have ignored the report of my heavy rifle.

There was not sufficient time for me to call up my men to skin the bear, so I set off to collect them at the hut and get back to the Rest House before nightfall, for somewhere in that area there was a man-eater. My men, and the dozen or so villagers who had collected at the hut, were too intent on gazing across the valley to observe my approach, and when I walked in among them, they were dumb with amazement. Bala Singh was the first to recover speech, and when I heard his story I was not surprised that the assembled men had looked at me as one returned from the dead. 'We advised you,' Bala Singh said, 'not to sit so close to the ground, and when we heard your first scream, followed by the tiger's roar, we were convinced that you had been pulled out of the tree and that you were fighting for your life with the tiger. Then, when the tiger stopped roaring and you continued to scream, we thought the tiger was carrying you away. Later we heard two reports from your rifle, followed by a third, and we were greatly mystified, for we could not understand how a man who was being carried away by a tiger could fire his rifle. And while we were consulting with these men what we should do, you suddenly appeared and we became speechless.' To men keyed-up and listening for sounds from where a tiger was being sat up for, the scream of a bear could easily be mistaken for the scream of a human being, for the two are very similar and at a distance would not be distinguishable from one another.

Bala Singh got a cup of tea ready for me while I told the men about the fight they had heard and about the bear I had shot. Bear's fat is greatly valued as a cure for rheumatism, and the men were delighted when I told them I did not want the fat and that they could share it with their friends. Next morning I set out to skin the bear, accompanied by a crowd of men who were anxious not only to get a share of the fat but also to see the animal that had fought a tiger. I have never measured or weighed a bear but have seen quite a few, and the one I skinned that morning was the biggest and the fattest Himalayan bear I have ever seen. When the fat and the other prized parts of the bear had been divided, a very happy throng of men turned their faces to Dabidhura, and the happiest and the most envied of all was Bala Singh who proudly carried, strapped to his back, the bear's skin I had given him.

The tiger did not return to finish his interrupted meal, and by evening the vultures had picked clean the bones of the cow and the bear.

5

Skinning a bear encased in fat is a very messy job, and as I plodded back to the Rest House for a hot bath and a late breakfast I met a very agitated forest guard, whose headquarters were at Dabidhura. He had been at an outlying beat the previous night and on his return to Dabidhura that morning had heard at the *bania*'s shop about the bear I had shot. Being in urgent need of bear's fat for his father, who was crippled with rheumatism, he was hurrying to try to get a share of the fat when he ran into a herd of stampeding cattle, followed by a boy who informed him that a tiger had killed one of his cows. The forest guard had a rough idea where the cattle had been grazing when attacked by the tiger, so while Bala Singh and the other men carried onto Dabidhura I set off with him to try to find the kill. Uphill and downhill we went for two miles or more until we came to a small valley. It was in this valley that the forest guard thought the cow had been killed.

There had been an auction of condemned stores at the Gurkha

depot at Almora a few days previously, and my companion had
treated himself to a pair of army boots many sizes too big for
his feet. In these he had clumped ahead of me until we came
to the lip of the valley. Here I made him remove his boots and
when I saw the condition of his feet I marvelled that a man who
had gone barefoot all his life had, for the sake of vanity, endured
such torture. 'I bought big boots,' he told me, 'because I thought
they would shrink.'

The boat-shaped valley, some five acres in extent, was like a
beautiful park dotted over with giant oak trees. On the side from
which I approached it the ground sloped gently down and was
free of bushes, but on the far side the hill went up more steeply
with a few scattered bushes on it. I stood on the lip of the
valley for a few minutes scanning every foot of ground in my
field of vision without seeing anything suspicious, and then went
down the grassy slope followed by the forest guard, now walking
silently on bare feet. As I approached the flat ground on the
floor of the valley I saw that the dead leaves and dry twigs over
a considerable area had been scratched together, and piled into
a great heap. Though no part of the cow was visible I knew that
under this pile of dead matter the tiger had hidden his kill, and
very foolishly I did not inform my companion of this fact, for
he told me later that he did not know that tigers were in the
habit of hiding their kills. When a tiger hides his kill it is usually
an indication that he does not intend lying up near it, but it is
not safe to assume this always. So, though I had scanned the
ground before entering the valley, I again stood perfectly still
while I had another look.

A little beyond the piled-up leaves and twigs the hill went up
at an angle of forty-five degrees, and forty yards up the hillside
there was a small clump of bushes. As I was looking at these I
saw the tiger, who was lying on a small bit of flat ground with
his feet towards me, turn over and present his back to me. I
could see part of his head, and a three-inch wide strip of his
body from shoulder to hindquarters. A head shot was out of

the question, and nothing would be gained by inflicting a flesh wound. I had the whole afternoon and evening before me and as the tiger would be bound to stand up sooner or later, I decided to sit down and wait on events. As I came to this decision I caught sight of a movement on my left, and on turning my head saw a bear coming stealthily up the valley towards the kill, followed by two half-grown cubs. The bear had evidently heard the tiger killing the cow and after giving the tiger time to settle down—as I have done on many occasions—she was now coming to investigate, for unless they have a special reason bears do not move about at midday. Had I been standing on the lip of the valley, instead of a few feet from the kill, I believe I should have witnessed a very interesting sight, for on finding the kill, which with their keen scent they would have had no difficulty in doing, the bears would have started to uncover it. This would have awakened the tiger and I cannot imagine that he would have relinquished his kill without a fight, and the fight would have been worth seeing.

The forest guard, who all this time had been standing quietly behind me seeing nothing but the ground at his feet, now caught sight of the bears and exclaimed in a loud voice, '*Dekho Sahib*, *bhalu*, *bhalu*'. The tiger was up and away in a flash, but he had some twenty yards of open ground to cover, and as I aligned my sights on him and pressed the trigger the forest guard, under the impression that I was facing in the wrong direction, grabbed my arm and gave it a jerk with the result that my bullet struck a tree a few yards from where I was standing. Losing one's temper anywhere does no good, least of all in a jungle. The forest guard, who did not know what the piled-up leaves implied and who had not seen the tiger, was under the impression that he had saved my life by drawing my attention to the dreaded bears, so there was nothing to be said. Alarmed by my shot the bears lumbered away while my companion urged me with a catch in his throat, '*Maro, maro!*' ('Shoot, shoot!').

A very dejected forest guard walked back with me to Dabidhura, and to cheer him up I asked him if he knew of any place where I could shoot a *ghooral*, for my men were still without meat. Not only did the game little man know of such a place but he also volunteered, blisters and all, to take me to it. So after a cup of tea we set off accompanied by two of my men who, the forest guard said, would be needed to carry back the bag.

From the veranda of the Rest House the hill falls steeply away. Down this hill the forest guard led me for a few hundred yards until we came to a foot-wide *ghooral* track running across the face of the hill. I now took the lead and had proceeded for about half a mile to the right when, on coming to a rocky ridge, I looked across a deep ravine and saw a *ghooral* on the far side standing on a projecting rock and looking into space, as all goats including *thar*, ibex, and *markor* have a habit of doing. It was a male *ghooral*, as I could see from the white disk on its throat, and the distance between us was a shade over two hundred yards. Here now was an opportunity not only of procuring meat for my men but also of testing the accuracy of my new rifle. So, lying down, I put up the two hundred-yard leaf sight and, taking very careful aim, fired. At my shot the *ghooral* sank down on the rock on which he had been standing, which was very fortunate, for below him was a sheer drop of many hundred feet. A second *ghooral*, which I had not seen, now ran up the far side of the ravine followed by a small kid, and after standing still and looking back at us several times, carried on round the shoulder of the hill.

While the forest guard and I had a smoke, my two men set off to retrieve the bag. Deprived of his share of the bear's fat the forest guard was made happy by being promised a bit of the *ghooral* and its skin, which he said he would make into a seat for his father who, owing to age and rheumatism, spent all his days basking in the sun.

6

A visit to the valley early next morning confirmed my suspicion that the tiger would not return to his kill, and that the bears would. Little but the bones were left when the three bears had finished with the kill, and that little was being industriously sought by a solitary king vulture when I arrived on the scene.

The morning was still young so, climbing the hill in the direction in which the tiger had gone the previous day, I went over the ridge and down the far side to the Loharghat road to look for tracks of the man-eating leopard. On my return to the Rest House at midday I was informed of yet another tiger kill. My informant was an intelligent young man who was on his way to Almora to attend a court case and, being unable to spare the time to show me where he had seen the tiger killing a cow, drew a sketch for me on the floor of the veranda with a piece of charcoal. After a combined breakfast and lunch I set out to try to find the kill which—if the young man's sketch was correct—had taken place five miles from where I had fired at the tiger the previous day. The tiger, I found, had come on a small herd of cattle grazing on the banks of the stream flowing down the main valley and, judging from the condition of the soft ground, had experienced some difficulty in pulling down the victim he had selected. Killing a big and vigorous animal weighing six or seven hundred pounds is a strenuous job and a tiger after accomplishing this feat usually takes a breather. On this occasion, however, the tiger had picked up the cow as soon as he had killed it—as the absence of blood indicated—and crossing the stream entered the dense jungle at the foot of the hill.

Yesterday the tiger had covered up his kill at the spot where he had done his killing, but today it appeared to be his intention to remove his kill to as distant a place as possible from the scene of killing. For two miles or more I followed the drag up the steep face of the densely wooded hill to where the tiger, when he had conveyed his heavy burden to within a few hundred yards of the crest, had got one of the cow's hind legs fixed between two oak saplings. With a mighty jerk *uphill*, the tiger tore the leg off a little below the hock, and leaving that fixed between the saplings went on with his kill. The crest of the hill at the point where the tiger arrived with his kill was flat and overgrown with oak saplings a foot or two feet in girth. Under these trees, where there were no bushes or cover of any kind, the tiger left his kill without making any attempt to cover it up.

I had followed the drag slowly, carrying only my rifle and a few cartridges; even so, when I arrived at the crest my shirt was wet and my throat dry. I could imagine, therefore, the thirst that the tiger must have acquired and his desire to quench it. Being in need of a drink myself I set out to find the nearest water, where there was also a possibility of finding the tiger. The ravine in which I had shot the bear was half a mile to the right and had water in it, but there was another ravine closer to the left and I decided to try that first.

I had gone down this ravine for the best part of a mile and had come to a place where it narrowed with steep shaly banks on either side when, on going round a big rock, I saw the tiger lying in front of me at a range of twenty yards. There was a small pool of water at this spot, and lying on a narrow strip of sand between the pool and the right-hand bank was the tiger. Here the ravine took a sharp turn to the right, and part of the tiger was on my side of the turn and part round the bend. He was lying on his left side with his back to the pool and I could see his tail and part of his hind legs. Between me and the sleeping animal was a great mass of dry branches that had been lopped from overhanging trees some time previously to feed buffaloes. It was not possible to negotiate this obstacle without making a noise, nor was it possible to go along either of the steep banks without causing small landslides of shale. So the only thing to do was to sit down and wait for the tiger to give me a shot.

After his great exertion and a good drink, the tiger was sleeping soundly and for half an hour he made no movement. Then he turned on to his right side and a little more of his legs came into view. In this position he lay for a few minutes and then stood up, and withdrew round the bend. With finger on trigger I waited for him to reappear, for his kill was up the hill behind me. Minutes passed and then a *kakar* a hundred yards away went dashing down the hill barking hysterically, and a little later a *sambhar* belled. The tiger had gone; why, I did not know, for he had already taken as much exercise as any tiger needed to take, and it was not a case of his having scented me, for tigers have no sense of smell. It did not matter, however, for presently he would return to the kill he had been at such pains to take to the top of the hill, and I would be there to receive him. The water in the pool where the tiger had drunk was ice-cold, and having slaked my thirst I was able to enjoy a long-deferred smoke.

The sun was near setting when I made myself comfortable on an oak tree ten yards to the east and a little to the right of the kill. The tiger would come up the hill from the west and it was not advisable to have the kill directly between us, for tigers have very good eyesight. From my seat on the tree I had a clear view of the valley and of the hills beyond; and when the setting sun, showing as a great ball of fire, was resting on the rim of the earth bathing the world in red, a *sambhar* belled in the valley below me. The tiger was on the move and there was plenty of time for him to arrive at his kill while there was still sufficient daylight for accurate shooting.

The ball of fire dipped below the horizon; the red glow died of the earth; twilight gave place to darkness; and all was silent in the jungle. The moon was in its third quarter, but the stars—nowhere more brilliant than in the Himalayas—were giving enough light for me to see the kill, which was white. The head of the kill was towards me and if the tiger came now and started to eat at the hindquarters I would not be able to see him, but by aligning my sights on the white kill and then raising the rifle and pressing the trigger, as the kill disappeared from view, there was a fifty-fifty chance of hitting the tiger. But here was no man-eater to be fired at under any conditions. Here was a 'temple' tiger who had never molested human beings and who, though he had killed four head of cattle in four consecutive days, had committed no crime against the jungle code. To kill him outright would benefit those who were suffering from his depredations, but to take an uncertain shot at night with the possibility of only wounding him and leaving him to suffer for hours, or if unrecovered to become a man-eater, was not justifiable in any circumstances.

Light was coming in the east, for the boles of the trees were beginning to cast vague shadows, and then the moon rose, flooding the open patches of the jungle with light. It was then that the tiger came. I could not see him but I knew he had come for I could feel and sense his presence. Was he crouching on the far side of the kill with just his eyes and the top of his head raised over the brow of the hill watching me? No, that was not possible, for from the time I had made myself comfortable on my seat I had become part of the tree and tigers do not go through a jungle scanning, without a reason, every tree they approach. And yet, the tiger was here, and he was looking at me.

There was sufficient light now for me to see clearly, and very carefully I scanned the ground in front of me. Then as I turned my head to the right, to look behind, I saw the tiger. He was sitting on his hunkers in a patch of moonlight, facing the kill, with his head turned looking up at me. When he saw me looking down on him he flattened his ears, and as I made no further movement, his ears regained their upright position. I could imagine him saying to himself, 'Well, you have now seen me, and what are you going to do about it?' There was little I could do about it, for in order to get a shot I would have to turn a half-circle and it would not be possible to do this without alarming the tiger, who was looking at me from a range of fifteen feet. There was, however, just a possibility of my getting a shot from my left shoulder, and this I decided to try to do. The rifle was resting on my knees with the muzzle pointing to the left, and as I lifted it and started turning it to the right the tiger lowered his head and again flattened his ears. In this position he remained as long as I was motionless, but the moment I started to move the rifle again, he was up and away into the shadows behind.

Well, that was that, and the tiger had very definitely won another round. As long as I sat on the tree he would not return, but if I went away he *might* come back and remove the kill; and as he could not eat a whole cow in a night I would have another chance next day.

The question that now faced me was where to spend the night. I had already walked some twenty miles that day and the prospect of doing another eight miles to the Rest House— through forest all the way—did not appeal to me. In any other locality I would have moved away from the kill for two or three hundred yards and slept peacefully on the ground, but in this locality there was a man-eating leopard, and man-eating leopards hunt at night. While sitting on the tree earlier in the evening, I had heard the distant pealing of cattle-bells, coming either from a village or from a cattle-station. I had pin-pointed the sound and I now set out to find where it had come from. Cattle-lifting is unknown in the Himalayas, and throughout Kumaon there are communal cattle-stations situated in the jungles close to the grazing grounds. I traced the bells I had heard to one of these stations, in which there were about a hundred head of cattle in a large open shed surrounded by a strong stockade. The fact that the station was in the depth of the jungle, and unguarded, was proof of the honesty of the hillfolk, and it was also proof that until my arrival cattle in the Dabidhura area had not been molested by tigers.

At night all animals in the jungle are suspicious, and if I was to spend the night under the protection of the inmates of the shed I would have to disarm their very natural suspicion. The tenants of our village at Kaladhungi keep about nine hundred head of cows and buffaloes, and having been associated with cattle from my earliest childhood I know the language they understand. Moving very slowly and speaking to the cattle I approached the shed, and on reaching the stockade sat down with my back to it to have a smoke. Several cows were standing near the spot where I sat and one of them now advanced and, putting its head through the bars of the stockade, started to lick the back of my head; a friendly gesture, but a wetting one, and here at an altitude of eight thousand feet the nights were cold. Having finished my cigarette, I unloaded my rifle and, covering it with straw, climbed the stockade.

Care was needed in selecting a place on which to sleep, for if there was an alarm during the night and the cattle started milling round it would be unsafe to be caught on the ground. Near the centre of the shed, and close to one of the roof-supports up which I could go if the need arose, there was an open space between two sleeping cows. Stepping over recumbent animals and moving the heads of standing ones to get past them, I lay down between the two that were lying back to back. There was no alarm during the night, so the necessity for me to shin up the roof-support did not arise, and with the warm bodies of the cows to keep off the night chills and with the honey-sweet smell of healthy cattle in my nostrils I slept as one at peace with all the world, tigers and man-eating leopards included.

The sun was just rising next morning when, on hearing voices,

I opened my eyes and saw three men, armed with milking pails, staring at me through the bars of the stockade. The water I had drunk at the tiger's pool was all that had passed my lips since breakfast the previous day, and the warm drink of milk the men gave me—after they had recovered from their amazement at finding me asleep with their cattle—was very welcome. Declining the men's invitation to accompany them back to their village for a meal, I thanked them for their board and lodging and, before returning to the Rest House for a bath and a square meal, set off to see where the tiger had taken his kill. To my surprise I found the kill lying just as I had left it, and after covering it over with branches to protect it from vultures and golden-headed eagles I went on to the Rest House.

In no other part of the world, I imagine, are servants as tolerant of the vagaries of their masters as in India. When I returned to the Rest House after an absence of twenty-four hours, no surprise was expressed, and no questions asked. A hot bath was ready, clean clothes laid out, and within a very short time I was sitting down to a breakfast of porridge, scrambled eggs, hot *chapatis* and honey—the last a present from the old priest—and a dish of tea. Breakfast over, I sat on the grass in front of the Rest House admiring the gorgeous view and making plans. I had set out from my home in Naini Tal with one object, and one object only, to try to shoot the Panar man-eating leopard; and from the night it had tried to drag the herdsman off the temple platform nothing had been heard of it. The priest, the *bania*, and all the people in near and distant villages that I questioned informed me that there were occasions when for long periods the man-eater seemed to disappear off the face of the earth and they were of the opinion that one of these periods had now started, but no one could say how long it would last. The area over which the man-eater was operating was vast, and in it there were possibly ten to twenty leopards. To find and shoot in that area one particular leopard—that had stopped killing human beings—without knowing where to look for it, was a hopeless job.

My mission as far as the man-eater was concerned had failed, and no useful purpose would be served by my prolonging my stay at Dabidhura. The question of the temple tiger remained. I did not feel that the killing of this tiger was any responsibility of mine; but I did feel, and felt very strongly, that my pursuit of him was inducing him to kill more cattle than he would otherwise have done. Why a male tiger started killing cattle on the day of my arrival at Dabidhura it was not possible to say, and whether he would stop when I went away remained to be seen. Anyway, I had tried my best to shoot him; had paid compensation for the damage he had done to the full extent of my purse; and he had provided me with one of the most interesting jungle experiences I had ever had. So I harboured no resentment against him for having beaten me at every point in the exciting game we had played during the past four days. These four days had been very strenuous for me, so I would rest today and make an early start next morning on the first stage of my journey back to Naini Tal. I had just come to this decision when a voice from behind me said, 'Salaam, Sahib. I have come to tell you that the tiger has killed one of my cows.' One more chance of shooting the tiger, and whether I succeeded or not I would stick to my plan of leaving next morning.

7

Annoyed at the interference of human beings and bears, the tiger had shifted his ground, and this last kill had taken place on the eastern face of the Dabidhura mountain several miles from where I had sat up for him the previous evening. The ground here was undulating, with patches of scrub and a few odd trees dotted here and there; ideal ground for *chukor* (hill partridge), but the last place in which I would have expected to find a tiger.

Running diagonally across the face of the mountain was a shallow depression. In this depression were patches of dense scrub, interspersed with open glades of short grass. At the edge of one of these glades the cow had been killed, dragged a few yards towards some bushes, and left in the open. On the opposite or downhill side of the glade to the kill, there was a big oak tree. On this tree, the only one for hundreds of yards around, I decided to sit.

While my men warmed a kettle of water for tea I scouted round to see if I could get a shot at the tiger on foot. The tiger I felt sure was lying up somewhere in the depression, but though I searched every foot of it for an hour I saw no sign of him.

The tree that was to provide me with a seat was leaning out towards the glade. Excessive lopping had induced a crop of small branches all along the trunk, which made the tree easy to climb but obscured a view of the trunk from above. Twenty feet up, a single big branch jutted out over the glade, offering the only seat on the tree but not a comfortable one or one easy to reach. At 4 p.m. I sent my men away, instructing them to go to a village farther up the hill and wait for me, for I had no intention of sitting up after sun-down.

The kill, as I have said, was lying in the open, ten yards from me and with its hindquarters a yard or so from a dense clump of bushes. I had been in position for an hour and was watching a number of red-whiskered bulbuls feeding on a raspberry bush to my right front, when on turning my eyes to look at the kill I saw the tiger's head projecting beyond the clump of bushes. He was evidently lying down, for his head was close to the ground, and his eyes were fixed on me. Presently a paw was advanced, then another, and then very slowly and with belly to ground the tiger drew himself up to his kill. Here he lay for several minutes without movement. Then, feeling with his mouth, and with his eyes still fixed on me, he bit off the cow's tail, laid it on one side and started to eat. Having eaten nothing since his fight with the bear three days before, he was hungry, and he ate just as a man would eat an apple, ignoring the skin and taking great bites of flesh from the hindquarters.

The rifle was across my knees pointing in the direction of the tiger, and all I had to do was to raise it to my shoulder. I would get an opportunity of doing this when he turned his eyes

away from me for a brief moment. But the tiger appeared to know his danger, for without taking his eyes off me he ate on steadily and unhurriedly. When he had consumed about fifteen or twenty pounds of flesh, and when the *bulbuls* had left the raspberry bush and, joined by two black-throated jays, were making a great chattering on the bushes behind him, I thought it was time for me to act. If I raised the rifle very slowly he would probably not notice the movement so, when the birds were chattering their loudest, I started to do this. I had raised the muzzle possibly six inches, when the tiger slid backwards as if drawn back by a powerful spring. With rifle to shoulder and elbows on knees I now waited for the tiger to project his head a second time, and this I felt sure he would presently do. Minutes passed, and then I heard the tiger. He had skirted round the bushes and, approaching from behind, started to claw my tree where the thick growth of small branches on the trunk made it impossible for me to see him. Purring with pleasure the tiger once and again clawed the tree with vigour, while I sat on my branch and rocked with silent laughter.

I know that crows and monkeys have a sense of humour, but until that day I did not know that tigers also possessed this sense. Nor did I know that an animal could have the luck, and the impudence, that particular tiger had. In five days he had killed five cows, four of them in broad daylight. In those five days I had seen him eight times and on four occasions I had pressed a trigger on him. And now, after staring at me for half an hour and eating while doing so, he was clawing the tree on which I was sitting and purring to show his contempt of me.

When telling me of the tiger the old priest said, 'I have one objection, Sahib, to your *trying* to shoot this tiger but neither you nor anyone else will ever succeed in *killing* it.' The tiger was now, in his own way, confirming what the priest had said. Well, the tiger had made the last move in the exciting game we had played without injury to either of us, but I was not going to give him the satisfaction of having the last laugh. Laying down the rifle and cupping my hands I waited until he stopped clawing, and then sent a full-throated shout echoing over the hills which sent him careering down the hill at full speed and brought my men down from the village at a run. 'We saw the tiger running away with his tail in the air,' the men said when they arrived, 'and just see what he has done to the tree.'

Next morning I bade farewell to all my friends at Dabidhura, and assured them I would return when the man-eater got active again.

I visited Dabidhura several times in subsequent years while hunting man-eaters, and I never heard of anyone having killed the temple tiger. So I hope that in the fullness of time this old warrior, like an old soldier, just faded away.

# THE MUKTESAR MAN-EATER

**EIGHTEEN MILES TO THE NORTH**—north-east of Naini Tal is a hill eight thousand feet high and twelve to fifteen miles long, running east and west. The western end of the hill rises steeply and near this end is the Muktesar Veterinary Research Institute, where lymph and vaccines are produced to fight India's cattle diseases. The laboratory and staff quarters are situated on the northern face of the hill and command one of the best views to be had anywhere of the Himalayan snowy range. This range, and all the hills that lie between it and the plains of India, run east and west, and from a commanding point on any of the hills an uninterrupted view can be obtained not only of the snows to the north but also of the hills and valleys to the east and to the west as far as the eye can see. People who have lived at Muktesar claim that it is the most beautiful spot in Kumaon, and that its climate has no equal.

A tiger that thought as highly of the amenities of Muktesar as human beings did, took up her residence in the extensive forests adjoining the small settlement. Here she lived very happily on *sambhar*, *kakar*, and wild pig, until she had the misfortune to have an encounter with a porcupine. In this encounter she lost an eye and got some fifty quills, varying in length from one to nine inches, embedded in the arm and under the pad of her right foreleg. Several of these quills after striking a bone had doubled back in the form of a U, the point and the broken-off end being close together. Suppurating sores formed where she endeavoured to extract the quills with her teeth, and while she was lying up in a thick patch of grass, starving and licking her wounds, a woman selected this particular patch of grass to cut as fodder for her cattle. At first the tigress took no notice, but when the woman had cut the grass right up to where she was lying, the tigress struck once, the blow crushing the woman's skull. Death was instantaneous, for, when found the following day, she was grasping her sickle with one hand and holding a tuft of grass, which she was about to cut when struck, with the other. Leaving the woman lying where she had fallen, the tigress limped off for a distance of over a mile and took refuge in a little hollow under a fallen tree. Two days later a man came to chip firewood off this fallen tree, and the tigress who was lying on the far side killed him also. The man fell across the tree, and as he had removed his coat and shirt and the tigress had clawed his back while killing him, it is possible that the sight of blood trickling down his body as he hung across the bole of the tree first gave her the idea that he was something that she could satisfy her hunger with. However that may be, before leaving him she ate a small portion from his back. A day later she killed her third victim deliberately, and without having received any provocation. Thereafter she became an established man-eater.

I heard of the tigress shortly after she started killing human beings, and as there were a number of sportsmen at Muktesar, all of whom were keen on bagging the tigress—who was operating right on their doorsteps—I did not consider it would be sporting of an outsider to meddle in the matter. When the toll of human beings killed by the tigress had risen to twenty-four, however, and the lives of all the people living in the settlement and neighbouring villages were endangered and work at the Institute slowed down, the veterinary officer in charge of the Institute requested the Government to solicit my help.

My task, as I saw it, was not going to be an easy one, for, apart from the fact that my experience of man-eaters was very limited, the extensive ground over which the tigress was operating was not known to me and I therefore had no idea where to look for her.

Accompanied by a servant and two men carrying a roll of bedding and a suitcase, I left Naini Tal at midday and walked ten miles to the Ramgarh Dak Bungalow, where I spent the night. The Dak Bungalow *khansama* (cook, bottle-washer, and general factotum) was a friend of mine, and when he learnt that I was on my way to Muktesar to try to shoot the man-eater, he warned me to be very careful while negotiating the last two miles into Muktesar for, he said, several people had recently been killed on that stretch of road.

Leaving my men to pack up and follow me I armed myself with a double-barrelled .500 express rifle using modified cordite, and making a very early start next morning arrived at the junction of the Naini Tal / Almora road with the Muktesar road just as it was getting light. From this point it was necessary to walk warily for I was now in the man-eater's country. Before zigzagging up the face of a very steep hill the road runs for some distance over flat ground on which grows the orange-coloured lily, the round hard seeds of which can be used as shot in a muzzle-loading gun. This was the first time I had ever climbed that hill and I was very interested to see the caves, hollowed out by wind, in the sandstone cliffs overhanging the road. In a gale I imagine these caves must produce some very weird sounds, for they are of different sizes and, while some are shallow, others appear to penetrate deep into the sandstone.

Where the road comes out on a saddle of the hill there is a small area of flat ground flanked on the far side by the Muktesar Post Office, and a small bazaar. The post office was not open at that early hour, but one of the shops was and the shopkeeper very kindly gave me directions to the Dak Bungalow which, he said, was half a mile away on the northern face of the hill. There are two Dak Bungalows at Muktesar, one reserved for government officials and the other for the general public. I did not know this and my shopkeeper friend, mistaking me for a government official, possibly because of the size of my hat, directed me to the wrong one and the *khansama* in charge of the bungalow, and I, incurred the displeasure of the red tape brigade, the *khansama* by providing me with breakfast, and I by partaking of it. However, of this I was at the time happily ignorant, and later I made it my business to see that the *khansama* did not suffer in any way for my mistake.

While I was admiring the superb view of the snowy range, and waiting for breakfast, a party of twelve Europeans passed me carrying service rifles, followed a few minutes later by a sergeant and two men carrying targets and flags. The sergeant, a friendly soul, informed me that the party that had just passed was on its way to the rifle range, and that it was keeping together because of the man-eater. I learnt from the sergeant that the officer in charge of the Institute had received a telegram from the Government the previous day informing him that I was on my way to Muktesar. The sergeant expressed the hope that I would succeed in shooting the man-eater for, he said, conditions in the settlement had become very difficult. No one even in daylight, dared to move about alone, and after dusk everyone had to remain behind locked doors. Many attempts had been made to shoot the man-eater but it had never returned to any of the kills that had been sat over.

After a very good breakfast I instructed the *khansama* to tell my men when they arrived that I had gone out to try get news of the man-eater, and that I did not know when I would return. Then, picking up my rifle, I went up to the post office to send a telegram to my mother to let her know I had arrived safely.

From the flat ground in front of the post office and the bazaar the southern face of the Muktesar hill falls steeply away, and is cut up by ridges and ravines overgrown with dense brushwood, with a few trees scattered here and there. I was standing on the edge of the hill, looking down into the valley and the well-wooded Ramgarh hills beyond, when I was joined by the Postmaster and several shopkeepers. The Postmaster had dealt with the Government telegram of the previous day, and on seeing my signature on the form I had just handed in, he concluded I was the person referred to in the telegram and his friends and he had now come to offer me their help. I was very glad of the offer for they were in the best position to see and converse with everyone coming to Muktesar, and as the man-eater was sure to be the main topic of conversation where two or more were gathered together, they would be able to collect information that would be of great value to me. In rural India, the post office and the *bania*'s shop are to village folk what taverns and clubs are to people of other lands, and if information on any particular subject is sought, the post office and the *bania*'s shop are the best places to seek it.

In a fold of the hill to our left front, and about two miles away and a thousand feet below us, was a patch of cultivation. This I was informed was Badri Sah's apple orchard. Badri, son of an old friend of mine, had visited me in Naini Tal some months previously and had offered to put me up in his guest house and to assist me in every way he could to shoot the man-eater.

This offer, for the reason already given, I had not accepted. Now, however, as I had come to Muktesar at the request of the Government I decided I would call on Badri and accept his offer to help me, especially as I had just been informed by my companions that the last human kill had taken place in the valley below his orchard.

Thanking all the men who were standing round me, and telling them I would rely on them for further information, I set off down the Dhari road. The day was still young and before calling on Badri there was time to visit some of the villages farther along the hill to the east. There were no milestones along the road, and after I had covered what I considered was about six miles and visited two villages, I turned back. I had retraced my steps for about three miles when I overtook a small girl having difficulties with a bullock. The girl, who was about eight years old, wanted the bullock to go in the direction of Muktesar, while the bullock wanted to go in the opposite direction, and when I arrived on the scene the stage had been reached when neither would do what the other wanted. The bullock was a quiet old beast, and with the girl walking in front holding the rope that was tied round his neck and I walking behind to keep him on the move he gave no further trouble. After we had proceeded a short distance I said:

'We are not stealing Kalwa, are we?' I heard her addressing the black bullock by that name.

'N—o,' she answered indignantly, turning her big brown eyes full on me.

'To whom does he belong?' I next asked.

'To my father,' she said.

'And where are we taking him?'

'To my uncle.'

'And why does uncle want Kalwa?'

'To plough his field.'

'But Kalwa can't plough uncle's field by himself.'

'Of course not,' she said. I was being stupid, but then you

could not expect a sahib to know anything about bullocks and ploughing.

'Has uncle only got one bullock?' I next asked.

'Yes,' she said; 'he has only got one bullock now, but he did have two.'

'Where is the other one?' I asked, thinking that it had probably been sold to satisfy a debt.

'The tiger killed it yesterday,' I was told. Here was news indeed, and while I was digesting it we walked on in silence, the girl every now and then looking back at me until she plucked up courage to ask:

'Have you come to shoot the tiger?'

'Yes,' I said, 'I have come to try to shoot the tiger.'

'Then why are you going away from the kill?'

'Because we are taking Kalwa to uncle.' My answer appeared to satisfy the girl, and we plodded on. I had got some very useful information, but I wanted more and presently I said:

'Don't you know that the tiger is a man-eater?'

'Oh, yes,' she said, 'it ate Kunthi's father and Bonshi Singh's mother, and lots of other people.'

'Then why did your father send you with Kalwa? Why did he not come himself?'

'Because he has *bhabari bokhar* (malaria).'

'Have you no brothers?'

'No. I had a brother but he died long ago.'

'A mother?'

'Yes, I have a mother; she is cooking the food.'

'A sister?'

'No, I have no sister.' So on this small girl had devolved the dangerous task of taking her father's bullock to her uncle, along a road on which men were afraid to walk except when in large parties, and on which in four hours I had not seen another human being.

We had now come to a path up which the girl went, the bullock following, and I bringing up the rear. Presently we came to a field on the far side of which was a small house. As we approached the house the girl called out and told her uncle that she had brought Kalwa.

'All right,' a man's voice answered from the house, 'tie him to the post, Putli, and go home. I am having my food.' So we tied Kalwa to the post and went back to the road. Without the connecting link of Kalwa between us, Putli (dolly) was now shy, and as she would not walk by my side I walked ahead, suiting my pace to hers. We walked in silence for some time and then I said:

'I want to shoot the tiger that killed uncle's bullock but I don't know where the kill is. Will you show me?'

'Oh, yes,' she said eagerly, 'I will show you.'

'Have you seen the kill?' I asked.

'No,' she said, 'I have not seen it, but I heard uncle telling my father where it was.'

'Is it close to the road?'

'I don't know.'

'Was the bullock alone when it was killed?'

'No, it was with the village cattle.'

'Was it killed in the morning or the evening?'

'It was killed in the morning when it was going out to graze with the cows.'

While talking to the girl I was keeping a sharp look-out all round, for the road and bordered on the left by heavy tree jungle, and on the right by dense scrub. We had proceeded for about a mile when we came to a well-used cattle track leading off into the jungle on the left. Here the girl stopped and said it was on this track that her uncle had told her father the bullock had been killed. I had now got all the particulars I needed to enable me to find the kill, and after seeing the girl safely to her home I returned to the cattle track. This track ran across a valley and I had gone along it for about a quarter of a mile when I came upon a spot where cattle had stampeded. Leaving the track, I now went through the jungle, parallel to and about fifty yards below the track. I had only gone a short distance when I came on a drag-mark. This drag-mark went straight down into the valley, and after I had followed it for a few hundred yards I found the bullock, from which only a small portion of the hindquarters had been eaten. It was lying at the foot of a bank about twenty feet high, and some forty feet from the head of a deep ravine. Between the ravine and the kill was a stunted tree, smothered over by a wild rose. This was the only tree within a reasonable distance of the kill on which I could sit with any hope of bagging the tiger, for there was no moon, and if the tiger came after dark—as I felt sure it would—the nearer I was to the kill the better would be my chance of killing the tiger.

It was now 2 p.m. and there was just time for me to call on Badri and ask him for a cup of tea, of which I was in need for I had done a lot of walking since leaving Ramgarh at four o'clock that morning. The road to Badri's orchard takes off close to where the cattle track joins the road, and runs down a steep hill for a mile through dense brushwood. Badri was near his guest house, attending to a damaged apple tree when I arrived, and on hearing the reason for my visit he took me up the guest house which was on a little knoll overlooking the orchard. While we sat on the veranda waiting for the tea and something to eat that Badri had ordered his servant to prepare for me, I told him why I had come to Muktesar, and about the kill the young girl had enabled me to find. When I asked Badri why this kill had

not been reported to the sportsmen at Muktesar, he said that
owing to the repeated failures of the sportsmen to bag the tiger
the village folk had lost confidence in them, and for this reason
kills were no longer being reported to them. Badri attributed
the failures to the elaborate preparations that had been made to
sit over kills. These preparations consisted of clearing the ground
near the kills of all abstractions in the way of bushes and small
trees, the building of big *machans*, and the occupation of the
*machans* by several men. Reasons enough for the reputation the
tiger had earned of never returning to a kill. Badri was convinced
that there was only one tiger in Muktesar district and that it
was slightly lame in its right foreleg, but he did not know
what had caused the lameness, nor did he know whether the
animal was male or female.

Sitting on the veranda with us was a big Airedale terrier.
Presently the dog started growling, and looking in the direction
in which the dog was facing, we saw a big *langur* sitting on the
ground and holding down the branch of an apple tree, and eating
the unripe fruit. Picking up a shotgun that was leaning against
the railing of the veranda, Badri loaded it with No. 4 shot and
fired. The range was too great for the pellets, assuming any hit
it, to do the *langur* any harm, but the shot had the
effect of making it canter up the hill with the dog
in hot pursuit. Frightened that the dog might
come to grief, I asked Badri to call it back,
but he said it would be all right for the dog
was always chasing this particular animal,
which he said had done a lot of
damage to his young trees. The
dog was now gaining on the
*langur*, and when it got
to within a few

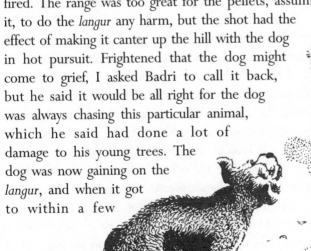

yards the *langur* whipped round, got the dog by the ears, and bit a lump off the side of its head. The wound was a very severe one, and by the time we had finished attending to it my tea and a plate of hot *puris* (unleavened bread fried in butter) was ready for me.

I had told Badri about the tree I intended sitting on, and when I returned to the kill he insisted on going with me accompanied by two men carrying materials for making a small *machan*. Badri and the two men had lived under the shadow of the man-eater for over a year and had no illusions about it, and when they saw that there were no trees near the kill—with the exception of the one I had selected—in which a *machan* could be built, they urged me not to sit up that night, on the assumption that the tiger would remove the kill and provide me with a more suitable place to sit up the following night. This was what I myself would have done if the tiger had not been a man-eater, but as it was I was disinclined to miss a chance which might not recur on the morrow, even if it entailed a little risk. There were bears in this forest and if one of them smelt the kill, any hope I had of getting a shot at the tiger would vanish, for Himalayan bears are no respecters of tigers and do not hesitate to appropriate their kills. Climbing into the tree, smothered as it was by the rose bush, was a difficult feat, and after I had made myself as comfortable as the thorn permitted and my rifle had been handed up to me Badri and his men left, promising to return early next morning.

I was facing the hill, with the ravine behind me. I was in clear view of any animal coming down from above, but if the tiger came from below, as I expected, it would not see me until it got to the kill. The bullock, which was white, was lying on its right side with its legs towards me, and at a distance of about fifteen feet. I had taken my seat at 4 p.m. and an hour later a *kakar* started barking on the side of the ravine two hundred yards below me. The tiger was on the move, and having seen it the *kakar* was standing still and barking. For a long time it barked and then it started to move away, the bark growing fainter and fainter until the sound died away round the shoulder of the hill. This indicated that after coming within sight of the kill, the tiger had lain down. I had expected this to happen after having been 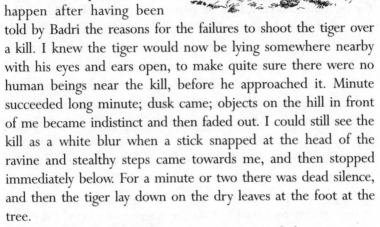 told by Badri the reasons for the failures to shoot the tiger over a kill. I knew the tiger would now be lying somewhere nearby with his eyes and ears open, to make quite sure there were no human beings near the kill, before he approached it. Minute succeeded long minute; dusk came; objects on the hill in front of me became indistinct and then faded out. I could still see the kill as a white blur when a stick snapped at the head of the ravine and stealthy steps came towards me, and then stopped immediately below. For a minute or two there was dead silence, and then the tiger lay down on the dry leaves at the foot at the tree.

Heavy clouds had rolled up near sunset and there was now a black canopy overhead blotting out the stars. When the tiger eventually got up and went to the kill, the night could best be described as pitch black. Strain my eyes as I would, I could see nothing of the white bullock, and still less of the tiger. On reaching the kill the tiger started blowing on it. In the Himalayas, and especially in the summer, kills attract hornets, most of which leave as the light fades but those that are too torpid to fly remain, and a tiger—possibly after bitter experience—blows off the hornets adhering to the exposed portion of the flesh before starting to feed. There was no need for me to hurry over my shot for, close though it was, the tiger would not see me unless I attracted its attention by some movement or sound. I can see reasonably well on a dark night by the light of the stars, but there were no stars visible that night nor was there a flicker of lightning in the heavy clouds.

The tiger had not moved the kill before starting to eat, so I knew he was lying broadside on to me, on the right-hand side of the kill.

Owing to the attempts that had been made to shoot the tiger I had suspicion that it would not come before dark, and it had been my intention to take what aim I could—by the light of the stars—and then move the muzzle of my rifle sufficiently for my bullet to go a foot or two to the right of the kill. But now that the clouds had rendered my eyes useless, I would have to depend on my ears (my hearing at that time was perfect). Raising the rifle and resting my elbows on my knees, I took careful aim at the sound the tiger was making, and while holding the rifle steady, turned my right ear to the sound, and then back again. My aim was a little too high, so, lowering the muzzle a fraction of an inch, I again turned my head and listened. After I had done this a few times and satisfied myself that I was pointing at the sound, I moved the muzzle a little to the right and pressed the trigger. In two bounds the tiger was up the twenty-foot bank. At the top there was a small bit of flat ground, beyond which the hill went up steeply. I heard the tiger on the dry leaves as far as the flat ground, and then there was silence. This silence could be interpreted to mean either that the tiger had died on reaching the flat ground or that it was unwounded. Keeping the rifle to my shoulder I listened intently for three or four minutes, and as there was no further sound I lowered the rifle. This movement was greeted by a deep growl from the top of the bank. So the tiger was unwounded, and had seen me. My seat on the tree had originally been about ten feet up but, as I had nothing solid to sit on, the rose bush had sagged under my weight and I was now possibly no more than eight feet above ground, with my dangling feet considerably lower. And a little above and some twenty feet from me a tiger that I had every reason to believe was a man-eater was growling deep down in his throat.

The near proximity of a tiger in daylight, even when it has

not seen you, causes a disturbance in the blood stream. When the tiger is not an ordinary one, however, but a man-eater and the time is ten o'clock on a dark night, and you know the man-eater is watching you, the disturbance in the blood stream becomes a storm. I maintain that a tiger does not kill beyond its requirements, except under provocation. The tiger that was growling at me already, had a kill that would last it for two or three days, and there was no necessity for it to kill me. Even so, I had an uneasy feeling that on this occasion this particular tiger might prove an exception to the rule. Tigers will at times return to a kill after being fired at, but I knew this one would not do so. I also knew that in spite of my uneasy feeling I was perfectly safe so long as I did not lose my balance—I had nothing to hold on to—or go to sleep and fall off the tree. There was no longer any reason for me to deny myself a smoke, so I took out my cigarette case and as I lit a match I heard the tiger move away from the edge of the bank. Presently it came back and again growled. I had smoked three cigarettes, and the tiger was still with me, when it came on to rain. A few big drops at first and then a heavy downpour. I had put on light clothes when I started from Ramgarh that morning and in a few minutes I was wet to the skin, for there was not a leaf above me to diffuse the raindrops. The tiger, I knew, would have hurried off to shelter under a tree or on the lee of a rock the moment the rain started. The rain came on at 11 p.m.; at 4 a.m. it stopped and the sky cleared. A wind now started to blow, to add to my discomfort, and where I had been cold before I was now frozen. When I get a twinge of rheumatism I remember that night and others like it, and am thankful that it is no more than a twinge.

Badri, good friend that he was, arrived with a man carrying a kettle of hot tea just as the sun was rising. Relieving me of my rifle the two men caught me as I slid off the tree, for my legs were too cramped to function. Then as I lay on the ground and drank the tea they massaged my legs and restored circulation. When I was able to stand, Badri sent his man off to light a fire in the guest house. I had never previously used my ears to direct a bullet and was interested to find that I had missed the tiger's head by only a few inches. The elevation had been all right but I had not moved the muzzle of the rifle far enough to the right, with the result that my bullet had struck the bullock six inches from where the tiger was eating.

The tea and the half-mile walk up to the road took all the creases out of me, and when we started down the mile-long track to Badri's orchard, wet clothes and an empty stomach were my only discomfort. The track ran over red clay which the rain had made very slippery. In this clay were three tracks: Badri's and his man's tracks going up, and the man's tracks going down. For fifty yards there were only these three tracks in the wet clay, and then, where there was a bend in the track, a tigress had jumped down from the bank on the right and gone down the track on the heels of Badri's man. The footprints of the man and the pug-marks of the tigress showed that both had been travelling at a fast pace. There was nothing that Badri and I could do, for the man had a twenty-minute start from us, and if he had not reached the safety of the orchard he would long have been beyond any help we could give him. With uneasy thoughts assailing us, we made what speed we could on the slippery ground and were very relieved to find, on coming to a footpath from where the orchard and a number of men working in it were visible, that the tigress had gone down the path while the man had carried on to the orchard.

Questioned later, the man said he did not know that he had been followed by the tigress.

While drying my clothes in front of a roaring wood-fire in the guest house, I questioned Badri about the jungle into which the tigress had gone. The path which the tigress had taken, Badri told me, ran down into a deep and densely wooded ravine which extended down the face of a very steep hill, for a mile or more, to where it was met by another ravine coming down from the right. At the junction of the two ravines there was a stream and here there was an open patch of ground which, Badri said, commanded the exit of both ravines. Badri was of the opinion that the tigress would lie up for the day in the ravine into which we had every reason to believe she had gone, and as this appeared to be an ideal place for a beat, we decided to try this method of getting a shot at the tigress, provided we could muster sufficient men to carry out the beat. Govind Singh, Badri's head gardener, was summoned and our plan explained to him. Given until midday, Govind Singh said he could muster a gang of thirty men to do the beat, and in addition carry out his master's orders to gather five *maunds* (four hundred and ten pounds) of peas. Badri had an extensive vegetable garden in addition to his apple orchard and the previous evening he had received a telegram informing him that the price of marrowfat peas on the Naini Tal market had jumped to four annas (four pence) a pound. Badri was anxious to take advantage of this good price and his men were gathering the peas to be dispatched by pack pony that night, to arrive in Naini Tal for the early morning market.

After cleaning my rifle and walking round the orchard, I joined Badri at his morning meal—which had been put forward an hour to suit me—and at midday Govind produced his gang of thirty men. It was essential for someone to supervise the pea-pickers, so Badri decided to remain and send Govind to carry out the beat. Govind and the thirty men were local residents and knew the danger to be apprehended from the man-eater. However, after I had told them what I wanted them to do, they expressed their willingness to carry out my instructions. Badri was to give me an hour's start to enable me to search the ravine for the tigress and, if I failed to get a shot, to take up my position on the open ground near the stream. Govind was to divide his men into two parties, take charge of one party himself, and put a reliable man in charge of the other. At the end of the hour Badri was to fire a shot and the two parties were to set off, one on either side of the ravine, rolling rocks down, and shouting and clapping their hands. It all sounded as simple as that, but I had my doubts, for I have seen many beats go wrong.

Going up the track down which I had come that morning, I followed the path that the tigress had taken, only to find after I had gone a short distance that it petered out in a vast expanse of dense brushwood. Forcing my way through for several hundred yards I found that the hillside was cut up by a series of deep ravines and ridges. Going down a ridge which I thought was the right-hand boundary of the ravine to be beaten, I came to a big drop at the bottom of which the ravine on my left met a ravine coming down from the right, and at the junction of the two ravines there was stream. While I was looking down and wondering where the open ground was on which I was to take my stand, I heard flies buzzing near me and on following the sound found the remains of a cow that had been killed about a week before. The marks on the animal's throat showed that it had been killed by a tiger. The tiger had eaten all of the cow, except a portion of the shoulders, and the neck and head. Without having any particular reason for doing so, I dragged the carcass to the edge and sent it crashing down the steep hill. After rolling for about a hundred yards the carcass fetched up in a little hollow a short distance from the stream. Working round to the left I found an open patch of ground on a ridge about three hundred yards from the hollow into which I had rolled the remains of the cow. The ground down here was very different from what I had pictured it to be. There was no place where I could stand to overlook the hillside that was to be beaten, and the tigress might break out anywhere without my seeing her. However, it was then too late to do anything, for Badri had fired the shot that was to let me know the beat had started. Presently, away in the distance, I heard men shouting. For a time I thought the beat was coming my way and then the sounds grew fainter and fainter until they eventually died away. An hour later I again heard the beaters. They were coming down the hill to my right, and when they were on a level with me I shouted to them to stop the beat and join me on the ridge. It was no one's fault that the beat had miscarried, for without knowing the ground and without previous preparation we had tried to beat with a handful of untrained men a vast area of dense brushwood that hundreds of trained men would have found difficult to cope with.

The beaters had had a very strenuous time forcing their way through the brushwood, and while they sat in a bunch removing thorns from their hands and feet and smoking my cigarettes, Govind and I stood facing each other, discussing his suggestion of carrying out a beat on the morrow in which every available man in Muktesar and the surrounding villages would take part. Suddenly, in the middle of a sentence, Govind stopped talking. I could see that something unusual had attracted his attention behind me, for his eyes narrowed and a look of incredulity came over his face. Swinging round I looked in the direction in which he was facing, and there, quietly walking along a field that had gone out of cultivation, was the tigress. She was about four hundred yards away on the hill on the far side of the stream, and was coming towards us.

When a tiger is approaching you in the forest—even when you are far from human habitations—thoughts course through your mind of the many things that can go wrong to spoil your chance of getting the shot, or the photograph, you are hoping for. On one occasion I was sitting on a hillside overlooking a

game track, waiting for a tiger. The track led to a very sacred jungle shrine known as *Baram ka Than*, Baram is a jungle God who protects human beings and does not permit the shooting of animals in the area he watches over. The forest in the heart of which this shrine is situated is well stocked with game and is a favourite hunting ground of poachers for miles around, and of sportsmen from all parts of India. Yet, in a lifetime's acquaintance with that forest, I do not know of a single instance of an animal having been shot in the vicinity of the shrine. When therefore I set out that day to shoot a tiger that had been taking toll of our village buffaloes, I selected a spot a mile from Baram's shrine. I was in position, behind a bush, at 4 p.m. and an hour later a *sambhar* belled in the direction from which I was expecting the tiger. A little later and a little nearer to me a *kakar* started barking; the tiger was coming along the track near which I was sitting. The jungle was fairly open and consisted mostly of young *jamun* trees, two to three feet in girth. I caught sight of the tiger—a big male—when he was two hundred yards away. He was coming slowly and had reduced the distance between us to a hundred yards when I heard the swish of leaves, and on looking up saw that one of the *jamun* trees whose branches were interlaced with another was beginning to lean over. Very slowly the tree heeled over until it came in contact with another tree of the same species and of about the same size. For a few moments the second tree supported the weight of the first and then it, too, started to keel over. When the two trees were at an angle of about thirty degrees from the perpendicular, they fetched up against a third and smaller tree. For a moment or two there was a pause, and then all three trees crashed to the ground. While watching the trees, which were only a few yards from me, I had kept an eye on the tiger. At the first sound of the leaves he had come to a halt and when the trees crashed to the ground he turned and, without showing any sign of alarm, went back in the direction from which he had come. What made the occurrence I had witnessed so unusual was that the trees were young and vigorous; that no rain had fallen recently to loosen their roots; that not a breath of air was stirring in the forest; and, finally, that the trees had fallen across the track leading to the shrine when the tiger had only another seventy yards to cover to give me the shot I was waiting for.

The chances of a shot being spoilt are greatly increased when the quarry is in an inhabited area in which parties of men may be travelling from one village to another or going to or from markets, or where shots may be fired to scare away *langurs* from apple orchards. The tigress still had three hundred yards to go to reach the stream, and two hundred yards of that was over open ground on which there was not a single tree or bush. The tigress was coming towards us at a slight angle and would see any movement we made, so there was nothing I could do but watch her, and no tigress had ever moved more slowly. She was known to the people of Muktesar as the lame tiger, but I could see no sign of her being lame. The plan that was forming in my head as I watched her was to wait until she entered the scrub jungle, and then run forward and try to get a shot at her either before or after she crossed the stream. Had there been sufficient cover between me and the point the tigress was making for, I would have gone forward as soon as I saw her and tried either to get a shot at her on the open ground or, failing that, to intercept her at the stream. But unfortunately there was not sufficient cover to mask my movements, so I had to wait until the tigress entered the bushes between the open ground and the stream. Telling the men not to move or make a sound until I returned, I set off at a run as the tigress disappeared from view. The hill was steep and as I ran along the contour I came to a wild rose bush which extended up and down the hill for many yards. Through the middle of the bush there was a low tunnel, and as I bent down to run through it my hat was knocked off, and raising my head too soon at the end of the tunnel I was nearly dragged off my feet by the thorns that entered my head. The thorns of these wild roses are curved and very strong and as I was not able to stop myself some embedded themselves and broke off in my head—where my sister Maggie had difficulty in removing them when I got home—while others tore through the flesh. With little trickles of blood running down my face I continued to run until I approached the hollow into which I had rolled the partly eaten kill from the hill above. This hollow was about forty yards long and thirty yards wide. The upper end of it where the kill was lying, the hill above the kill, and the further bank, were overgrown with dense brushwood. The lower half of the hollow and the bank on my side were free of bushes. As I reached the edge of the hollow and peered over, I heard a bone crack. The tigress had reached the hollow before me and, on finding the old kill, was trying to make up for the meal she had been deprived of the previous night.

If after leaving the kill, on which there was very little flesh, the tigress came out on to the open ground I would get a shot at her, but if she went up the hill or up the far bank I would not see her. From the dense brushwood in which I could hear the tigress, a narrow path ran up the bank on my side and passed within a yard to my left; a yard beyond the path, there was a sheer drop of fifty feet into the stream below. I was considering the possibility of driving the tigress out of the brushwood on to the open ground by throwing a stone on to the hill above her, when I heard a sound behind me. On looking round I saw Govind standing behind me with my hat in his hand. At that time no European in India went about without a hat, and having seen mine knocked of by the rose bush Govind had retrieved it and brought it to me. Near us there was a hole in the hill. Putting my finger to my lips I got Govind by the arm and pressed him into the hole. Sitting on his hunkers with his chin resting on his drawn-up knees, hugging my hat, he just fitted into the hole and looked a very miserable object, for he could hear the tigress crunching bones a few yards away. As I straightened up and resumed my position on the edge of the bank, the tigress stopped eating. She had either seen me or, what was more probable, she had not found the old kill to her liking. For a long minute there was no movement or sound, and then I caught sight of her. She had climbed up the opposite bank, and was now going along the top of it towards the hill. At this point there were a number of six-inch-thick poplar saplings, and I could only see the outline of the tigress as she went through them. With the forlorn hope that my bullet would miss the saplings and find the tigress I threw up my rifle and took a hurried shot. At my shot the tigress whipped round, came down the bank, across the hollow, and up the path on my side, as hard as she could go. I did not know, at the time, that my bullet had struck a sapling near her head, and that she was blind of one eye. So what looked like a very determined charge might only have been a frightened animal running away from danger, for in that restricted space she would not have known from which direction the report of my rifle had come. Be that as it may, what I took to be a wounded and a very angry tigress was coming straight at me; so, waiting until she was two yards away, I leant forward and with great good luck managed to put the remaining bullet in the rifle into the hollow where her neck joined her shoulder. The impact of the heavy .500 bullet deflected her just sufficiently for her to miss my left shoulder, and her impetus carried her over the fifty-foot drop into the stream below, where she landed with a great splash. Taking a step forward I looked over the edge and saw the tigress lying submerged in a pool with her feet in the air, while the water in the pool reddened with her blood.

Govind was still sitting in the hole, and at a sign he joined me. On seeing the tigress he turned and shouted to the men on the ridge, 'The tiger is dead. The tiger is dead.' The thirty men on the ridge now started shouting, and Badri on hearing them got hold of his shot gun and fired off ten rounds. These shots were heard at Muktesar and in the surrounding villages, and presently men from all sides were converging on the stream. Willing hands drew the tigress from the pool, lashed her to a sapling, and carried her in triumph to Badri's orchard. Here she was put down on a bed of straw for all to see, while I went to the guest house for a cup of tea. An hour later

by the light of hand lanterns, and with a great crowd of men standing round, among whom were several sportsmen from Muktesar, I skinned the tigress. It was then that I found she was blind of one eye and that she had some fifty porcupine quills, varying in length from one to nine inches, embedded in the arm and under the pad of her right foreleg. By ten o'clock my job was finished, and declining Badri's very kind invitation to spend the night with him I climbed the hill in company with the people who had come down from Muktesar, among whom were my two men carrying the skin. On the open ground in front of the post office the skin was spread out for the Postmaster and his friends to see. At midnight I lay down in the Dak Bungalow reserved for the public, for a few hour's sleep. Four hours later I was on the move again and at midday I was back in my home at Naini Tal after an absence of seventy-two hours.

The shooting of a man-eater gives one a feeling of satisfaction. Satisfaction at having done a job that badly needed doing. Satisfaction at having outmanoeuvred, on his own ground, a very worthy antagonist. And, the greatest satisfaction of all, at having made a small portion of the earth safe for a brave little girl to walk on.

# THE PANAR MAN-EATER

1

**WHILE I WAS HUNTING** the Champawat man-eater in 1907, I heard of a man-eating leopard that was terrorizing the inhabitants of villages on the eastern border of Almora district. This leopard, about which questions were asked in the House of Commons, was known under several names and was credited with having killed four hundred human beings. I knew the animal under the name of the Panar man-eater, and I shall therefore use this name for the purpose of my story.

No mention is made in government records of man-eaters prior to the year 1905 and it would appear that until the advent of the Champawat tiger and the Panar leopard, man-eaters were unknown in Kumaon. When therefore these two animals—who between them killed eight hundred and thirty-six human beings—made their appearance, the Government was faced with a difficult situation for it had no machinery to put in action against them and had to rely on personal appeals to sportsmen. Unfortunately there were very few sportsmen in Kumaon at that time who had any inclination for this new form of sport which, rightly or wrongly was considered as hazardous as Wilson's solo attempt—made a few years later—to conquer Everest. I myself was as ignorant of man-eaters as Wilson was of Everest and that I succeeded in my attempt, where he apparently failed in his, was due entirely to luck.

When I returned to my home in Naini Tal after killing the Champawat tiger I was asked by the Government to undertake the shooting of the Panar leopard. I was working hard for a living at the time and several weeks elapsed before I was able to spare the time to undertake this task, and then just as I was ready to start for the outlying area of Almora district in which the leopard was operating, I received an urgent request from Berthoud, the Deputy Commissioner of Naini Tal, to go to the help of the people of Muktesar where a man-eating tiger had established a reign of terror. After hunting down the tiger, an account of which I have given, I went in pursuit of the Panar leopard.

As I had not previously visited the vast area over which this leopard was operating, I went via Almora to learn all I could about the leopard from Stiffe, the Deputy Commissioner of Almora. He kindly invited me to lunch, provided me with maps, and then gave me a bit of a jolt when wishing me goodbye by asking me if I had considered all the risks and prepared for them by making my will.

My maps showed that there were two approaches to the affected area, one via Panwanaula on the Pithoragarh road, and the other via Lamgara on the Dabidhura road. I selected the latter route and after lunch set out in good heart—despite the reference to a will—accompanied by one servant and four men carrying my luggage. My men and I had already done a stiff march of fourteen miles from Khairna, but being young and fit we were prepared to do another long march before calling it a day.

As the full moon was rising we arrived at a small isolated building which, from the scribbling on the walls and the torn bits of paper lying about, we assumed was used as a school. I had no tent with me and as the door of the building was locked I decided to spend the night in the courtyard with my men, a perfectly safe proceeding for we were still many miles from the man-eater's hunting grounds. This courtyard, which was about twenty feet square, abutted on the public road and was surrounded on three sides by a two-foot-high wall. On the fourth side it was bounded by the school building.

There was plenty of fuel in the jungle behind the school and my men soon had a fire burning in a corner of the courtyard for my servant to cook my dinner. I was sitting with my back to the locked door, smoking, and my servant had just laid a leg of mutton on the low wall nearest the road and turned to attend to the fire, when I saw the head of a leopard appear over the wall close to the leg of mutton. Fascinated, I sat motionless and watched—for the leopard was facing me—and when the man had moved away a few feet the leopard grabbed the meat and bounded across the road into the jungle beyond. The meat had been put down on a big sheet of paper, which had stuck to it, and when my servant heard the rustle of paper and saw what he thought was a dog running away with it he dashed forward shouting, but on realizing that he was dealing with a leopard and not with a mere dog he changed direction and dashed towards me with even greater speed. All white people in the East are credited with being a little mad—for other reasons than walking about in the midday sun—and I am afraid my good servant thought I was a little more mad than most of my kind when he found I was laughing, for he said in a very aggrieved voice, 'It was your dinner that the leopard carried away and I have nothing else for you to eat.' However, he duly produced a meal that did him credit, and to which I did as much justice as I am sure the hungry leopard did to his leg of prime mutton.

Making an early start next morning, we halted at Lamgara for a meal, and by evening reached the Dol Dak Bungalow on the border of the man-eater's domain. Leaving my men at the bungalow I set out the following morning to try to get news of the man-eater. Going from village to village, and examining the connecting footpaths for leopard pug-marks, I arrived in the late evening at an isolated homestead consisting of a single stone-built slate-roofed house, situated in a few acres of cultivated land and surrounded by scrub jungle. On the footpath leading to this homestead I found the pug-marks of a big male leopard.

As I approached the house a man appeared on the narrow balcony and, climbing down a few wooden steps, came across the courtyard to meet me. He was a young man, possibly twenty-two years of age, and in great distress. It appeared that the previous night while he and his wife were sleeping on the floor of the single room that comprised the house, with the door open for it was April and very hot, the man-eater climbed on to the balcony and getting a grip of his wife's throat started to pull her head-foremost out of the room. With a strangled scream the woman flung an arm round her husband who, realizing in a flash what was happening, seized her arm with one hand and placing the other against the lintel of the door, for leverage, jerked her away from the leopard and closed the door. For the rest of the night the man and his wife cowered in a corner of the room, while the leopard tried to tear down the door. In the hot unventilated room the woman's wounds started to turn septic and by morning her suffering and fear had rendered her unconscious.

Throughout the day the man remained with his wife, too frightened to leave her for fear the leopard should return and carry her away, and too frightened to face the mile of scrub jungle that lay between him and his nearest neighbour. As day was closing down and the unfortunate man was facing another night of terror he saw me coming towards the house, and when I had heard his story I was no longer surprised that he had run towards me and thrown himself sobbing at my feet.

A difficult situation faced me. I had not up to that time approached Government to provide people living in areas in which a man-eater was operating with first-aid sets, so there was no medical or any other kind of aid nearer than Almora, and

Almora was twenty-five miles away. To get help for the woman I would have to go for it myself and that would mean condemning the man to lunacy, for he had already stood as much as any man could stand and another night in that room, with the prospect of the leopard returning and trying to gain entrance, would of a certainty have landed him in a mad-house.

The man's wife, a girl of about eighteen, was lying on her back when the leopard clamped its teeth into her throat, and when the man got a grip of her arm and started to pull her back, the leopard—to get a better purchase—drove the claws of one paw into her breast. In the final struggle the claws ripped through the flesh, making four deep cuts. In the heat of the small room, which had only one door and no windows and in which a swarm of flies were buzzing, all the wounds in the girl's throat and on her breast had turned septic, and whether medical aid could be procured or not, the chances of her surviving were very slight; so, instead of going for help, I decided to stay the night with the man. I very sincerely hope that no one who reads this story will ever be condemned to seeing and hearing the sufferings of a human being, or of an animal, that has had the misfortune of being caught by the throat by either a leopard or a tiger and not having the means—other than a bullet—of alleviating or of ending the suffering.

The balcony which ran the length of the house, and which was boarded up at both ends, was about fifteen feet long and four feet wide, accessible by steps hewn in a pine sapling. Opposite these steps was the one door of the house, and under the balcony was an open recess four feet wide and four feet high, used for storing firewood.

The man begged me to stay in the room with him and his wife but it was not possible for me to do this, for, though I am not squeamish, the smell in the room was overpowering and more than I could stand. So between us we moved the firewood from one end of the recess under the balcony, clearing a small space where I could sit with my back to the wall. Night

was now closing in, so after a wash and a
drink at a near-by spring I settled down in
my corner and told the man to go up to
his wife and keep the door of the room
open. As he climbed the steps the man said,
'The leopard will surely kill you, Sahib,
and then what will I do?' 'Close the door,'
I answered, 'and wait for morning.'

The moon was two nights off the full and
there would be a short period of darkness.
It was this period of darkness
that was worrying me. If

the leopard had remained scratching at the door until daylight,
as the man said it had, it would not have gone far and even
now it might be lurking in the bushes watching me. I had been
in position for half an hour, straining my eyes into the darkening
night and praying for the moon to top the hills to the east, when
a jackal gave its alarm call. This call, which is given with the full
force of the animal's lungs, can be heard for a very long distance
and can be described as 'pheaon, pheaon', repeated over and
over again as long as the danger that has alarmed the jackal is in
sight. Leopards when hunting or when approaching a kill move
very slowly, and it would be many minutes before this one—
assuming it was the man-eater—covered the half mile between
us, and even if in the meantime the moon had not risen it would
be giving sufficient light to shoot by, so I was able to relax and
breathe more freely.

Minutes dragged by. The jackal stopped calling. The moon

rose over the hills, flooding the ground in front of me with brilliant light. No movement to be seen anywhere, and the only sound to be heard in all the world was the agonized fight for breath of the unfortunate girl above me. Minutes gave way to hours. The moon climbed the heavens and then started to go down in the west, casting the shadow of the house on the ground I was watching. Another period of danger, for if the leopard had seen me he would, with a leopard's patience, be waiting for these lengthening shadows to mask his movements. Nothing happened, and one of the longest nights I have ever watched through came to an end when the light from the sun lit up the sky where, twelve hours earlier, the moon had risen.

The man, after his vigil of the previous night, had slept soundly and as I left my corner and eased my aching bones—only those who have sat motionless on hard ground for hours know how bones can ache—he came down the steps. Except for a few wild raspberries I had eaten nothing for twenty-four hours, and as no useful purpose would have been served by my remaining any longer, I bade the man goodbye and set off to rejoin my men at the Dol Dak Bungalow, eight miles away, and summon aid for the girl. I had only gone a few miles when I met my men. Alarmed at my long absence they had packed up my belongings, paid my dues at the Dak Bungalow, and then set out to look for me. While I was talking to them the Road Overseer, whom I have mentioned in my story of the Temple tiger, came along. He was well mounted on a sturdy Bhootia pony, and as he was on his way to Almora he gladly undertook to carry a letter from me to Stiffe. Immediately on receipt of my letter Stiffe dispatched medical aid for the girl, but her sufferings were over when it arrived.

It was this Road Overseer who informed me about the human kill that took me to Dabidhura, where I met with one of the most interesting and the most exciting *shikar* experiences I have ever had. After that experience I asked the old priest of the Dabidhura temple if the man-eater had as effective protection from his temple as the tiger I had failed to shoot, and he answered, 'No, no, Sahib. This *Shaitan* (devil) has killed many people who worshipped at my temple and when you come back to shoot him, as you say you will, I shall offer prayers for your success morning and evening.'

2

No matter how full of happiness our life may have been, there are periods in it that we look back to with special pleasure. Such a period for me was the year 1910, for in that year I shot the Muktesar man-eating tiger and the Panar man-eating leopard, and in between these two—for me—great events, my men and I set up an all-time record at Mokameh Ghat by handling, without any mechanical means, five thousand five hundred tonnes of goods in a single working day.

My first attempt to shoot the Panar leopard was made in April 1910, and it was not until September of the same year that I was able to spare the time to make a second attempt. I have no idea how many human beings were killed by the leopard between April and September, for no bulletins were issued by Government and beyond a reference to questions asked in the House of Commons no mention of the leopard—as far as I am aware— was made in the Indian press. The Panar leopard was credited with having killed four hundred human beings, against one hundred and twenty-five killed by the Rudraprayag leopard, and the fact that the former received such scant publicity while the latter was headline news throughout India was due entirely to the fact that the Panar leopard operated in a remote area far from the beaten track, whereas the Rudraprayag leopard operated in an area visited each year by sixty thousand pilgrims ranging from the humblest in the land to the highest, all of whom had to run the gauntlet of the man-eater. It was these pilgrims, and the daily bulletins issued by the Government, that made the Rudraprayag leopard so famous, though it caused far less human suffering than the Panar leopard.

Accompanied by a servant and four men carrying my camp kit and provisions, I set out from Naini Tal on 10 September on my second attempt to shoot the Panar leopard. The sky was overcast when we left home at 4 a.m. and we had only gone a few miles when a deluge of rain came on. Throughout the day it rained and we arrived at Almora, after a twenty-eight-mile march, wet to the bone. I was to have spent the night with Stiffe, but not having a stitch of dry clothing to put on I excused myself and spent the night at the Dak Bungalow. There were no other travellers there and the man in charge very kindly put two rooms at my disposal, with a big wood fire in each, and by morning my kit was dry enough for me to continue my journey.

It had been my intention to follow the same route from Almora that I had followed in April, and start my hunt for the leopard from the house in which the girl had died of her

wounds. While I was having breakfast a mason by the name of Panwa, who did odd jobs for us in Naini Tal, presented himself. Panwa's home was in the Panar valley, and on learning from my men that I was on my way to try to shoot the man-eater he asked for permission to join our party, for he wanted to visit his home and was frightened to undertake the journey alone. Panwa knew the country and on his advice I altered my plans and instead of taking the road to Dabidhura via the school where the leopard had eaten my dinner, I took the road leading to Pithoragarh. Spending the night at the Panwa Naula Dak Bungalow, we made an early start next morning and after proceeding a few miles left the Pithoragarh road for a track leading off to the right. We were now in the man-eater's territory where there were no roads, and where the only communication was along footpaths running from village to village.

Progress was slow, for the villages were widely scattered over many hundreds of square miles of country, and as the exact whereabouts of the man-eater were not known it was necessary to visit each village to make inquiries. Going through Salan and Rangot *pattis* (*patti* is a group of villages), I arrived late on the evening of the fourth day at Chakati, where I was informed by the headman that a human being had been killed a few days previously at a village called Sanouli on the far side of the Panar river. Owing to the recent heavy rain the Panar was in flood and the headman advised me to spend the night in his village, promising to give me a guide next morning to show me the only safe ford over the river, for the Panar was not bridged.

The headman and I had carried on our conversation at one end of a long row of double-storied buildings and when, on his advice, I elected to stay the night in the village, he said he would have two rooms vacated in the upper storey for myself and my men. I had noticed while talking to him that the end room on the ground floor was untenanted, so I told him I would stay in it and that he need only have one room vacated in the upper storey for my men. The room I had elected to spend the night in had no door, but this did not matter for I had been told that the last kill had taken place on the far side of the river and I knew the man-eater would not attempt to cross the river while it was in flood.

The room had no furniture of any kind, and after my men had swept all the straw and bits of rags out of it, complaining as they did so that the last tenant must have been a very dirty person, they spread my groundsheet on the mud floor and made up my bed. I ate my dinner—which my servant cooked on an open fire in the courtyard—sitting on my bed, and as I had done a lot of walking during the twelve hours I had been on my feet, it did not take me long to get to sleep. The sun was just rising next morning, flooding the room with light, when on hearing a slight sound in the room I opened my eyes and saw a man sitting on the floor near my bad. He was about fifty years of age, and in the last stage of leprosy. On seeing that I was awake this unfortunate living death said he hoped I had spent a comfortable night in his room. He went on to say that he had been on a two-days' visit to friends in an adjoining village, and finding me asleep in his room on his return had sat near my bed and waited for me to awake.

Leprosy, the most terrible and the most contagious of all diseases in the East, is very prevalent throughout Kumaon, and especially bad in Almora district. Being fatalists the people look upon the disease as a visitation from God, and neither segregate the afflicted nor take any precautions against infection. So quite evidently, the headman did not think it necessary to warn me that the room I had selected to stay in had for years been the home of a leper. It did not take me long to dress that morning, and as soon as our guide was ready we left the village.

Moving about as I have done in Kumaon I have always gone in dread of leprosy, and I have never felt as unclean as I did after my night in that poor unfortunate's room. At the first stream we came to I called a halt, for my servant to get breakfast ready for me and for my men to have their food. Then, telling my men to wash my groundsheet and lay my bedding out in the sun, I took a bar of carbolic soap and went down the stream to where there was a little pool surrounded by great slabs of rock. Taking off every stitch of clothing I had worn in that room, I washed it all in the pool and, after laying it out on the slabs of rock, I used the remainder of the soap to scrub myself as I had never scrubbed myself before. Two hours later, in garments that had shrunk a little from the rough treatment they had received, I returned to my men feeling clean once again, and with a hunter's appetite for breakfast.

Our guide was a man about four feet six inches tall with a big head crowned with a mop of long hair; a great barrel of a body, short legs, and few words. When I asked him if we had any stiff climbing to do, he stretched out his open hand, and answered, 'Flat as that.' Having said this he led us down a very steep hill into a deep valley. Here I expected him to turn and follow the valley down to its junction with the river. But no. Without saying a word or even turning his head he crossed the open ground and went straight up the hill on the far side. This hill, in addition to being very steep and overgrown with thorn bushes, had loose gravel on it which made the going difficult, and as the sun was now overhead and very hot, we reached the top in a bath of sweat. Our guide, whose legs appeared to have been made for climbing hills, had not turned a hair.

There was an extensive view from the top of the hill, and when our guide informed us that we still had the two high hills in the foreground to climb before reaching the Panar river, Panwa, the mason, who was carrying a bundle containing presents for his family and a great coat made of heavy dark material, handed the coat to the guide and said that as he was making us climb all the hills in Kumaon he could carry the coat for the rest of the way. Unwinding a length of goat hair cord from round his body the guide folded up the coat and strapped it securely to his back. Down and up we went, and down and up again, and then away down in a deep valley we saw the river. So far we had been going over trackless ground, without a village in sight, but we now came on a narrow path running straight down to the river. The nearer we got to the river the less I liked the look of it. The path leading to the water and up the far side showed that there was a ford here, but the river was in flood and the crossing appeared to me to be a very hazardous one. The guide assured us, however, that it was perfectly safe to cross, so removing my shoes and stockings I linked arms with Panwa and stepped into the water. The river was about forty yards wide and from its broken surface I judged it was running over a very rough bed. In this I was right, and after stubbing my toes a few times and narrowly avoiding being washed off our feet, we struggled out on the far bank.

Our guide had followed us into the river and on looking back, I saw that the little man was in difficulties. The water which for us had been thigh deep was for him waist deep and on reaching the main stream, instead of bracing his back against it and walking crab fashion, he very foolishly faced up-stream with the result that he was swept over backwards and submerged under the fast-running current. I was barefoot and helpless on the sharp stones, but Panwa—to whom sharp stones were no obstacle—threw down the bundle he was carrying and without a moment's hesitation sprinted along the bank to where fifty yards farther down, a big slab of rock jutted into the river at the head of a terrifying rapid. Running out on to this wet and slippery rock Panwa lay down, and as the drowning man was swept past, grabbed him by his long hair and after a desperate struggle drew him on to the rock. When the two men rejoined me—the guide looking like a drowned rat—I complimented Panwa on his noble and brave act in having saved the little man's life, at great risk to his own. After looking at me in some surprise Panwa said, 'Oh, it was not his life that I wanted to save, but my new coat that was strapped to his back.' Anyway, whatever the motive, a tragedy had been averted, and after my men had linked arms and crossed safely I decided to call it a day and spend the night on the river bank. Panwa, whose village was five miles farther up the river, now left me, taking with him the guide, who was frightened to attempt a second crossing of the river.

3

Next morning we set out to find Sanouli, where the last human kill had taken place. Late in the evening of that day we found ourselves in a wide open valley, and as there were no human habitations in sight, we decided to spend the night on the open ground. We were now in the heart of the man-eater's country and after a very unrestful night, spent on cold wet ground, arrived about midday at Sanouli. The inhabitants of this small village were overjoyed to see us and they very gladly put a room at the disposal of my men, and gave me the use of an open platform with a thatched roof.

The village was built on the side of a hill overlooking a valley in which there were terraced fields, from which a paddy crop had recently been harvested. The hill on the far side of the valley sloped up gradually, and a hundred yards from the cultivated land there was a dense patch of brushwood, some twenty acres in extent. On the brow of the hill, above this patch of brushwood, there was a village, and on the shoulder of the hill to the right another village. To the left of the terraced fields the valley was closed in by a steep grassy hill. So, in effect, the patch of brushwood was surrounded on three sides by cultivated land, and on the fourth by open grass land.

While breakfast was being got ready, the men of the village sat round me and talked. During the second half of March and the first half of April, four human beings had been killed in this area by the man-eater. The first kill had taken place in the village on the shoulder of the hill, the second and third in the village on the brow of the hill, and the fourth in Sanouli. All four victims had been killed at night and carried some five hundred yards into the patch of brushwood, where the leopard had eaten them at his leisure, for——having no firearms——the inhabitants of the

three villages were too frightened to make any
attempt to recover the bodies. The last
kill had taken place six days before,
and my informants were convinced
that the leopard was still in the patch
of brushwood.

I had purchased two young male
goats in a village we passed through
earlier that day, and towards evening
I took the smaller one and tied it at
the edge of the path of brushwood
to test the villager's assertion that
the leopard was still in the cover. I did not sit
over the goat, because there were no suitable trees nearby and
also because clouds were banking up and it looked as though
there might be rain during the night. The platform that had been
placed at my disposal was open all round, so I tied the second
goat near it in the hope that if the leopard visited the village
during the night it would prefer a tender goat to a tough human
being. Long into the night I listened to the two goats calling to
each other. This convinced me that the leopard was not within
hearing distance. However, there was no reason why he should
not return to the locality, so I went to sleep hoping for the best.

There was a light shower during the night and when the sun
rose in a cloudless sky every leaf and blade of grass was sparkling
with raindrops and every bird that had a song to sing was singing
a joyful welcome to the day. The goat near my platform was
contentedly browsing off a bush and bleating occasionally, while
the one across the valley was silent. Telling my servant to keep
my breakfast warm, I crossed the valley and went to the spot
where I had tied up the smaller goat. Here I found that, some
time before the rain came on, a leopard had killed the goat,
broken the rope, and carried away the kill. The rain had washed
out the drag-mark, but this did not matter for there was only

one place to which he leopard could have taken his kill, and that was into the dense patch of brushwood.

Stalking a leopard, or a tiger, on its kill is one of the most interesting forms of sport I know of, but it can only be indulged in with any hope of success when the conditions are favourable. Here the conditions were not favourable, for the brushwood was too dense to permit of a noiseless approach. Returning to the village, I had breakfast and then called the villagers together, as I wanted to consult them about the surrounding country. It was necessary to visit the kill to see if the leopard had left sufficient for me to sit over and, while doing so, I would not be able to avoid disturbing the leopard. What I wanted to learn from the villagers was whether there was any other heavy cover, within a reasonable distance, to which the leopard could retire on being disturbed by me. I was told that there was no such cover nearer than two miles, and that to get to it the leopard would have to cross a wide stretch of cultivated land.

At midday I returned to the patch of brushwood and, a hundred yards from where he had killed it, I found all that the leopard had left of the goat—its hooves, horns, and part of its stomach. As there was no fear of the leopard leaving the cover at that time of day for the jungle two miles away, I tried for several hours to stalk it, helped by *bulbuls*, drongos, thrushes, and scimitar-babblers, all of whom kept me informed of the leopard's every movement. In case any should question why I did not collect the men of the three villages and get them to drive the leopard out on to the open ground, where I could have shot it, it is necessary to say that this could not have been attempted without grave danger to the beaters. As soon as the leopard found he was being driven towards open ground, he would have broken back and attacked anyone who got in his way.

On my return to the village after my unsuccessful attempt to get a shot at the leopard, I went down with a bad attack of malaria and for the next twenty-four hours I lay on the platform in a stupor. By the evening of the following day the fever had left me and I was able to continue the hunt. On their own initiative the previous night my men had tied out the second goat where the first had been killed, but the leopard had not touched it. This was all to the good, for the leopard would now be hungry, and I set out on that third evening full of hope.

On the near side of the patch of brushwood, and about a hundred yards from where the goat had been killed two nights previously there was an old oak tree. This tree was growing out of a six-foot-high bank between two terraced fields and was leaning away from the hill at an angle that made it possible for me to walk up the trunk in my rubber soled shoes. On the underside of the trunk and about fifteen feet from the ground there was a branch jutting out over the lower field. This branch, which was about a foot thick, offered a very uncomfortable and a very unsafe seat for it was hollow and rotten. However, as it was the only branch on the tree, and as there were no other trees within a radius of several hundred yards, I decided to risk the branch.

As I had every reason to believe—from the similarity of the pug-marks I had found in the brushwood to those I had seen in April on the path leading to the homestead where the girl was killed—that the leopard I was dealing with was the Panar man-eater, I made my men cut a number of long blackthorn shoots. After I had taken my seat with my back to the tree and my legs stretched out along the branch, I made the men tie the shoots into bundles and lay them on the trunk of the tree and lash them to it securely with strong rope. To the efficient carrying out of these small details I am convinced I owe my life.

Several of the blackthorn shoots, which were from ten to twenty feet long, projected on either side of the tree; and as I had nothing to hold on to, to maintain my balance, I gathered the shoots on either side of me and held them firmly pressed between my arms and my body. By five o'clock my preparations were complete. I was firmly seated on the branch with my coat collar pulled up well in front to protect my throat, and my soft hat pulled down well behind to protect the back of my neck. The goat was tied to a stake driven into the field thirty yards in front of me, and my men were sitting out in the field smoking and talking loudly.

Up to this point all had been quiet in the patch of brushwood, but now, a scimitar-babbler gave its piercing alarm call followed a minute or two later by the chattering of several white-throated laughing thrushes. These two species of birds are the most reliable informants in the hills, and on hearing them I signalled to my men to return to the village. This they appeared to be very glad to do, and as they walked away, still talking loudly, the goat started bleating. Nothing happened for the next half-hour and then, as the sun was fading off the hill above the village, two drongos that had been sitting on the tree above me, flew off and started to bait some animal on the open ground between me and the patch of brushwood. The goat while calling had been facing in the direction of the village, and it now turned round, facing me, and stopped calling. By watching the goat I could follow the movements of the animal that the drongos were baiting and that the goat was interested in, and this animal could only be a leopard.

The moon was in her third quarter and there would be several hours of darkness. In anticipation of the leopard's coming when light conditions were not favourable, I had armed myself with a twelve-bore double-barrelled shot gun loaded with slugs, for there was a better chance of my hitting the leopard with eight slugs than with a single rifle bullet. Aids to night shooting, in the way of electric lights and torches, were not used in India at the time I am writing about, and all that one had to rely on for accuracy of aim was a strip of white cloth tied round the muzzle of the weapon.

Again nothing happened for many minutes, and then I felt a gentle pull on the blackthorn shoots I was holding and blessed my forethought in having had the shoots tied to the leaning tree, for I could not turn round to defend myself and at best the collar of my coat and my hat were poor protection. No question now that I was dealing with a man-eater, and a very determined man-eater at that. Finding that he could not climb over the thorns, the leopard, after his initial pull, had now got the butt ends of the shoots between his teeth and was jerking them violently, pulling me hard against the trunk of the tree. And now the last of the daylight faded out of the sky and the leopard, who did all his human killing in the dark, was in his element and I was out of mine, for in the dark a human being is the most helpless of all animals and—speaking for myself— his courage is at its lowest ebb. Having killed four hundred human beings at night, the leopard was quite unafraid of me, as was evident from the fact that while tugging at the shoots, he was growling loud enough to be heard by the men anxiously listening in the village. While this growling terrified the men, as they told me later, it had the opposite effect on me, for it let me know where the leopard was and what he was doing. It was when he was silent that I was most terrified, for I did not know what his next move would be. Several times he had nearly unseated me by pulling on the shoots vigorously and then suddenly letting them go, and now that it was dark and I had nothing stable to hold on to, I felt sure that if he sprang up he would only need to touch me to send me crashing to the ground.

After one of these nerve-racking periods of silence the leopard jumped down off the high bank and dashed towards the goat. In the hope that the leopard would come while there was still sufficient light to shoot by, I had tied the goat thirty yards from the tree to give me time to kill the leopard before it got to the goat. But now, in the dark, I could not save the goat—which, being white, I could only just see as an indistinct blur—so I waited until it had stopped struggling and then aimed where I thought the leopard would be and pressed the trigger. My shot was greeted with an angry grunt and I saw a white flash as the leopard went over backwards, and disappeared down another high bank into the field beyond.

For ten or fifteen minutes I listened anxiously for further sounds from the leopard, and then my men called out and asked if they should come to me. It was now quite safe for them to do so, provided they kept to the high ground. So I told them to light pine torches, and thereafter carry out my instructions. These torches, made of twelve to eighteen inches long splinters of resin-impregnated pine-wood cut from a living tree, give a brilliant light and provide the remote villages in Kumaon with the only illumination they have ever known.

After a lot of shooting and running about, some twenty men each carrying a torch left the village and, following my instructions, circled round above the terraced fields and approached my tree from behind. The knots in the ropes securing the blackthorn shoots to the tree had been pulled so tight by the leopard that they had to be cut. After the thorns had been removed men climbed the tree and helped me down, for the uncomfortable seat had given me cramps in my legs.

The combined light from the torches lit up the field on which the dead goat was lying, but the terraced field beyond was in shadow. When cigarettes had been handed round I told the men I had wounded the leopard but did not know how badly, and that we would return to the village now and I would look for the wounded animal in the morning. At this, great disappointment was expressed. 'If you have wounded the leopard it must surely be dead by now. There are many of us, and you have a gun, so there is no danger.' 'At least let us go as far as the edge of the field and see if the leopard has left a blood trail.' After all arguments for and against going to look for the leopard immediately had been exhausted, I consented against my better judgement to go as far as the edge of the field, from where we could look down on the terraced field below.

Having acceded to their request, I made the men promise that they would walk in line behind me, hold their torches high, and not run away and leave me in the dark if the leopard charged. This promise they very willingly gave, and after the torchers had been replenished and were burning brightly we set off, I walking in front and the men following five yards behind.

Thirty yards to the goat, and another twenty yards to the edge of the field. Very slowly, and in silence, we moved forward. When we reached the goat—no time now to look for a blood trail— the farther end of the lower field came into view. The nearer we approached the edge, the more of this field became visible, and then, when only a narrow strip remained in shadow from the torches, the leopard, with a succession of angry grunts, sprang up the bank and into full view.

There is something very terrifying in the angry grunt of a charging leopard, and I have seen a line of elephants that were staunch to tiger turn and stampede from a charging leopard; so I was not surprised when my companions, all of whom were unarmed, turned as one man and bolted. Fortunately for me, in their anxiety to get away they collided with each other and some of the burning splinters of pine—held loosely in their hands— fell to the ground and continued to flicker, giving me sufficient light to put a charge of slugs into the leopard's chest.

On hearing my shot the men stopped running, and then I heard one of them say, '*Oh, no.* He won't be angry with us, for he knows that this devil has turned our courage to water.' Yes, I knew, from my recent experience on the tree, that fear of a man-eater robs a man of courage. As for running away, had I been one of the torchbearers I would have run with the best. So there was nothing for me to be angry about. Presently, while I was making believe to examine the leopard, to ease their embarrassment, the men returned in twos and threes. When they were assembled, I asked, without looking up, 'Did you bring a bamboo pole and rope to carry the leopard back to the village?' 'Yes,' they answered eagerly, 'we left them at the foot of the tree.' 'Go and fetch them,' I said, 'for I want to get back to the village for a cup of hot tea.' The cold night-wind blowing down from the north had brought on another attack of malaria, and now that all the excitement was over I was finding it difficult to remain on my feet

That night, for the first time in years, the people of Sanouli slept, and have since continued to sleep, free from fear.

# THE CHUKA MAN-EATER

## 1

**CHUKA—WHICH GAVE ITS NAME** to the man-eating tiger of the Ladhya valley—is a small village of some ten ploughs on the right bank of the Sarda river near its junction with the Ladhya. From the north-west corner of the village a path runs for a quarter of a mile along a fire track before it divides, one arm going straight up a ridge to Thak village and the other diagonally up and across the hills to Kotekindri, a village owned by the people of Chuka.

Along this latter path a man was driving two bullocks in the winter of 1936, and as he approached Chuka, a tiger suddenly appeared on the fire track. With very commendable courage the man interposed himself between the tiger and his bullocks and, brandishing his stick and shouting, attempted to drive the tiger away. Taking advantage of the diversion created in their favour the bullocks promptly bolted to the village and the tiger, baulked of his prey, turned his attention to the man. Alarmed at the threatening attitude of the tiger the man turned to run and, as he did so, the tiger sprang on him. Across his shoulders the man had a heavy wooden plough, and on his back he was carrying a bag containing the provisions he needed for his stay at Chuka. While the tiger was expending its teeth and claws on the plough and bag, the man, relieved of his burdens, sprinted towards the village shouting for help as he ran. His relatives and friends, hearing his shouts, rallied to his assistance and he reached the village without further incident. One claw of the tiger had ripped his right arm from shoulder to wrist, inflicting a deep wound.

Some weeks later two men returning from the market at Tanakpur were climbing the steep path to Kotekindri, when a tiger crossed the path fifty yards ahead of them. Waiting for a few minutes to give the tiger time to move away from the vicinity of the path, the men proceeded on their way, shouting as they went. The tiger had not moved away, however, and as the leading man came abreast of it, it sprang on him. This man was carrying a sack of *gur* (unrefined sugar), half of which was on his head and the other half on his back. The tiger's teeth caught in the sack and he carried it away down the hillside, without doing the man any injury. There is no record of what the tiger thought of the captures he had made so far—a plough and a sack of *gur*—but it can be assumed he was not satisfied with his bag, for, from now on, he selected human beings who were not burdened with either ploughs or sacks.

Thak, which is about three thousand feet above Chuka, has quite a large population for a hill village. The Chand Rajas who ruled Kumaon before the advent of the Gurkhas, gave the lands of Thak to the forefathers of the present holders for their maintenance, and appointed them hereditary custodians of the Purnagiri temples. Rich lands and a considerable income from the temples have enabled the people of Thak to build themselves good substantial houses, and to acquire large herds of cattle.

On a day early in June 1937, seven men and two boys were herding the village cattle, two hundred yards to the west of Thak. At 10 a.m. it was noticed that some of the cattle were beginning to stray off the open ground towards the jungle and one of the boys, aged fourteen, was sent to turn them back. Six hours later the men, who had been sleeping through the heat of the day, were aroused by the barking of a *kakar* in the jungle bordering the open ground, into which all the cattle had by now strayed,

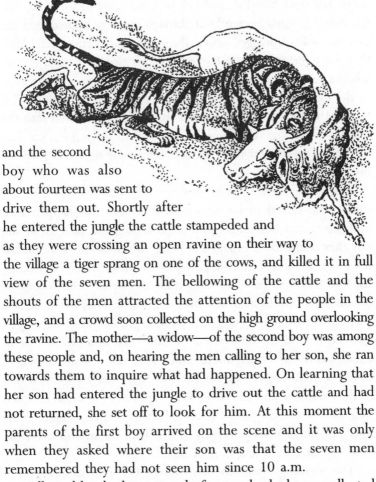

and the second
boy who was also
about fourteen was sent to
drive them out. Shortly after
he entered the jungle the cattle stampeded and
as they were crossing an open ravine on their way to
the village a tiger sprang on one of the cows, and killed it in full
view of the seven men. The bellowing of the cattle and the
shouts of the men attracted the attention of the people in the
village, and a crowd soon collected on the high ground overlooking
the ravine. The mother—a widow—of the second boy was among
these people and, on hearing the men calling to her son, she ran
towards them to inquire what had happened. On learning that
her son had entered the jungle to drive out the cattle and had
not returned, she set off to look for him. At this moment the
parents of the first boy arrived on the scene and it was only
when they asked where their son was that the seven men
remembered they had not seen him since 10 a.m.

Followed by the large crowd of men who had now collected
in the ravine near the dead cow, the distraught mother went into
the jungle and found her son where the tiger had killed and left
him, and under a near-by bush the parents of the first boy found
their son dead and partly eaten. Close to this boy was a dead
calf. From the accounts the villagers subsequently gave me of
the tragic happenings of that day, I believe that the tiger was
lying up in the jungle overlooking the ground on which the cattle
were grazing, and when the calf, unseen by the men, entered the

jungle the tiger killed it, and before it was able to carry it away, the boy either inadvertently or through curiosity approached the calf, was killed, dragged under the bush, and partly eaten. After this the tiger apparently lay up near his two kills until 4 p.m. when a *kakar* on its way to drink at the small pool on the edge of the clearing either saw or smelt it and started barking. This aroused the men to the fact that the cattle had strayed into the jungle, and the second boy who was sent to drive them out had the ill luck to go straight to the spot where the tiger was guarding his kills.

The killing of the second boy was evidently witnessed by the cattle, who rallied to his rescue—I have seen this happen with both cows and buffaloes—and after driving the tiger from the boy they stampeded. Enraged at being driven off his kills, and at the rough treatment he had quite possibly received in the process, the tiger followed the stampeding cattle and wreaked his vengeance on the first one he was able to get hold of. Had the herd not run right on into the village he would probably not have been satisfied with killing only one of his attackers. In a similar case of attempted rescue I once saw an entire herd of five buffaloes wiped out in a titanic fight with an enraged tiger. The tiger killed one of their number and the other four big-hearted animals attacked him and fought on until the last of them had been killed. The tiger evidently suffered severely in the fight, for when he left the battle-ground he left a trail of blood.

The seemingly wanton slaughter of two human beings and two animals on the same day—resulting I am convinced from the tiger's having been disturbed on his first kill—caused a great outcry in the districts on Naini Tal and Almora, and every effort was made to kill the tiger. On several occasions district officials sat up all night on *machans* over kills, and though the tiger had been wounded on two occasions—unfortunately only with buckshot—he continued to prey on human beings, and claimed yet another victim from the ill-fated village of Thak.

Two hundred yards above Thak there is a wheat field. The

crop had been cut from this field and two boys were grazing a few cattle on the stubble. For safety's sake the boys, who were brothers and orphans ten and twelve years of age, were sitting in the middle of the field. On the far side of the field, from the village, there was a light fringe of bushes. From these the hill went steeply up for a thousand feet, and from anywhere on the hill the two boys sitting in the open would have been visible. Towards the afternoon a cow strayed towards the bushes and the boys, keeping close together, set off to drive it back on to the field. The elder boy was leading and as he passed a bush the tiger, who was lying in wait, pounced on him and carried him away. The younger boy fled back to the village and dashing up to a group of men fell sobbing at their feet. When the boy was able to speak coherently he told the men that big red animal—it was the first tiger he had ever seen—had carried away his brother. A search party was hastily organized and with very commendable bravery the blood trail was followed for about a mile into the densely wooded Suwar Gadh ravine to the east of the village. Night was now closing in, so the party returned to Thak. The following day, assisted by men from adjoining villages, a day-long search was made but all that was found of the boy was his red cap and his torn and bloodstained clothes. That was the Chuka man-eater's last human victim.

I do not think it is possible to appreciate courage until danger that brought it into being has been experienced. Those who have never lived in an area in which a man-eating tiger is operating may be inclined to think that there was nothing courageous in a mother going to look for her son, in two boys grazing cattle, or in a party of men going out to look for a missing boy. But to one who has lived in such an area the entry of the mother into a dense patch of jungle in which she knew there was an angry tiger; the two small boys sitting close together for protection; and the party of unarmed men following on the blood trail left by a man-eater were acts calling for a measure of courage that merits the greatest admiration.

2

The Chuka man-eater was now disorganizing life for everyone in the Ladhya valley, and shortly after Ibbotson had been appointed Deputy Commissioner-in-Charge of the three districts of Naini Tal, Almora, and Garhwal, we joined forces to try to rid his division of the menace.

It was early afternoon on a sweltering hot day in April 1937 that Ibby, his wife Jean, and I, alighted from our motor bus at the Boom above Baramdeo. We had left Naini Tal in the early hours of the morning and, travelling via Haldwani and Tanakpur, arrived at the Boom at the hottest time of the day, covered in dust from head to foot, and with many sore spots in unseen and tender places. A cup of tea drunk while sitting on yielding sand on the bank of the Sarda river helped restore our spirits, and taking the short cut along the river bank we set off on foot to Thuli Gadh where our tents, sent in advance, had been pitched.

Starting after breakfast next morning we went to Kaladhunga. The distance between Thuli Gadh and Kaladhunga via the Sarda gorge is eight miles, and via Purnagiri, fourteen miles. The Ibbotsons and I went through the gorge while our servants and the men carrying our kit went via Purnagiri. The gorge is four miles long and was at one time traversed by a tramway line blasted out of the rock cliff by J. V. Collier when extracting the million cubic feet of *sal* timber presented by the Nepal Durbear to the Government of India as a thank-offering after the First World War. The tramway line has long since been swept away by landslides and floods, and these four miles necessitate a great deal of rock climbing where a false step or the slipping of a hand-hold would inevitably precipitate one into the cold river. We negotiated the gorge without mishap, and at the upper end, where Collier's tramline entered the forest, we caught two fish in a run where a rock of the size of a house juts out into the river.

Word had been sent ahead for the *patwaris* and forest guards working in the area to met us at Kaladhunga and give us the latest news of the man-eater. We found four men awaiting our arrival at the bungalow and the reports they gave us were encouraging. No human beings had been killed within the past few days, and the tiger was known to be in the vicinity of Thak village where three days previously it had killed a calf.

Kaladhunga is a gently rising cone-shaped peninsula roughly four miles long and a mile wide, surrounded on three sides by the Sarda river and backed on the fourth by a ridge of hills five thousand feet high. The bungalow, a three-roomed house with a wide veranda, faces east and is situated at the northern or upper end of the peninsula. The view from the veranda as the morning sun rises over the distant hills and the mist is lifting is one of the most pleasing prospects it is possible to imagine. Straight in front, and across the Sarda, is a wide open valley running deep into Nepal. The hills on either side are densely wooded, and winding through the valley is a river fringed with emerald-green elephant grass. As far as the eye can see there are no human habitations and, judging from the tiger and other animal calls that can be heard from the bungalow, there appears to be an abundant stock of game in the valley. It was from this valley that Collier extracted the million cubic feet of timber.

We spent a day at Kaladhunga, and while our men went on to Chuka to pitch our tents and make camp we fished, or, to be correct, the Ibbotsons fished while I, who had been laid up with malaria the previous night, sat on the bank and watched. From the broken water below the bungalow to the point of the peninsula—a stretch of some five hundred yards—the Ibbotsons, who are expert thread-line casters, combed the river with their one-inch spoons without moving a fish. The small river that flows down the Nepal valley joins the Sarda opposite the point of the peninsula. Here the Sarda widens out and shallows, and flows for two hundred yards over rocks before entering a big pool. It was at the upper end of this run and well out in the river that Ibby hooked his first fish—an eight-pounder—which needed careful handling on the light tackle before it was eventually brought to the bank and landed.

All keen anglers delight in watching others of the craft indulging in this, one of the best of outdoor sports. As for myself, I would just as soon watch another fishing than fish myself, especially when fish are on the take, the foothold uncertain—as it always is in the Sarda—and the river fairly fast. Shortly after Ibby killed his fish, Jean—who was fishing in broken water thirty yards from the bank—hooked a fish. Her reel only held a hundred yards of thread line, and fearing that the fish would make for the pool and break her, she attempted to walk backwards while playing the fish, and in doing so lost her footing and for a long minute all that was visible of her was the toe of one foot and the point of her rod. You will naturally assume that I, forgetting my recent attack of malaria, dashed out to her rescue. As a matter of fact I did nothing of the kind and only sat on the bank and laughed, for to attempt to rescue either of the Ibbotsons from a watery grave would be as futile as trying to save an otter from drowning. After a long and a violent struggle Jean upended herself, and reaching the bank killed her fish, which weighed six pounds. Hardly had she done so when Ibby, in making a long cast, slipped off the rock on which he was standing and disappeared under water, rod and all.

From the bottom end of the pool below the run, the river turns to the right. On the Nepal side of this bend in the river there had stood a giant *semul* tree, in the upper branches of which a pair of ospreys had for many years built their nest. The tree had been an ideal home for the birds, for not only had it commanded an extensive view of the river, but the great branches growing out at right angles to the trunk had also provided tables on which to hold and devour their slippery prey. The monsoon floods of the previous year had cut into the bank and washed away the old tree and the ospreys had built themselves a new nest in a tall *shisham* tree standing at the edge of the forest, a hundred yards from the river.

The run was evidently the favourite fishing ground of ospreys, and while the female sat in the nest the male kept flying backwards and forwards over the Ibbotsons' heads. Eventually tiring of this unprofitable exercise it flew farther down the river to where a few partly submerged rocks broke the surface of the water, making a small run. Fish were evidently passing this spot, and a dozen times the osprey banked steeply, closed his wings, and dropped like a plummet and, checking himself with widespread wings and tail before reaching the water, rose flapping to regain height for his next cast. At last his patience was rewarded. An unwary fish had come to the surface directly below him, and without a moment's pause he went from flat flight into a lightning dive through a hundred feet of air and plunged deep into the broken water. His needle-sharp and steel-strong talons took hold, but the catch was evidently heavier than he anticipated. Time and time again with wildly threshing wings he attempted to launch himself into the air, only to sink down again on his breast feathers. I believe he would have had to relinquish his catch had not a gust of wind blowing up river come at this critical moment to help him. As the wind reached him he turned downstream and, making one last desperate effort, got the

fish clear of the water. Home was in the opposite direction from that in which he was now heading but to turn was impossible, so, selecting a great slab of rock on the bank on which to land, he made straight for it.

I was not the only one who had been watching the osprey, for he had hardly landed on the rock when a woman who had been washing clothes on the Nepal side of the river called out excitedly, and a boy appeared on the high bank above her. Running, down the steep track to where the woman was standing, he received his instructions and set off along the boulder-strewn bank at a pace that threatened his neck and limbs at every stride. The osprey made no attempt to carry off his prey, and as the boy reached the rock it took to the air, circling round his head as he held up the fish—which appeared to be about four pounds in weight—for the woman to see.

For some time thereafter I lost sight of the osprey, and we had finished our lunch before I again saw him quartering the air above the run in which he had caught the fish of which the boy had deprived him. Back and forth he flew for many minutes, always at the same height, and then he banked, dropped fifty feet, again banked and then plunged straight into the water. This time his catch was lighter—a *kalabas* about two pounds in weight—and without effort he lifted it clear of the water and, holding it like a torpedo to reduce wind pressure, made for his nest. His luck was out that day, however, for he had only covered half the distance he had to go, when a Pallas fish-eagle twice his weight and size came up from behind, rapidly overtaking him. The osprey saw him coming and altering his course a point to the right headed for the forest with the object of shaking off his pursuer among the branches of the trees. The eagle realizing the object of this manoeuvre emitted a scream of rage and increased his speed. Only twenty yards more to go to reach safety, but the risk was too great to take and, relinquishing his hold of the *kalabas*, the osprey—only just in time—hurled himself straight into the air. The fish had not fallen a yard before the eagle caught it and, turning in a graceful sweep, made off down river in the direction from which he had come. He was not to escape with his booty as easily as he expected, however, for he had only gone a short distance on his return journey when the pair of crows that fed on the osprey's leavings set off to bait him, and to shake them off he too was compelled to take to the forest. At the edge of the forest the crows turned back and the eagle had hardly disappeared from view when falling out of the sky came two Tawny eagles going at an incredible speed in the direct line the Pallas eagle had taken. I very greatly regret I did not see the end of the chase for, from the fact that while I watched neither of the birds rose out of the forest, I suspect that the Pallas eagle retained his hold on the fish too long. I have only once seen a more interesting chase. On that occasion I was taking a line of eighteen elephants through grass and the ten guns and five spectators who were sitting on the elephants, shooting black partridge, saw a bush chat pass—without once touching the ground—from a sparrow-hawk that killed it just in front of our line of elephants to a red-headed merlin, then to a honey buzzard, and finally to a peregrine falcon who swallowed the little bird whole. If any of the guns or spectators who were with me that February morning read this chapter, they will recall the occurrence as having taken place on the Rudrapur Maidan.

After an early breakfast next morning we moved from Kaladhunga to Chuka, an easy march of five miles. It was one of those gorgeous days that live long in the memory of a fisherman. The sun was pleasantly warm; a cool wind blowing down from the north; a run of *chilwa* (fingerlings) in progress; and the river full of big fish madly on the take. Fishing with light tackle we had many exciting battles, all of which we did not win. We ended the day, however, with enough fish to feed our camp of thirty men.

## 3

To assist us in our campaign against the man-eater, and to try to prevent further loss of human life, six young male buffaloes had been sent up from Tanakpur in advance of us, to be used as bait for the tiger. On our arrival at Chuka we were told that the buffaloes had been tied out for three nights, and that though a tiger's pug-marks had been seen near several of them, none had been killed. During the next four days we visited the buffaloes in the early morning; tried to get in touch with the tiger during the day, and in the evening accompanied the men engaged in tying out the buffaloes. On the fifth morning we found that a buffalo we had tied up at Thak, at the edge of the jungle in which the two boys had lost their lives, had been killed and carried off by a tiger. Instead of taking its kill into the dense jungle as we had expected, the tiger had taken it across an open patch of ground, and up on to a rocky knoll. This it had evidently done to avoid passing near a *machan* from which it had been fired at—and quite possibly wounded—on two previous occasions. After the buffalo had been dragged for a short distance its horns got jammed between two rocks, and being unable to free it, the tiger had eaten a few pounds of flesh from the hindquarters of the kill and then left it. In casting round to see in which direction the tiger had gone, we found its pug-marks in a buffalo wallow, between the kill and the jungle. These pug-marks showed that the killer of the buffalo was a big male tiger.

It was generally believed by the District Officials—on what authority I do not know—that the man-eater was a tigress. On showing them the tracks in the buffalo wallow we were told by the villagers that they could not distinguish between the pug-marks of different tigers and that they did not know whether the man-eater was male or female, but that they did know it had a broken tooth. In all the kills, human as well as animal, that had taken place near their village they had noticed that one of the tiger's teeth only bruised the skin and did not penetrate it. From this they concluded that one of the man-eater's canine teeth was broken.

Twenty yards from the kill there was a *jamun* tree. After we had dragged the kill out from between the rocks we sent a man up the tree to break a few twigs that were obstructing a view of the kill from the only branch of the tree in which it was possible to sit. This isolated tree on the top of the knoll was in full view of the surrounding jungle, and though the man climbed it and broke the twigs with the utmost care, I am inclined to think he was seen by the tiger.

It was now 11 a.m., so, sending our men back to the village to have their midday meal, Ibby and I selected a bush under which to shelter from the sun and talked and dozed, and dozed and talked throughout the heat of the day. At 2.30 p.m., while we were having a picnic lunch, some *kalege* pheasants started chattering agitatedly at the edge of the jungle where the buffalo had been killed, and on hearing them our men returned from the village. While Ibby and his big-hearted man, Sham Singh, went into the jungle where the pheasants were chattering—to

attract the tiger's attention—I climbed silently into the *jamun* tree. Giving me a few minutes in which to settle down, Ibby and Sham Singh came out of the jungle and returned to our camp at Chuka, leaving my two men at Thak.

Shortly after Ibby had gone the pheasants started chattering again and a little later a *kakar* began barking. The tiger was evidently on the move, but there was little hope of his crossing the open ground and coming to the kill until the sun had set and the village had settled down for the night. The *kakar* barked for a quarter of an hour or more before it finally stopped, and from then until sunset, except for the natural calls of a multitude of birds, the jungle—as far as the tiger was concerned—was silent.

The red glow from the setting sun had faded from the Nepal hills on the far side of the Sarda river, and the village sounds had died down, when a *kakar* barked in the direction of the buffalo wallow; the tiger was returning to his kill along the line he had taken when leaving it. A convenient branch in front of me gave a perfect rest for my rifle, and the only movement it would be necessary to make when the tiger arrived would be to lower my head on to the rifle butt. Minute succeeded minute until a hundred had been added to my age and then, two hundred yards up the hillside, a *kakar* barked in alarm and my hope of getting a shot, which I had put at ten to one, dropped to one in a thousand. It was now quite evident that the tiger had seen my man breaking the twigs off the tree, and that between sunset and the barking of this last *kakar* he had stalked the tree and seeing me on it had gone away. From then on *kakar* and *sambhar* called at intervals, each call a little farther away than the last. At midnight these alarm calls ceased altogether, and the jungle settled down to that nightly period of rest ordained by Nature, when strife ceases and the jungle fold can sleep in peace. Others who have spent nights in an Indian jungle will have noticed this period of rest, which varies a little according to the season of the year and the phases of the moon, and which as a rule extends from midnight to 4 a.m. Between these hours killers sleep. And those who go in fear of them are at peace. It may be natural for carnivores to sleep from midnight to 4 a.m., but I would prefer to think that Nature had set apart these few hours so that those who go in fear of their lives can relax and be at peace.

Day was a few minutes old when, cramped in every joint, I descended from the tree and, unearthing the thermos flask Ibby had very thoughtfully buried under a bush, indulged in a much needed cup of tea. Shortly after my two men arrived and while we were covering the kill with branches, to protect it from vultures, the tiger called three times on a hill half a mile away. As I passed through Thak on my way back to camp the greybeards of the village met me and begged me not to be discouraged by my night's failure, for, they said, they had consulted the stars and offered prayers and if the tiger did not die this day it would certainly die on the next or, may be, the day after.

A hot bath and a square meal refreshed me and at 1 p.m. I again climbed the steep hill to Thak and was told on my arrival that a *sambhar* had belled several times on the hill above the village. I had set out from camp with the intention of sitting up over a live buffalo; and, to ensure while doing so that the tiger did not feed in one place while I was waiting for him in another, I placed several sheets of newspaper near the kill I had sat over the previous night. There was a well-used cattle track through the jungle in which the villagers said the *sambhar* had called. In a tree on the side of this track I put up a rope seat, and to a root on the track I tied the buffalo. I climbed into the tree at three o'clock, and an hour later first a *kakar* and then a tiger called on the far side of the valley a thousand yards away. The buffalo had been provided with a big feed of green grass, and throughout the night it kept the bell I had tied round its neck ringing, but it failed to attract the tiger. At daylight my men came for me and they told me that *sambhar* and *kakar* had called during the night in the deep ravine in which the boy's red cap and torn clothes had been found, and at the lower end of which we had tied up a buffalo at the request of the villagers.

When I got back to Chuka I found that Ibby had left camp before dawn. News had been received late the previous evening that a tiger had killed a bullock eight miles up the Ladhya valley. He sat up over the kill all night without seeing anything of the tiger, and late the following evening he returned to camp.

4

Jean and I were having breakfast after my night in the tree over the live buffalo, when the men engaged in tying out our remaining five buffaloes came in to report that the one they had tied up at the lower end of the ravine in which my men had heard the *sambhar* and *kakar* calling the previous night was missing. While we were being given this news MacDonald, Divisional Forest Officer, who was moving camp that day from Kaladhunga to Chuka, arrived and told us he had seen the pug-marks of a tiger at the lower end of a ravine where he presumed one of our buffaloes had been tied up. These pug-marks, Mac said, were similar to those he had seen at Thak when on a previous visit he had tried to shoot the man-eater.

After breakfast, Jean and Mac went down the river to fish while I went off with Sham Singh to try to find out what had become of the missing buffalo. Beyond the broken rope and the tiger's pug-marks there was nothing to show that the buffalo had been killed. However, on casting round I found where one of the buffalos' horns had come in contact with the ground and from here on there was a well-defined blood trail. Whether the tiger lost his bearings after killing the buffalo or whether he was trying to cover up his tracks I do not know, for after taking the kill over most difficult ground for several miles he brought it back to the ravine two hundred yards from where he had started. At this point the ravine narrowed down to a bottle-neck some ten feet wide. The tiger was probably lying up with his kill on the far side of the narrow neck, and as I intended sitting up for him all night I decided to join the anglers and share their lunch before sitting up.

After fortifying the inner man, I returned with Sham Singh and three men borrowed from the fishing party, for if I found the kill and sat up over it it would not have been safe for Sham Singh to have gone back to camp alone. Walking well ahead of the four men I approached the bottle-neck for the second time, and as I did so the tiger started growling. The ravine here was steep and full of boulders and the tiger was growling from behind a dense screen of bushes, about twenty yards straight in front of me. An unseen tiger's growl at close range is the most terrifying sound in the jungle, and is a very definite warning to intruders not to approach any nearer. In that restricted space, and with the tiger holding a commanding position, it would have been foolish to have gone any farther. So, signalling to the men to retire, and giving them a few minutes to do so, I started to walk backwards very slowly—the only safe method of getting away from any animal with which one is anxious not to make contact. As soon as I was well clear of the bottle-neck I turned and, whistling to the men to stop, rejoined them a hundred yards farther down the ravine. I now knew exactly where the tiger was, and felt confident I would be able to deal with him; so, on rejoining the men, I told them to leave me and return to the fishing party. This, however, they were very naturally frightened to do. They believed, as I did, that the tiger they had just heard growling was a man-eater and they wanted to have the protection of my rifle. To have taken them back myself would have lost me two hours, and as we were in a *sal* forest and there was not a climbable tree in sight, I had of necessity to keep them with me.

Climbing the steep left bank we went straight away from the ravine for two hundred yards. Here we turned to the left and after I had paced out two hundred yards we again turned to the left and came back to the ravine a hundred yards above where we had heard the tiger growling. The tables were now turned and we held the advantage of position. I knew the tiger would not go down the ravine, for he had seen human beings in that direction, only a few minutes before; nor would he go up the ravine, for in order to do so he would have to pass us. The bank on our side was thirty feet high and devoid of undergrowth, so the only way the tiger could get out of the position we had manoeuvred him into would be to go up the opposite hillside. For ten minutes we sat on the edge of the ravine scanning every foot of ground in front of us. Then, moving back a few paces, we went thirty yards to the left and again sat down on the edge and, as we did so, the man sitting next to me whispered 'sher', and pointed across the ravine. I could see nothing, and on asking the man how much of the tiger he could see, and to describe its position, he said he had seen its ears move and that it was near some dry leaves. A tiger's ears are not conspicuous objects at fifty yards, and as the ground was carpeted with dead leaves his description did nothing to help me locate the tiger. From the breathing of the men behind me it was evident that excitement was rising to a high pitch. Presently one of the men stood up to get a better view, and the tiger, who had been lying down facing us, got up and started to go up the hill, and as his head appeared from behind a bush I fired. My bullet, I subsequently found, went through the ruff on his neck and striking a rock splintered back, making him spring straight up into the air, and on landing he got involved with a big creeper from which he found some difficulty in freeing himself. When we saw him struggling on the ground we thought he was down for good, but when he regained his feet and galloped off Sham Singh expressed the opinion, which I shared, that he was unwounded. Leaving the men I crossed the ravine and on examining the ground found the long hairs the bullet had clipped, the splintered rock, and the torn and bitten creeper, but I found no blood.

Blood does not always flow immediately after an animal has been hit, and my reconstruction of the shot may have been faulty; so it was necessary to find the kill, for it would tell me on the morrow whether or not the tiger was wounded. Here we had some difficulty, and it was not until we had gone over the ground twice that we eventually found the kill in a pool of water four feet deep, where the tiger had presumably put it to preserve it from hornets and blowflies. Sending the three men I had borrowed back to the fishing party—it was safe to do so now—Sham Singh and I remained hidden near the kill for an hour to listen for jungle sounds and then, hearing none, returned to camp. After an early breakfast next morning Mac and I returned to the ravine and found that the tiger had removed the kill from the pool, carried it a short distance, and eaten it out leaving only the head and hooves. This, together with the absence of blood on the ground on which he had been lying while eating, was proof that the tiger was not wounded and that he had recovered from his fright.

When we got back to camp we were informed that a cow had been killed in a wide open ravine on the far side of the Ladhya river, and that the men who had found it had covered it with branches. Ibby had not returned from his visit to the village eight miles up the Ladhya, and after lunch Mac and I went out to look at the cow. It had been covered up at midday and shortly afterwards the tiger had returned, dug it out from under the branches, and carried it away without leaving any mark of a drag. The forest here consisted of great big *sal* trees without any undergrowth, and it took us an hour to find the kill where the tiger had hidden it under a great pile of dead leaves. In a nearby tree Mac very gallantly put up a *machan* for me while I smoked and emptied his water-bottle—the shade temperature was about a hundred and ten degrees—and after seeing me into the tree he returned to camp. An hour later a small stone rolling down the steep hill on the far side of the ravine attracted my attention, and shortly after a tigress came into view, followed by two small cubs. This was quite evidently the first occasion on which the cubs had ever been taken to a kill, and it was very interesting to see the pains the mother took to impress on them the danger of the proceeding and the great caution it was necessary to exercise. The behaviour of the cubs was as interesting as their mother's. Step by step they followed in her tracks; never trying to pass each other, or her; avoiding every obstruction that she avoided no matter how small it was, and remaining perfectly rigid when she stopped to listen, which she did every few yards. The ground was carpeted with big *sal* leaves as dry as tinder over which it was impossible to move silently; however, every pad was put down carefully and as carefully lifted, and as little sound as possible was made.

Crossing the ravine, the tigress, closely followed by the cubs, came towards me and passing behind my tree lay down on a flat piece of ground overlooking the kill, and about thirty yards from it. Her lying down was apparently intended as a signal to the cubs to go forward in the direction in which her nose was pointing, and this they proceeded to do. By what means the mother conveyed the information to her cubs that there was food for them at this spot I do not know, but that she had conveyed this information to them there was no question. Passing their mother—after she had lain down—and exercising the same caution they had been made to exercise when following her, they set out with every appearance of being on a very definite quest. I have repeatedly asserted that tigers have no sense of smell, and the cubs were providing me with ample proof of that assertion. Though the kill had only been reported to us that morning the cow had actually been killed the previous day, and before hiding it under the pile of dead leaves the tigress had eaten the greater portion of it. The weather, as I have said, was intensely hot, and it was the smell that eventually enabled Mac and me to find the kill. And here, now, were two hungry cubs ranging up and down, back and forth, passing and repassing a dozen times within a yard of the kill and yet not being able to find it. It was the blowflies that disclosed its position and at length enabled them to find it. Dragging it out from under the leaves the cubs sat down together to have their meal. The tigress had watched her cubs as intently as I had and only once, when they were questing too far afield, had she spoken to them. As soon as the kill had been found the mother turned on to her back with her legs in the air and went to sleep.

As I watched the cubs feeding I was reminded of a scene I had witnessed some years previously at the foot of Trisul, I was lying on a ridge scanning with field glasses a rock cliff opposite me for *thar*, the most sure-footed of all Himalayan goats. On a ledge halfway up the cliff a *thar* and her kid were lying asleep. Presently the *thar* got to her feet, stretched herself, and the kid immediately started to nuzzle her and feed. After a minute or so the mother freed herself, took a few steps along the ledge, poised for a moment, and then jumped down on to another and a narrower ledge some twelve to fifteen feet below her. As soon as it was left alone the kid started running backwards and forwards, stopping every now and then to peer down at its mother, but unable to summon the courage to jump down to her for, below the few-inches-wide ledge, was a sheer drop of a thousand feet. I was too far away to hear whether the mother was encouraging her young, but from the way her head was turned I believe she was doing so. The kid was now getting more and more agitated and, possibly fearing that it would do something foolish, the mother went to what looked like a mere crack in the vertical rock face and, climbing it, rejoined her young. Immediately on doing so she lay down, presumably to prevent the kid from feeding. After a little while she again got to her feet, allowed the kid to drink for a minute, poised carefully on the brink, and jumped down, while the kid again ran backwards and forwards above her. *Seven* times in the course of the next half-hour this procedure was gone through, until finally the kid, abandoning itself to its fate, jumped, and landing safely beside its mother was rewarded by being allowed to drink its fill. The lesson, to teach her young that it was safe to follow where she led, was over for that day. Instinct helps, but it is the infinite patience of the mother and the unquestioning obedience of her offspring that enable the young of all animals in the wild to grow to maturity. I regret I lacked the means, when I had the opportunity, of making cinematographic records of the different species of animals I have watched training their young, for there is nothing more interesting to be seen in a jungle.

When the cubs finished their meal they returned to their mother and she proceeded to clean them, rolling them over and licking off the blood they had acquired while feeding. When this job was finished to her entire satisfaction she set off, with the cubs following close behind, in the direction of a shallow ford in the Ladhya, for nothing remained of the kill and there was no suitable cover for her cubs on this side of the river.

I did not know, and it would have made no difference if I had, that the tigress I watched with such interest that day would later, owing to gunshot wounds, become a man-eater and a terror to all who lived or worked in the Ladhya valley and the surrounding villages.

5

The kill at Thak, over which I had sat the first night, had been uncovered to let the vultures eat it, and another buffalo had been tied up at the head of the valley to the west of the village and about two hundred yards from the old kill. Four mornings later the headman of Thak sent word to us that this buffalo had been killed by a tiger and carried away.

Our preparations were soon made, and after a terribly hot climb Ibby and I reached the scene of the kill at about midday. The tiger, after killing the buffalo and breaking a very strong rope, had picked up the kill and gone straight down into the valley. Telling the two men we had brought to carry our lunch to keep close behind us, we set off to follow the drag. It soon became apparent that the tiger was making for some definite spot, for he led us for two miles through dense undergrowth, down steep banks, through beds of nettles and raspberry bushes, over and under fallen trees, and over great masses of rock until finally he deposited the kill in a small hollow under a box tree shaped like an umbrella. The buffalo had been killed the previous night and the fact that the tiger had left it without having a meal was disquieting. However, this was to a great extent offset by the pains he had taken in getting the kill to this spot, and if all went well there was every reason to hope that he would return to his kill, for, from the teeth-marks on the buffalo's neck, we knew he was the man-eater we were looking for and not just an ordinary tiger.

Our hot walk up to Thak and subsequent descent down the densely wooded hillside, over difficult ground, had left us in a bath of sweat, and while we rested in the hollow having lunch and drinking quantities of tea, I cast my eyes round for a convenient tree on which to sit and, if necessary in which to pass the night. Growing on the outer edge of the hollow and leaning away from the hill at an angle of forty-five degrees was a *ficus* tree. This, starting life in some decayed part of a giant of the forest, had killed the parent tree by weaving a trellis round it, and this trellis was now in course of coalescing to form a trunk for the parasite. Ten feet from the ground, and where the trellis had stopped and the parent tree had rotted and fallen away, there appeared to be a comfortable seat on which I decided to sit.

Lunch eaten and a cigarette smoked, Ibby took our two men sixty yards to the right and sent them up a tree to shake the branches and pretend they were putting up a *machan*, to distract the tiger's attention in case he was lying up close by and watching us, while I as silently as possibly climbed into the *ficus* tree. The seat I had selected sloped forward and was cushioned with rotten wood and dead leaves and, fearing that if I brushed them off the sound and movement might be detected by the tiger, I left them as they were and sat down on them, hoping devoutly that there were no snakes in the hollow trunk below me or scorpions in the dead leaves. Placing my feet in an opening in the the trellis, to keep from slipping forward, I made myself as comfortable as conditions permitted, and when I had done so Ibby called the men off the tree and went away talking to them in a loud voice.

The tree in which I had elected to sit was, as I have already said, leaning outwards at an angle of forty-five degrees, and ten feet immediately below me there was a flat bit of ground about ten feet wide and twenty feet long. From this flat piece of ground the hill fell steeply away and was overgrown with tall grass and dense patches of brushwood, beyond which I could hear a stream running; an ideal place for a tiger to lie up in.

Ibby and the two men had been gone about fifteen minutes when a red monkey on the far side of the valley started barking to warn the jungle folk of the presence of a tiger. From the fact that this monkey had not called when we were coming down the hill, following the drag, it was evident that the tiger had not moved off at our approach and that he was now coming to investigate—as tigers do—the sounds he had heard in the vicinity of his kill. Monkeys are blessed with exceptionally good eyesight, and though the one that was calling was a quarter of a mile away, it was quite possible that the tiger he was calling at was close to me.

I was sitting facing the hill with the kill to my left front, and the monkey had only called eight times when I heard a dry stick snap down the steep hillside behind me. Turning my head to the right and looking through the trellis, which on this side extended a little above my head, I saw the tiger standing and looking in the direction of my tree, from a distance of about forty yards. For several minutes he stood looking alternately in my direction and then in the direction of the tree the two men had climbed, until eventually, deciding to come in my direction, he started up the steep hillside. It would not have been possible for a human being to have got over that steep and difficult ground without using his hands and without making considerable noise, but the tiger accomplished the feat without making a sound. The nearer he came to the flat ground the more cautious he became and the closer he kept his belly to the ground. When he was near the top of the bank he very slowly raised his head, took a long look at the tree the men had climbed, and satisfied that it was not tenanted sprang up on to the flat ground and passed out of sight under me. I expected him to reappear on my left and go towards the kill, and while I was waiting for him to do so I heard the dry leaves under the tree being crushed as he lay down on them.

For the next quarter of an hour I sat perfectly still, and as no further sounds came to me from the tiger I turned my head to the right, and craning my neck looked through an opening in the trellis, and saw the tiger's head. If I had been able to squeeze a tear out of my eye and direct it through the opening it would, I believe, have landed plumb on his nose. His chin was resting on the ground and his eyes were closed. Presently he opened them blinked a few times to drive away the flies, then closed them again and went to sleep. Regaining my position I now turned my head to the left. On this side there was no trellis nor were there any branches against which I could brace myself, and when I had craned my neck as far as I could without losing my balance I looked down and found I could see most of the tiger's tail, and a part of one hind leg.

The situation needed consideration. The bole of the tree against which I had my back was roughly three feet thick and afforded ideal cover, so there was no possibility of the tiger seeing me. That he would go to the kill if not disturbed was certain; the question was, when would he go? It was a hot afternoon, but the spot he had selected to lie on was in deep shade from my tree and, further, there was a cool breeze blowing up the valley. In these pleasant conditions he might sleep for hours and not approach the kill until day light had gone, taking with it my chance of getting a shot. The risk of waiting on the tiger's pleasure could not be taken, therefore, for apart from the reason given the time at our disposal was nearly up and this might be the last chance I would get of killing the tiger, while on that chance might depend the lives of many people. Waiting for a shot being inadvisable, then, there remained the possibility of dealing with the tiger where he lay. There were several openings in the trellis on my right through which I could have inserted the barrel of my rifle, but having done this it would not have been possible to depress the muzzle of the rifle sufficiently to get the sights to bear on the tiger's head. To have stood up, climbed the trellis, and fired over the top of it would not have been difficult. But this could not have been done without making a certain amount of noise, for the dry leaves I was sitting on would have crackled when relieved of my weight, and within ten feet of me was an animal with the keenest hearing of any in the jungle. A shot at the head end of the tiger not being feasible, there remained the tail end.

When I had both my hands on the rifle and craned my neck to the left, I had been able to see most of the tiger's tail and a portion of one hind leg. By releasing my right hand from the rifle and and getting a grip of the trellis I found I could lean out far enough to see one-third of the tiger. If I could maintain this position after releasing my hold, it would be possible to disable him. The thought of disabling an animal, and a sleeping one at that, simply because he occasionally liked a change of diet was hateful. Sentiment, however, where a man-eater was concerned was out of place. I had been trying for days to shoot this tiger to save further loss of human life, and now that I had a chance of doing so the fact that I would have to break his back before killing him would not justify my throwing away that chance. So the killing would have to be done no matter how unpleasant the

method might be, and the sooner it was done the better, for in bringing his kill to this spot the tiger had laid a two-mile-long scent trail, and a hungry bear finding that trail might at any moment take the decision out of my hands. Keeping my body perfectly rigid I gradually released my hold of the trellis, got both hands on the rifle, and fired a shot behind and under me which I have no desire ever to repeat. When I pressed the trigger of the 450/400 high-velocity rifle, the butt was pointing to heaven and I was looking under, not over, the sights. The recoil injured but did not break either my fingers or my wrist, as I had feared it would, and as the tiger threw the upper part of his body round and started to slide down the hill on his back, I swung round on my seat and fired the second barrel into his chest. I should have felt less a murderer if, at my first shot, the tiger had stormed and raved but—being the big-hearted animal that he was—he never opened his mouth, and died at my second shot without having made a sound.

Ibby had left me with the intention of sitting up in the *jamun* tree over the buffalo which had been killed four days previously and which the vultures had, for some unknown reason, not eaten. He thought that if the tiger had seen me climbing into the *ficus* tree it might abandon the kill over which I was sitting and go back to its old kill at Thak and give him a shot. On hearing my two shots he came hurrying back to see if I needed his help, and I met him half a mile from the *ficus* tree. Together we returned to the scene of the killing to examine the tiger. He was a fine big male in the prime of life and in perfect condition, and would have measured—if we had had anything to measure him with—nine feet six inches between pegs, or nine feet ten over curves. And the right canine tooth in his lower jaw was broken. Later I found several pellets of buckshot embedded in different parts of his body.

The tiger was too heavy for the four of us to carry back to camp so we left him where he lay, after covering him up with grass, branches, and deadwood heaped over with big stones, to protect him from bears. Word travelled round that night that the man-eating tiger was dead and when we carried him to the foot of the *ficus* tree next morning to skin him, more than a hundred men and boys crowded round to see him. Among the latter was the ten-year-old brother of the Chuka man-eater's last human victim.

# THE TALLA DES MAN-EATER

## 1

**NOWHERE ALONG THE FOOTHILLS** of the Himalayas is there a more beautiful setting for a camp than under the Flame of the Forest trees at Bindukhera, when they are in full bloom. If you can picture white tents under a canopy of orange-coloured bloom; a multitude of brilliantly plumaged red and gold minivets, golden orioles, rose-headed parakeets, golden backed woodpeckers, and wire-crested drongos flitting from tree to tree and shaking down the bloom until the ground round the tents resembled a rich orange-coloured carpet; densely wooded foothills in the background topped by ridge upon rising ridge of the Himalayas, and they in turn topped by the eternal snows, then, and only then, will you have some idea of our camp at Bindukhera one February morning in the year 1929.

Bindukhera, which is only a name for the camping ground, is on the western edge of a wide expanse of grassland some twelve miles long and ten miles wide. When Sir Henry Ramsay was king of Kumaon the plain was under intensive cultivation, but at the time of my story there were only three small villages, each with a few acres of cultivation dotted along the banks of the sluggish stream that meanders down the length of the plain. The grass on the plain had been burnt a few weeks before our arrival, leaving islands of varying sizes where the ground was damp and the grass too green to burn. It was on these islands that we hoped to find the game that had brought us to Bindukhera for a week's shooting. I had shot over this ground for ten years and knew every foot of it, so the running of the shoot was left to me.

Shooting from the back of a well-trained elephant on the grasslands of the Tarai is one of the most pleasant forms of sport I know of. No matter how long the day may be, every moment of it is packed with excitement and interest, for in addition to the variety of game to be shot—on a good day I have seen eighteen varieties brought to bag ranging from quail and snipe to leopard and swamp deer—there is a great wealth of bird life to ordinarily be seen when walking through grass on foot.

There were nine guns and five spectators in camp on the first day of our shoot that February morning, and after an early breakfast we mounted our elephants and formed a line, with a pad elephant between every two guns. Taking my position in the centre of the line, with four guns and four pad elephants on either side of me, we set off due south with the flanking gun on the right—fifty yards in advance of the line—to cut off birds that rose out of range of the other guns and were making for the forest on the right. If you are ever given choice of position in a line of elephants on a mixed-game shoot select a flank, but only if you are good with both gun ad rifle. Game put up by a line of elephants invariably try to break out at a flank, and one of the most difficult objects to hit is a bird or an animal that has been missed by others.

When the air is crisp and laden with all the sweet scents that are to be smelt in an Indian jungle in the early morning, it goes to the head like champagne, and has the same effect on birds, with the result that both guns *and* birds tend to be too quick off the mark. A too eager gun and a wild bird do not produce a heavy bag, and the first few minutes of all glorious days are usually as unproductive as the last few minutes when muscles are tired and eyes strained. Birds were plentiful that morning, and, after the guns had settled down, shooting improved and in our first beat along the edge of the forest we picked up five peafowl, three red jungle fowl, ten black partridges, four grey partridges, two bush quails, and three hares. A good *sambhar* had been put up but he gained the shelter of the forest before rifles could be got to bear on him.

Where a tongue of forest extended out on to the plain for a few hundred yards, I halted the line. This forest was famous for the number of peafowl and jungle fowl that were always to be found in it, but as the ground was cut up by a number of deep nullahs that made it difficult to maintain a straight line, I decided not to take the elephants through it, for one of the guns was inexperienced and was shooting from the back of an elephant that morning for the first time. It was in this forest—when Wyndham and I some years previously were looking for a tiger—that I saw for the first time a cardinal bat. These beautiful bats, which look like gorgeous butterflies as they flit from cover to cover, are, as far as I know, only to be found in heavy elephant-grass.

After halting the line I made the elephants turn their heads to the east move off in single file. When the last elephant had cleared the ground over which we had just beaten, I again halted them and made them turn their heads to the north. We were now facing the Himalayas, and hanging in the sky directly in front of us was a brilliantly lit white cloud that looked solid enough for angels to dance on.

The length of a line of seventeen elephants depends on the ground that is being beaten. Where the grass was heavy I shortened the line to a hundred yards, and where it was light I extended it to twice that length. We had beaten up to the north for a mile or so, collecting thirty more birds and a leopard, when a ground owl got up in front of the line. Several guns were raised and lowered when it was realized what the bird was. These ground owls, which live in abandoned pangolin and porcupine burrows, are about twice the size of a partridge, look white on the wing, and have longer legs than the ordinary run of owls. When flushed by a line of elephants they fly low for fifty to a hundred yards before alighting. This

I believe they do to allow the line to clear their burrows, for when flushed a second time they invariably fly over the line and back to the spot from where they originally rose. The owl we flushed that morning, however, did not behave as these birds usually do, for after flying fifty to sixty yards in a straight line it suddenly started to gain height by going round and round in short circles. The reason for this was apparent a moment later when a peregrine falcon, flying at great speed, came out of the forest on the left. Unable to regain the shelter of its burrow the owl was now making a desperate effort to keep above the falcon. With rapid wing beats he was spiralling upwards, while the falcon on widespread wings was circling up and up to get above his quarry. All eyes, including those of the *mahouts*, were now on the exciting flight, so I halted the line.

It is difficult to judge heights when there is nothing to make a comparison with. At a rough guess the two birds had reached a height of a thousand feet, when the owl—still moving in circles—started to edge away towards the big white cloud, and one could imagine the angels suspending their dance and urging it to make one last effort to reach the shelter of their cloud. The falcon was not slow to see the object of this manoeuvre, and he too was now beating the air with his wings and spiralling up in ever-shortening circles. Would the owl make it or would he now, as the falcon approached nearer to him, lose his nerve and plummet down in a vain effort to reach mother earth and the sanctuary of his burrow? Field glasses were now out for those who needed them, and up and down the line excited exclamations—in two languages—were running.

'Oh! he can't make it.'

'Yes he can, he can.'

'Only a little way to go now.'

'But look, look, the falcon is gaining on him.' And then, suddenly, only one bird was to be seen against the cloud. 'Well done! well done! *Shahbash*! *shahbash*! 'The owl had made it, and while hats were being waved and hands were being clapped, the falcon in a long graceful glide came back to the *semul* tree from which he had started.

The reactions of human beings to any particular event are unpredictable. Fifty-four birds and four animals had been shot that morning—and many more missed—without a qualm or the batting of an eyelid. And now, guns, spectators, and *mahouts* were unreservedly rejoicing that a ground owl had escaped the talons of a peregrine falcon.

At the northern end of the plain I again turned the line of elephants south, and beat down along the right bank of the stream that provided irrigation water for the three villages. Here on the damp ground the grass was unburnt and heavy, and rifles were got ready, for there were many hog deer and swamp deer in this area, and there was also a possibility of putting up another leopard.

We had gone along the bank of the stream for about a mile, picking up five more peafowl, four cock florican—hens were barred—three snipe, and a hog deer with very good horns when the accidental (please turn your eyes away, Recording Angel) discharge of a heavy high-velocity rifle in the hands of a spectator sitting behind me in my howdah, scorched the inner lining of my left ear and burst the eardrum. For me the rest of that February day was torture. After a sleepless night I excused myself on the plea that I had urgent work to attend to (again, please, Recording Angel) and at dawn, while the camp was asleep, I set out on a twenty-five-mile walk to my home at Kaladhungi.

The doctor at Kaladhungi, a keen young man who had recently completed his medical training, confirmed my fears that my eardrum had been destroyed. A month later we moved up to our summer home at Naini Tal, and at the Ramsay Hospital I received further confirmation of this diagnosis from Colonel Barber, Civil Surgeon of Naini Tal. Days passed, and it became apparent that abscesses were forming in my head. My condition was distressing my two sisters as much as it was distressing me, and as the hospital was unable to do anything to relieve me I decided—much against the wishes of my sisters and the advice of Colonel Barber—to go away.

I have mentioned this 'accident' not with the object of enlisting sympathy but because it has a very important bearing on the story of the Talla Des man-eater which I shall now relate.

2

Bill Baynes and Ham Vivian were Deputy Commissioners of, respectively, Almora and Naini Tal in the year 1929, and both were suffering from man-eaters, the former from the Talla Des man-eating tiger, and the latter from the Chowgarh man-eating tiger.

I had promised Vivian that I would try to shoot his tiger first, but as it had been less active during the winter months than Baynes's, I decided, with Vivian's approval, to try for the other first. The pursuit of this tiger would, I hoped, tide me over my bad time and enable me to adjust myself to my new condition. So to Talla Des I went.

My story concerns the Talla Des tiger, and I have refrained

from telling it until I had written *Jungle Lore*. For without first reading *Jungle Lore*, and knowing that I had learnt—when a boy and later—how to walk in a jungle and use a rifle, and the credulity of all who were not present in Kumaon at that time would have been strained and this, after my previous stories had been accepted at their face value, was the last thing I desired.

My preparations were soon made and on 4 April I left Naini Tal accompanied by six Garhwalis, among whom were Madho Singh and Ram Singh, a cook named Elahai, and a Brahmin, Ganga Ram, who did odd jobs and was very keen to go with me. Walking the fourteen miles down to Kathgodam we caught the evening train and, travelling through Bareilly and Pilibhit, arrived at noon next day at Tanakpur. Here I was met by the *peshkar*, who informed me that a boy had been killed the previous day by the Talla Des man-eater, and that under Baynes's orders two young buffaloes—to be used as bait—had been dispatched for me via Champawat to Talla Des. After my men had cooked and eaten their food and I had breakfasted at the dak bungalow, we started off in good heart to try to walk the twenty-four miles to Kaladhunga (not to be confused with Kaladhungi) the same night.

The first twelve miles of the road—through Baramdeo to the foot of the sacred Purnagiri mountain—runs through forest most of the way. At the foot of the mountain the road ends, and there is the choice of two tracks to Kaladhunga. One, the longer, goes steeply up the left-hand side of the mountain to the Purnagiri temples, over a shoulder of the mountain, and down to Kaladhunga. The other track follows the alignment of the tramway line made by Collier when extracting the million cubic feet of *sal* timber that I have already spoken of. Collier's tramline—where it ran for four miles through the Sarda river gorge—has long since been washed away, but portions of the track he blasted across the perpendicular rock face of the mountain still remain. The going over this portion of the track was very difficult for my heavily laden Garhwalis, and night came on when we were only halfway through the gorge. Finding a suitable place on which to camp for the night was not easy, but after rejecting several places made dangerous by falling stones we eventually found a narrow shelf where the overhanging rock offered measure of safety. Here we decided to spend the night, and after I had eaten my dinner and while the men were cooking their food with driftwood brought up from the river I undressed and lay down on my camp bed, the only article of camp equipment, excluding a washbasin and a forty-pound tent, that I had brought with me.

The day had been hot and we had covered some sixteen miles since detraining at Tanakpur. I was comfortably tired and was enjoying an after-dinner cigarette, when on the hill on the far side of the river I suddenly saw three lights appear. The forests in Nepal are burnt annually, the burning starting in April. Now, on seeing the lights, I concluded that the wind blowing down the gorge had fanned to flame the smouldering embers in some dead wood. As I idly watched these fires two more appeared a little above them. Presently the left-hand one of these two new fires moved slowly down the hill and merged into the central one of the original three. I now realized that what I had assumed were fires, were not fires but lights, all of a uniform size of about two feet in diameter, burning steadily without a flicker or trace of smoke. When presently more lights appeared, some to the left and others farther up the hill, an explanation to account for them presented itself. A potentate out on *shikar* had evidently lost some article he valued and had sent men armed with lanterns to search for it. Admittedly a strange explanation, but many strange things happen on the far side of that snow-fed river.

My men were as interested in the lights as I was, and as the river below us flowed without a ripple and the night was still, I asked them if they could hear voices or any other sounds—the distance across was about a hundred and fifty yards—but they said they could hear nothing. Speculation as to what was happening on the opposite hill was profitless, and as we were tired out after our strenuous day the camp was soon wrapped in slumber. Once during the night a *ghooral* sneezed in alarm on the cliff above us, and a little later a leopard called.

A long march and a difficult climb lay before us. I had warned my men that we would make an early start, and light was just showing in the east when I was given a cup of hot tea. Breaking camp, when only a few pots and pans had to be put away and a camp bed dismantled, was soon accomplished. As the cook and my Garhwalis streamed off in single file down a goat track into a deep ravine, which in Collier's day had been spanned by an iron bridge, I turned my eyes to the hill on which we had seen the lights. The sun was not far from rising, and distant objects were now clearly visible. From crest to water's edge and from water's edge to crest I scanned every foot of the hill, first with my naked eyes and then with field glasses. Not a sign of any human being could I see, or, reverting to my first theory, was there any smouldering wood, and it only needed a glance to see that the vegetation in this area had not been burnt for a year. The hill was rock from top to bottom, a few stunted trees and bushes growing where roothold had been found in crack or cranny. Where the lights had appeared was a perpendicular rock where no human being, unless suspended from above, could possibly have gone.

Nine days later, my mission to the hill people accomplished, I camped for a night at Kaladhunga. For a lover of nature, or for a keen fisherman, there are few places in Kumaon to compare with Kaladhunga. From the bungalow Collier built when extracting the timber Nepal gave India, the land slopes gently down in a series of benches to the Sarda river. On these benches, where crops grew in the bygone days, there is now a luxuriant growth of grass. Here *sambhar* and *cheetal* are to be seen feeding morning and evening, and in the beautiful forests behind the bungalow live leopards and tigers, and a wealth of bird life including peafowl, jungle fowl, and *kalega* pheasants. In the big pools and runs below

the bungalow some of the best fishing in the Sarda river is to be had, either on a spinning rod with plug bait or on a light rod with salmon fly or fly spoon.

At crack of dawn next morning we left Kaladhunga, Ganga Ram taking the mountain track to Purnagiri and the rest of us the shorter way through the Sarda gorge. Ganga Ram's mission—which would entail an additional ten-miles walk—was to present our thank-offerings to the sacred Purnagiri shrine. Before he left me I instructed him to find out all he could, from the priests who served the shrine, about the lights we had seen when on our way up to Talla Des. When he rejoined me that evening at Tanakpur he gave me the following information, which he had gleaned from the priests and from his own observations.

Purnagiri, dedicated to the worship of the Goddess Bhagbatti and visited each year by tens of thousands of pilgrims, is accessible by two tracks. These, one from Baramdeo and the other from Kaladhunga, meet on the northern face of the mountain a short distance below the crest. At the junction of the tracks is situated the less sacred of the two Purnagiri shrines. The more sacred shrine is higher up and to the left. This holy of holies can only be reached by going along a narrow crack, or fault, running across the face of a more or less perpendicular rock cliff. Nervous people, children, and the aged are carried across the cliff in a basket slung on the back of a hillman. Only those whom the Goddess favours are able to reach the upper shrine; the others are struck blind and have to make their offerings at the lower shrine.

*Puja* (prayer) at the upper shrine starts at sunrise and ends at midday. After this hour no one is permitted to pass the lower shrine. Near the upper and more sacred shrine is a pinnacle of rock a hundred feet high, the climbing of which is forbidden by the Goddess. In the days of long ago a *sadhu*, more ambitious than his fellows, climbed the pinnacle with the object of putting himself on an equality with the Goddess. Incensed at his disregard of her orders, the Goddess hurled the *sadhu* from the pinnacle to the hill on the far side of the snow-fed river. It is this *sadhu* who, banished for ever from Purnagiri, worships the Goddess two thousand feet above him by lighting lamps to her. These votive lights only appear at certain times (we saw them on 5 April) and are only visible to favoured people. This favour was accorded to me and to the men with me, because I was on a mission to the hillfolk over whom the Goddess watches.

That in brief was the information regarding the light which Ganga Ram brought back from Purnagiri and imparted to me while we were waiting for our train at Tanakpur. Some weeks later I received a visit from the Rawal (High Priest) of Purnagiri. He had come to see me about an article I had published in a local paper on the subject of the Purnagiri lights, and to congratulate me on being the only European ever to have been privileged to see them. In my article I gave the explanation for the lights as I have given it in these pages, and I added that if my readers were unable to accept this explanation and desired to find one for themselves, they should bear the following points in mind:

The lights did not appear simultaneously.

They were of a uniform size (about two feet in diameter).

They were not affected by wind.

They were able to move from one spot to another.

The High Priest was emphatic that the lights were an established fact which no one could dispute—in this I was in agreement with him for I had seen them for myself—and that no other explanation than the one I had given could be advanced to account for them.

The following year I was fishing the Sarda with Sir Malcolm (now Lord) Hailey, who was Governor of the United Provinces at the time. Sir Malcolm had seen my article and as we approached the gorge he asked me to point out the spot where I had seen the lights. We had four *dhimas* (fishermen) with us who were piloting the *sarnis* (inflated skins) on which we were floating down the river from one fishing stand to the next. These men were part of a gang of twenty engaged by a contractor in floating pine sleepers from the high-level forests in Kumaon and Nepal to the boom at Baramdeo. This was a long, difficult, and very dangerous task, calling for great courage and a thorough knowledge of the river and its many hazards.

Below the shelf blasted out of the cliff by Collier, on which my men and I had spent the night when on our way up to Talla Des, was a narrow sandy beach. Here the *dhimas* at my request brought the *sarnis* to the bank, and we went ashore. After I had pointed out where the lights had appeared, and traced their movements on the hill, Sir Malcolm said the *dhimas* could possibly provide an explanation, or at least throw some light on the subject. So he turned to them—he knew the correct approach to make to an Indian when seeking information and could speak the language perfectly—and elicited the following information. Their homes were in the Kangra Valley where they had some cultivation, but not sufficient to support them. They earned their living by floating sleepers down the Sarda river for Thakur Dan Singh Bist. They knew every foot of the river as far down as Baramdeo, for they had been up and down it countless times. They knew this particular gorge very well, for there were backwaters in it that hung up the sleepers and gave them a great deal of trouble. They had never seen anything unusual in this part of the river in the way of lights, or anything else.

As he turned away from the *dhimas* I asked Sir Malcolm to put one more question to them. Had they in all the years they had been working on the Sarda ever spent a night in the gorge? Their answer to this question was a very emphatic No! Questioned further they said that not only had they never spent a night in the gorge but that they had never heard of anyone else ever having done so. The reason they gave for this was that the gorge was haunted by evil spirits.

Two thousand feet above us a narrow crack, worn smooth by the naked feet of generations upon generations of devotees, ran for fifty yards across a perpendicular rock cliff where there was no handhold of any kind. In spite of the precautions taken by the priests to safeguard the lives of pilgrims, casualties while negotiating that crack were heavy until H. H. The Maharaja of Mysore provided funds a few years ago for a steel cable to be stretched across the face of the cliff, from the lower shrine to the upper.

So there well might be spirits at the foot of that cliff but not, I think, evil ones.

3

Now to get back to my story.

Ganga Ram, who could cover the ground as fast as any man in Kumaon, had stayed back with me to carry my camera, and we caught up with the cook and the six Garhwalis two miles from where we had spent the night. For the next six hours we walked with never a pause, at times through dense forests and at times along the bank of the Sarda river. Our way took us through Kaladhunga and through Chuka to the foot of the mountain, on the far side of which was our objective, the hunting grounds of the Talla Des man-eater. At the foot of the mountain we halted for two hours—to cook and eat our midday meal—before essaying the four-thousand-foot climb.

In the afternoon, with the hot April sun blazing down on our backs and without a single tree to shade us, we started on one of the steepest and most exhausting climbs my men and I had ever undertaken. The so-called road was only a rough track which went straight up the face of the mountain without a single hairpin bend to ease the gradient. After repeated and many halts we arrived at sunset at a little hamlet, a thousand feet from the crest. We had been warned at Chuka to avoid this hamlet, for, being the only inhabited place on the southern face of the mountain, it was visited regularly by the man-eater. However, man-eater or no man-eater, we could go no farther, so to the hamlet—which was a few hundred yards from the track—we went. The two families in the hamlet were delighted to see us and after we had rested and eaten our evening meal, my men were provided with accommodation behind locked doors, while I settled down on my camp bed under a tree that sheltered the tiny spring which provided the two families with drinking water, with a rifle and a lantern to keep me company.

Lying on my bed that night I had ample time to review the situation. Instructions had been issued by Bill Baynes to headmen of villages not to disturb any human or other kills, pending my arrival. The boy the *peshkar* of Tanakpur had told me about, had been killed on the fourth and it was now the night of the sixth. Since leaving the train at Tanakpur we had not spared ourselves in an effort to try to get to the scene of the killing with as little delay as possible. I knew the tiger would have eaten out his kill before our arrival and that, if he was not disturbed, he would probably remain in the vicinity for a day or two. I had hoped when leaving camp that morning that we would reach our destination in time to tie out one of the young buffaloes, but the climb up from the Sarda had been too much for us. Regrettable as the loss of one day was, it could not be helped, and I could only hope that if the tiger had moved away from the scene of his kill, he had not gone far. One of the disadvantages I had to contend with was that I did not know this part of Kumaon. The tiger had been operating for eight years and had made one hundred and fifty human kills, so it was reasonable to assume he was working over a very large area. If contact with him was once lost it might be weeks before it could again be made. However, worrying over what the tiger had done, or what he might do, was profitless, so I went to sleep.

I was to make an early start and it was still quite dark when Ganga Ram roused me by lighting the lantern which had gone out during the night. While breakfast was being got ready I had a bath at the spring, and the sun was just rising over the Nepal mountains when, having cleaned and oiled my .275 Rigby Mauser rifle and put five rounds in the magazine, I was ready to start. Inter-village communication had been interrupted by the man-eater and the two men in the hamlet had not heard about the tiger's last kill, so they were unable to give me any information as to the direction, or the distance, we would have to go. Not knowing when my men would get their next meal I told them to have a good one now and to follow me when they were ready, keeping close together and selecting open places to sit down in when they wanted to rest.

Rejoining the track up which we had laboured the previous evening, I halted for a spell to admire the view. Below me the valley of the Sarda was veiled in shadow and a wisp of mist showed where the river wound in and out through the foothills to emerge at Tanakpur. Beyond Tanakpur the eye could follow the river as a gleaming silver ribbon, until lost to sight on the horizon. Chuka was in shadow and partly obscured by mist, but I could see the path winding up to Thak, every foot of which I was to know when hunting the Thak man-eater ten years later. Thak village, gifted hundreds of years ago by the Chand Rajas of Kumaon to the priests who see the Purnagiri shrines, was bathed in the morning sun, as was also the pinnacle of Purnagiri.

Twenty-five years have come and gone since I turned away from that view to complete the last stage of my journey to Talla Des—a long period, in which much has happened. But time does not efface events graven deep on memory's tablets, and the events of the five days I spent hunting the man-eating tiger of Talla Des are as clear-cut and fresh in my memory today as they were twenty-five years ago.

On the far side of the hill I found the track that I was on joined a quite good forest road some six feet wide, running east and west. Here I was faced with a dilemma, for there were no villages in sight and I did not know in which direction to go. Eventually, on the assumption that the road to the east could only take me out of my way as far as the Sarda, I decided to try it first.

Given the option of selecting my own time and place for a walk anywhere, I would unhesitatingly select a morning in early April on the northern face of a well-wooded hill in the Himalayas. In April all Nature is at her best; deciduous trees are putting out new leaves, each of a different shade of green or bronze; early violets, buttercups, and rhododendrons are giving way to later primulas, larkspurs, and orchids; and the birds—thrushes, babblers, minivets, tits, and a host of others—that migrated to the foothills for the winter are back on their nesting grounds and vie with each other in their joyous mating songs. Walking carefree and at ease in a forest in which there is no danger, only those objects and sounds which please the senses are looked at and listened to with any degree of attention, and all the other less-arresting sights and sounds blend together to form a pleasing whole. When there is danger from a man-eating tiger, however, the carefree feeling gives way to intense awareness.

Danger not only adds zest to all forms of sport, it also tends to sharpen the faculties and to bring into focus all that is to be seen and heard in a forest. Danger that is understood, and which you are prepared to face, does not detract in any way from pleasure. The bank of violets does not lose any of its beauty because the rock beyond it may shelter a hungry tiger, and the song of the black-headed sibia, poured out from the topmost branch of an oak tree, is none the less pleasing because a scimitar-babbler at the foot of the tree is warning the jungle folk of the presence of danger.

Fear may not be a heritage to some fortunate few, but I am not of their number. After a lifelong acquaintance with wild life I am no less afraid of a tiger's teeth and claws today than I was the day that a tiger shooed Magog and me out of the jungle in which he wanted to sleep. But to counter that fear and hold it in check I now have the experience that I lacked in those early years. Where formerly I looked for danger all round me and was afraid of every sound I heard, I now knew where to look for danger, and what sounds to ignore or pay special attention to. And, further, where there was uncertainty where a bullet would go, there was now a measure of certainty that it would go in the direction I wanted it to. Experience engenders confidence, and without these two very important assets the hunting of a man-eating tiger on foot, and alone, would be a very unpleasant way of committing suicide.

The forest road I was walking on that April morning ran through an area in which a man-eating tiger was operating and had been used by the tiger frequently, as was evident from the scratch marks on it. In addition to these marks, none of which was fresh enough to show the pug-marks of the tiger which had made them, there were many tracks of leopard, *sambhar*, bear, *kakar*, and pig. Of birds there were many varieties, and of flowers there was great profusion, the most beautiful of which was the white butterfly orchid. These orchids hang down in showers and veil the branch or the trunk of the tree to which their roots are attached. One of the most artistic nests I have ever seen was that of a Himalayan black bear, made in a tree on which orchids were growing. A big oak tree had snapped off, either by weight of snow or in a storm, some forty feet above ground. Where the break had taken place a ring of branches, the thickness of a man's arm, had sprouted out at right angles to the trunk. Here moss had grown and in the moss butterfly orchids had found root-hold. It was here among these orchids that a bear had made its nest by bending over and pressing down the branches on to the broken-off tree trunk. The trees selected by bears in which to make their nests are of the variety whose branches will bend without snapping. The nests have nothing to do with family affairs and I have seen them at altitudes of from two thousand to eight thousand feet. At the lower altitudes, to which bears descend during the winter months to feed on wild plums and honey, the nests give protection from ants and flies, and at the higher altitudes they enable the animals to bask undisturbed in the sun.

When a road is interesting its length does not register on one's consciousness. I had been walking for about an hour when the forest ended and I came out on a grassy ridge overlooking a village. My approach over the open ground was observed, and when I reached the village the whole population appeared to have

turned out to greet me. I often wonder whether in any other part of the world a stranger whose business was not known, arriving unexpectedly at a remote village, would be assured of the same welcome and hospitality as he would receive at any village throughout the length and breadth of Kumaon. I was possibly the first white man who had ever approached that village alone and on foot, and yet, by the time I reached the assembled people, a square of carpet had been produced, a *morha* (rush seat) placed on it, and I had hardly sat down before a brass vessel containing milk was placed in my hands. A lifelong association with the hillfolk enables me to understand the different dialects that are spoken in Kumaon and, what is just as important, to follow their every thought. As I had arrived armed with a rifle it was taken for granted that I had come to rid them of the man-eater, but what was puzzling them was my arrival on foot at that early hour when the nearest bungalow at which I could have spent the night was thirty miles away.

Cigarettes, passed round while I was drinking the milk, loosened tongues, and after I had answered the many questions put to me I put a few of my own. The name of the village, I learnt, was Tamali. The village had suffered for many years from the man-eater. Some said eight years and others said ten, but all were agreed that the man-eater had made its appearance the year that Bachi Singh had cut off his toes while splitting wood with an axe, and Dan Singh's black bullock, for which he had paid thirty rupees, had fallen down the hill and got killed. The last person killed at Tamali by the man-eater had been Kundan's mother. She had been killed on the twentieth day of the previous month (March), while working with other women in a field below the village. No one knew whether the tiger was a male or a female, but all knew it was a very big animal, the fear of which was now so great that the outlying fields were no longer being cultivated and no one was willing to go to Tanakpur to get the food that was needed for the village. The tiger was never absent from Tamali for long, and if I stayed with them, which they begged me to do, I would have a better chance of shooting it than anywhere else in Talla Des.

To leave people who place implicit trust in you to the tender mercies of a man-eater is not easy. However, my reason for doing so was accepted, and, after I had assured the fifty or more people gathered round me that I would return to Tamali at the first opportunity, I bade them goodbye and set off to try to find the village where the last kill had taken place.

At the point where the track from the hamlet met the forest road I removed the sign I had placed on the road to indicate to my men that I had gone east, and replaced it on the road to the west, and, to ensure that there would be no mistake, I put a 'road closed' sign on the road to the east. The two signs I have mentioned are known throughout the hills, and, though I had not told my men that I would use them, I knew they would understand that I had laid them and would interpret

them correctly. The first sign consists of a small branch laid in the middle of the road, held in position with a stone or bit of wood, with the leaves pointing in the direction in which it is intended that the person following should go. The second sign consists of two branches crossed, in the form of an X.

The road to the west was level most of the way and ran through a forest of giant oak trees standing knee-deep in bracken and maidenhair fern. Where there were openings in this forest there were magnificent views of hills upon rising hills backed by the snowy range extending to east and west as far as the eye could see.

4

After going for some four miles due west the forest road turned to the north and crossed the head of a valley. Flowing down the valley was a crystal-clear stream which had its birth in the dense oak forest on the hill that towered above me on my left. Crossing the stream on stepping-stones, and going up a short rise, I came out on an open stretch of ground on the far side of which was a village. Some girls coming down from the village on their way to the stream caught sight of me as I came out on the open ground, and they called out in great excitement, 'The Sahib has come! The Sahib has come!' The cry was caught up from house to house and before I reached the village I was surrounded by an excited throng of men, women, and children.

From the headman I learnt that the name of the village was Talla Kote. That a *patwari* had arrived two days previously (5 April) from Champawat, to meet me and to tell all the people in the district that a sahib was coming from Naini Tal to try to shoot the man-eater. That shortly after the arrival of the *patwari* a woman of the village had been killed by the man-eater, and that in obedience to orders received from the Deputy Commissioner, Almora, the kill had not been disturbed. And finally, that in anticipation of my arrival a party of men had been sent that morning to look for the kill and, if there was anything left of it, to put up a *machan* for me. While the headman was giving me this information the party, numbering some thirty men, returned. These men told me that they had searched the ground where the tiger had eaten its kill and that all they had been able to find were the woman's teeth. Even her clothes, they said, were missing. When I asked where the kill had taken place, a lad of about seventeen who was with the party of men said that if I would accompany him to the other side of the village he would point out to me where his mother had been killed by the man-eater. With the lad leading and the throng of men, women, and children following me, we went through the village to a narrow saddle some fifty yards long connecting two hills. This saddle was the apex of two great valleys. The one on the left, or western side, swept down towards the Ladhya river; the one on the right fell steeply away and down ten or fifteen miles to the Kali river. Halting on the saddle the lad turned and faced the valley on the right. The left-hand or northern, side of this valley was under short grass with an odd bush scattered here and there, and the right-hand side was under dense scrub and tree jungle. Pointing to a bush on the grassy side eight hundred to a thousand yards away and a thousand to fifteen hundred feet below us, the lad said his mother had been killed near it while cutting grass in company with several other women. Then pointing to an oak tree in the ravine, the branches of which had been broken by *langurs*, he said it was under that tree that they had found the remains of his mother. Of the tiger, he said, neither he nor any of the party of men with him had seen or heard anything, but that when they were on their way down the hill they had heard first a *ghooral*, and then a little later, a *langur* calling.

A *ghooral* and a *langur* calling. *Ghooral* do occasionally call on seeing human beings, but not *langurs*. Both will call on seeing a tiger, however. Was it possible that the tiger had lingered near the scene of its kill and on being disturbed by the party of men had moved off and been seen, first by the *ghooral*, and then by the *langur*? While I was speculating on this point, and making a mental map of the whole country that stretched before me, the *patwari*, who had been having his food when I arrived, joined me. Questioned about the two young buffaloes for which I had asked Baynes, the *patwari* said he had started out with them from Champawat and that he had left them at a village then miles from Talla Kote, where a boy had been killed by the man-eater on 4 April within sight of the village. As there was no one on the spot to deal with the man-eater, the body had been recovered, and after a report of the occurrence had been sent to Champawat, from where it had been telegraphed to Tanakpur for my information, he had given orders for the body of the boy to be cremated.

My men had not yet arrived from the hamlet where we spent the night, so, after instructing the headman to have my tent pitched on the open ground near the stream, I decided to go down and have a look at the ground where the tiger had eaten his kill, with the object of finding out if the man-eater was male or female, and if the latter, whether she had cubs. This part of Kumaon was, as I have already said, unknown to me, and when I asked the headman if he could tell me the easiest way to get down into the valley the lad, who had pointed out to me where his mother had been killed and eaten, stepped forward and said very eagerly, 'I will come with you, Sahib, and show you the way.'

The courage of people living in an area in which there is danger from a man-eater, and the trust they are willing to place in absolute strangers, has always been a marvel to me. The lad, whose name I learnt was Dungar Singh, was yet another example of that courage and trust. For years Dungar Singh had lived in fear of the man-eater and only an hour previously he had seen the pitiful remains of his mother. And yet, alone and unarmed, he was willing to accompany an absolute stranger into an area in which he had every reason to believe—from the alarm call of a *ghooral* and a *langur*—that the killer of his mother was lurking. True, he had only recently visited that area, but on that occasion he had been accompanied by thirty of his friends, and in numbers there was safety.

There was no way down the steep hillside from the saddle, so Dungar Singh led me back through the village to where there was a goat track. As we went down through scattered bushes I told him that my hearing was defective, that if he wanted to draw my attention to any particular thing to stop and point to it, and that if he wanted to communicate with me to come close and whisper into my right ear. We had gone about four hundred yards when Dungar Singh stopped and looked back. Turning round and looking in the same direction, I saw the *patwari* followed by a man carrying a shotgun hurrying down the hill after us. Thinking they had important information for me, I awaited their arrival and was disappointed to find that all the *patwari* wanted was to accompany me with his gun-bearer. This, very reluctantly, I permitted him to do for neither he nor his gun-bearer—both of whom were wearing heavy boots—looked like men who could move in a jungle without making considerable noise.

We had gone another four hundred yards through dense scrub jungle, when we came out on a clearing a few yards square. Here, where the goat track divided, one arm going towards a deep ravine on the left while the other followed the contour of the hill to the right, Dungar Singh stopped, and pointing in the direction of the ravine whispered that it was down there that the tiger had eaten his mother. As I did not wish the ground on which I wanted to look for pug-marks to be disturbed by booted men, I told Dungar Singh to stay on the open ground with the two men, while I went down alone into the ravine. As I stopped talking Dungar Singh whipped round and looked up the hill. When I looked in the same direction I saw a crowd of men standing on the saddle of the hill where I had stood a little while before. With a hand stretched out towards us to ensure silence, and the other cupped to his ear, Dungar Singh was intently listening, occasionally nodding his head. Then with a final nod he turned to me and whispered. 'My brother says to tell you that in the *wyran* field below you, there is something red lying in the sun.'

A *wyran* field is one that has gone out of cultivation, and below us on such a field there was something red lying in the sun. Maybe the red object was only a bit of dry bracken, or a *kakar* or young *sambhar*, but it might be a tiger. Anyway, I was not going to risk spoiling what might turn out to be a heaven-sent chance. So, handing my rifle to Dungar Singh, I took the *patwari* and his man, each by an arm, and led them to a medlar tree growing near by. Unloading the *patwari's* gun and laying it under a bush, I told the two men to climb the tree and on pain of death to remain quietly in it until I ordered them to come down. I do not think any two men ever climbed into a tree more gladly and from the way they clung to the branches after they had climbed as high as it was safe to go, it was evident that their views on man-eater hunting had undergone a drastic change since they followed me from the village.

The goat track to the right led on to a terraced field which had long been out of cultivation, and on which there was a luxuriant growth of oat grass. This field, about a hundred yards long, was ten feet wide at my end and thirty feet wide at the other, where it terminated on a ridge. For fifty yards the field was straight and then it curved to the left. As Dungar Singh saw me looking at it, he said that from the farther end we would be able to see down on to the *wyran* field on which his brother had seen the red object. Bending down and keeping to the inner edge of the field we crept along until we came to the far end. Here we lay down, and, crawling on hands and knees to the edge of the field, parted the grass and looked down.

Below us was a small valley with, on the far side, a steep grassy slope fringed on the side farthest from us by a dense growth of oak saplings. Beyond the saplings was the deep ravine in which the man-eater had eaten Dungar Singh's mother. The grassy slope was about thirty yards wide and below it was a rock cliff which, judging from the trees growing at the foot, was from eighty to a hundred feet high. On the near side of the slope was a terraced field, a hundred yards long and some ten yards wide. The field, which was in a straight line with us, had a small patch of short emerald-green grass at our end. On the remainder was a dense growth of an aromatic type of weed which grows to a height of four or five feet and has leaves like chrysanthemums, the undersides of which are white. Lying in brilliant sunlight on the patch of grass, and about ten feet apart, were two tigers.

The nearer tiger had its back to us with its head towards the hill, and the farther one had its stomach to us with its tail towards the hill. Both were fast asleep. The nearer offered the better shot, but I was afraid that on hearing the smack of the bullet the farther one would go straight down the hill into dense cover, in the direction in which its head was pointing. Whereas if I fired at the farther one first, the smack of the bullet—not to be confused with the crack of the rifle—would either drive the nearer one up the hill where there was less cover or else drive it towards me. So I decided to take the farther one first. The distance was approximately one hundred and twenty yards, and the angle of fire was not so steep that any allowance had to be made for the lift of the bullet, a point which has to be kept in mind when shooting downhill on the Himalayas. Resting the back of my hand on the edge of the field, to form a cushion, and holding the rifle steady, I took careful aim at where I thought the animal's heart would be and gently pressed the trigger. The tiger never moved a muscle, but the other one was up like a flash and in one bound landed on a five-foot-high bank of earth that divided the field from a rainwater channel. Here the second tiger stood, broadside on to me, looking back over its right shoulder at its companion. At my shot it reared up and fell over backwards into the rainwater channel, and out of sight.

After my second shot I saw a movement in the aromatic weeds which started close to where the dead tiger was lying. A big animal

was going at full gallop straight along the field. Having started from so close to where the two tigers had been lying, this third animal could only be another tiger. I could not see the animal, but I could follow its movements by the parting of the weeds, the leaves of which were white on the underside. Flicking up the two-hundred-yard leaf-sight I waited for the animal to break cover. Presently out on to the grassy slope dashed a tiger. I now noticed that the slope the tiger was on curved to the right, in the same way as the field I was lying on curved to the left. As the tiger was keeping to the contour of the hill this curve in the slope enabled me to get a near-broadside shot at it.

I have seen animals fall over at a shot, and I have seen them crumple up, but I have never seen an animal fall as convincingly dead as that tiger fell at my shot. For a few moments it lay motionless and then it started to slide down, feet foremost, gaining momentum as it went. Directly below it, and within a few feet of the brink of the rock cliff, was an oak sapling eight to ten inches thick. The tiger struck this sapling with its stomach and came to rest with its head and forelegs hanging down on side and its tail and hindlegs hanging down on the other. With rifle to shoulder and finger on trigger I waited, but there was not so much as a quiver in the tiger. Getting to my feet I beckoned to the *patwari*, who from his seat on the medlar tree had obtained a grandstand view of the whole proceedings. Dungar Singh, who had lain near me breathing in short gasps, was now dancing with excitement and from the way he was glancing at the tigers and then up at the crowd of people on the saddle, I knew he was thinking of the tale he would have to tell that night and for many moons thereafter.

When I saw the two tigers lying asleep I concluded that the man-eater had found a mate, but later, when my third shot flushed a third tiger, I knew I was dealing with a tigress and her two cubs. Which of the three was the mother and which the cubs it was not possible to say, for all three looked about the same size when I had viewed them over the sights of my rifle. That one of the three was the man-eater of Talla Des there could be no question, for tigers are scarce in the hills, and these three tigers had been shot close to where a human being had recently been killed and eaten. The cubs had died for the sins of their mother. They had undoubtedly eaten the human flesh their mother had provided for them from the time they were weaned; this, however, did not mean that when they left the protection of their mother they would have become man-eaters themselves. For in spite of all that has been said since *Man-eaters of Kumaon* was published I still maintain that the cubs of man-eating tigers—in that part of India about which I am writing—do not become man-eaters simply because they have eaten human flesh when young.

Sitting on the edge of the field with my feet dangling down and the rifle resting on my knees, I handed cigarettes to my companions and told them I would go and have a look at the tiger that had fallen into the rainwater channel, after we had finished our smoke. That I would find the tiger dead I had no doubt whatsoever; even so, nothing would be lost by waiting a few minutes, if for no other reason than to give myself a little time to rejoice over the marvellous luck I had met with. Within an hour of my arrival at Talla Des I had, quite by accident, got in touch with a man-eater that had terrorized an area of many hundreds of square miles for eight years, and in a matter of a few seconds had shot dead the man-eater and her two cubs. To the intense pleasure that all sportsmen feel at having held a rifle steady when every drop of blood in one's body is pounding with excitement, was added the pleasure and relief of knowing that there would be no necessity to follow up a wounded animal, a contingency that has to be faced when hunting tigers on foot.

My men would not ascribe my good fortune to luck. To avoid the possibility of failure they had consulted the old priest at the temple in Naini Tal and he had selected the propitious day for us to start on our journey to Talla Des, and evil omens when we started had been absent. My success would not be ascribed to good luck, therefore; nor, if I had failed to shoot the tigers, would my failure have been ascribed to bad luck, for no matter how well aimed a bullet might be it could do no harm to an animal whose time to die had not come. The superstitions of those whom I have been associated with on *shikar* have always been of interest to me. Being myself unwilling to begin a journey on a Friday, I am not inclined to laugh at a hillman's rooted aversion to begin a journey to the north on Tuesday or Wednesday, to the south on Thursday, to the east on Monday or Saturday, or to the west on Sunday or Friday. To permit those who accompany one on a dangerous mission to select the day for the start of the journey is a small matter, but it makes all the difference between having cheerful and contented companions and companions who are oppressed by a feeling of impending disaster.

The four of us sitting on the edge of the field had nearly finished our cigarettes, when I noticed that the tiger that was resting against the oak sapling was beginning to move. The blood from the body had evidently drained into the forward end of the animal, making that end heavier than the tail end, and it was now slowly slipping down head foremost. Once it was clear of the sapling the tiger glissaded down the grassy slope, and over the brink of the rock cliff. As it fell through space I threw up the rifle and fired. I fired that shot on the spur of the moment to give expression to my joy at the saucers of my mission to Talla Des, and also, I am ashamed to admit, to demonstrate that there was nothing—not even a tiger falling through space—that I could not hit on a day like this. A moment after the tiger disappeared among the tree tops, there was a rending of branches, followed by a dull and heavy thud. Whether or not I had hit the falling tiger did not matter, but what did matter was that the men of the village would have farther to carry it now than if it had remained on the slope.

My cigarette finished, I told my companions to sit still while I went down to look at the tiger in the rainwater channel. The hill was very steep and I had climbed down some fifty feet when Dungar Singh called out in a very agitated voice. 'Look, Sahib, look. There goes the tiger.' With my thoughts on the tiger below me, I sat down and raised my rifle to meet the charge I thought was coming. On seeing my preparations, the lad called out, 'Not here, but there, Sahib, there.' Relieved of the necessity of guarding my front I turned my head and looked at Dungar Singh and saw he was pointing across the main valley to the lower slopes of the hill on which his mother had been killed. At first I could see nothing, and then I caught sight of a tiger going diagonally up towards a ridge that ran out from the main hill. The tiger was very lame and could only take three or four steps at a time, and on its right shoulder was a big patch of blood. The patch of blood showed it was the tiger that had crashed through the trees, for the tiger that had fallen into the rainwater channel had been shot in the left shoulder.

Growing on the hill close to where I was sitting was a slender pine sapling. Putting up the three-hundred-yard leaf-sight I got a firm grip of the sapling with my left hand and resting the rifle on my wrist took a careful and an unhurried shot. The distance was close on four hundred yards and the tiger was on a slightly higher elevation than I was, so, taking a very full sight, I waited until it again came to a stand and then gently pressed the trigger. The bullet appeared to take an incredibly long time to cover the distance, but at last I saw a little puff of dust and at the same moment the tiger lurched forward, and then carried on with its slow walk. I had taken a little too full a sight, and the bullet had gone a shade too high. I now had the range to a nicety and all that I needed to kill the tiger was one more cartridge; the cartridge I had foolishly flung away when the tiger was falling through the air. With an empty rifle in my hands, I watched the tiger slowly and painfully climb to the ridge, hesitate for a few moments, and then disappear from view.

Sportsmen who have never shot in the Himalayas will

question my wisdom in having armed myself with a light .275 rifle, and only carrying five rounds of ammunition. My reasons for having done so were:

(a) The rifle was one I had used for over twenty years, and with which I was familiar.

(b) It was light to carry, accurate, and sighted up to three hundred yards.

(c) I had been told by Colonel Barber to avoid using a heavy rifle, and not to fire more shots than were necessary with a light one.

With regard to ammunition, I had not set out that morning to shoot tigers but to find the village where the last human kill had taken place and, if I had the time, to tie out a young buffalo as bait. As it turned out, both the light rifle and the five rounds would have served my purpose if I had not thrown away that vital round.

My men arrived at the village in time to join the crowd on the saddle, and to witness the whole proceedings. They knew that the five rounds in the magazine of the rifle were all the ammunition I had with me, and when after my fifth shot they saw the wounded tiger disappear over the ridge, Madho Singh came tearing down the hill with a fresh supply of ammunition.

The tiger on the patch of green grass, and the tiger in the rainwater channel—which I found lying dead where it had fallen—were both nearly full-grown, and the one that had got away wounded was quite evidently their mother, the man-eater of Talla Des. Leaving Madho Singh and Dungar Singh to make arrangements for the cubs to be carried up to the village, I set out alone to try to get in touch with the wounded tigress. From the bed of bracken on to which she had fallen after crashing through the trees, I followed a light blood-trail to where she had been standing when I fired my last shot. Here I found a few cut hairs clipped from her back by my bullet, and a little extra blood which had flowed from her wound when she lurched forward on hearing my bullet strike the ground above her. From this spot to the ridge there was only an occasional drop of blood, and on the short stiff grass beyond the ridge I lost the trail. Close by was a dense patch of scrub, a hundred yards wide, extending up the side of a steep hill for three hundred yards, and I suspected that the tigress had taken shelter in this scrub. But as night was now closing in and there was not sufficient light for accurate shooting, I decided to return to the village and leave the searching of the scrub until the following day.

5

The next morning was spent in skinning the cubs and in pegging out their skins with the six-inch nails I had brought with me from Naini Tal. While I was performing this task at least a hundred vultures alighted on the trees fringing the open ground on which my tent was pitched. It was these that brought to light the missing clothes of the man-eater's victim, for the cubs had torn the blood-soaked garments into strips and swallowed them.

The men of the village sat round me while I was skinning the cubs and I told them I wanted them to assist my Garhwalis in beating out the patch of scrub in which I thought the wounded tigress had taken shelter. This they were very willing to do. At about midday we set off, the men going through the village and along the saddle to the top of the hill above the cover, while I went down the goat track into the valley and up to the ridge over which I had followed the tigress the previous evening. At the lower edge of the scrub there was an enormous boulder—from which I was visible to the men at the top of the hill—I waved my hat as a signal for them to start the beat. To avoid the risk of anyone getting mauled, I had instructed the men to stay on the top of the hill and, after clapping their hands and shooting, to roll rocks down the hillside into the scrub I have spoken of. One *kakar* and a few *kalege* pheasants came out of the bushes, but nothing else. When the rocks had searched out every foot of the ground, I again waved my hat as a signal for the men to stop the beat and return to the village.

When the men had gone I searched the cover, but without any hope of finding the tigress. As I watched her going up the hill the previous evening I could see that she was suffering from a very painful wound, and when I examined the blood where she had lurched forward, I knew the wound was a surface one and not internal. Why then had the tigress fallen to my bullet as if poleaxed, and why had she hung suspended from the oak sapling for a matter of ten to fifteen minutes without showing any signs of life? To these questions I could not at the time nor can I now find any reasonable answer. Later I found my soft-nose, nickel-encased bullet firmly fixed in the ball-and-socket joint of the right shoulder. When the flight of a high-velocity bullet is arrested by impact with a bone the resulting shock to an animal is very considerable. Even so, a tiger is a heavy animal with a tremendous amount of vitality, and why a light .275 bullet should knock such an animal flat and render it unconscious for ten or fifteen minutes is to me inexplicable. Returning to the ridge, I stood and surveyed the country. The ridge appeared to be many miles long and divided two valleys. The valley to the left at the upper end of which was the patch of scrub was open grass country, while the valley to the right at the upper end of which the tigers had eaten the woman had dense tree and scrub jungle on the right-hand side, and a steep shaly slope edging in a rock cliff on the left.

Sitting down on a rock on the ridge to have a quiet smoke, I reviewed the events of the previous evening, and came to the following conclusions:

(a) From the time the tigress fell to my shot to the time she crashed through the trees, she had been unconscious.

(b) Her fall, cushioned by the trees and the bed of bracken, had restored consciousness but had left her dazed.

(c) In this dazed condition she had just followed her nose and on coming up against the hill she had climbed it without knowing where she was going.

The question that now faced me was: How far and in what direction had the tigress gone? Walking downhill with an injured leg is far more painful than walking uphill and as soon as the tigress recovered from her dazed condition she would stop going downhill and would make for cover in which to nurse her injury. To get to cover she would have to cross the ridge, so the obvious thing was to try to find out if she had done so. The task of finding if a soft-footed animal had crossed a ridge many miles long would have been a hopeless one if the ridge had not had a knife-edge. Running along the top was a game track, with an ideal surface for recording the passages of all the animals that used it. On the left of the track was a grassy slope and on the right a steep shale scree ending in a sheer drop into the ravine below.

Finishing my smoke I set off along the game track on which I found the tracks of *ghooral*, *sarao*, *sambhar*, *langur*, porcupine, and the pug-marks of a male leopard. The farther I went the more despondent I grew, for I knew that if I did not find the tigress's pug-marks on this track there was little hope of my ever seeing her again. I had gone about a mile along the ridge, disturbing two *ghooral* who bounded away down the grassy slope to the left, when I found the pug-marks of the tigress, and a spot of dry blood. Quite evidently, after disappearing from my view over the ridge the previous evening, the tigress had gone straight down the grassy slope until she recovered form her dazed condition and then had kept to the contour of the hill, which brought her to the game track. For half a mile I followed her pug-marks to where the shale scree narrowed to about fifteen yards. Here the tigress attempted to go down the scree, evidently with the intention of gaining the shelter of the jungle on the far side of the ravine. Whether her injured leg failed her or whether dizziness overcame her, I do not know; anyway, after falling forward and sliding head-foremost for a few yards she turned round and with legs widespread clawed the ground in a desperate but vain effort to avoid going over the sheer drop into the ravine below. I am as sure-footed as a goat, but that scree was far too difficult for me to attempt to negotiate, so I carried on along the track for a few hundred yards until I came to a rift in the hill. Down this rift I climbed into the ravine.

As I walked up the thirty-yard-wide ravine I noted that the rock cliff below the shale scree was from sixty to eighty feet high. No animal, I was convinced, could fall that distance on to rocks without being killed. On approaching the spot where the tigress had fallen I was overjoyed to see the white underside of a big animal. My joy, however, was short lived, for I found the animal was a *sarao* and not the tigress. The *sarao* had evidently been lying asleep on a narrow ledge near the top of the cliff and, on being awakened by hearing, and possibly scenting, the tigress above him, had lost his nerve and jumped down, breaking his neck on the rocks at the foot of the cliff. Close to where the *sarao* had fallen there was a small patch of loose sand. On this the tigress had landed without doing herself any harm beyond tearing open the wound in her shoulder. Ignoring the dead *sarao*, within a yard of which she passed, the tigress crossed the ravine, leaving a well-defined blood trail. The bank on the right-hand side of the ravine was only a few feet high, and several times the tigress tried but failed to climb it. I knew now that I would find her in the first bit of cover she could reach. But my luck was out. For some time heavy clouds had been massing overhead, and before I found where the tigress had left the ravine a deluge of rain came on, washing out the blood trail. The evening was now well advanced and as I had a long and a difficult way to go, I turned and made for camp.

Luck plays an important part in all sport, and the tigress had—so far—had her full share of it. First, instead of lying out in the open with her cubs where I would have been able to recognize her for what she was, she was lying out of sight in thick cover. Then, the flight of my bullet had been arrested by striking the one bone that was capable of preventing it from inflicting a fatal wound. Later the tigress had twice fallen down a rock cliff, where she would undoubtedly have been killed had her fall in the one case not been cushioned by branches and a bed of bracken and in the other by a soft patch of sand. And finally, when I was only a hundred yards from where she was lying up, the rain came down and washed out the blood trail. However, I too

had had a measure of luck, for my fear that the tigress would wander away down the greasy slope where I would lose touch with her had not been realized, and, further, I knew now where to look for her.

6

Next morning I returned to the ravine, accompanied by my six Garhwalis. Throughout Kumaon the flesh of *sarao* is considered a great delicacy, and as the young animal that had broken its neck was in prime condition, it would provide a very welcome meat ration for my men. Leaving the men to skin the *sarao*, I went to the spot from where I had turned back the previous evening. Here I found that two deep and narrow ravines ran up the face of the hill on the right. As it was possible that the tigress had gone up one of these, I tried the nearer one first only to find, after I had gone up it for a few hundred yards, that the sides were too steep for any tiger to climb, and that it ended in what in the monsoon rains must have been a thirty-foot-high waterfall. Returning to my starting point I called out to the men, who were about fifty yards away up the main ravine, to light a fire and boil a kettle of water for my tea. I then turned to examine the second ravine and as I did so I noticed a well-used game track coming down the hill on the left-hand side. On the game track I found the pug-marks of the tigress, partly obliterated by the rain of the previous evening. Close to where I was standing was a big rock. On approaching this rock I saw that there was a little depression on the far side. The dead leaves in the depression had been flattened down, and on them were big clots of blood. After her fall into the ravine—which may have been forty hours earlier—the tigress had come to this spot and had only moved off on hearing me call to the men to boil the kettle for tea.

Owing to differences in temperament it is not possible to predict what a wounded tiger will do when approached by a human being on foot, nor is it possible to fix a period during which a wounded tiger can be considered as being dangerous—

that is liable to charge when disturbed. I have seen a tiger with an inch-long cut in a hind pad, received while running away, charge full out from a distance of a hundred yards five minutes after receiving the wound; and I have seen a tiger that had been nursing a very painful jaw wound for many hours allow an approach to within a few feet without making any attempt to attack. Where a wounded man-eating tiger is concerned the situation is a little complicated, for, apart from not knowing whether the wounded animal will attack on being approached, there is the possibility—when the wound is not an internal one—of its attacking to provide itself with food. Tigers, except when wounded or when man-eaters, are on the whole very good-tempered. Were this not so it would not be possible for thousands of people to work as they do in tiger-infested jungles, nor would it have been possible for people like me to have wandered for years through the jungles on foot without coming to any harm. Occasionally a tiger will object to too close an approach to its cubs or to a kill that it is guarding. The objection invariably takes the form of growling, and if this does not prove effective it is followed by short rushes accompanied by terrifying roars. If these warnings are disregarded, the blame for any injury inflicted rests entirely with the intruder. The following experience with which I met some years ago is a good example of my assertion that tigers are good-tempered. My sister Maggie and I were fishing one evening on the Boar river three miles from our home at Kaladhungi. I had caught two small *mahseer* and was sitting on a rock smoking when Geoff Hopkins, who later became Conservator of Forests, Uttar Pradesh, turned up on his elephant. He was expecting friends, and being short of meat he had gone out with a .240 rook-rifle to try to shoot a *kakar* or a peafowl. I had caught all the fish we needed, so we fell in with Geoff's suggestion that we should accompany him and help him to find the game he was looking for. Mounting the elephant we crossed the river and I directed the *mahout* to a part of the jungle where kakar and peafowl were to be found. We were going through short grass and plum jungle when I caught sight of a dead *cheetal* lying under a tree. Stopping the elephant I slipped to the ground and went to see what had killed the *cheetal*. She was an old hind that had been dead for twenty-four hours, and as I could find no marks of injury on her I concluded that she had died of snake-bite. As I turned to rejoin the elephant I saw a drop of fresh blood on a leaf. The shape of the drop of blood showed that the animal from which it had come had been moving away from the dead *cheetal*. Looking a little farther in the direction in which the splash from the blood indicated the animal had gone, I saw another spot of blood. Puzzled by this fresh blood-trail I set off to see where it led to, and signalled to the elephant to follow me. After going over short grass for sixty or seventy yards the trail led towards a line of thick bushes some five feet high. Going up to the bushes where the trail ended I stretched out both arms—I had left my rod on the elephant—and parted the bushes wide, and there under my outstretched hands was a *cheetal* stag with horns in velvet, and lying facing me and eating the stag was a tiger. As I parted the bushes the tiger looked up and the expression on its face said, as clearly as any words, 'Well, I'll be damned!' Which was exactly what I was saying to myself. Fortunately I was so surprised that I remained perfectly still— possibly because my heart had stopped beating—and after looking straight into my face for a moment the tiger, who was close enough to have stretched out a paw and stroked my head, rose, turned, and sprang into the bushes behind him all in one smooth graceful movement. The tiger had killed the stag among the plum bushes shortly before our arrival, and in taking it to cover he went past the dead hind, leaving the blood trail that I followed. The three on the elephant did not see the tiger until he was in the air, when the *mahout* exclaimed with horror, '*Khabardar*, Sahib. *Sher hai*.' He was telling me that it was a tiger and to be careful.

Rejoining my men I drank a cup of tea while they cut up the *sarao* into convenient bits to carry, and returned with them to the depression in which I had found the clots of blood. All six men had been out on *shikar* with me on many occasions, and on seeing the quantity of blood they were of the opinion that the tigress had a body wound which would prove fatal in a matter of hours. On this point we were not in agreement, for I knew the wound was a superficial one from which the tigress, given time, would recover, and that the longer she lived the more difficult it would be to get in touch with her.

If you can imagine a deep and narrow ravine running up the face of a steep hill with the ground on the right sloping towards the ravine and well wooded but free of undergrowth, and the ground on the left-hand side of the ravine sloping upwards and covered with dense patches of *ringal* (stunted bamboo), bracken, and brushwood of all kinds, you will have some idea of the country my men and I worked over for the rest of that day.

My plan was for the men to go up on the right-hand side of the ravine, to keep me in sight by climbing into the highest trees they could find, and, if they wished to attract my attention, to whistle—hillmen, like some boys, are very good at whistling through their teeth. They would be in no danger from the tigress, for there was no cover on their side, and all of them were expert tree-climbers. The tracks of the tigress after she left the depression near the big rock showed that she had gone up the hill on the left-hand side of the ravine. Up this hill I now started to follow her.

I have emphasized elsewhere that jungle lore is not a science that can be learnt from textbooks, but that it can be absorbed a little at a time, and that the absorption process can go on indefinitely. The same applies to tracking. Tracking, because of its infinite variations, is one of the most interesting forms of sport I know and it can, at times, be also the most exciting. There are two generally accepted methods of tracking. One, following a trail on which there is blood, and the other, following a trail on which there is no blood. In addition to these two methods I have also at times been able to find a wounded animal by following blowflies, or by following meat-eating birds. Of the two generally accepted methods, following a blood-trail is the more sure way of finding a wounded animal. But as wounds do not always bleed, wounded animals have at times to be tracked by their foot-prints or by the disturbance to vegetation caused by their passage. Tracking can be easy or difficult according to the nature of the ground, and also according to whether the animal being tracked has hard hooves or soft pads. When the tigress left the depression—on hearing me calling to my men—her wound had stopped bleeding and the slight discharge that was coming from the wound owing to its having turned septic was not sufficient to enable me to follow her, so I had to resort to tracking her by her foot-prints and by disturbed vegetation. This, on the ground I was on, would not be difficult, but it would be slow, and time was on the side of the tigress. For the longer the trail the better the chances would be of her recovering from her wound and the less chance there would be of my finding her, for the strain of the past few days was now beginning to tell on me.

For the first hundred yards the trail led through knee-high bracken. Here tracking was easy, for the tigress had kept to a more or less straight line. Beyond the bracken was a dense thicket of *ringal*. I felt sure the tigress would be lying up in this thicket, but unless she charged there was little hope of my getting a shot at her, for it was not possible to move silently through the matted *ringals*. When I was halfway through the thicket a *kakar* started barking. The tigress was on the move, but instead of going straight up the hill she had gone out on the left, apparently on to open ground, for the *kakar* was standing still and barking. Retracing my steps I worked round to the left but found no open ground in that direction, nor did I appear to be getting any nearer the barking deer. The *kakar*, soon after, stopped barking and a number of *kalege* pheasants started chattering. The tigress was still on the move, but, turn my head as I would, I could not locate the sound.

Pin-pointing, that is fixing the exact direction and distance of all sounds heard, is a jungle accomplishment which I have reduced to a fine art and of which I am very proud. Now, for the first time, I realized with a shock that my accident had deprived me of this accomplishment and that no longer would I be able to depend on my ears for safety and for the pleasure of listening intimately to the jungle folk whose language it had taken me years to learn. Had my remaining ear been sound it would not have mattered so much, but unfortunately the drum of that ear also had been injured by a gun 'accident' many years previously. Well, there was nothing that could be done about it now, and handicapped though I was I was not going to admit at this stage of the proceedings that any tiger, man-eater or other, had any advantage over me when we were competing for each other's lives under conditions that favoured neither side.

Returning to the bracken, I started to try to find the tigress, depending on my eyes only. The jungle appeared to be well stocked with game, and I repeatedly heard *sambhar*, *kakar*, and *langur* giving their alarm calls, and more than once I heard pheasants, jays, and white-capped laughing thrush mobbing the tigress. Paying no attention to these sounds, which ordinarily I would have listened for eagerly, I tracked the tigress foot by foot as, resting frequently, she made her way up the hill, at times in a straight line and at times zigzagging from cover to cover. Near the top of the hill was a stretch of short stiff grass about a hundred yards wide. Beyond this open ground were two patches of dense brushwood divided by a narrow lane which ran up to the top of the hill. On the short stiff grass I lost the tracks. The tigress knew she was being closely followed and would therefore expose herself as little as possible. The patch of brushwood to my right front was thirty yards nearer than the patch to the left, so I decided to try it first. When I was within a yard or two of the cover I heard a dry stick snap under the weight of some heavy animal. I was positive on this occasion that the sound had come from the left, so I turned and went to the patch of brushwood from which the sound appeared to have come. This was the second mistake I made that day—the first was calling to my men to boil the kettle for tea—for my men told me later that I crossed the open stretch of ground on the heels of the tigress, and that when I turned and walked away to the left she was lying on an open bit of ground a few yards inside the bushes, evidently waiting for me.

Finding no trace of the tigress in the brushwood on the left I came back to the open ground, and, on hearing my men whistling, looked in the direction in which I expected them to be. They had climbed to the top of a tree a few hundred yards to my right, and when I lifted my hand to indicate that I had seen them, they waved me up, up, up, and then down, down, down. They were letting me know that the tigress had climbed to the top of the hill, and that she had gone down on the far side. Making what speed I could I went up the narrow lane and on reaching the top found an open hillside. On this the grass had been burnt recently, and in the ashes, which were still damp from the rain of the previous evening, I found the pug-marks of the tigress. The hill sloped gently down to a stream, the one that I had crossed several miles higher up on the day of my arrival at Talla Kote. After lying down and quenching her thirst the tigress had crossed the stream and gone up into the thick jungle beyond. It was now getting late, so I retraced my steps to the top of the hill and beckoned to my men to join me.

From the big rock where I took up the tracks of the tigress to the stream where I left them was only some four miles, and it had taken me seven hours to cover the distance. Though it had ended in failure the day had been an interesting and exciting one. Not only for me who, while doing the tracking, had to avoid being ambushed by a wounded man-eating tiger, but also for my Garhwalis who by climbing trees had kept both the tigress and myself in view most of the time. And it had been a long day also, for we had started at daylight, and it was 8 p.m. when we got back to camp.

7

The following morning while my men were having their food I attended to the skins, re-pegging them on fresh ground and rubbing wood ashes and powdered alum on the damp parts. Tiger skins need a lot of care, for if every particle of fat is not removed and the lips, ears, and pads properly treated, the hair slips, ruining the skin. A little before midday I was ready to start, and accompanied by four of my men—I left the other two men in camp to attend to the *sarao's* skin—I set out for the place where I had stopped tracking the tigress the previous evening.

The Valley through which the stream flowed was wide and comparatively flat, and ran from west to east. On the left-hand side of the valley was the hill on the far side of which I had followed the tigress the previous day, and on the right-hand side was the hill along which ran the road to Tanakpur. Before the advent of the man-eater the valley between these two hills had been extensively grazed over by the cattle of Talla Kote, and in consequence the ground was criss-crossed by a maze of cattle paths, and cut up with narrow eroded water-channels. Dotted about the valley were open glades of varying sizes surrounded by dense scrub and tree jungle. Good ground on which to hunt *sambhar*, *kakar*, and bear, all of whose tracks were to be seen on the cattle paths, but not the ground one would select on which to hunt a man-eating tiger. The hill on the left commanded an extensive view of the valley, so I spaced my men in trees along the crest at intervals of two hundred yards to keep a look-out and to be on hand in case they were needed. I then went down to the spot where I had left the tracks of the tigress the previous evening.

I had wounded the tigress on 7 April, and it was now the

10th. As a general rule a tiger is not considered to be dangerous—that is, liable to charge at sight—twenty-four hours after being wounded. A lot depends on the nature of the wound, however, and on the temper of the wounded individuals. Twenty-four hours after receiving a light flesh wound a tiger usually moves away on being approached, whereas a tiger with a painful body-wound might continue to be dangerous for several days. I did not know the nature of the wound the tigress was suffering from, and as she had made no attempt to attack me the previous day I believed I could now ignore the fact that she was wounded and look upon her only as a man-eater, and a very hungry man-eater at that, for she had eaten nothing since killing the woman whom she had shared with the cubs.

Where the tigress had crossed the stream there was a channel, three feet wide and two feet deep, washed out by rainwater. Up this channel, which was bordered by dense brushwood, the tigress had gone. Following her tracks I came to a cattle path. Here she had left the channel and gone along the path to the right. Three hundred yards along was a tree with heavy foliage and under this tree the tigress had lain all night. Her wound had troubled her and she had tossed about, but on the leaves on which she had been lying there was neither blood nor any discharge from her wound. From this point on I followed her fresh tracks, taking every precaution not to walk into an ambush. By evening I had tracked her for several miles along cattle paths, water channels, and game tracks, without having set eyes on so much as the tip of the her tail. At sunset I collected my men, and as we returned to camp they told me they had been able to follow the movements of the tigress through the jungle by the animals and birds that had called at her, but that they too had seen nothing of her.

When hunting unwounded man-eating tigers the greatest danger, when walking into the wind, is of an attack from behind, and to a lesser extent from either side. When the wind is from behind, the danger is from either side. In the same way, if the wind is blowing from the right the danger is from the left and from behind, and if blowing from the left the danger is from the right and from behind. In none of these cases is there any appreciable danger of an attack from in front, for in my experience all unwounded tigers, whether man-eaters or not, are disinclined to make a head-on attack. Under normal conditions man-eating tigers limit the range of their attack to the distance they can spring, and for this reason they are more difficult to cope with than wounded tigers, who invariably launch an attack from a little distance, maybe only ten or twenty yards, but possibly as much as a hundred yards. This means that whereas the former have to be dealt with in a matter of split seconds, the latter give one time to raise a rifle and align the sights. In either case it means rapid shooting and a fervent prayer that an ounce or two of lead will stop a few hundred pounds of muscle and bone.

In the case of the tigress I was hunting, I knew that her wound would not admit of her springing and that if I kept out of her reach I would be comparatively safe. The possibility that she had recovered from her wound in the four days that had elapsed since I had last seen her had, however, to be taken into account. When therefore I started out alone on the morning of 11 April to take up the tracks where I had left them the previous evening, I resolved to keep clear of any rock, bush, tree, or other object behind which the tigress might be lying up in wait for me.

She had been moving the previous evening in the direction of the Tanakpur road. I again found where she had spent the night, this time on a soft bed of dry grass, and from this point I followed her fresh tracks. Avoiding dense cover—possibly because she could not move through it silently—she was keeping to water channels and game tracks and it became apparent that she was not moving about aimlessly but was looking for something to kill and eat. Presently, in one of these water channels she found and killed a few-weeks-old *kakar*. She had come on the young deer as it was lying asleep in the sun on a bed of sand, and had eaten every scrap of it, rejecting nothing but the tiny hooves. I was now only a minute or two behind her, and knowing that the morsel would have done no more than whet her appetite, I redoubled my precautions. In places the channels and game tracks to which the tigress was keeping twisted and turned and ran through dense cover or past rocks. Had my condition been normal I would have followed on her footsteps and possibly been able to catch up with her, but unfortunately I was far from normal. The swelling on my head, face, and neck, had now increased to such proportions that I was no longer able to move my head up or down or from side to side, and my left eye was closed. However, I still had one good eye, fortunately my right one, and I could still hear a little.

During the whole of that day I followed the tigress without seeing her and without, I believe, her seeing me. Where she had gone along water channels, game tracks, or cattle paths that ran through dense cover I skirted round the cover and picked up her pug-marks on the far side. Not knowing the ground was a very great handicap, for not only did it necessitate walking more miles than I need have done, but it also prevented my anticipating the movements of the tigress and ambushing her. When I finally gave up the chase for the day, the tigress was moving up the valley in the direction of the village.

Back in camp I realized that the 'bad time' I had foreseen and dreaded was approaching. Electric shocks were stabbing through the enormous abscess, and the hammer blows were increasing in intensity. Sleepless nights and a diet of tea had made a coward of me, and I could not face the prospect of sitting on my bed through another long night, racked with pain and waiting for something, I knew not what, to happen. I had come to Talla Des to try to rid the hill people of the terror that menaced them and to tide over my bad time, and all that I had accomplished so far was to make their condition worse. Deprived of the ability to secure her natural prey, the tigress, who in eight years had only killed a hundred and fifty people would now, unless she recovered from her wound, look to her easiest prey—human beings—to provide her with most of the food she needed. There was therefore an account to be settled between the tigress and myself, and that night was as suitable a time as any to settle it.

Calling for a cup of tea—made hill-fashion with milk—which served me as dinner, I drank it while standing in the moonlight. Then, calling my eight men together, I instructed them to wait for me in the village until the following evening, and if I did not return by then to pack up my things and start early the next morning for Naini Tal. Having done this I picked up my rifle from where I put it on my bed, and headed down the valley. My men, all of whom had been with me for years, said not a word either to ask me where I was going or to try to dissuade me from going. They just stood silent in a group and watched me walk away. Maybe the glint I saw on their cheeks was only imagination, or maybe it was only the reflection of the moon. Anyway, when I looked back not a man had moved. They were just standing in a group as I had left them.

8

One of my most pleasant recollections—of the days when I was young—are the moonlight walks along forest roads that ten or a dozen of us used to take during the winter months, and the high teas we consumed on our return home. These walks tended to dispel all the fears that assail a human being in a forest at night, and, further, they made us familiar with the sounds to be heard in a forest by night. Later, years of experience added to my confidence and to my knowledge. When therefore I left my camp on the night of 11 April—in brilliant moonlight—to try conclusions with the Talla Des man-eating tigress, I did not set out with any feeling of inferiority on what might appear to have been a suicidal quest.

I have been interested in tigers from as far back as I can

remember, and having spent most of my life in an area in which they were plentiful I have had ample opportunities of observing them. My ambition when I was very young was to see a tiger, just that, and no more. Later my ambition was to shoot a tiger, and this I accomplished on foot with an old army rifle which I bought for fifty rupees from a seafaring man, who I am inclined to think had stolen it and converted it into a sporting rifle. Later still, it was my ambition to photograph a tiger. In the course of time all three of these ambitions were fulfilled. It was while trying to photograph tigers that I learnt the little I know about them. Having been favoured by Government with the 'freedom of the forests', a favour which I very greatly appreciate and which I shared with only one other sportsman in India, I was able to move about without let or hindrance in those forests in which tigers were most plentiful. Watching tigers for days or weeks on end, and on one occasion for four and a half months, I was able to learn a little about their habits and in particular their method of approaching and of killing their victims. A tiger does not run down its prey; it either lies in wait or stalks it. In either case contact with its victim is made by a single spring, or by a rush of a few yards followed by a spring. If therefore an animal avoids passing within striking distance of a tiger, avoids being stalked, and reacts instantly to danger whether conveyed by sight, scent, or by hearing, it has a reasonable chance of living to an old age. Civilization has deprived human beings of the keen sense of scent and hearing enjoyed by animals, and when a human being is menaced by a man-eating tiger he has to depend for his safety almost entirely on sight. When restlessness and pain compelled me to be on the move that night, I was handicapped to the extent that I only had one effective eye. But against this handicap was the knowledge that the tigress could do me no harm if I kept out of her reach, whereas I could kill her at a distance. My instructions therefore to my men to go back to Naini Tal if I thought I could not cope with the tigress, but because I failed to return by the following evening were not given since I feared there was a possibility of my becoming unconscious and unable to defend myself.

One of the advantages of making detailed mental maps of ground covered is that finding the way back to any given spot presents no difficulty. Picking up the pug-marks of my quarry where I had left them, I resumed my tracking, which was now only possible on game tracks and on cattle paths, to which the tigress was, fortunately, keeping. *Sambhar* and *kakar* had now come out to the open glades, some to feed and others for protection, and though I could not pin-point their alarm calls they let me know when the tigress was on the move and gave me a rough idea of the direction in which she was moving.

On a narrow, winding cattle path running through dense cover I left the pug-marks of the tigress and worked around through scattered brushwood to try to pick them up on the far side. The way round was longer than I had anticipated, and I eventually came out on an open stretch of ground with short grass and dotted about with big oak trees. Here I came to a halt in the shadow of a big tree. Presently, by a movement of this shadow, I realized that the tree above me was tenanted by a troop of *langurs*. I had covered a lot of ground during the eighteen hours I had been on my feet that day, and here now was safe place for me to rest awhile, for the *langurs* above would give warning of danger. Sitting with my back against the tree and facing the cover round which I had skirted, I had been resting for half an hour when an old *langur* gave his alarm call; the tigress had come out into the open and the *langur* had caught sight of her. Presently I too, caught sight of the tigress just as she started to lie down.

She was a hundred yards to my right and ten yards from the cover, and she lay down broadside on to me with her head turned looking up at the calling *langur*.

I have had a lot of practice in night shooting, for during the winter months I assisted our tenants at Kaladhungi to protect their crops against marauding animals such as pig and deer. On a clear moonlit night I can usually count on hitting an animal up to a range of about a hundred yards. Like most people who have taught themselves to shoot, I keep both eyes open when shooting. This enables me to keep the target in view with one eye, while aligning the sights of the rifle with the other. At any other time I would have waited for the tigress to stand up and then fired at her, but unfortunately my left eye was now closed and a hundred yards was too far to risk a shot with only one eye. On the two previous nights the tigress had lain in the one spot and had possibly slept most of the night, and she might do the same now. If she lay right down on her side—she was now lying on her stomach with her head up—and went to sleep I could either go back to the cattle path on which I had left her pug-marks and follow her tracks to the edge of the cover and get to within ten yards of her, or I could creep up to her over the open ground until I got close enough to make sure of my shot. Anyway, for the present I could do nothing but sit perfectly still until the tigress made up her mind what she was going to do.

For a long time, possibly half an hour or a little longer, the tigress lay in one position, occasionally moving her head from side to side, while the old *langur* in a sleepy voice continued to give his alarm call. Finally she got to her feet and very slowly and very painfully started to walk away to my right. Directly in the line in which she was going there was an open ravine ten to fifteen feet deep and twenty to twenty-five yards wide, which I had crossed lower down when coming to the spot where I now was. When the tigress had increased the distance between us to a hundred and fifty yards, and the chances of her seeing me had decreased, I started to follow her. Slipping from tree to tree, and moving a little faster than she, I reduced her lead to fifty yards by the time she reached the edge of the ravine. She was now in range, but was standing in shadow, and her tail end was a very small mark to fire at. For a long and anxious minute she stood in the one position and then, having made up her mind to cross the ravine, very gently went over the edge.

As the tigress disappeared from view I bent down and ran forward on silent feet. Bending my head down and running was a very stupid mistake for me to have made, and I had only run a few yards when I was overcome by vertigo. Near me were two oak saplings, a few feet apart and with inter-laced branches. Laying down my rifle I climbed up the saplings to a height of ten or twelve feet. Here I found a branch to sit on, another for my feet, and yet other small branches for me to rest against. Crossing my arms on the branches in front of me, I laid my head on them, and at that moment the abscess burst, not into my brain as I feared it would, but out through my nose and left ear.

'No greater happiness can man know, than the sudden cessation of great pain,' was said by someone who had suffered and suffered greatly, and who knew the happiness of sudden relief. It was round about midnight when relief came to me, and the grey light was just beginning to show in the east when I raised my head from my crossed arms. Cramp in my legs resulting from my having sat on a thin branch for four hours had roused me, and for a little while I did not know where I was or what had happened to me. Realization was not long in coming. The great swelling on my head, face, and neck had gone and with it had gone the pain. I could now move my head as I liked, my left eye was open, and I could swallow without discomfort. I had lost an opportunity of shooting the tigress, but what did that matter now, for I was over my bad time and no matter where or how for the tigress went I would follow her, and sooner or later I would surely get another chance.

When I last saw the tigress she was heading in the direction of the village. Swinging down from the saplings, up which I had

climbed with such difficulty, I retrieved my rifle and headed in the same direction. At the stream I stopped and washed and cleaned myself and my clothes as best I could. My men had not spent the night in the village as I had instructed them to, but had sat round a fire near my tent keeping a kettle of water on the boil. As, dripping with water, they saw me coming towards them they sprang up with a glad cry of 'Sahib! Sahib! You have come back, and you are well.' 'Yes,' I answered, 'I have come back, and I am now well.' When an Indian gives his loyalty, he gives it unstintingly and without counting the cost. When we arrived at Talla Kote the headman put two rooms at the disposal of my men, for it was dangerous to sleep anywhere except behind locked doors. On this my bad night, and fully alive to the danger, my men had sat out in the open in case they could be of any help to me, and to keep a kettle on the boil for my tea—if I should return. I cannot remember if I drank the tea, but I can remember my shoes being drawn off by willing hands, and a rug spread over me as I lay down on my bed.

Hours and hours of peaceful sleep, and then a dream. Someone was urgently calling me, and someone was as urgently saying I must not be disturbed. Over and over again the dream was repeated with slight variations, but with no less urgency, until the words penetrated through the fog of sleep and became a reality. 'You *must* wake him or he will be very angry.' And the rejoinder, 'We will *not* wake him for he is very tired.' Ganga Ram was the last speaker, so I called out and told him to bring the man to me. In a minute my tent was besieged by an excited throng of men and boys all eager to tell me that the man-eater had just killed six goats on the far side of the village. While pulling on my shoes I looked over the throng and on seeing

Dungar Singh, the lad who was with me when I shot the cubs, I asked him if he knew where the goats had been killed and if he could take me to the spot. 'Yes, yes,' he answered eagerly, 'I know where they were killed and I can take you there.' Telling the headman to keep the crowd back, I armed myself with my .275 rifle and, accompanied by Dungar Singh, set off through the village.

My sleep had refreshed me, and as there was now no need for me to put my feet down gently—to avoid jarring my head— I was able, for the first time in weeks, to walk freely and without discomfort.

### 9

The day I arrived at Talla Kote, Dungar Singh, the lad who was with me now, had taken me through the village to a narrow saddle from where there was an extensive view into two valleys. The valley to the right fell steeply away in the direction of the Kali river. At the upper end of this valley I had shot the cubs and wounded the tigress. The other valley, the one to the left, was less steep and from the saddle a goat track ran down into it. It was in this valley that the goats had been killed. Down the goat track the lad now started to run, with me close on his heels. After winding down over steep and broken ground for five or six hundred yards, the track crossed a stream and then continued down the valley on the left bank. Close to where the track crossed the stream there was an open bit of comparatively flat ground. Running from left to right across this open ground was a low ridge of rock, on the far side of which was a little hollow, and lying in the hollow were three goats.

On the way down the hill the lad had told me that round about midday a large flock of goats in charge of ten or fifteen boys was feeding in the hollow, when a tiger—which they suspected was the man-eater—suddenly appeared among them and struck down six goats. On seeing the tiger the boys started yelling and were joined by some men collecting firewood near by. In the general confusion of goats dashing about and human beings yelling, the tiger moved off and no one appeared to have seen in which direction it went. Grabbing hold of three dead goats the men and boys dashed back to the village to give me the news, leaving three goats with broken backs in the hollow.

That the killer of the goats was the wounded man-eater there could be no question, for when I last saw her the previous night she was going straight towards the village. Further, my men told me that an hour or so before my return to camp a *kakar* had barked near the stream, a hundred yards from where they were sitting, and thinking that the animal had barked on seeing me they had built up the fire. It was fortunate that they had done so, for I later found the pug-marks of the tigress where she had skirted round the fire and had then gone through the village, obviously with the object of securing a human victim. Having failed in her quest she had evidently taken cover near the village, and at the first opportunity of securing food had struck down the goats. This she had done in a matter of seconds, while suffering from a wound that made her limp badly.

As I was not familiar with the ground, I asked Dungar Singh in which direction he thought the tigress had gone. Pointing down the valley he said she had probably gone in that direction, for there was heavy jungle farther down. While I was questioning him about this jungle, with the idea of going down and looking for the tigress, a *kalege* pheasant started chattering. On hearing this the lad turned round and looked up the hill, giving me an indication of the direction in which the bird was calling. To our left the hill went up steeply, and growing on it were a few bushes and stunted trees. I knew the tigress would not have attempted to climb this hill, and on seeing me looking at it Dungar Singh said the pheasant was not calling on the hill but in a ravine round the shoulder of it. As we were not within sight of the pheasant, there was only one thing that could have alarmed it, and that was the tigress. Telling Dungar Singh to leave me and run back to the village as fast as he could go, I covered his retreat with my rifle until I considered he was clear of the danger zone and then turned round to look for a suitable place in which to sit.

The only trees in this part of the valley were enormous pines which, as they had no branches for thirty or forty feet, it would be quite impossible to climb. So of necessity I would have to sit on the ground. This would be all right during daylight, but if the tigress delayed her return until nightfall, and preferred human flesh to mutton, I would need a lot of luck to carry me through the hour or two of darkness before the moon rose.

On the low ridge running from left to right on the near side of the hollow was a big flat rock. Near it was another and smaller one. By sitting on this smaller rock I found I could shelter behind the bigger, exposing only my head to the side from which I expected the tigress to come. So here I decide to sit. In front of me was a hollow some forty yards in width with a twenty-foot-high bank on the far side. Above this bank was a ten—to twenty-yard—wide flat stretch of ground sloping down to the right. Beyond this the hill went up steeply. The three goats in the hollow, which were alive when the boys and men ran away, were now dead. When striking them down the tigress had ripped the skin on the back of one of them.

The *kalege* pheasant had now stopped chattering, and I speculated as to whether it had called at the tigress as she was going up the ravine after the lad and I had arrived or whether it had called on seeing the tigress coming back. In the one case it would mean a long wait for me, and in the other a short one. I had taken up my position at 2 p.m., and half an hour later a pair of blue Himalayan magpies came up the valley. These beautiful birds, which do a lot of

destruction in the nesting season among tits and other small birds, have an uncanny instinct for finding in a jungle anything that is dead. I heard the magpies long before I saw them, for they are very vocal. On catching sight of the goats they stopped chattering and very cautiously approached. After several false alarms they alighted on the goat with the ripped back and started to feed. For some time a king vulture had been quartering the sky, and now, on seeing the magpies on the goat, he came sailing down and landed as lightly as a feather on the dead branch of a pine tree. These king vultures with their white shirt-fronts, black coats, and red heads and legs, are always the first of the vultures to find a kill. Being smaller than other vultures it is essential for them to be first at the table, for when the others arrive they have to take a back seat.

I welcomed the vulture's coming, for he would provide me with information I lacked. From his perch high up on the pine tree he had an extensive view, and if he came down and joined the magpies it would mean that the tigress had gone, whereas if he remained where he was it would mean that she was lying up somewhere close by. For the next half hour the scene remained unchanged—the magpies continued to feed, and the vulture sat on the dead branch—and then the sun was blotted out by heavy rain-clouds. Shortly after, the *kalege* pheasant started chattering again and the magpies flew screaming down the valley. The tigress was coming, and here, sooner than I had expected, was the chance of shooting her that I had lost the previous night when overcome by vertigo.

A few light bushes on the shoulder of the hill partly obstructed my view in the direction of the ravine, and presently through these bushes I saw the tigress. She was coming, very slowly, along the flat bit of ground above the twenty-foot-high bank and was looking straight towards me. With only head exposed and my soft hat pulled down to my eyes, I knew she would not notice me if I made no movement. So, with the rifle resting on the flat rock, I sat perfectly still. When she had come opposite to me the tigress sat down, with the bole of a big pine tree directly between us. I could see her head on one side of the tree and her tail and part of her hindquarters on the other. Here she sat for minutes, snapping at the flies that, attracted by her wound, were tormenting her.

## 10

Eight years previously, when the tigress was a comparatively young animal, she had been seriously injured in an encounter with a porcupine. At the time she received this injury she may have had cubs, and unable for the time being to secure her natural prey to feed herself in order to nourish her cubs, she had taken to killing human beings. In doing this she had committed no crime against the laws of Nature. She was a carnivorous animal, and flesh, whether human or animal, was the only food she could assimilate. Under stress of circumstances an animal, and a human being also, will eat food that under normal conditions they are averse to eating. From the fact that during the whole of her man-eating career the tigress had only killed a hundred and fifty human beings—fewer than twenty a year—I am inclined to think that she only resorted to this easily procured form of food when she had cubs and when, owing to her injury, she was unable to get the requisite amount of natural food needed to support herself and her family.

The people of Talla Des had suffered and suffered grievously from the tigress, and for the suffering she had inflicted she was now paying in full. To put her out of her misery I several times aligned the sights of my rifle on her head, but the light, owing to the heavy clouds, was not good enough for me to make sure of hitting a comparatively small object at sixty yards.

Eventually the tigress stood up, took three steps and then stood broadside on to me, looking down at the goats. With my elbows resting on the flat rock I took careful aim at the spot where I thought her heart would be, pressed the trigger, and saw a spurt of dust go up on the hill on the far side of her. On seeing the dust the thought flashed through my mind that not only had I missed the tigress's heart, but that I had missed the whole animal. And yet, after my careful aim, that could not be. What undoubtedly had happened was that my bullet had gone clean through her without meeting any resistance. At my shot the tigress sprang forward, raced over the flat ground like a very frightened but unwounded animal, and before I could get in another shot, disappeared from view.

Mad with myself for not having killed the tigress when she had given me such a good shot, I was determined now that she would not escape from me. Jumping down from the rock, I sprinted across the hollow, up the twenty-foot bank and along the flat ground until I came to the spot where the tigress had disappeared. Here I found there was a steep forty-foot drop down a loose shale scree. Down this the tigress had gone in great bounds. Afraid to do the same for fear of spraining my ankles, I sat down on my heels and tobogganed to the bottom. At the foot of the scree was a well-used footpath, along which I felt sure the tigress had gone, though the surface was too hard to show pug-marks. To the right of the path was a boulder-strewn stream, the one that Dungar Singh and I had crossed farther up, and flanking the stream was a steep grassy hill. To the left of the path was a hill with a few pine trees growing on it. The path for some distance was straight, and I had run along it for fifty or more yards when I heard a *ghooral* give its alarm sneeze. There was only one place where the *ghooral* could be and that was on the grassy hill to my right. Thinking that the tigress had possibly crossed the stream and gone up this hill, I pulled up to see if I could see her. As I did so, I thought I heard men shouting. Turning around, I looked up in the direction of the village and saw a crowd of men standing on the saddle of the hill. On seeing me look around they shouted again and waved me on, straight along the path. In a moment I was on the run again, and on turning a corner found fresh blood on the path.

The skin of animals is loose. When an animal that is standing

still is hit in the body by a bullet and it dashes away at full speed, the hole made in the skin does not coincide with the hole in the flesh, with the result that, as long as the animal is running at speed, little if any blood flows from the wound. When, however, the animal slows down and the two holes come closer together, blood flows and continues to flow more freely the slower the animal goes. When there is any uncertainty as to whether an animal that has been fired at has been hit or not, the point can be very easily cleared up by going to the exact spot where the animal was when fired at, and looking for cut hairs. These will indicate that the animal was hit, whereas the absence of such hairs will show that it was clean missed.

After going round the corner the tigress had slowed down, but she was still running, as I could see from the blood splashes, and in order to catch up with her I put on a spurt. I had not gone very far when I came to spur jutting out from the hill on my left. Here the path bent back at a very acute angle, and not being able to stop myself, and there being nothing for me to seize hold of on the hillside, I went over the edge of the narrow path all standing. Ten to fifteen feet below was a small rhododendron sapling, and below the sapling a sheer drop into a dark and evil-looking ravine where the stream, turning at right angles, had cut away the toe of the hill. As I passed the sapling with my heels cutting furrows in the soft earth, I gripped it under my right arm. The sapling, fortunately, was not uprooted, and though it bent it did not break. Easing myself round very gently, I started to kick footholds in the soft loamy hill-face which had a luxuriant growth of maidenhair fern.

The opportunity of catching up with the tigress had gone, but I now had a well-defined blood-trail to follow, so there was no longer any need for me to hurry. The footpath which at first had run north now ran west along the north face of a steep and well-wooded hill. When I had gone for another two hundred yards along the path, I came to flat ground on a shoulder of the hill. This was the limit I would have expected a tiger shot through the body to have travelled, so I approached the flat ground, on which there was a heavy growth of bracken and scattered bushes, very cautiously.

A tiger that has made up its mind to avenge an injury is the most terrifying animal to be met with in an Indian jungle. The tigress had a very recent injury to avenge and she had demonstrated—by striking down six goats and by springing and dashing away when I fired at her—that the leg wound she had received five days before was no handicap to rapid movement. I felt sure, therefore, that as soon as she became aware that I was following her and she considered that I was within her reach, she would launch an all-out attack on me, which I would possibly have to meet with a single bullet. Drawing back the bolt of the rifle, I examined the cartridge very carefully and satisfied that it was one of a fresh lot I had recently got from Manton in Calcutta, I replaced it in the chamber, put back the bolt, and threw off the safety catch.

The path ran through the bracken, which was waist high and which met over it. The blood trail led along the path into the bracken, and the tigress might be lying up on the path or on the right or the left-hand side of it. So I approached the bracken foot by foot and looking straight ahead for, on these occasions, it is unwise to keep turning the head, when I was within three yards of the bracken I saw a movement a yard from the path on the right. It was the tigress gathering herself together for a spring.

Wounded and starving though she was, she was game to fight it out. Her spring, however, was never launched, for, as she rose, my first bullet raked her from end to end, and the second bullet broke her neck.

Days of pain and strain on an empty stomach left me now trembling in every limb, and I had great difficulty in reaching the spot where the path bent back at an acute angle and where, but for the chance dropping of a rhododendron seed, I would have ended my life on the rocks, below.

The entire population of the village, plus my own men, were gathered on the saddle of the hill and on either side of it, and I had hardly raised my hat to wave when, shouting at the top of their voices, the men and boys came swarming down. My six Garhwalis were the first to arrive. Congratulations over, the tigress was lashed to a pole and six of the proudest Garhwalis in Kumaon carried the Talla Des man-eater in triumph to Talla Kote village. Here the tigress was laid down on a bed of straw for the women and children to see, while I went back to my tent for my first solid meal in many weeks. An hour later with a crowd of people around me, I skinned the tigress.

My first bullet, a .275 soft-nose with split nickel case fired on 7 April, was bushed and firmly fixed in the ball-and-socket joint of the tigress's right shoulder. The second and third bullets, fired as she was falling through the air and climbing up the hill, had missed her. The fourth, fired on 12 April, had gone clean through without striking any bones, and the fifth and sixth had killed her. From her right foreleg and shoulder I found some twenty porcupine quills, ranging in length from two to six inches, which were firmly embedded in muscle and were undoubtedly the cause of the tigress's having become a man-eater.

I spent the following day in partly drying the skin, and three days later I was safely back in my home with my bad time behind me. Baynes very kindly sent for Dungar Singh and his brother, and at a public function at Almora thanked them for the help they had given me and presented them with my token of gratitude.

A week after my return to Naini Tal, Sir Malcolm Hailey gave me an introduction to Colonel Dick, an ear specialist, who treated me for three months in his hospital in Lahore and restored my hearing sufficiently for me to associate with my fellow men without embarrassment, and gave me back the joy of hearing music and the song of birds.

# EPILOGUE

**THE STORY OF THE TALLA** Des man-eater—which I refrained from telling until I had written *Jungle Lore*—has now been told. I am aware that to many the story will seem incredible, and to none more so than to those who have themselves hunted tigers. None knows better than I that the hunting of tigers on foot is not a popular sport, and that the hunting of man-eaters on foot is even less so. I also know that the following-up of a wounded tiger on foot is a task that is sought by none and dreaded by all. And yet, knowing these things, I have told of the hunting of a man-eating tiger on foot, not only by day but also by night, and the chasing on foot of a wounded tiger. Small wonder, then, if my story to many should seem incredible.

There are few places in Kumaon where a fortnight's holiday could be more pleasantly spent than along the eastern border of the Almora district. Hiking in the Himalayas is becoming a very popular pastime, and I could suggest no more pleasant hike for a sportsman or for a party of young army men or students than the following:

Start from Tanakpur, but before doing so get the *peshkar* to give you a *tahsil peon* to show you where the epic fight took place between the elephant and the two tigers. From Tanakpur go via Baramdeo to Purnagiri. Here, after doing *darshan* at the temple, learn all you can from the High Priest and the temple *pujaris* about the lights that appear on the far side of the Sarda, and similar manifestations, as for example the fire with an old man sitting near it telling his beads that is to be seen during certain seasons at the foot of the Pindari glacier. From Purnagiri a track used by the priests will take you to Thak village. This is beautifully situated, and while you rest and admire the view, get the headman or any of the other men sitting round to give you his version of the shooting of the Thak and of the Chuka man-eating tigers. Tewari, a relative of the headman and as fine a type of a hill Brahmin as you will see, will then show you where his brother whose body he helped me find was killed, the mango tree with a spring at its roots, and the rock on the way down to Chuka where I shot the Thak man-eater. He will also, if you have the time, show you the *ficus* tree from which I shot the Chuka man-eater. At Chuka inquire for Kunwar Singh, and hear his story of the hunting of the two tigers.

From Chuka to Talla Kote is a long march, and it will be advisable to start at the crack of dawn. Having forded the Ladhya near its junction with the Sarda, you will come to Sem. The headman of Sem, who was a boy when I knew him, will show you where the man-eater killed his mother while she was cutting grass near their home. With Sem behind you and a stiff climb accomplished, you will pass the small hamlet where I spent a night under a mango tree. After going over the ridge you will come to a forest road. Take the turn to the left and follow the road until you come to a stream. Cross the stream and the small patch of open ground on which my 40-1b tent was pitched, and you have reached you destination, Talla Kote.

Dungar Singh, *malguzar* (land-holder) of Talla Kote, will now be about forty years of age. Give him my *salams* and ask him to take you to the *ling* or saddle from which there is an extensive view into two valleys. Face first the valley to the east and get Dungar Singh to point out the bush where his mother was killed, the oak tree under which she was eaten, the *wyran* field on which the young tigers were shot, and the grassy hill up which the wounded tigress went. Then turn round, walk a few steps, and face the valley to the west. Dungar Singh will now point out where the six goats were killed, where the tigress was standing when my bullet went through her, and the footpath along which she dashed and along which I ran after her.

The hunting of no other tiger has ever been witnessed by a greater number of non-participants than witnessed the hunting of the Talla Des man-eating tiger. Some of those will have passed away, but many will still remain and they will not have forgotten my visit or the thrilling events of the week I spent with them.

# THE MAN-EATING LEOPARD OF
RUDRAPRAYAG

# CONTENTS

# THE PILGRIM ROAD

**IF YOU ARE A HINDU FROM** the sun-scorched plains of India and you desire—as all good Hindus do—to perform the pilgrimage to the age-old shrines of Kedarnath and Badrinath, you must start on your pilgrimage from Hardwar and, in order to acquire a full measure of the merits vouch-safed to you for the correct performance of the pilgrimage, you must walk every step of the way from Hardwar to Kedarnath and, thence, over the mountain track to Badrinath, barefoot.

Having purified yourself by immersion in the sacred Har-ki-pauri pool, done *darshan* at the many shrines and temples in Hardwar, and added your mite to their coffers, you must not omit to toss a coin within reach of the festering stumps—which once were hands—of the lepers who line the narrowest part of the pilgrim road above the sacred pool, for if you make this omission, they will call down curses on your head. What matter if these unfortunate ones have wealth beyond your dreams secreted in their filthy rags, or in the rock caves they call their homes? The curses of such as they were best avoided, and immunity will cost you but a few coppers.

You have now done all that custom and religion require of a good Hindu and are at liberty to start on your long and hard pilgrimage.

The first place of interest you will come to after leaving Hardwar is Rishikesh. Here you will make your first acquaintance with the Kalakamli Wallahas, so called because of the black blanket their founder wore—and which many of his disciples still wear—in the form of a habit or loose cloak bound round the middle with a cord of goat's hair; and who are renowned throughout the land for their good deeds. I do not know if any of the other religious brotherhoods you will meet on your pilgrimage have any claim to renown, but I do know that the Kalakamli Wallahas have such a claim, and justly so, for out of the offerings they receive at their many shrines and temples, they have built—and they maintain—hospitals, dispensaries, and pilgrim shelters, and they feed the poor and the needy.

With Rishikesh behind you, you will come next to Lachman Jhula, where the pilgrim road crosses from the right to the left bank of the Ganges on a suspension bridge. Here beware of the red monkeys who infest the bridge, for they are even more importunate than the lepers of Hardwar, and if you omit to propitiate them with offerings of sweets, or parched gram, your passage across the long and narrow bridge is likely to be both difficult and painful.

Three-day's journey up the left bank of the Ganges and you have reached the ancient capital of Garhwal—Shreenagar—an historic, religious, and trading centre of considerable importance and of great beauty, nestling in a wide, open valley surrounded by high mountains. It was here, in the year 1805, that the forebears of the Garhwali soldiers who have fought so gallantly in two world wars made their last, and unsuccessful, stand against the Gurkha invaders, and it is a matter of great regret to the people of Garhwal that their ancient city of Shreenagar, together with the palaces of their kings, was swept away, to the last stone, by the bursting of the Gohna Lake dam in 1894. This dam, caused by a landslide in the valley of the Birehi Ganga, a tributary of the Ganges, was 11,000 feet wide at the base, 2,000 feet wide at the summit, and 900 feet high and, when it burst, ten billion cubic feet of water were released in the short space of six hours. So well was the bursting of the dam timed that though the flood devastated the valley of the Ganges right down to Hardwar and swept away every bridge, only one family was lost, the members of which had returned to the danger-zone after having been forcibly removed from it.

From Shreenagar you have to face a stiff climb to Chatikhal, which is compensated for by the magnificent views you will get of the Ganges valley and of the eternal snows above Kedarnath.

A day's march from Chatikhal and you see in front of you Golabrai with its row of grass-thatched pilgrim shelters, a one-roomed stone-built house, and its drinking trough. This big and imposing drinking trough is fed by a tiny crystal-clear stream which, in summer, is sedately conducted down the mountain-side by a series of channels rough-hewn from pine saplings. At other seasons of the year the water cascades unconfined and merrily over rocks draped with moss and maidenhair fern, through luxuriant beds of vivid green watercress and sky-blue strobilanthes.

A hundred yards beyond the pilgrim shelters, and on the right-hand side of the road, stands a mango tree. This tree and the two-storied house above it which is the home of the pundit, who owns the Golabrai pilgrim shelters, are worthy of note, for they play an important part in the tale I have to tell.

Another two miles, along the last flat bit of ground you will see for many a day, and you have reached Rudraprayag, where you and I, my pilgrim friend, must part, for your way lies across the Alaknanda and up the left bank of the Mandakini to Kedarnath, while mine lies over the mountains to my home in Naini Tal.

The road in front of you, which has been trodden by the feet of millions of pilgrims like you, is excessively steep and incredibly rough; and you, whose lungs have never breathed air above sea level, who have never climbed anything higher than the roof of your house, and whose feet have never trodden anything harder than yielding sand, will suffer greatly. Times there will be, a-many, when, gasping for breath, you toil up the face of steep mountains on feet torn and bleeding by passage over rough rocks, sharp shale, and frozen ground, when you will question whether the prospective reward you seek is worth the present price you pay in suffering; but being a good Hindu you will toil on, comforting yourself with the thought that merit is not gained without suffering, and the greater the suffering in this world, the greater the reward in the next.

# THE MAN-EATER

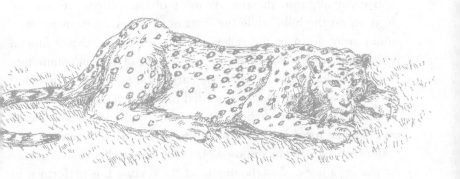

**'PRAYAG' IS THE HINDI WORD FOR** 'confluence'. At Rudraprayag, two rivers—the Mandakini coming down from Kedarnath, and the Alaknanda from Badrinath—meet, and from here onwards the combined waters of the two rivers are known to all Hindus as Ganga Mai, and to the rest of the world as the Ganges.

When an animal, be it a leopard or be it a tiger, becomes a man-eater, it is given a place-name for purposes of identification. The name so given to a man-eater does not necessarily imply that the animal began its man-eating career at, or that all its kills were confined to, that particular place. It is quite natural that the leopard which started its man-eating career at a small village twelve miles from Rudraprayag, on the Kedarnath pilgrim route, should have been known for the rest of its career as the Man-eating Leopard of Rudraprayag.

Leopards do not become man-eaters for the same reasons that tigers do. Though I hate to admit it, our leopards—the most beautiful and the most graceful of all the animals in our jungles, and who when cornered or wounded are second to none in courage—are scavengers to the extent that they will, when driven by hunger, eat any dead thing they find in the jungle, just as lions will in the African bush.

The people of Garhwal are Hindus, and as such cremate their dead. The cremation invariably takes place on the bank of a stream or river in order that the ashes may be washed down into the Ganges and eventually into the sea. As most of the villages are situated high up on the hills, while the streams of rivers are in many cases miles away down in the valleys, it will be realized that a funeral entails a considerable tax on the man-power of a small community when, in addition to the carrying party, labour has to be provided to collect and carry the fuel needed for the cremation. In normal times these rites are carried out very effectively; but when disease in epidemic form sweeps through the hills, and the inhabitants die faster than they can be disposed of, a very simple rite, which consists of placing a live coal in the mouth of the deceased, is performed in the village, and the body is then carried to the edge of the hill and cast into the valley below.

A leopard, in an area in which his natural food is scarce, finding these bodies, very soon acquires a taste for human flesh, and when the disease dies down and normal conditions are re-established, he, very naturally, on finding his food-supply cut off, takes to killing human beings. In the wave of epidemic influenza that swept through the country in 1918 and that cost India over a million lives, Garhwal suffered very severely, and it was at the end of this epidemic that the Garhwal man-eater made his appearance.

The first human kill credited to the man-eating leopard of Rudraprayag is recorded as having taken place at Bainji village on 9 June 1918, and the last kill for which the man-eater was responsible took place at Bhainswara village on 14 April 1926. Between these two dates the number of human kills recorded by Government was one hundred and twenty-five.

While I do not think that this figure, of one hundred and twenty-five, is our to the extent claimed by Government officials who served in Garhwal at that time and by residents in the area in which the man-eater was operating, I do know that the figure given is not correct, for some kills which took place while I was on the ground have not been shown in the records.

In crediting the man-eater with fewer kills than he was actually responsible for, I do not wish to minimize in any way the sufferings endured by the people of Garhwal for eight long years, nor do I wish to detract in any way from the reputation of the animal which the people of Garhwal claim as having been the most famous man-eating leopard of all time.

However, be the number of human kills what they may, Garhwal can claim that this leopard was the most publicized animal that has ever lived, for he was mentioned—to my knowledge—in the press of the United Kingdom, America, Canada, South Africa, Kenya, Malaya, Hong Kong, Australia, New Zealand, and in most of the dailies and weeklies in India.

In addition to this newspaper publicity, tales of the man-eater were carried to every part of India by the sixty thousand pilgrims who annually visit the shrines of Kedarnath and Badrinath.

The procedure laid down by Government in all cases of human beings alleged to have been killed by man-eaters is for the relatives or friends of the deceased to lodge a report with the village *patwari* as soon after the occurrence as possible. On receipt of the report the *patwari* proceeds to the spot, and if the body of the victim has not been found before his arrival he organizes a search party, and with their aid endeavours to find the victim. If the body has been found before his arrival, or if the search party finds it, the *patwari* holds an inquiry on the spot and when satisfied that it is a genuine kill by a man-eater, and not a case of murder, he gives the relatives permission to remove the remains for cremation or for burial, according to the caste or creed of the victim. The kill is duly recorded in his register against the man-eater operating in that area, and a full report of occurrence is submitted to the administrative head of the district—the Deputy Commissioner—who also keeps a register in which all the man-eater's kills are recorded. In the event, however, of the body, or any portion of it, not being found— as sometimes happens, for man-eaters have an annoying habit of carrying their victims for long distances—the case is held over for further inquiry, and the man-eater is not credited with the kill. Again, when people are mauled by a man-eater and subsequently die from their injuries, the man-eater concerned is not credited with their deaths.

It will thus be seen that though the system adopted for recording the kills of man-eaters is as good as it can be, it is possible for one of these abnormal animals to be responsible for more human kills than he is finally credited with, especially when his operations extend over a long period of years.

# TERROR

**THE WORD 'TERROR' IS SO** generally and universally used in connection with everyday trivial matters that it is apt to fail to convey, when intended to do so, its real meaning. I should like therefore to give you some idea of what terror—real terror—meant to the fifty thousand inhabitants living in the five hundred square miles of Garhwal in which the man-eater was operating, and to the sixty thousand pilgrims who annually passed through that area between the years 1918 and 1926. And I will give you a few instances to show you what grounds the inhabitants, and the pilgrims, had for that terror.

No curfew order has ever been more strictly enforced, and more implicitly obeyed, than the curfew imposed by the man-eating leopard of Rudraprayag.

During the hours of sunlight life in that area carried on in a normal way. Men went long distances to the bazaars to transact business, or to outlying villages to visit relatives or friends; women went up the mountain-sides to cut grass for thatching or for cattle-fodder; children went to school or into the jungles to graze goats or to collect dry sticks, and, if it was summer, pilgrims, either singly or in large numbers, toiled along the pilgrim routes on their way to and from the sacred shrines of Kedarnath and Badrinath.

As the sun approached the western horizon and the shadows lengthened, the behaviour of the entire population of the area underwent a very sudden and a very noticeable change. Men who had sauntered to the bazaars or to outlying villages were hurrying home; women carrying great bundles of grass were stumbling down the steep mountain-sides; children who had loitered on their way from school, or who were late in bringing in their flocks of goats or the dry sticks they had been sent out to collect, were being called by anxious mothers, and the weary pilgrims were being urged by any local inhabitant who passed them to hurry to shelter.

When night came, an ominous silence brooded over the whole area—no movement and no sound anywhere. The entire local population was behind fast-closed doors and, in many cases, had sought further protection by building additional doors. Those of the pilgrims who had not been fortunate enough to find accommodation inside houses were huddled close together in pilgrim shelters. And all, whether in house or shelter, were silent for fear of attracting the dread man-eater.

This is what terror meant to the people of Garhwal, and to the pilgrims, for eight long years.

I will now give a few instances to show you what grounds there were for that terror.

A boy, an orphan aged fourteen, was employed to look after a flock of forty goats. He was of the depressed—untouchable—class, and each evening when he returned with his charges he was given his food and then shut into a small room with the goats. The room was on the ground floor of a long row of double-storied buildings and was immediately below the room occupied by the boy's master, the owner of the goats. To prevent the goats crowding in on him as he slept, the boy had fenced off the far left-hand corner of the room.

This room had no windows and only one door, and when the

boy and the goats were safely inside, the boy's master pulled the door to, and fastened it by passing the hasp, which was attached by a short length of chain to the door, over the staple fixed in the lintel. A piece of wood was then inserted in the staple to keep the hasp in place, and on his side of the door the boy, for his better safety, rolled a stone against it.

On the night the orphan was gathered to his fathers, his master asserts the door was fastened as usual, and I have no reason to question the truth of his assertion. In support of it, the door showed many deep claw-marks, and it is possible that in his attempts to claw open the door the leopard displaced the piece of wood that was keeping the hasp in place, after which it would have been easy for him to push the stone aside and enter the room.

Forty goats packed into a small room, one corner of which was fenced off, could not have left the intruder much space to manoeuvre in, and it is left to conjecture whether the leopard covered the distance from the door to the boy's corner of the room over the backs of the goats or under their bellies, for at this stage of the proceedings all the goats must have been on their feet.

It were best to assume that the boy slept through all the noise the leopard must have made when trying to force open the door, and that the goats must have made when the leopard had entered the room, and that he did not cry for help to deaf ears, only screened from him and the danger that menaced him by a thin plank.

After killing the boy in the fenced-off corner, the leopard carried him across the empty room—the goats had escaped into the night—down a steep hillside, and then over some terraced fields to a deep boulder-strewn ravine. It was here, after the sun had been up a few hours, that the master found all that the leopard had left of his servant.

Incredible as it may seem, not one of the forty goats had received so much as a scratch.

A neighbour had dropped in to spend the period of a long smoke with a friend. The room was L-shaped and the only door in it was not visible from where the two men sat on the floor with their backs to the wall, smoking. The door was shut but not fastened, for up to that night there had been no human kills in the village.

The room was in darkness and the owner of it had just passed the hookah to his friend when it fell to the ground, scattering a shower of burning charcoal and tobacco. Telling his friend to be more careful or he would set the blanket on which they were sitting on fire, the man bent forward to gather up the embers and, as he did so, the door came into view. A young moon was near setting and, silhouetted against it, the man saw a leopard carrying his friend through the door.

When recounting the incident to me a few days later the man said: 'I am speaking the truth, sahib, when I tell you I never heard even so much as the intake of a breath, or any other sound, from my friend who was sitting only an arm's-length from me, either when the leopard was killing him, or when it was carrying him away. There was nothing I could do for my friend, so I waited until the leopard had been gone some little while, and then I crept up to the door and hastily shut and secured it.'

The wife of the headman of a village was ill from a fever, and two friends had been called in to nurse her.

There were two rooms in the house. The outer room had two doors, one opening on to a small flagged courtyard, and the other leading into the inner room. This outer room also had a narrow slip of a window set some four feet above floor level, and in this window, which was open, stood a large brass vessel containing drinking-water for the sick woman.

Except for the one door giving access to the outer room, the inner room had no other opening in any of its four walls.

The door leading out on to the courtyard was shut and securely fastened, and the door between the two rooms was wide open.

The three women in the inner room were lying on the ground, the sick woman in the middle with a friend on either side of her. The husband in the outer room was on a bed on the side of the room nearest the window, and on the floor beside his bed, where its light would shine into the inner room, was a lantern, turned down low to conserve oil.

Round about midnight, when the occupants of both the rooms were asleep, the leopard entered by way of the narrow slip of a window, avoiding in some miraculous way knocking over the brass vessel which nearly filled it, skirted round the man's low bed and, entering the inner room, killed the sick woman. It was only when the heavy brass vessel crashed to the floor as the leopard attempted to lift its victim through the window that the sleepers awoke.

When the lantern had been turned up the woman who had been sick was discovered lying huddled up under the window, and in her throat were four great teeth-marks.

A neighbour, whose wife had been one of the nurses on that night, when relating the occurrence to me said, 'The woman was very ill from her fever and was likely to have died in any case, so it was fortunate that the leopard selected her.'

Two Gujars were moving their herd of thirty buffaloes from one grazing-ground to another, and accompanying them was the twelve-year-old daughter of the older of the two men, who were brothers.

They were strangers to the locality and either had not heard of the man-eater or, which is more probable, thought the buffaloes would give them all the protection they needed.

Near the road and at an elevation of eight thousand feet was a narrow strip of flat ground below which was a sickle-shaped terraced field, some quarter of an acre in extent, which had long been out of cultivation. The men selected this site for their camp and having cut stakes from the jungle which surrounded them on all sides, they drove them deep into the field and tethered their buffaloes in a long row.

After the evening meal prepared by the girl had been eaten, the party of three laid their blankets on the narrow strip of ground between the road and the buffaloes and went to sleep.

It was a dark night, and some time towards the early hours of the morning the men were awakened by the booming of their buffalo-bells and by the snorting of the frightened animals. Knowing from long experience that these sounds indicated the presence of carnivora, the men lit a lantern and went among the buffaloes to quieten them, and to see that none had broken the ropes tethering them to the stakes.

The men were absent only a few minutes. When they returned to their sleeping-place they found that the girl whom they had left asleep was missing. On the blanket on which she had been lying were big splashes of blood.

When daylight came the father and the uncle followed the blood trail. After skirting round the row of tethered buffaloes, it went across the narrow field and down the steep hillside for a few yards, to where the leopard had eaten his kill.

'My brother was born under an unlucky star, sahib, for he has no son, and he had only this one daughter who was to have been married shortly, and to whom he looked in the fullness of time to provide him with an heir, and now the leopard has come and eaten her.'

I could go on and on, for there were many kills, and each one has its own tragic story, but I think I have said enough to convince you that the people of Garhwal had ample reason to be terrified of the man-eating leopard of Rudraprayag, especially when it is remembered that Garhwalis are intensely superstitious and that, added to their fear of physical contact with the leopard, was their even greater fear of the supernatural, of which I shall give you an example.

I set out from the small one-roomed Rudraprayag Inspection Bungalow one morning just as day was breaking, and as I stepped off the veranda I saw in the dust, where the ground had been worn away by human feet, the pug-marks of the man-eater.

The pug-marks were perfectly fresh and showed that the leopard had stepped out of the veranda only a few minutes in advance of me, and from the direction in which they were pointing it was evident that the leopard, after his fruitless visit to the bungalow, was making for the pilgrim road some fifty yards away.

Tracking between the bungalow and the road was not possible owing to the hard surface of the ground, but as I reached the gate I saw the pug-marks were heading in the direction of Golabrai. A large flock of sheep and goats had gone down the road the previous evening, and in the dust they had kicked up the leopard's tracks showed up as clearly as they would have on fresh-fallen snow.

I had, by then, become quite familiar with the man-eater's pug-marks and could with little difficulty have distinguished them from the pug-marks of any hundred leopards.

A lot can be learnt from the pug-marks of carnivora, as for instance the sex, age, and size of the animal. I had examined the pug-marks of the man-eater very carefully the first time I had seen them, and I knew he was an out-sized male leopard, long past his prime.

As I followed the tracks of the man-eater on this morning I

could see that he was only a few minutes ahead of me, and that he was moving at a slow, even pace.

The road, which had no traffic on it at this early hour of the morning, wound in and out of a number of small ravines, and as it was possible that the leopard might on this occasion break his rule of never being out after daylight, I crept round each corner with the utmost care until I found, a mile farther on, where the leopard had left the road and gone up a great track into dense scrub and tree jungle.

A hundred yards from where the leopard left the road there was a small field, in the centre of which was a thorn enclosure, erected by the owner of the field to encourage packmen to camp there and fertilize it. In this enclosure was the flock of sheep and goats that had come down the road the previous evening.

The owner of the flock, a rugged fellow who by the looks of him had been packing trade commodities up and down the pilgrim road for nigh on half a century, was just removing the thornbush closing the entrance to the enclosure when I came up. In reply to my inquiries he informed me that he had seen nothing of the leopard but that, just as dawn was breaking, his two sheep-dogs had given tongue and, a few minutes later, a kakar had barked in the jungle above the road.

When I asked the old packman if he would sell me one of his goats, he asked for what purpose it was wanted; and when I told him it was to tie up for the man-eater, he walked through the opening in the fence, replaced the bush, accepted one of my cigarettes, and sat down on a rock by the side of the road.

We remained smoking for a while, with my question still unanswered, and then the man began to talk.

'You, sahib, are undoubtedly he whom I have heard tell of on my way down from my village near Badrinath, and it grieves me that you should have come all this long way from your home on a fruitless errand. The evil spirit that is responsible for all the human deaths in this area is not an animal, as you think it is, that can be killed by ball or shot, or by any of the other means that you have

tried and that others have tried before you; and
in proof of what I say I will tell you a story
while I smoke this second cigarette. The story
was told to me by my father, who, as
everyone knows, had never been heard
to tell a lie.'

'My father was a young man then,
and I unborn, when an evil spirit, like
the one that is now troubling this land,
made its appearance in our village,
and all said it was a leopard. Men,
women, and children were killed
in their homes and every effort was
made, as has been made here, to kill the animal.
Traps were set, and far-famed marksmen sat in trees and fired
ball and shot at the leopard; and when all these attempts to kill it
had failed, a great terror seized the people and none dared leave
the shelter of his home between the hours of sunset and sunrise.'

'And then the headmen of my father's village, and of the villages
round about, bade all the men attend a *panchayat*, and when all were
assembled the *panch* addressed the meeting and said they were
assembled to devise some fresh means to rid themselves of this
man-eating leopard. Then an old man, fresh back from the burning-
ghat, whose grandson had been killed the previous night, arose and
said it was no leopard that had entered his house and killed his
grandson as he lay asleep by his side, but one from among their
own community who, when he craved for human flesh and blood,
assumed the semblance of a leopard, and that such a one could
not be killed by the methods already tried, as had been amply
proved, and could only be killed by fire. His suspicions, he said,
fell on the fat *sadhu* who lived in the hut near the ruined temple.'

'At this there was a great uproar, some exclaiming that the old
man's sorrow at the loss of his grandson had demented him; others
averring he was right. And these later recalled that the *sadhu* had
arrived at the village at about the time the killings had started, and

it was further recalled that on the day succeeding a killing the *sadhu* had been wont to sleep all day, stretched on his bed in the sun.'

'When order had been restored the matter was long debated and the *panchayat* eventually decided that no immediate action would be taken, but that the *sadhu's* movements should in future be watched. The assembled men were then divided into three parties, the first party to start its watch from the night the next kill could be expected; for the kills had taken place at more or less regular intervals.'

'During the nights the first and the second parties were on watch, the *sadhu* did not leave his hut.'

'My father was with the third party, and at nightfall he silently took up his position. Soon after, the door of the hut slowly opened, and the *sadhu* emerged and vanished into the night. Some hours later an agonized scream came floating down on the night air from the direction of a charcoal-burner's hut far up the mountain-side, and thereafter there was silence.'

'No man of my father's party closed an eye that night, and as the grey dawn was being born in the east they saw the *sadhu* hurrying home, and his hands and his mouth were dripping blood.'

'When the *sadhu* had gone inside his hut and had closed the door, the watchers went up to it, and fastened it from the outside by passing the chain that was dangling from it over the staple in the lintel. Then they went each to his haystack and returned with a big bundle of straw, and when the sun rose that morning there was nothing but smouldering ash where the hut had been. From that day the killing stopped.'

'Suspicion has not yet fallen on any one of the many *sadhus* in these parts, but when it does the method employed in my father's time will be adopted in mine, and until that day comes, the people of Garhwal must suffer.'

'You have asked if I will sell you a goat. I will not sell you a goat, sahib, for I have none to spare. But if, after hearing my story, you still want an animal to tie up for what you think is a man-eating leopard, I will lend you one of my sheep. If it is killed you shall pay me its price, and if it is not killed no money shall pass between us. Today and tonight I rest here, and tomorrow at the rising of the Bhootia star I must be on my way.'

Near sundown that evening I returned to the thorn enclosure and my packman friend very cheerfully let me select from his flock a fat sheep which I considered was heavy enough to give the leopard two nights' feed. This sheep I tied in the scrub jungle close to the path up which the leopard had gone some twelve hours earlier.

Next morning I was up betimes. As I left the bungalow I again saw the pug-marks of the man-eater where he had stepped off the veranda, and at the gate I found he had come up the road from the direction of Golabrai, and, after calling at the bungalow, had gone away towards the Rudraprayag bazaar.

The fact that the leopard was trying to secure a human kill was proof that he had no interest in the sheep I had provided for him, and I was therefore not surprised to find that he had not eaten any portion of the sheep which he had apparently killed shortly after I had tied it up.

'Go back to your home, sahib, and save your time and your money,' was the parting advice of the old packman as he whistled to his flock, and headed down the road for Hardwar.

A parallel case, happily without as tragic an ending, occurred a few years previously near Rudraprayag.

Incensed at the killing of their relatives and friends, and convinced that a human being was responsible for their deaths, an angry crowd of men seized an unfortunate *sadhu* of Kothgi village, Dasjulapatty, but before they were able to wreak their vengeance on him Philip Mason, then Deputy Commissioner of Garhwal, who was camping in the vicinity, arrived on the scene. Seeing the temper of the crowd, and being a man of great experience, Mason said he had no doubt that the real culprit had been apprehended but that before the *sadhu* was lynched justice demanded that his guilt should be established. To this end he suggested that the *sadhu* should be placed under arrest and closely guarded, night and day. To this suggestion the crowd agreed, and for seven days and seven nights the *sadhu* was carefully guarded by the police, and as carefully watched by the populace. On the eighth morning, when the guard and the watchers were being changed, word was brought that a house in a village some miles away had been broken into the previous night, and a man carried off.

The populace raised no objection to the *sadhu* being released that day, contenting themselves by saying that on this occasion the wrong man had been apprehended, but that next time no mistake would be made.

In Garhwal all kills by man-eaters are attributed to *sadhus*, and in Naini Tal and Almora districts all such kills are attributed to the Bokhsars, who dwell in the unhealthy belt of grass at the foot of the hills called the Terai, living chiefly on game. The *sadhus* are believed to kill for the lust of human flesh and blood, and the Bokhsars are believed to kill for the jewellery their victims are wearing, or for other valuables they have on their person. More women than men have been killed by man-eaters in Naini Tal and Almora districts, but for this there is a better reason than the one given.

I have lived too long in silent places to be imaginative. Even so there were times a-many during the months I spent at Rudraprayag sitting night after night—on one occasion for twenty-eight nights in succession—watching bridges, or cross-roads, or approaches to villages, or over animal or human kills, when I could imagine the man-eater as being a big, light-coloured animal—for so he had appeared to me the first time that I saw him—with the body of a leopard and the head of a fiend.

A fiend who, while watching me through the long night hours, rocked and rolled with silent fiendish laughter at my vain attempts to outwit him, and licked his lips in anticipation of the time when, finding me off my guard for one brief moment, he would get the opportunity he was waiting for, of burying his teeth in my throat.

It may be asked what the Government was doing all the years the Rudraprayag man-eater menaced the people of Garhwal. I hold no brief for the Government, but after having spent ten weeks on the ground, during which time I walked many hundreds of miles and visited most of the villages in the affected area, I assert that the Government did everything in its power to remove the menace. Rewards were offered: the local population believed they amounted to ten thousand rupees in cash and the gift of two villages, sufficient inducement to make each one of the four thousand licensed gun-holders of Garhwal a prospective slayer of the man-eater. Picked *shikaris* were employed on liberal wages and were promised special rewards if their efforts were successful. More than three hundred special gun licences over and above the four thousand in force were granted for the specific purpose of shooting the man-eater. Men of the Garhwal Regiments stationed in Lansdowne were permitted to take their rifles with them when going home on leave, or were provided with sporting arms by their officers. Appeals were made through the press to sportsmen all over India to assist in the destruction of the leopard. Scores of traps of the drop-door type, with goats as bait, were erected on approaches to villages and on roads frequented by the man-eater. *Patwaris* and other Government officials were supplied with poison for the purpose of poisoning human kills, and, last but not least, Government servants, often at great personal risk, spent all the time they could spare from their official duties in pursuit of the man-eater.

The total results from all these many and combined efforts were a slight gunshot wound which creased the pad of the leopard's left hind foot and shot away a small piece of skin from one of its toes, and an entry in Government records by the Deputy Commissioner of Garhwal that, so far from suffering any ill effects, the leopard appeared to thrive on, and be stimulated by, the poison he absorbed via human kills.

Three interesting incidents are recorded in a Government report and I will summarize them here.

First: In response to the press appeal to sportsmen, two young

British officers arrived at Rudraprayag in 1921 with the avowed object of shooting the man-eater. What reason they had for thinking that the leopard crossed from bank to bank of the Alaknanda river by the Rudraprayag suspension bridge I do not know; anyway they decided to confine their efforts to this bridge and shoot the leopard as it was crossing at night. There are towers at each end of the bridge to carry the suspending cables, so one of the young sportsmen sat on the tower on the left bank of the river, and his companion sat on the tower on the right bank.

After they had been sitting for two months on these towers, the man on the left bank saw the leopard walk out on to the bridge from the archway below him. Waiting until the leopard had got well on to the bridge, he fired, and as it dashes across, the man on the tower on the right bank emptied the six chambers of his revolver at it. Next morning blood was found on the bridge and on the hill up which the leopard had gone, and as it was thought that the wound, or wounds, would be fatal, a search was kept up for many days. The report goes on to say that for six months after it was wounded the leopard did not kill any human beings.

I was told about this incident by men who had heard the seven shots, and who had assisted in trying to recover the wounded animal. It was thought by the two sportsmen, and also by my informants, that the leopard had been hit in the back by the first bullet and possibly in the head by some of the subsequent bullets, and it was for this reason that a diligent and prolonged search had been made for it. From the particulars given me of the blood trail I was of opinion that the sportsmen were wrong in thinking that they had inflicted a body and head wound on the leopard, for the blood trail as described to me could only have been made by a foot wound, and I was very gratified to find later that my deductions were correct and that the bullet fired by the man on the tower on the left bank had only creased the pad of the leopard's left hind foot and shot away a portion of one of its toes, and that the man on the right bank had missed all his shots.

Second: After some twenty leopards had been caught and killed in traps of the drop-door type, a leopard which everyone thought was the man-eater was caught in one of these traps; and as the Hindu population were unwilling to kill it for fear the spirits of the people whom the man-eater had killed would torment them, an Indian Christian was sent for. This Christian was living in a village thirty miles away, and before he could arrive on the scene, the leopard had dug its way out of the trap, and escaped.

Third: After killing a man the leopard lay up with his kill in a small isolated patch of jungle. Next morning, when search was being made for the victim, the leopard was detected leaving the jungle. After a short chase it was seen to enter a cave, the mouth of which was promptly closed with thornbushes heaped over with big rocks. Every day a growing crowd of men visited the spot. On the fifth day, when some five hundred were assembled, a man whose name is not given but whom the report described as 'a man of influence' came, and, to quote the report, 'said scornfully "there is no leopard in this cave" and took the thorns off the cave. As he took the thorns up, the leopard suddenly rushed out of the cave and made his way safely through a crowd of some five hundred persons who had gathered there.'

These incidents took place shortly after the leopard had become a man-eater, and had the leopard been killed on the bridge, shot in the trap, or sealed up in the cave, several hundred people need not have died, and Garhwal would have been saved many years of suffering.

# ARRIVAL

**IT WAS DURING ONE OF** the intervals of Gilbert and Sullivan's *Yeomen of the Guard,* which was showing at the Chalet Theatre in Naini Tal in 1925, that I first had any definite news of the Rudraprayag man-eater.

I had heard casually that there was a man-Eating leopard in Garhwal and had read articles in the press about the animal, but knowing that there were over four thousand licensed gun-holders in Garhwal, and host of keen sportsmen in Lansdowne, only some seventy miles from Rudraprayag, I imagined that people were falling over each other in their eagerness to shoot the leopard and that a stranger under these circumstances would not be welcome.

It was with no little surprise therefore that, as I stood at the Chalet bar that night having a drink with a friend, I heard Michael Keene—then Chief Secretary to the Government of the United Provinces and later Governor of Assam—telling a group of men about the man-eater and trying to persuade them to go after it. His appeal, judging from the remark of one of the group, and endorsed by the others, was not received with any enthusiasm. The remark was, 'Go after a man-eater that has killed a hundred people? Not on your life!'

Next morning I paid Michael Keene a visit and got all the particulars I wanted. He was not able to tell me exactly where the man-eater was operating, and suggested my going to Rudraprayag and getting in touch with Ibbotson. On my return home I found a letter from Ibbotson on my table.

Ibbotson—now Sir William Ibbotson, and lately Adviser to the Governor of the United Provinces—had very recently been posted to Garhwal as Deputy Commissioner, and one of his first acts had been to try to rid his district of the man-eater. It was in this connection that he had written to me.

My preparations were soon made, and by travelling via Ranikhet, Adbadri, and Karanprayag, I arrived on the evening of the tenth day at a road Inspection Bungalow near Nagrasu. When leaving Naini Tal I did not know it was necessary to arm myself with a permit to occupy this bungalow, and as the caretaker had orders not to allow anyone to occupy it unless so armed, the six Garhwalis carrying my kit, my servant, and I toiled on for another two miles down the Rudraprayag road until we found a suitable place on which to camp for the night.

While my men busied themselves getting water and dry sticks, and my servant collected stones for a cooking-place, I picked up an axe and went to cut down thornbushes to make an enclosure to protect us during the night, for we had been warned ten miles farther up the road that we had entered the man-eater's territory.

Shortly after the fires to cook our evening meal had been lit, a very agitated call came down to us from a village far up the mountain-side, asking us what we were doing out in the open, and warning us that if we remained where we were one or more of us would surely be killed by the man-eater. When the good samaritan had delivered his warning, to do which he had possibly taken a great risk—for it was then dark—Madho Singh, whom you have met elsewhere,[1] expressed the wishes of all present when he said,

[1] See 'The Chowgarh Tigers' in *Man-eaters of Kumaon*.

'We will stay here, sahib, for there is sufficient oil in the lantern to keep it alight all night, and you have your rifle.'

There was sufficient oil in the lantern to keep it alight all night, for I found it burning when I awoke in the morning, and my loaded rifle lay across my bed. But the thorn enclosure was very flimsy and we were dead tired after our ten days' march, and if the leopard had paid us a visit that night he would have secured a very easy victim.

Next day we arrived at Rudraprayag and were given a warm welcome by the men whom Ibbotson had instructed to meet us.

# INVESTIGATION

**I SHALL NOT ATTEMPT TO GIVE** you a day-by-day account of my activities during the ten weeks I spent at Rudraprayag, for it would be difficult after this lapse of time to write such an account and, if written, it would be boring for you to read. I shall confine myself to relating a few of my experiences, sometimes while alone and at other times in company with Ibbotson. But before doing so I should like to give you some idea of the country over which the leopard ranged for eight years, and in which I hunted him for ten weeks.

If you were to climb the hill to the east of Rudraprayag you would be able to see the greater portion of the five hundred square miles of country that the Rudraprayag man-eater ranged over. This area is divided into two more or less equal parts by the Alaknanda river, which, after passing Karanprayag, flows south to Rudraprayag, where it is met by the Mandakini coming down from the north-west. The triangular bit of country between the two rivers is less steep than the country along the left bank of the Alaknanda, and there are consequently more villages in the former area than in the latter.

From your elevated position, the cultivated land in the distance shows up as a series of lines drawn across the face of the steep mountains. These lines are terraced fields which vary in width from a yard to, in some cases, fifty or more yards. The village buildings, you will note, are invariably set at the upper end of the cultivated land; this is done with the object of overlooking and protecting the cultivation from stray cattle and wild animals, for except in very rare cases there are no hedges or fences round the fields. The brown and the green patches that make up most of the landscape are, respectively, grassland and forests. Some of the villages, you will observe, are entirely surrounded by grasslands, while others are entirely surrounded by forests. The whole country, as you look down on it, is rugged and rough, and is cut up by innumerable deep ravines and rock cliffs. In this area there are only two roads, one starting from Rudraprayag and going up to Kedarnath, and the other the main pilgrim road to Badrinath. Both roads, up to the time I am writing about, were narrow and rough and had never had a wheel of any kind on them.

The number of human beings killed between 1918 and 1926 is shown on page 457.

# THE MAN-EATING LEOPARD OF RUDRAPRAYAG
## CASUALTY LIST (by villages), 1918–1926

*Six kills*
CHOPRA

*Five kills*
KOTHKI, RATAURA

*Four kills*
BIJRAKOT

*Three kills*
NAKOT, GANDHARI, KOKHANDI, DADOLI, QUETHI, JHIRMOLI
GOLABRAI, LAMERI

*Two kills*
BAJADU, RAMPUR, MAIKOTI, CHHATOLI, KOTI, MADOLA, RAUTA,
KANDE (JOGI), BAWRUN, SARI, RANAU, PUNAR, TILANI,
BAUNTHA, NAGRASU, GWAR, MARWARA

*One kill*
ASON, PILU, BHAUNSAL, MANGU, BAINJI, BHATWARI, KHAMOLI,
SWANRI, PHALSI, KANDA DHARKOT, DANGI, GUNAUN, BHATGAON,
BAWAL, BARSIL, BHAINSGAON, NARI, SANDAR, TAMEND,
KHATYANA, SEOPURI, SAN, SYUND, KAMERA, DARMARI, DHAMKA
BELA, BELA-KUND, SAUR, BHAINSARI, BAJNU, QUILI, DHARKOT,
BHAINGAON, CHHINKA, DHUNG, KIURI, BAMAN KANDAI,
POKHTA, THAPALGAON, BANSU, NAG, BAISANI, RUDRAPRAYAG,
GWAR, KALNA, BHUNKA, KAMERA, SAIL, PABO, BHAINSWARA

### ANNUAL TOTALS

| Year | | | | | Total |
|------|---|---|---|---|-------|
| 1918 | . | . | . | . | 1 |
| 1919 | . | . | . | . | 3 |
| 1920 | . | . | . | . | 6 |
| 1921 | . | . | . | . | 23 |
| 1922 | . | . | . | . | 24 |
| 1923 | . | . | . | . | 26 |
| 1924 | . | . | . | . | 20 |
| 1925 | . | . | . | . | 8 |
| 1926 | . | . | . | . | 14 |
| | | | | | 125 |

It would be reasonable to assume that more human beings would have been killed in villages surrounded by forests than in villages surrounded by cultivated land. Had the man-eater been a tiger this would undoubtedly have been the case, but to a man-eating leopard, which only operates at night, the presence or absence of cover makes no difference, and the only reason why there were more kills in one village than in another was due, in the one case, to lack of precautions, and in the other, to the observance of them.

I have mentioned that the man-eater was an out-sized male leopard long past his prime, but though he was old he was enormously strong. The ability of carnivora to carry their kills to a place where they can feed undisturbed determines, to a great extent, the place they choose to do their killing. To the Rudraprayag man-eater all places were alike, for he was capable of carrying the heaviest of his human victims for distances up to—on one occasion that I know of—four miles. On the occasion I refer to the leopard killed a fully grown man in his own house and carried his victim for two miles up the steep slope of a well-wooded hill, and down the far side for another two miles through dense scrub jungle. This was done for no apparent reason, for the kill had taken place in the early hours of the night and the leopard had not been followed up until noon of the next day.

Leopards—other than man-eaters—are the most easily killed of all animals in our jungles, for they have no sense of smell.

More methods are employed in killing leopards than are employed in killing any other animal. These methods vary according to whether the leopard is being killed for sport, or for profit. The most exciting, and the most interesting, method of killing leopards for sport is to track them down in the jungles and, when they are located, stalk and shoot them. The easiest, and the most cruel, method of killing leopards for profit is to insert a small and very highly explosive bomb in the flesh of an animal which are been killed by a leopard. Many villagers have learnt to make these bombs, and when one of them comes in contact with the leopard's teeth, it explodes and blows the leopard's jaws off. Death is instantaneous in some cases, but more often than not the unfortunate animal crawls away to die a lingering and very painful death, for the people who use the bombs have not the courage to follow the blood trail left by the leopard to dispatch it.

The tracking, locating, and stalking of leopards, besides being exciting and interesting, is comparatively easy. For leopards have tender pads and keep to footpaths and game tracks as far as possible; they are not hard to locate, for practically every bird and animal in the jungle assists the hunter; and they are easy to stalk, for, though they are blessed with very keen sight and hearing, they are handicapped by having no sense of smell. The sportsman can therefore select the line of approach that best suits him, irrespective of the direction in which the wind is blowing.

Having tracked, located, and stalked a leopard, far more pleasure is got from pressing the button of a camera than is ever got from pressing the trigger of a rifle. In the one case the leopard can be watched for hours, and there is no more graceful and interesting animal in the jungles to watch. The button of the camera can be pressed as fancy dictates to make a record which never loses its interest. In the other case a fleeting glimpse, one press of the trigger, and—if the aim has been true—the acquisition of a trophy which soon loses both its beauty and its interest.

# THE FIRST KILL

**SHORTLY BEFORE MY ARRIVAL AT** Rudraprayag, Ibbotson had organized a beat which if it had been successful would have saved the lives of fifteen human beings. The beat, and the circumstances leading up to it, are worthy of record.

Twenty pilgrims toiling up the road to Badrinath arrived towards evening at a small roadside shop. After the shopkeeper had met their wants he urged them to be on their way, telling them there was only just sufficient daylight left for them to reach the pilgrim shelters four miles farther up the road, where they would get food and safe shelter. The pilgrims were unwilling to accept this advice; they said they had done a long march that day and were too tired to walk another four miles, and that all they wanted were facilities to prepare and cook their evening meal, and permission to sleep on the platform adjoining the shop. To this proposal the shopkeeper vigorously objected. He told the pilgrims that his house was frequently visited by the man-eater, and that to sleep out in the open would be to court death.

While the argument was at its height a *sadhu* on his way from Mathura to Badrinath arrived on the scene and championed the cause of the pilgrims. He said that if the shopkeeper would give shelter to the women of the party he would sleep on the platform with the men, and if any leopard—man-eater or otherwise—dared to molest them he would take it by the mouth and tear it in half.

To this proposal the shopkeeper had perforce to agree. So while the ten women of the party took shelter in the one-roomed shop behind a locked door, the ten men lay down in a row on the platform, with the *sadhu* in the middle.

When the pilgrims on the platform awoke in the morning they found the *sadhu* missing, the blanket on which he had slept rumpled, and the sheet he had used to cover himself with partly dragged off the platform and spotted with blood. At the sound of the men's excited chattering the shopkeeper opened the door, and at a glance saw what had happened. When the sun had risen, the shopkeeper, accompanied by the men, followed the blood trail down the hill and across three terraced fields, to a low boundary wall; here, lying across the wall, with the lower portion of his body eaten away, they found the *sadhu*.

Ibbotson was staying at Rudraprayag at this time, trying to get in touch with the man-eater. There had been no kills during his stay, so he decided to beat, on spec, a very likely looking bit of cover, on the far side of the Alaknanda, which the locals suspected was used by the man-eater as a lying-up place during the hours of daylight. So while the twenty pilgrims were toiling up the road towards the little shop, the *patwaris* and other members of Ibbotson's staff were going round the near-by villages warning men to be ready for the beat which was to take place on the morrow.

After an early breakfast next morning Ibbotson accompanied by his wife and a friend whose name I have forgotten, and followed by some members of his staff and two hundred beaters, crossed the Alaknanda by the suspension bridge, went up the hill on the far side for a mile or so, and took up positions for the beat.

While the beat was still in progress, word was brought by runner of the killing of the *sadhu*.

The beat, which proved to be a blank, was completed and a hurried council held, the upshot of which was that Ibbotson, his

party, and the two hundred beaters set off up the right bank, to cross the river four miles farther up by a swing bridge, to make their way back along the left bank to the scene of the kill, while the staff dispersed over the countryside to collect as many men as possible and assemble them at the shop.

By late afternoon two thousand beaters and several additional guns had gathered, and the high rugged hill above the shop was beaten from top to bottom. If you know Ibbotson, there is no need for me to tell you that the beat was very efficiently organized, and as efficiently carried out, and the only reason why it failed in its object was that the leopard was not in that area.

When a leopard, or a tiger, leaves of his own accord a kill in the open, in an exposed spot, it is an indication that the animal has no further interest in the kill. After its feed it invariably removes itself to a distance, maybe only two or three miles, or in the case of man-eaters, maybe to a distance of ten or more miles. So it is quite possible that, while the hill was being beaten, the man-eater was peacefully slumbering ten miles away.

# LOCATING THE LEOPARD

**MAN-EATING LEOPARDS ARE OF RARE** occurrence, and for this reason very little is known about them.

My own experience of these animals was very limited, amounting to no more than a brief encounter with one many years previously, and though I suspected that the change-over from animal to human-and-animal diet would affect the habits of a leopard as much as it does those of a tiger, I did not know to what extent a leopard's habits would change, and meanwhile I decided to try to kill the man-eater by the methods usually employed for killing leopards.

The most common method of killing leopards is to sit up for them, either over a kill or over live bait in the form of a goat or a sheep. To carry out either one of these methods it is necessary in the one case to find a kill, and in the other to locate the quarry.

My object in going to Rudraprayag was to try to prevent further loss of human life, and I had no intention of waiting for another human kill to occur over which I could sit, therefore the obvious thing to do was to locate the man-eater and shoot it over live bait.

Here a formidable difficulty, which I hoped in time partly to overcome, presented itself. From the maps I had been supplied with I found that the man-eater was operating over an area of roughly five hundred square miles. Five hundred square miles of country anywhere would have been a considerable area in which to find and shoot any animal, and in this mountainous and rugged part of Garhwal the task of finding an animal that only operated at night appeared, at first glance, to be well-nigh impossible—until I took the Alaknanda river, which divided the area into two more or less equal parts, into consideration.

It was generally believed that the Alaknanda offered no obstacle to the man-eater and that when he found it difficult to obtain a human kill on one bank, he crossed over to the other bank, by swimming the river.

I discounted this belief. No leopard in my opinion would under any circumstances voluntarily commit itself to the swift-flowing, ice-cold waters of the Alaknanda, and I was convinced that when the man-eater crossed from one bank to the other he did so by one of the suspension bridges.

There were two suspension bridges in the area, one at Rudraprayag, and the other about twelve miles farther up the river, at Chatwapipal. Between these two bridges there was a swing bridge—the one by which Ibbotson, his party, and the two hundred men had crossed the river on the day of the beat. This swing bridge, which no animal excepting a rat could possibly have crossed, was the most fear-compelling structure of its kind that I have ever seen. The two hand-twisted grass cables, blackened by age and mouldy from the mists rising from the river, spanned some two hundred feet of foaming white water which, a hundred yards farther down, surged with a roar like thunder between two walls of rock, where a *kakar*, driven by wild dogs, is credited with having leapt across the Alaknanda. Between the cables, and forming the footway, were odd bits of sticks an inch and a half to two inches in diameter set about two feet apart and loosely tied to the cables with wisps of grass. To add to the difficulty in crossing this cobweb structure, one of the cables had sagged, with the result that the sticks on which one had to place one's feet were at an angle of forty-five degrees. The first time I met this fearsome *jhula* I was foolish enough to ask the toll-collector, who for the payment of one pice permitted me to risk my life on it, whether the bridge was ever tested or repaired. His answer, given as he ran a speculative eye over me, that the bridge was never tested or repaired but was replaced when it broke under the weight of someone who was trying to cross it, gave me a cold feeling down my spine, a feeling that remained with me long after I had got safely to the other side.

This *jhula* being beyond the powers of the man-eater to cross, there remained the two suspension bridges, and I felt sure that if I could close them against the leopard I should be able to confine him to one side of the Alaknanda, and so reduce by half the area in which to look for him.

The first thing therefore was to try to find out on which bank of the river the leopard was. The last kill, of the sadhu, had taken place on the left bank of the river a few miles from the Chatwapipal suspension bridge, and I felt sure that the leopard had crossed this bridge, after abandoning his kill, for no matter what precautions the locals and the pilgrims may have taken before a kill, their precautions were redoubled immediately after one, and made it almost impossible for the leopard to secure consecutive kills in the same area. Looking at the map you will ask why, if this was so, as many as six kills have been shown against a single village. I can only answer that an effort cannot be sustained indefinitely. The houses are small and without conveniences or means of sanitation,

and it would not be surprising if, hearing the man-eater was operating in a village ten, fifteen, or twenty miles away, some man, woman, or child should, at the urgent dictate of nature, open a door for a brief minute and so give the leopard the chance for which he had perhaps been waiting many nights.

# THE SECOND KILL

**NO PHOTOGRAPHS OR OTHER MEANS** by which I could identify the man-eater by his pug-marks were available, so,until I had been given an opportunity of acquiring this information for myself, I decided to treat all leopards in the vicinity of Rudraprayag as suspect, and to shoot any that gave me a chance.

The day I arrived at Rudraprayag, I purchased two goats. One of these I tied up the following evening a mile along the pilgrim road; the other I took across the Alaknanda and tied up on a path running through some heavy scrub jungle where I found the old pug-marks of a big male leopard. On visiting the goats the following morning I found the one across the river had been killed and a small portion of it eaten. The goat had unquestionably been killed by a leopard, but had been eaten by a small animal, possibly a pine-marten.

Having received no news about the man-eater during the day, I decided to sit up over the goat, and at 3 p.m. took up my position in the branches of a small tree about fifty yards from the kill. During the three hours I sat in the tree I had no indication, from either animals or birds, that the leopard was anywhere in the vicinity, and as dusk was falling I slipped off the tree, cut the cord tethering the goat—which the leopard had made no attempt to break the previous night—and set off for the bungalow.

I have already admitted that I had very little previous experience of man-eating leopards, but I had met a few man-eating tigers, and from the time I left the tree until I reached the bungalow I took every precaution to guard against a sudden attack; and it was fortunate that I did so.

I made an early start next morning, and near the gate of the bungalow I picked up the tracks of a big male leopard. These tracks I followed back to a densely wooded ravine which crossed the path close to where the goat was lying. The goat had not been touched during the night.

The leopard that had followed me could only have been the man-eater, and for the rest of the day I walked as many miles as my legs would carry me, telling all the people in the villages I visited, and all whom I met on the roads, that the man-eater was on our side of the river, and warning them to be careful.

Nothing happened that day, but next day, just as I was finishing breakfast after a long morning spent in prospecting the jungles beyond Golabrai, a very agitated man dashed into the bungalow to tell me that a woman had been killed by the man-eater the previous night in a village on the hill above the bungalow—the same hill and almost at the exact spot from where you obtained your bird's-eye view of the five hundred square miles of country the man-eater was operating over.

Within a few minutes I collected all the things I needed—a spare rifle and a shotgun, cartridges, rope, and a length of fishing-line—and set off up the steep hill accompanied by the villager and two of my men. It was a sultry day, and though the distance was not great—three miles at the most—the climb of four thousand feet in the hot sun was very trying and I arrived at the village in a bath of sweat.

The story of the husband of the woman who had been killed was soon told. After their evening meal, which had been eaten by the light of the fire, the woman collected the metal pots and pans that had been used and carried them to the door to wash, while the man sat down to have a smoke. On reaching the door the woman sat down on the doorstep, and as she did so the utensils clattered to the ground. There was not sufficient light for the man to see what had happened, and when he received no answer to his urgent call he dashed forward and shut and barred the door. 'Of what use', he said, 'would it have been for me to risk my life in trying to recover a dead body?' His logic was sound, though heartless; and I gathered that the grief he showed was occasioned not so much by the loss of his wife, as by the loss of that son and heir whom he had expected to see born within the next few days.

The door, where the woman had been seized, opened on to a four-foot-wide lane that ran for fifty yards between two rows of houses. On hearing the clatter of the falling pots and pans, followed by the urgent call of the man to his wife, every door in the lane had been instantaneously shut. The marks on the ground showed that the leopard had dragged the unfortunate woman the length of the lane, then killed her, and carried her down the hill for a hundred yards into a small ravine that bordered some terraced fields. Here he ate his meal, and here he left the pitiful remains.

The body lay in the ravine at one end of a narrow terraced field, at the other end of which, forty yards away, was a leafless and stunted walnut tree in whose branches a hayrick had been built, four feet from the ground and six feet tall. In this hayrick I decided to sit.

Starting from near the body, a narrow path ran down into the ravine. On this path were the pug-marks of the leopard that had killed the woman, and they were identical with the pug marks of the leopard that had followed me two nights previously from the killed goat to the Rudraprayag bungalow. The pug-marks were of an out-sized male leopard long past his prime, with a slight defect where a bullet fired four years previously had creased the pad of his left hind paw.

I procured two stout eight-foot bamboos from the village and

drove them into the ground close to the perpendicular bank that divided the field where the body was laying from the field below. To these bamboos I fixed my spare rifle and shotgun securely, tied lengths of dressed silk fishing-line to the triggers, looped the lines back over the trigger-guards, and fastened them to two stakes driven into the hillside on the far side of, and a little above, the path. If the leopard came along the path he had used the previous night there was a reasonable chance of his pulling on the lines and shooting himself; on the other hand, if he avoided them, or came by any other way, and I fired at him while he was on the kill, he would be almost certain to run into the trap which lay on his most natural line of retreat. Both the leopard, because of its protective colouring, and the body, which had been stripped of all clothing, would be invisible in the dark; so to give me an idea of the direction in which to fire, I took a slab of white rock from the ravine and put it on the edge of the field, about a foot from the near side of the body.

My ground arrangements completed to my satisfaction, I made myself a comfortable seat on the rick, throwing out some of the straw, and heaping some behind me and up to my waist in front. As I was facing the kill and had my back to the tree, there was little chance of the leopard seeing me, no matter at what time he came; and that he would come during the night, in spite of his reputation of not returning to his kills, I was firmly convinced. My clothes were still wet after the stiff climb, but a comparatively dry jacket kept out the chill wind; so I settled down into my soft and comfortable seat and prepared for an all-night vigil. I sent my men away, and told them to remain in the headman's house until I came for them, or until the sun was well up next morning. (I had stepped from the bank on to the rick and there was nothing to prevent the man-eater from doing the same.)

The sun was near setting, and the view of the Ganges valley, with the snowy Himalayas in the background showing bluish pink under the level rays of the setting sun, was a feast for the eyes. Almost before I realized it, daylight had faded out of the sky and night had come.

Darkness, when used in connection with night, is a relative term and has no fixed standard; what to one man would be pitch dark, to another would be dark, and to a third moderately dark. To me, having spent so much of my life in the open, the night is never dark, unless the sky is overcast with heavy clouds. I do not wish to imply that I can see as well by night as by day; but I can see quite well enough to find my way through any jungle or, for that matter, over any ground. I had placed the white stone near the body only as a precaution, for I hoped that the starlight, with the added reflection from the snowy range, would give me sufficient light to shoot by.

But my luck was out; for night had hardly fallen when there was a flash of lightning, followed by distant thunder, and in a few minutes the sky was heavily overcast. Just as the first big drops of a deluge began to fall, I heard a stone roll into the ravine, and a minute later the loose straw on the ground below me was being scratched up. The leopard had arrived; and while I sat in torrential rain with the icy-cold wind whistling through my wet clothes, he lay dry and snug in the straw below. The storm was one of the worst I have ever experienced, and while it was at its height, I saw a lantern being carried towards the village, and marvelled at the courage of the man who carried it. It was not until some hours later that I learnt that the man who so gallantly braved both the leopard and the storm had done a forced march of over thirty miles

from Pauri to bring me the electric night-shooting light the Government had promised me; the arrival of this light three short hours earlier *might* . . . But regrets are vain, and who can say that the fourteen people who died later would have had a longer span of life if the leopard had not buried his teeth in their throats? And again, even if the light had arrived in time there is no certainty that I should have killed the leopard that night.

The rain was soon over—leaving me chilled to the bone—and the clouds were breaking up when the white stone was suddenly obscured, and a little later I heard the leopard eating. The night before, he had lain in the ravine and eaten from that side; so, expecting him to do the same this night, I had placed the stone on the near side of the kill. Obviously, the rain had formed little pools in the ravine, and to avoid them the leopard had taken up a new position and in doing so had obscured my mark. This was something I had not foreseen; however, knowing the habits of leopards, I knew I should not have to wait long before the stone showed up again. Ten minutes later the stone was visible, and almost immediately thereafter I heard a sound below me and saw the leopard as a light-yellowish object disappearing under the rick. His light colour could be accounted for by old age, but the sound he made when walking I could not then, nor can I now, account for; it was like the soft rustle of a woman's silk dress, and could not be explained by stubble in the field—for there was none—or by the loose straw lying about.

Waiting a suitable length of time, I raised the rifle and covered the stone, intending to fire the moment it was again obscured; but there is a limit to the time a heavy rifle can be held to the shoulder, and when the limit had been reached I lowered the rifle to ease my aching muscles. I had hardly done so when the stone for the second time disappeared from view. Three times within the next two hours the same thing happened, and in desperation, as I heard the leopard approaching the rick for the fourth time, I leant over and fired at the indistinct object below me.

The narrow terrace to which I have given the usual name of

'field' was only about two feet wide at this point, and when I examined the ground next morning I found my bullet-hole in the centre of the two-foot-wide space with a little hair, cut from the leopard's neck, scattered round it.

I saw no more of the leopard that night, and at sunrise I collected my men and set off down the steep hill to Rudraprayag, whilst the husband and his friends carried away the woman's remains for cremation.

# PREPARATIONS

**MY THOUGHTS AS, COLD AND STIFF,** I walked down the hill to Rudraprayag from the scene of my night's failure were very bitter, for, from whatever angle it was viewed, there was no question that the fickle jade chance had played both Garhwal and myself a scurvy trick which we did not deserve.

However little I merit it, the people of our hills credit me with supernatural powers where man-eaters are concerned. News that I was on my way to try to rid Garhwal of the man-eater had preceded me, and while I was still many days' march from Rudraprayag the men I met on the roads, and those who from their fields or village homes saw me passing, greeted me with a faith in the accomplishment of my mission that was as touching as it was embarrassing, and which increased in intensity the nearer I approached my destination. Had any been there to witness my entry into Rudraprayag, he would have found it hard to believe that the man whom the populace thronged round was no hero returning from the wars, but a man, very sensible of his limitations, who greatly feared that the task he had undertaken was beyond his powers of accomplishment.

Five hundred square miles, much of which was clothed with dense scrub jungle, and all of which was rugged and mountainous, was an enormous area in which to find and shoot one particular leopard out of possibly fifty that inhabited it, and the more I saw of the grand and beautiful country the less I liked it from the viewpoint of the task I had undertaken. The populace quite naturally did not share my misgivings; to them I was one who had rid others of man-eaters and who had now come among them to rid them of the menace they had lived under for eight long years. And then, with incredible good luck, I had within a few hours of my arrival got the animal I was in pursuit of to kill one of my goats and, by staying out a little after dark, to follow me to that side of the Alaknanda where I believed it would be less difficult to deal with it than it would have been on the other side. Following on this initial success had been the kill of the unfortunate woman. I had tried to prevent the further loss of human life, and had failed, and my failure had presented me with an opportunity of shooting the leopard which otherwise I might not have got for many months.

As I had been toiling uphill behind my guide the previous day, I had weighed up my chances of killing the leopard and assessed them at two-to-one, despite the facts that the animal had in recent years earned the reputation of never returning to a kill, that it was a dark night, and that I had no aid to night shooting. The day I visited Michael Keene and told him I would go to Garhwal he had asked me if I had everything I wanted; and hearing that I only lacked a night-shooting light and would telegraph to Calcutta for one, he said the least the Government could do for me was to provide me with a light; and he promised to have the best one procurable waiting for me at Rudraprayag.

Though my disappointment was great when I found that the light had not arrived, it was mitigated by my ability to see in the dark, the ability on which I had assessed my chances at two-to-one. So much depended on the success of that night's venture, that I had armed myself with a spare rifle and shot gun, and when from my concealed position on the hayrick I viewed the scene—the short range at which I should get my shot, and the perfectly camouflaged gun-trap into which the leopard would of a certainty run if I missed or wounded him—my hopes rose high and I put my chances of success at ten-to-one. Then had come the storm. With visibility reduced to practically nil, and without the electric light, I had failed, and my failure would in a few hours be known throughout the stricken area.

Exercise, warm water, and food have a wonderfully soothing effect on bitter thoughts, and by the time I had picked my way down the steep hillside, had a hot bath, and breakfast, I had ceased to rail at fate and was able to take a more reasonable view of my night's failure. Regret over a bullet fired into the ground was as profitless as regret over milk spilt on sand, and provided the leopard had not crossed the Alaknanda my chances of killing it had improved, for I now had the electric shooting light which the runner had braved both the leopard and the storm to bring me.

The first thing to do was to find out if the leopard had crossed the Alaknanda, and as I was firm in my conviction that the only way it could do this was by way of the suspension bridges, I set out after breakfast to glean this information. I discounted the possibility of the leopard having crossed the Chatwapipal bridge, for no matter how great the shock he had received by the discharge of my heavy rifle a few feet from his head, it was not possible that he would have covered the fourteen miles that separated the kill from the bridge in the few hours that remained between the firing of my shot and daylight, so I decided to confine my search to the Rudraprayag bridge.

There were three approaches to the bridge; one from the north, one from the south, and between these two a well-beaten footpath from the Rudraprayag bazaar. After examining these approaches very carefully I crossed the bridge and examined the Kedarnath pilgrim road for half a mile, and then the footpath on

which three nights previously my goat had been killed. Satisfied that the leopard had not crossed the river. I determined to put in operation my plan for closing the two bridges at night and thus confining the leopard to my side of the river. The plan was a simple one and, given the co-operation of the caretakers of the bridges, both of whom lived on the left bank and close to the bridge abutments, was certain of success.

To close the only means of communication between the two banks of the river over a stretch of some thirty miles would appear to be a very high-handed proceeding, but actually it was not so, for no human being dared to use the bridges between sunset and sunrise owing to the curfew imposed by the leopard.

The bridges were closed by wedging thornbushes in the four-foot-wide archway in the towers carrying the steel cables from which the plank footway was suspended, and during the whole period that the bridges were closed with thorn, or were guarded by me, no human being demanded passage across them.

I spent in all some twenty nights on the tower on the left bank of the Rudraprayag bridge, and those nights will never be forgotten. The tower was built out on a projecting rock and was twenty feet high, and the platform on the top of it, which had been worn smooth by the wind, was about four feet wide and eight feet long. There were two means of reaching this platform, one by swarming along the cables, which ran through holes near the top of the tower and were anchored in the hillside some fifty feet from the tower, and the other by climbing up a very rickety bamboo ladder. I chose the latter way, for the cables were coated over with some black and very evil-smelling matter which clung to one's hands and permanently stained one's clothes.

The ladder—two uneven lengths of bamboo connected with thin sticks loosely held in position with string—only reached to within four feet of the platform. Standing on the top rung of the ladder and dependent for a handhold on the friction of the palms of my hands on the smooth masonry, the safe gaining of the platform was an acrobatic feat that had less appeal the oftener it was tried.

All the rivers in this part of the Himalayas flow from north to south, and in the valleys through which they flow blows a wind which changes direction with the rising and the setting of the sun. During daylight hours the wind—locally called *dadu*—blows from the south, and during the hours of night it blows from the north.

At the time when I used to take up my position on the platform there was usually a lull in the wind, but shortly thereafter it started blowing as a light zephyr gaining in strength as daylight faded, and amounting by midnight to a raging gale. There was no handhold on the platform and even when lying flat on my stomach to increase friction and reduce wind-pressure, there was imminent risk of being blown off on to the rocks sixty feet below, off which one would have bounced into the ice-cold Alaknanda—not that the temperature of the water would have been of any interest after a fall of sixty feet on to sharp and jagged rocks. Strangely enough, whenever I felt in fear of falling it was always the water, and never the rocks, that I thought of. Added to the discomfort of the wind, I suffered torment from a multitude of small ants, which entered my clothes and ate away patches of skin. During the twenty nights I guarded the bridge, the thornbushes were not placed in position; and in all that long period the bridge was only crossed by one living thing—a jackal.

# MAGIC

**EACH EVENING WHEN I WENT TO** the bridge I was accompanied by two men who carried the ladder that enabled me to climb to the platform, and which they removed after handing me my rifle.

On the second day, as we arrived at the bridge, we saw a man dressed in flowing white robes with something glinting on his head and breast. He carried a six-foot silver cross, and was approaching the bridge from the direction of Kedarnath. On reaching the bridge the man knelt down and, holding the cross in front of him, bowed his head. After remaining in this position for a little while he raised the cross high, rose to his feet, took a few steps forward, and again knelt down and bowed his head. This he continued to do at short intervals all the way across the long bridge.

As he passed me the man raised his hand in salutation, but since he appeared to be deep in prayer I did not speak to him. The glints I had seen on his head-dress and breast were, I perceived, silver crosses.

My men had been as interested in this strange apparition as I had been, and watching him climb the steep footpath to the

Rudraprayag bazaar, they asked me what manner of man he was, and from what country he had come. That he was a Christian was apparent, and as I had not heard him speak I assumed from his long hair, jet-black luxuriant beard, and what I could see of his features, that he was a man from Northern India.

The following morning, when with the help of the ladder I had climbed down from the tower and was proceeding to the Inspection Bungalow, where I passed that portion of the daylight hours that I did not spend in visiting near and distant villages in search of news of the man-eater, I saw the tall white-robed figure standing on a great slab of rock near the road, surveying the river. At my approach he left the rock and greeted me, and when I asked him what had brought him to these parts he said he had come—from a distant land—to free the people of Garhwal from the evil spirit that was tormenting them. When I asked how he proposed accomplishing this feat, he said he would make an effigy of a tiger and after he had, by prayer, induced the evil spirit to enter it, he would set the effigy afloat on the Ganges and the river would convey it down to the sea from where it could not return, and where it would do no farther harm to human beings.

However much I doubted the man's ability to accomplish the task he had set himself, I could not help admiring his faith and his industry. He arrived each morning before I left the tower, and I found him still at work when I returned in the evening, labouring with split bamboos, string, paper, and cheap coloured cloth on his 'tiger'. When the effigy was nearing completion a heavy rainstorm one night made the whole structure come unstuck, but, nothing daunted, he cheerfully started on it again next morning, singing as he worked.

Came at last the great day when the 'tiger'—about the size of a horse, and resembling no known animal—was fashioned to his satisfaction.

Who is there among our hill-folk who does not whole-heartedly enjoy taking part in a *tamasha*? When the effigy, tied to a long pole, was carried down a steep path to a small sandy beach, it had an escort of over a hundred men, many of whom were beating gongs and blowing long trumpets.

At the river's edge the effigy was unlashed from the pole. The white-robed man, with his silver crosses on headgear and breast and his six-foot cross in his hands, knelt on the sand, and with earnest prayer induced the evil spirit to enter his handiwork, and then the effigy, with a crash of gongs and blare of trumpets, was consigned to the Ganges, and speeded on its way to the sea by a liberal offering of sweets and flowers.

Next morning the familiar figure was absent from the rock, and when I asked some men who were on their way to have an early dip in the river where my friend of the flowing robes had come from, and where he had gone, they answered, 'Who can tell whence a holy man has come, and who dare question whither he has departed?'

These men with sandalwood-paste caste-marks on their foreheads, who spoke of the man as 'holy', and all those others who had taken part in the launching ceremony, were Hindus.

In India, where there are no passports or identity discs, and where religion counts for so much—except among those few who have crossed the 'black water'—I believe that a man wearing a saffron robe, or carrying a beggar's bowl, or with silver crosses on his headgear and chest, could walk from the Khyber Pass to Cape Comorin without once being questioned about his destination, or the object of his journey.

# A NEAR ESCAPE

**WHILE I WAS STILL GUARDING THE** bridge, Ibbotson and his wife Jean arrived from Pauri, and as the accommodation in the Inspection Bungalow was very limited I moved out to make room for them, and set up my forty-pound tent on the hill on the far side of the pilgrim road.

A tent afforded little protection against an animal that had left his claw-marks on every door and window for miles round, so I helped my men to put a thorn fence round the ground we intended to camp on. Overhanging this plot of ground was a giant prickly-pear-tree, and as its branches interfered with the erection of the tent I told the men to cut it down. When the tree had been partly cut through I changed my mind, for I saw that I should be without shade during the heat of the day, so instead of felling the tree I told the men to lop the overhanging branches. This tree, which was leaning over the camp at an angle of forty-five degrees, was on the far side of the fence.

There were eight of us in the little camp, and when we had eaten our evening meal I wedged a thornbush securely into the opening in the fence we had entered by, and as I did so I noticed that it would be very easy for the man-eater to climb the tree and drop down on our side of the fence. However, it was too late then to do anything about it, and if the leopard left us alone for that one night, the tree could be cut down and removed in the morning.

I had no tents for my men, and had intended that they should sleep with Ibbotson's men in the outbuildings of the Inspection Bungalow, but this they had refused to do, asserting that there was no more danger for them than there was for me in the open tent. My cook—who was, I discovered, a very noisy sleeper—was lying next to and about a yard from me, and beyond him, packed like sardines in the little enclosure, were the six Garhwalis I had brought from Naini Tal.

The weak spot in our defence was the tree, and I went to sleep thinking of it.

It was a brilliant moonlit night, and round about midnight I was suddenly awakened by hearing the leopard climbing the tree. Picking up the riffle, which was lying ready loaded on the bed, I swung my legs off the bed and had just slipped my feet into my slippers—to avoid the thorns which were scattered all round—when there was an ominous crack from the partly-cut-through tree, followed by a yell from the cook of 'Bagh! Bagh!' In one jump I was outside the tent and, swinging round, was just too late to get the

rifle to bear on the leopard as it sprang up the bank on to a terraced field. Pulling the bush out of the gap I dashed up to the field which was about forty yards in width and bare of crops, and as I stood scanning the hillside dotted over with thornbushes and a few big rocks, the alarm call of a jackal far up the hill informed me that the leopard had gone beyond my reach.

The cook informed me later that he had been lying on his back—a fact of which I had long been aware—and hearing the tree crack he had opened his eyes and looked straight into the leopard's face just as it was preparing to jump down.

The tree was cut down next day and the fence strengthened, and though we stayed in that camp for several weeks our slumbers were not again disturbed.

# THE GIN-TRAP

**FROM REPORTS RECEIVED FROM NEARBY** villages where unsuccessful attempts had been made to break into houses, and from the pug-marks I had seen on the roads, I knew that the man-eater was still in the vicinity, and a few days after the arrival of the Ibbotsons, news was brought that a cow had been killed in a village two miles from Rudraprayag, and about half a mile from the village where I had sat on the hayrick in a walnut tree.

Arrived at the village we found that a leopard had broken down the door of a one-roomed house and had killed and dragged to the door one of the several cows that were in it, and not being able to drag it through the door, had left it on the threshold after eating a good meal.

The house was in the heart of the village, and on prospecting round, we found that by making a hole in the wall of a house a few yards away we could overlook the kill.

The owner of this house, who was also the owner of the dead cow, was only too willing to fall in with our plans, and as evening closed in we locked ourselves very securely into the room, and after eating our sandwiches and drinking the tea we had brought with us, we mounted guard in turns over the hole in the wall throughout the long night without either seeing or hearing anything of the leopard.

When we emerged in the morning the villagers took us round the village, which was of considerable size, and showed us the claw-marks on doors and windows made by the man-eater in the course of years, in his attempts to get at the inmates. One door in particular had more and deeper claw-marks than any other—it was the door the leopard had forced to enter the room in which the forty goats and the boy had been secured.

A day or two later another cow was reported to have been killed in a small village on the hill a few hundred yards from the bungalow. Here again we found that the cow had been killed inside a house, dragged as far as the door, and partly eaten. Facing the door, and distant from it about ten yards, was a newly built hayrick, sixteen feet tall and built on a wooden platform two feet above ground.

News of the kill was brought to us early in the morning, so we had the whole day before us, and the *machan* we built by evening was I am sure not only the most effective, but also the most artistic, that has ever been constructed for a similar purpose.

To start with, the rick was dismantled, and a scaffolding of poles was set round the platform. With these poles to support it, a second, and smaller, platform was built four feet above the lower one. Two-inch-mesh wire-netting was then wound round the whole structure, leaving only the space bare between the lower platform and the ground. Wisps of straw were then looped into the meshes of the netting, and a little straw was spread round the rick and under the platform, just as it had been before we started work. One of the joint owners of the hayrick, who had been absent from the village for a day or two and who returned just as we had finished our task, would not believe that the rick had been disturbed until he felt it all round, and had been shown the second rick we had built with the spare hay in an adjoining field.

As the sun was setting we crawled through the hole we had left in the netting and entered the *machan*, securely closing the entrance behind us. Ibbotson is a little shorter than me, so he took the upper platform, and when we had made ourselves comfortable we each made a small hole in the straw to shoot through. As it would not be possible for us to communicate with each other once the leopard arrived, we agreed that whoever saw it first was to fire. It was a bright moonlit night, so there was no need for either of us to use the electric light.

Sounds in the village quietened down after the evening meal had been eaten, and at about 10 p.m. I heard the leopard coming down the hill behind us. On arriving at the rick it paused for a few minutes and then started to crawl under the platform I was sitting on. Immediately below me, and with only the thickness of a plank between my seat and his head, he paused for a long minute and then started to crawl forward; and just as I was expecting him to emerge from under the platform and give me an easy shot at a range of three or four feet, there was a loud creak in the platform above me. The leopard dashed out to the right, where I could not see him, and went up the hill. The creaking of the planks at the critical moment had resulted from Ibbotson changing his position to relieve a very painful cramp in both legs. After the fright he had got, the leopard abandoned the kill and did not return that night, or the next night.

Two nights later another cow was killed a few hundred yards above the Rudraprayag bazaar.

The owner of this cow lived alone in an isolated house which contained only one room, a room which was divided by a rough partition made of odd bits of plank into a kitchen and living-room. Sometime during the night a noise in the kitchen—the door of which he had forgotten to shut—awakened the man, and a little later, in the dim moonlight which the open door was admitting, he saw the leopard through the wide chinks in the partition, trying to tear one of the planks out.

For a long time the man lay and sweated, while the leopard tried plank after plank. Eventually, being unable to find a weak place in the partition, the leopard left the kitchen, and killed the man's cow, which was tethered in a grass lean-to against the side of the house. After killing the cow the leopard broke the rope by which it was tethered, dragged it a short distance from the lean-to, and left it out in the open after partaking of a good meal.

On the very edge of the hill, and about twenty yards from where the dead cow was lying, there was a fair-sized tree, in the upper branches of which a hayrick had been built; on this natural *machan*—from which there was a sheer drop of several hundred feet into the valley below—Ibbotson and I decided to sit.

To assist in killing the man-eater, the Government a few days previously had sent us a gin-trap. This trap, which was five feet long and weighed eighty pounds, was the most fearsome thing of its kind I have ever seen. Its jaws, armed with sharp teeth three inches long, had a spread of twenty-four inches, and were actuated by two powerful springs, which needed two men to compress.

When leaving the kill the leopard had followed a footpath across a field about forty yards wide, up a three-foot bank, and across another field bordered by a densely scrub-covered hill. At this three-foot step from the upper to the lower field, we set the trap, and to ensure the leopard stepping on to it we planted a few thorn twigs on either side of the path. To one of the traps was attached a short length of half-inch-thick chain, terminating in a ring three inches in diameter; through this ring we drove a stout peg, chaining the trap to the ground.

When these arrangements had been completed, Jean Ibbotson returned to the bungalow with our men, and Ibbotson and I climbed up to the hayrick. After tying a stick in front of us and looping a little hay over it, to act as a screen, we made ourselves comfortable, and waited for the leopard, which we felt sure would not escape us on this occasion.

As evening closed in heavy clouds spread over the sky, and as the moon was not due to rise until 9 p.m., we had of necessity to depend on the electric light for the accuracy of our shooting until then. This light was a heavy and cumbersome affair, and as Ibbotson insisted on my taking the shot, I attached it to my riffle with some little difficulty.

An hour after dark a succession of angry roars apprised us of the fact that the leopard was in the trap. Switching on the electric light, I saw the leopard rearing up with the trap dangling from his forelegs, and taking a hurried shot, my .450 bullet struck a link in the chain and severed it.

Freed from the peg the leopard went along the field in a series of great leaps, carrying the trap in front of him, followed up by the bullet from my left barrel, and two lethal bullets from Ibbotson's shot gun, all of which missed him. In trying to reload my rifle I displaced some part of the light, after which it refused to function.

Hearing the roars of the leopard and our four shots, the people in Rudraprayag bazaar, and in nearby villages, swarmed out of their houses carrying lanterns and pinetorches, and converged from all sides on the isolated house. Shouting to them to keep clear was of no avail, for they were making so much noise that they could not hear us; so while I climbed down the tree, taking my rifle with me—a hazardous proceeding in the dark—Ibbotson lit and pumped up the petrol lamp we had taken into the machan with us. Letting the lamp down to me on the end of a length of rope, Ibbotson joined me on the ground, and together we went in the direction the leopard had taken. Halfway along the field there was a hump caused by an outcrop of rock; this hump we approached, with Ibbotson holding the heavy lamp high above his head, while I walked by his side with rifle to shoulder. Beyond the hump was little depression, and crouching down in this depression and facing us and growling, was the leopard. Within a few minuets of my bullet crashing into his head, we were surrounded by an excited crowd, who literally danced with joy round their long-dreaded enemy.

The animal that lay dead before me was an out-sized male leopard, who the previous night had tried to tear down a partition to get at a human being, and who had been shot in an area in which dozens of human beings had been killed, all good and sufficient reasons for assuming that he was the man-eater. But I could not make myself believe that he was the same animal I had seen the night I sat over the body of the woman. True, it had been a dark night and I had only vaguely seen the outline of the leopard; even so, I was convinced that the animal that was now being lashed to a pole by willing hands was not the man-eater.

With the Ibbotsons leading the way, followed by the men carrying the leopard and a crowd of several hundred men, we set off via the bazaar for the bungalow.

As I stumbled down the hill in the wake of the procession—the only one in all that throng who did not believe that the man-eating leopard of Rudraprayag was dead—my thoughts went back to an occurrence that had taken place not far from our winter home when I was a small boy, and which I saw recounted many years later in a book entitled *Brave Deeds*, or perhaps it was *Bravest Deeds*. The occurence concerned two men: Smeaton of the Indian Civil Service and Braidwood of the Forest Department. One dark stormy night, in pre-railway days, these two men were travelling in a *dak-gharry* from Moradabad to Kaladhungi, and on going round a bend in the road they ran into a rogue elephant. In killing the driver and the two horses, the elephant overturned the *gharry*. Braidwood had a rifle, and while he got it out of its case, put it together, and loaded it, Smeaton climbed on to the *gharry* and released the one unbroken lamp from its socket. Then Smeaton, holding the oil lamp which only gave a glimmer of light over his head, advanced up to the elephant and shone the light on his forehead, to enable Braidwood to get in a killing shot. Admittedly there was a great difference between a rogue elephant and a leopard; even so, there are few who would care to walk up to a pain-maddened leopard—which we later found had practically torn its paw free and was only held by a thin strip of skin—holding a lamp above his head and depending for safety on a companion's bullet.

For the first night in many years every house in the bazaar was open, with women and children standing in the doorways. Progress was slow, for every few yards the leopard was put down to let the children cluster round and get a better view of it. At the farther end of the long street our escort left us, and the leopard was carried in triumph to the bungalow by our men.

Returning to the bungalow after a wash at my camp, the Ibbotsons and I, both during and long after it, put forward our arguments for and against the dead leopard being the man-eater. Eventually, without either side convincing the other, we decided that as Ibbotson had to get back to his work at Pauri, and I was tired out after my long stay at Rudraprayag, we would spend the next day in skinning the leopard and drying the skin, and on the day after would break camp and make for Pauri.

From early morning to late evening relays of men kept coming in from near and distant villages to see the leopard, and as most of these men asserted that they recognized the animal as the man-eater, the conviction of the Ibbotsons, that they were right and I was wrong, grew. Two concessions at my request Ibbotson made: he added his warning to the people to mind, not to relax precautions against the man-eater, and he refrained from telegraphing to tell the Government that we had shot the man-eater.

We went early to bed that night, for we were to start at daybreak next morning. I was up while it was still dark and was having *chota hazri* when I heard voices on the road. As this was very unusual, I called out to ask what men were doing on the road at that hour. On seeing me, four men climbed up the path to my camp, and informed me they had been sent by the *patwari* to tell me that a woman had been killed by the man-eater on the far side of the river, about a mile from the Chatwapipal bridge.

# THE HUNTERS HUNTED

**IBBOTSON WAS JUST UNBOLTING THE** door to admit his man with early tea when I arrived, and after he had countermanded his move to Pauri we sat on Jean's bed with a large-scale map between us, drinking tea and discussing our plans.

Ibbotson's work at his headquarters at Pauri was pressing, and at most he could only spare two more days and nights. I had telegraphed to Naini Tal the previous day to say I was returning home via Pauri and Kotdwara; this telegram I decided to cancel, and instead of going by rail, I would return on foot the way I had come. These details settled, and the village where the woman had been killed found on the map, I returned to camp to tell my men of our change of plans, and to instruct them to pack up and follow us, accompanied by the four men who had brought news of the kill.

Jeans was to remain at Rudraprayag, so after breakfast Ibbotson and I set off on two of his horses, a Gulf Arab and an English mare, two of the most surefooted animals I have ever had the good fortune to ride.

We took our rifles, a blue-flame stove, a petrol-lamp, and some provisions with us, and were accompanied by one of Ibbotson's syces on a borrowed horse, carrying food for our horses.

We left the horses at the Chatwapipal bridge. This bridge had not been closed the night we shot the leopard, with the result that the man-eater had got across the river and secured a kill at the first village he visited.

A guide was waiting for us at the bridge, and he took us up a very steep ridge and along a grassy hillside, and then down into a deep and densely wooded ravine with a small stream flowing through it. Here we found the *patwari* and some twenty men guarding the kill.

The kill was a very robust and fair girl, some eighteen or twenty years of age. She was lying on her face with her hands by her sides. Every vestige of clothing had been stripped from her, and she had been licked by the leopard from the soles of her feet to her neck, in which were four great teeth-marks; only a few pounds of flesh had been eaten from the upper portion of her body, and a few pounds from the lower portion.

The drums we had heard as we came up the hill were being beaten by the men who were guarding the kill, and as it was then about 2 p.m. and there was no chance of the leopard being anywhere in the vicinity, we went up to the village to brew ourselves some tea, taking the *patwari* and the guard with us.

After tea we went and had a look at the house where the girl had been killed. It was a stone-built house, consisting of one room, situated in the midst of terraced fields some two or three acres in extent, and it was occupied by the girl, her husband, and their six-month-old child.

Two days previous to the kill, the husband had gone to Pauri to give evidence in a land dispute case, and had left his father in charge of the house. On the night of the kill, after the girl and her father-in-law had partaken of their evening meal and it was getting near time to retire for the night, the girl, who had been nursing her child, handed it over to her father-in-law, unlatched the door, and stepped outside to squat down—I have already mentioned that there are no sanitary conveniences in the houses of our hill-folk.

When the child was transferred from the mother to the grandfather, it started crying, so even if there had been any sound from outside—and I am sure there was none—he would not have heard it. It was a dark night. After waiting for a few minutes the man called to the girl; and receiving no answer he called again. Then he got up and hurriedly closed and latched the door.

Rain had fallen earlier in the evening and it was easy to reconstruct the scene. Shortly after the rain had stopped, the leopard, coming from the direction of the village, had crouched down behind a rock in the field, about thirty yards to the left front of the door. Here it had lain for some time— possibly listening to the man and the girl talking. When the girl opened the door she squatted down on its right-hand side, partly turning her back on the leopard, who had crept round the far side of the rock, covered the twenty yards separating him from the corner of the house with belly to ground and, creeping along close to the wall of the house, had caught the girl from behind, and dragged her to the rock. Here, when the girl was dead, or possibly when the man called out in alarm, the leopard had picked her up and, holding her high, so that no mark of hand or foot showed on the soft newly ploughed ground, had carried her across one field, down a three-foot bank, and across another field which ended in a twelve-foot drop on to a well-used footpath. Down this drop

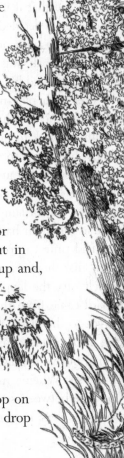

the leopard had sprung with the girl—who weighed about eleven stone—in his mouth, and some idea of his strength will be realized from the fact that when he landed on the footpath he did not let any portion of her body come in contact with the ground.

Crossing the footpath he had gone straight down the hill for half a mile, to the spot where he had undressed the girl. After eating a little of her, he had left her lying in a little glade of emerald-green grass, under the shade of a tree roofed over with dense creepers.

At about four o'clock we went down to sit over the kill, taking the petrol-lamp and night-shooting light with us.

It was reasonable to assume that the leopard had heard the noise the villagers made when searching for the girl, and later when guarding the body, and that if it returned to the kill it would do so with great caution; so we decided not to sit near the kill, and selected a tree about sixty yards away on the hill overlooking the glade.

This tree, a stunted oak, was growing out of the hill at almost a right angle, and after we had hidden the petrol-lamp in a little hollow and covered it over with pine-needles, Ibbotson took his seat in a fork of the tree from where he had a clear view of the kill, while I sat on the trunk with my back to him and facing the hill; Ibbotson was to take the shot, while I saw to our safety. As the shooting light was not functioning—possibly because the battery had faded out—our plan was to sit up as long as Ibbotson could see to shoot and then, with the help of the petrol-lamp, get back to the village where we hoped to find that our men had arrived from Rudraprayag.

We had not had time to prospect the ground, but the villagers had informed us that there was heavy jungle to the east of the kill, to which they felt sure the leopard had retired when they drove it off. If the leopard came from this direction, Ibbotson would see it long before it got to the glade and would get an easy shot, for his rifle was fitted with a telescopic sight which not only made for accurate shooting, but which also gave us an extra half-hour, as we had found from tests. When a minute of daylight more or less may make the difference between success and failure, this modification of the light factor is very important.

The sun was setting behind the high hills to the west, and we had been in shadow for some minutes when a *kakar* dashed down the hill, barking, from the direction in which we had been told there was heavy jungle. On the shoulder of the hill the animal pulled up, and after barking in one spot for some time went away on the far side, and the sound dies away in the distance.

The *kakar* had undoubtedly been alarmed by a leopard, and though it was quite possible that there were other leopards in that area, my hopes had been raised, and when I looked round at Ibbotson I saw that he too was keyed up, and that he had both hands on his rifle.

Light was beginning to fade, but was good enough to shoot by even without the aid of the telescopic sight, when a pine-cone dislodged from behind some low bushes thirty yards above us came rolling down the hill and struck the tree close to my feet. The leopard had arrived and, possibly suspecting danger, had taken a line that would enable him to prospect from a safe place on the hill all the ground in the vicinity of his kill. Unfortunately, in so doing he had got our tree in a direct line with the kill, and though I, who was showing no outline, might escape observation, he would be certain to see Ibbotson, who was sitting in a fork of the tree.

When sufficient light for me to shoot by had long since gone, and Ibbotson's telescopic sight was no longer of any use to him, we heard the leopard coming stealthily down towards the tree. It was then time to take action, so I asked Ibbotson to take my place, while I retrieved the lamp. This lamp was of German make and was called a petromax. It gave a brilliant light but, with its long body and longer handle, was not designed to be used as a lantern in a jungle.

I am a little taller than Ibbotson, and suggested that I should carry the lamp, but Ibbotson said he could manage all right, and, moreover, that he would rather depend on my rifle than his own. So we set off, Ibbotson leading and I following with both hands on my rifle.

Fifty yards from the tree, while climbing over a rock, Ibbotson slipped, the base of the lamp came in violent contact with the rock, and the mantle fell in dust to the bottom of the lamp. The streak of blue flame directed from the nozzle on to the petrol reservoir gave sufficient light for us to see where to put our feet, but the question was how long we should have even this much light. Ibbotson was of the opinion that he could carry the lamp for three minutes before it burst. Three minutes, in which to do a stiff climb of half a mile, over ground on which it was necessary to change direction every few steps to avoid huge rocks and thornbushes, and possibly followed—and actually followed as we found later—by a man-eater, was a terrifying prospect.

There are events in one's life which, no matter how remote, never fade from memory; the climb up that hill in the dark was for me one of them. When we eventually reached the footpath our troubles were not ended, for the path was a series of buffalo wallows, and we did not know where our men were. Alternately slipping on wet ground and stumbling over unseen rocks, we at last came to some stone steps which took off from the path and went up to the right. Climbing these steps we found a small courtyard, on the far side of which was a door. We had heard the gurgling of a hookah as we came up the steps, so I kicked the door and shouted to the inmates to open. As no answer came, I took out a box of matches and shook it, crying that if the door was not opened in a minute I would set the thatch alight. On this an agitated voice came from inside the house, begging me not to set the house on fire, and saying that the door was being opened—a minute later first the inner door and then the outer door were opened, and in two strides Ibbotson and I were in the house, slamming the inner door, and putting our backs to it.

There were some twelve or fourteen men, women, and children of all ages in the room. When the men had regained their wits after the unceremonious entry, they begged us to forgive them for not having opened the doors sooner, adding that they and their families had lived so long in terror of the man-eater that their courage had gone. Not knowing what form the man-eater might

take, they suspected every sound they heard at night. In their fear they had our full sympathy, for from the time Ibbotson had slipped and broken the mantle, and a few minutes later had extinguished the red-hot lamp to prevent it bursting, I had been convinced that one, and possibly both, of us would not live to reach the village.

We were told that our men had arrived about sundown, and that they had been housed in a block of buildings farther along the hill. The two able-bodied men in the room offered to show us the way, but as we knew it would be murder to let them return to their homes alone, we declined their offer—which had been made with the full realization of the risk it would entail—and asked if they could provide us with a light of some kind. After rummaging about in a corner of the room, an old and decrepit lantern with a cracked globe was produced, and when vigorous shaking had revealed that it contained a few drops of oil, it was lit, and with the combined good wishes of the inmates we left the house—the two doors being shut and bolted on our heels.

More buffalo wallows and more sunken rocks, but with the glimmer of light to help us we made good progress and, finding the second lot of steps we had been instructed to climb, we mounted them and found ourselves in a long courtyard facing a row of double-storied buildings extending to the right and to the left, every door of which was fast shut, and not a glimmer of light showing anywhere.

When we called a door was opened, and by climbing a short flight of stone steps we gained the veranda of the upper story, and found the two adjoining rooms which had been placed at the disposal of our men and ourselves. While the men were relieving us of the lamp and our rifles, a dog arrived from nowhere. He was just a friendly village pye, and after sniffing round our legs and wagging his tail, he went towards the steps up which we had just come. The next second, with a scream of fear followed by hysterical barking, he backed towards us with all his hair on end.

The lantern we had been lent had died on us as we reached the courtyard, but our men had procured its twin brother. Though

Ibbotson held it at all angles while I hurriedly reloaded my rifle, he could not get its light to illuminate the ground eight feet below.

By watching the dog it was possible to follow the movements of the leopard. When the leopard had crossed the yard and gone down the steps leading to the footpath, the dog gradually stopped barking and lay down intently watching in that direction, and growling at intervals.

The room that had been vacated for us had no windows, and as the only way in which we could have occupied it in safety would have been by closing the solid door, and excluding all air and light, we decided to spend the night on the veranda. The dog evidently belonged to the late occupant of the room and had been accustomed to sleeping there, for he lay contentedly at our feet and gave us a feeling of safety as we watched in turn through the long hours of the night.

# RETREAT

**AT DAYBREAK NEXT MORNING WE** very carefully stalked the kill, and were disappointed to find that the leopard had not returned to it, which we felt sure he would do after his failure to bag one of us the previous evening.

During the day, while Ibbotson dealt with some office work that had been sent out to him, I took a rifle and went off to see if I could get a shot at the leopard. Tracking on the hard and pine-needle-covered ground was not possible, so I made for the shoulder of the hill beyond which the villagers had told us there was heavy jungle. Here I found the ground very difficult to negotiate, for, in addition to dense scrub jungle through which it was not possible to penetrate, there was a series of rock cliffs on which it was impossible for a human being to find foothold. In this area there was a surprisingly large head of game, and on the paths that intersected it I found the tracks of *kakar*, *ghooral*, pig, and a solitary *sarao*. Of the leopard—except for a few old scratch-marks—I found no trace.

The gin-trap that had been sent off from Rudraprayag the previous day arrived while we were having lunch, and in the early evening we took it down to the glade and, after setting it, poisoned the kill with cyanide. I had no experience of poisons, nor had Ibbotson, but in a conversation with a doctor friend before leaving Naini Tal I had mentioned that Government wanted me to try every means to kill the man-eater, and that there was little use in my trying poison, as the records showed that the leopard throve on it. I told him what poisons had hitherto been tried, and he then recommended my using cyanide, which was the best poison for the cat family. I had passed this information on to Ibbotson, and a few days previously a supply had arrived, with capsules with which to use it. We inserted a few of these capsules in the kill at the places where the leopard had eaten.

There was every hope of the leopard returning to the kill this second night, and as he had seen us on the tree the previous evening we decided not to sit up, but to leave him to the gin-trap and to the poison.

In a big pine-tree near the footpath we built a *machan*, which we padded with hay and on which we took up our position after we had eaten the dinner which Ibbotson cooked on the blue-flame stove. Here on the comfortable *machan* we were able to lie at full stretch and talk and smoke, for our only reason for being there was to listen for sounds from the direction of the kill. We watched and slept by turns, hoping to hear the angry roar of the leopard if by accident it walked into the trap, for here there was no well-used track along which to direct the leopard to it.

Once during the night a *kakar* barked, but in the opposite direction to that from which we expected the leopard to come.

At the first streak of dawn we climbed out of the tree and, after brewing ourselves a cup of tea, visited the kill, which we found lying just as we had left it.

Ibbotson left for Rudraprayag after an early breakfast, and I was packing my things and having a final word with the villagers before starting on my fifteen-day journey back to Naini Tal when a party of men arrived to give the news that a cow had been killed by a leopard in a village four miles away. They suspected that the cow had been killed by the man-eater, for the previous night—the night

the leopard had followed Ibbotson and myself from the tree to the veranda—and towards the small hours of the morning, the leopard had made a determined attempt to break down the door of the headman's house; late the following evening, the cow had been killed in the jungle three hundred yards from this house. At the urgent request of these men I postponed my departure to Naini Tal and accompanied them back to their village, taking the gin-trap and a supply of poison with me.

The headman's house was on a little knoll surrounded by cultivated land, and was approached by a footpath which for a short distance ran over soft and boggy ground; here I found the pug-marks of the man-eater.

The headman had seen me approaching across the valley and had a steaming dish of tea brewed in fresh milk and sweetened with jaggery, waiting for me. While I drank this rich and over-sweetened liquid on the courtyard, sitting on a reed couch upholstered with *ghooral* skins, he drew my attention to the condition of the door which two nights previously the leopard had attempted to break down, in which attempt it would undoubtedly have succeeded if he had not fortunately had some sawn timber in the house—intended for repairing the roof—which he had used to shore up the door from inside.

The headman was old and crippled with rheumatism, so he sent his son to show me the kill while he made room in the house for myself and my men.

I found the kill—a young cow in grand condition—lying on a flat bit of ground just above the cattle track, in an ideal position for setting up the gin-trap. Its back was against a tangle of wild rose-bushes, and its hooves were against a foot-high bank; while eating, the leopard had sat on the bank with its forepaws between the cow's legs.

Having dug away the ground between the cow's legs and removed it to a distance, I set the trap where the leopard had placed his paws and covered it over with big green leaves. Then, after sprinkling on a layer of earth, I replaced the deal leaves, bits of dry sticks, and splinters of bone in the exact position between the cow's legs in which I had found them. Not one of a hundred human beings going to the kill would have noticed that the ground had in any way been disturbed, and a deadly trap set.

My arrangements made to my satisfaction I retraced my steps and climbed a tree half-way between the kill and the headman's house, where I would be handy if needed at the trap.

Near sundown a pair of *kalege* pheasants and their brood of five chicks, which I had been watching for some time, suddenly took alarm and went scuttling down the hill, and a few seconds later a *kakar* came dashing towards me and after barking under my tree for a little while, went off up the hill on tiptoe. Nothing happened after that, and when it was getting too dark under the shade of the trees for me to see the sights of my rifle, I slipped off the tree and myself tiptoed away on rubber-shod feet towards the village.

A hundred yards from the headman's house the track ran across an open glade, some thirty yards long and twenty yards wide. On the upper, hill side of the glade was a big rock. As I reached this open ground I felt I was being followed, and, determined to exploit the situation, I left the track and, taking two long steps over soft and spongy ground, lay down behind the rock, with only one eye showing in the direction of the kill.

For ten minutes I lay on the wet ground. When daylight had all but gone I regained the path and, taking every precaution, covered the remaining distance to the headman's house.

Once during the night the headman roused me from a sound sleep to tell me he had heard the leopard scratching on the door, and when I opened the door next morning I saw the pug-marks of the man-eater in the dust in front of it. These pug-marks I followed back to the glade, and found that the leopard had done just what I had done the previous evening. He had left the track where I had; had crossed the soft ground to the rock and, after regaining the track, had followed me to the house, round which he had walked several times.

On leaving the house the leopard had gone back along the track, and as I followed his pug-marks towards the kill my hopes rose high, for up to that time I had not fully realized the degree of cunning that a man-eating leopard can acquire after eight years of close association with human beings.

I left the track and approached from the high ground, and from a little distance away saw that the kill had gone, and that the ground where the trap had been buried was, except for two pug-marks, undisturbed.

Sitting on the foot-high bank, as he had done the first night, the leopard had put both front paws between the cow's legs, but on this occasion he had spread them wide apart and rested them on the buried levers of the trap which, released, would have closed the great jaws. Here, safe from the trap, he had eaten his meal, and when he had done, he skirted round the flat ground and, getting hold of the cow by the head, had dragged it through the rose-thorns and rolled it down the hill, where fifty yards lower down it had fetched up against an oak sapling. Content with his night's work, the leopard had then gone along the cattle track, and after following him for a mile I lost his tracks on hard ground.

There was no hope of the leopard returning to the kill. However, to salve my conscience for not having done so the previous night, I put a liberal dose of cyanide in the carcass of the cow. Truth to tell I hated the very thought of using poison then, and I hate it no less now.

I visited the kill in the morning and found that a leopard had eaten all that portion of the cow that I had poisoned. So sure was I that the poison had been eaten by a leopard that had accidentally come across the kill, and not by the man-eater, that on my return to the village I told the headman that I would not stay to recover the leopard, though I would pay a hundred rupees to anyone who found it and took its skin to the *patwari*. A month later the reward was claimed, and the skin of a leopard which had been dead many days was buried by the *patwari*.

It did not take my men long to pack up, and shortly after midday we started on our long journey back to Naini Tal. As we went down a narrow footpath to the Chatwapipal bridge a big rat snake leisurely crossed the path, and as I stood and watched it slip away Madho Singh, who was behind me, said, 'There goes the evil spirit that has been responsible for your failure.'

My action in leaving Garhwal to the tender mercies of the man-eater may appear heartless to you—it did so to me—and was adversely criticized in the press, for the leopard at that time was daily mentioned in the Indian papers. In extenuation I would urge that an effort entailing great strain cannot be indefinitely sustained. There were twenty-four hours in every day of the many weeks I spent in Garhwal, and time and time again after sitting up all night, I walked endless miles next day, visiting distant villages from which reports had come of unsuccessful attacks by the man-eater. On many moonlit nights, when sitting in an uncomfortable position physical endurance had reached its limit, and when sitting where it would have been easy for the leopard to have got at me I had no longer been able to keep my eyes open. I had for hours walked the roads which were alone open to me and to the leopard, trying every trick I knew of to outwit my adversary, and the man-eater had, with luck beyond his deserts or with devilish cunning, avoided the bullet that a press of my finger would have sent into him, for on retracing my steps in the morning after these night excursions I had found from the pug-marks on the road that I was right in assuming I had been closely followed. To know that one is being followed at night—no matter how bright the moon may be—by a man-eater intent on securing a victim, gives one an inferiority complex that is very unnerving, and that is not mitigated by repetition.

Tired out in mind and in body, my longer stay at Rudraprayag would not have profited the people of Garhwal, and it might have cost me my own life. Knowing that the temporary abandonment of my self-imposed task would be severely criticized by the press, but that what I was now doing was right, I plodded on towards my distant home, having assured the people of Garhwal that I would return to help them as soon as it was possible for me to do so.

# FISHING INTERLUDE

**I LEFT THE SCENE OF MY** failure, weary and dispirited, in the late autumn of 1925, and returned to continue my labour, refreshed and full of hope, in the early spring of 1926.

On this my second visit to Garhwal in pursuit of the man-eater, I travelled by train to Kotdwara and went from there by foot to Pauri, thus saving eight days on the journey. At Pauri, Ibbotson joined me and accompanied me to Rudraprayag.

During my three months' absence from Garhwal the man-eater had killed ten human beings, and during these three months no attempt had been made by the terror-stricken inhabitants to kill the leopard.

The last of these ten kills—the victim was a small boy—had taken place on the left bank of the Alaknanda, two days before our arrival at Rudraprayag. We had received telegraphic news of this kill at Pauri, and though we had travelled as fast as it was possible for us to do, we were disappointed to learn from the *patwari*, who was awaiting our arrival at the Inspection Bungalow, that the leopard disposed of the entire kill the previous night, leaving nothing of its small victim over which we could sit.

The boy had been killed at midnight in a village four miles from

Rudraprayag, and as it was unlikely that the leopard had crossed the river after his undisturbed feed, we took steps immediately on our arrival to close the two suspension bridges.

During the winter Ibbotson had organized a very efficient intelligence service throughout the area in which the man-eater was operating. If in this area a dog, goat, cow, or human being was killed, or an attempt made to force open a door, news of the occurrence was conveyed to us by the service, and in this way we were able to keep in constant touch with the man-eater. Hundreds of false rumours of alleged attacks by the man-eater were brought to us, entailing endless miles of walking, but this was only to be expected, for in an area in which an established man-eater is operating everyone suspects their own shadows, and every sound heard at night is attributed to the man-eater.

One of these rumours concerned a man by the name of Galtu, a resident of Kunda, a village seven miles from Rudraprayag on the right bank of the Alaknanda. Galtu left the village in the evening to spend the night in his cattle shed a mile away from the village, and when his son went to the shed next morning he found his father's blanket half in and half out of the door of the shed, and in a patch of soft ground nearby he found what he thought was drag mark, and near it the pug-marks of the man-eater. Returning to the village he raised an alarm, and while sixty men went off to search for the body, four men were dispatched to Rudraprayag to inform us. Ibbotson and I were beating a hillside on the left bank of the river for the man-eater when the men arrived, and as I was convinced that the leopard was on our side of the river, and that there was no truth in the rumour that Galtu had been killed, Ibbotson sent a *patwari* back to Kunda with the four men, with instructions to make a personal search and report back to us. Next evening we received the *patwari's* report, with a sketch of the pug-marks in the soft earth near the door of the shed. The report stated that an all-day search of the surrounding country, with two hundred men, had not resulted in finding Galtu's remains, and that the search would be continued. The sketch showed six circles, the inner one as large as a plate, with five equally spaced circles round it, each the size of a tea cup; all the circles had been made with a compass. Five days later, and just as Ibbotson and I were setting out to sit up on the tower of the bridge, a procession came up to the bungalow led by an irate man who was protesting loudly that he had committed no offence that justified his being arrested and brought to Rudraprayag. The irate man was Galtu. After we had pacified him, he gave us his story. It appeared that just as he was leaving his house on the night he was alleged to have been carried off by the man-eater, his son arrived and informed him that he had paid Rs 100 for a pair of bullocks which Galtu asserted were not worth more than Rs 70. The wanton waste of good money had so angered him that, after sleeping the night in the cattle shed, he had got up early next morning and gone to a village ten miles away, where a married daughter of his was living. On his return to his village that morning, he had been arrested by the *patwari*, and he wanted to know what crime he had committed that justified his arrest. It was some little time before he saw the humour of the situation, but once having done so, he laughed as heartily as any of the assembled throng at the thought of an important person like a *patwari*, and two hundred of his friends, searching for five days for his remains, what time he was cooling off in a village ten miles away.

Ibbotson was averse to lying all night on the wind-swept tower of the Rudraprayag suspension bridge, and as wood and carpenters were available, he had a platform built in the arch of the tower, and on this platform we sat for the five nights Ibbotson was able to spend at Rudraprayag.

After Ibbotson's departure the leopard killed one dog, four goats, and two cows. The dog and goats had been eaten out on the nights on which they had been killed, but I sat over each of the cows for two nights. On the second night on which I was sitting up over the first cow, the leopard came, but just as I was raising my rifle and preparing to switch on the torch I had provided myself with, a woman in the house adjoining the one I was sitting in, thumped on the door preparatory to opening it, and unfortunately frightened the leopard away.

No human beings had been killed during this period, but a woman and her baby had been badly mauled. The leopard had forced open the door of the room in which she was sleeping with her baby, and seizing her arm had attempted to drag her out of the room. The woman fortunately was stout of heart, and had not fainted or lost her wits, and after the leopard—dragging her along the floor—had backed out of the room, she shut the door on it, and escaped with a badly lacerated arm and several deep wounds on her breast, while the baby escaped with one head wound. I sat in this room for the following two nights, but the leopard did not return.

I was returning one day towards the latter end of March, after visiting a village on the Kedarnath pilgrim route, when, as I approached a spot where the road runs close alongside the Mandakini river, and where there is a water fall ten to twelve feet high, I saw a number of men sitting on the rock at the head of the fall on the far side of the river, armed with a triangular net attached to a long bamboo pole. The roar of the water prevented conversation, so leaving the road I sat down on the rocks on my side of the fall, to have a rest and a smoke—for I had walked for that day—and to see what the men were doing.

Presently one of the men got to his feet, and as he pointed down excitedly into the foaming white water at the foot of the fall, two of his companions manning the long pole held the triangular net close to the fall. A large shoal of *mahseer* fish, varying

in size from five to fifty pounds, were attempting to leap the fall. One of these fish, about ten pounds in weight, leapt clear of the fall and when falling back was expertly caught in the net. After the fish had been extracted and placed in a basket, the net was again held out close to the fall. I watched the sport for about an hour, during which time the men caught four fish, all about the same size—ten pounds.

On my previous visit to Rudraprayag I had been informed by the *chowkidar* in charge of the Inspection Bungalow that there was good fishing in the spring—before the snow-water came down— in both the Alaknanda and Mandakini rivers, so I had come armed on this my second visit with a fourteen-foot split cane salmon rod, a silex reel with two hundred and fifty yards of line, a few stout traces, and an assortment of home-made brass spoons varying in size from one to two inches.

The following morning—as no news had come in of the man-eater—I set off for the waterfall with my rod and tackle.

No fish were leaping the fall as they had been doing the previous day, and the men on the far side of the river were sitting in a group round a small fire smoking a hookah which was passing from hand to hand. They watched me with interest.

Below the waterfall was a pool thirty to forty yards wide, flanked on both sides by a wall of rock, and about two hundred yards long, one hundred yards of which was visible from where I stood at the head of the pool. The water in this beautiful and imposing pool was crystal-clear.

The rock face at the head of the pool rose sheer up out of the water to a height of twelve feet, and after keeping at this height for twenty yards, sloped gradually upwards to a height of a hundred feet. It was not possible to get down to water level anywhere on my side of the pool, nor would it be possible, or profitable, to follow a fish—assuming that I hooked one—along the bank, for at the top of the high ground there were trees and bushes, and at the tail of the pool the river cascaded down in a foaming torrent to its junction with the Alaknanda. To land a fish in this pool would be a difficult

and a hazardous task, but the crossing of that bridge could be deferred until the fish had been hooked—and I had not yet put together my rod.

On my side of the pool the water—shot through with millions of small bubbles—was deep, and from about half-way across a shingle bottom was showing, over which four to six feet of water was flowing. Above this shingle bottom, every stone and pebble of which was visible in the clear water, a number of fish, ranging in size from three to ten pounds, were slowly moving upstream.

As I watched these fish, standing on the rocks twelve feet above the water with a two-inch spoon mounted with a single strong treble hook in my hand, a flight of fingerlings flashed out of the deep water and went skimming over the shingle bottom, hotly pursued by three big *mahseer*. Using the good salmon rod as friend Hardy had never intended that it should be used—and as it had been used on many previous occasions—I slung the spoon out, and in my eagerness over-estimated the distance, with the result that the spoon struck the rock on the far side of the pool, about two feet above the water. The falling of the spoon into the water coincided with the arrival of the fingerlings at the rock, and the spoon had hardly touched the water, when it was taken by the leading *mahseer*.

Striking with a long line from an elevated position entails a very heavy strain, but my good rod stood the strain, and the strong treble hook was firmly fixed in the *mahseer's* mouth. For a moment or two the fish did not appear to realize what had happened as, standing perpendicularly in the water with his white belly towards me, he shook his head from side to side, and then, possibly frightened by the dangling spoon striking against his head, he gave a mighty splash and went tearing downstream, scattering in all directions the smaller fish that were lying on the shingle bottom.

In his first run the *mahseer* ripped a hundred yards of line off the reel, and after a moment's check carried on for another fifty yards. There was plenty of line still on the reel, but the fish had now gone round the bend and was getting dangerously near the tail of the pool. Alternately easing and tightening the strain on the line, I eventually succeeded in turning his head upstream, and having done so, very gently pulled him round the bend, into the hundred yards of water I was overlooking.

Just below me a projection of rock had formed a backwater, and into this backwater the fish, after half an hour's game fight, permitted himself to be drawn.

I had now very definitely reached my bridge and had just regretfully decided that, as there was no way of crossing it, the fish would have to be cut adrift, when a shadow fell across the rock beside me. Peering over the rock into the backwater, the new arrival remarked that it was a very big fish, and in the same breath asked what I was going to do about it. When I told him that it would not be possible to draw the fish up the face of the rock, and that therefore the only thing to do was to cut it free, he said, 'Wait, sahib, I will fetch my brother.' His brother—a long and lanky stripling with dancing eyes—had quite evidently been cleaning out a cow shed when summoned, so telling him to go upstream and wash himself lest he should slip on the smooth rock, I held council with the elder man.

Starting from where we were standing, a crack, a few inches wide, ran irregularly down the face of the rock, ending a foot above the water in a ledge some six inches wide. The plan we finally agreed on was that the stripling—who presently returned with his arms and legs glistening with water—should go down to the ledge, while the elder brother went down the crack far enough to get hold of the stripling's left hand, while I lay on the rock holding the elder brother's other hand. Before embarking on the plan I asked the brothers whether they knew how to handle a fish and whether they could swim, and received the laughing answer that they had handled fish and swum in the river from childhood.

The snag in the plan was that I could not hold the rod and at the same time make a link in the chain. However, some risk had to be taken, so I put the rod down and held the line in my hand, and when the brothers had taken up position I sprawled on the rock and, reaching down, got hold of the elder brother's hand. Then very gently I drew the fish towards the rock, holding the line alternately with my left hand and with my teeth. There was no question that the stripling knew how to handle a fish, for before the fish had touched the rock, he had inserted his thumb into one side of the gills and his fingers into the other, getting a firm grip on the fish's throat. Up to this point the fish had been quite amenable, but on having its throat seized, it lashed out, and for seconds it appeared that the three of us would go headlong into the river.

Both brothers were bare-footed, and when I had been relieved of the necessity of holding the line and was able to help with both hands, they turned and, facing the rock, worked their way up with their toes, while I pulled lustily from on top.

When the fish at last had been safely landed, I asked the brothers if they ate fish, and on receiving their eager answer that they most certainly did, when they could get any, I told them I would give them the fish we had just landed—a *mahseer* in grand condition weighing a little over thirty pounds—if they would help me to land another fish for my men. To this they very readily agreed.

The treble had bitten deep into the leathery underlip of the *mahseer*, and as I cut it out, the brothers watched interestedly. When the hook was free, they asked if they might have a look at it. Three hooks in one, such a thing had never been seen in their village. The bit of bent brass of course acted as a sinker. With what were the hooks baited? Why should fish want to eat brass? And was it really brass, or some kind of hardened bait? When the spoon, and the trace with its three swivels, had been commented on and marvelled at, I made the brothers sit down and watch while I set about catching the second fish.

The biggest fish in the pool were at the foot of the fall, but here in the foaming white water, in addition to *mahseer* were some very big goonch, a fish that takes a spoon of dead bait very readily, and which is responsible for 90 per cent of the tackle lost in our hill rivers through its annoying habit of diving to the bottom of the pool when hooked and getting its head under a rock from where it is always difficult, and often impossible, to dislodge it.

No better spot than the place from where I had made my first cast was available, so here I again took up my position, with rod in hand and spoon held ready for casting.

The fish on the shingle bottom had been disturbed while I was playing the *mahseer* and by our subsequent movements on the face of the rock but were now beginning to return, and presently an exclamation from the brothers, and an excited pointing of fingers, drew my attention to a big fish downstream where the shingle bottom ended and the deep water began. Before I was able to make a cast, the fish turned and disappeared in the deep water, but a little later it reappeared, and as it came into the shallow water I made a cast, but owing to the line being wet the cast fell short. The second cast was beautifully placed and beautifully timed, the spoon striking the water exactly where I wanted it to. Waiting for a second to give the spoon time to sink, I started to wind in the line, giving the spoon just the right amount of spin, and as I drew it along in little jerks, the *mahseer* shot forward, and next moment, with the hook firmly fixed in his mouth, jumped clean out of the water, fell back with a great splash, and went madly downstream, much to the excitement of the spectators, for the men on the far bank had been watching the proceedings as intently as the brothers.

As the reel spun round and the line paid out, the brothers—now standing one on either side of me—urged me not to let the fish go down the run at the trail of the pool. Easier said than done, for it is not possible to stop the first mad rush of a *mahseer* of any size with risking certain break, or the tearing away of the hook-hold. Our luck was in, or else the fish feared the run, for when there was less than fifty yards of line on the reel he checked, and though he continued to fight gamely he was eventually drawn round the bend, and into the little backwater at the foot of the rock.

The landing of this second fish was not as difficult as the landing of the first had been, for we each knew our places on the rock and exactly what to do.

Both fish were the same length, but the second was a little heavier than the first, and while the elder brother set off in triumph

for his village with his fish carried over his shoulder—threaded
on a grass cable he had made—the stripling begged to be allowed
to accompany me back to the Inspection Bungalow, and to carry
both my fish and my rod. Having in the days of long ago been a
boy myself, and having had a brother who fished, there was no
need for the stripling when making his request to have said, 'If
you will let me carry both the fish and the rod, and will walk a
little distance behind me, sahib, all the people who see me on the
road, and in the bazaar, will think that I have caught this great fish,
the like of which they have never seen.'

# DEATH OF A GOAT

**IBBOTSON RETURNED FROM PAURI ON** the last day of March, and the following morning, while we were having breakfast, we received a report that a leopard had called very persistently the previous night near a village to the north-west of Rudraprayag, about a mile from the place where we had killed the leopard in the gin-trap.

Half a mile to the north of the village, and on the shoulder of the great mountain, there was a considerable area of rough and broken ground where there were enormous rocks and caves, and deep holes in which the locals said their forefathers had quarried copper. Over the whole of this area there was scrub jungle, heavy in some places and light in others, extending down the hillside to within half a mile of the terraced fields above the village.

I had long suspected that the man-eater used this ground as a hide-out when he was in the vicinity of Rudraprayag, and I had frequently climbed to a commanding position above the broken ground in the hope of finding him basking on the rocks in the early morning sun, for leopards are very fond of doing this in a cold climate, and it is a very common way of shooting them, for all that is needed is a little patience, and accuracy of aim.

After an early lunch Ibbotson and I set out armed with our ·275 rifles, and accompanied by one of Ibbotson's men carrying a short length of rope. At the village we purchased a young male goat—the leopard having killed all the goats that I had purchased from time to time.

From the village, a rough goat track ran straight up the hill to the edge of the broken ground, where it turned left, and after running across the face of the hill for a hundred yards carried on round the shoulder of the mountain. The track where it ran across the hill was bordered on the upper side by scattered bushes, and on the steep lower side by short grass.

Having tied the goat to a peg firmly driven into the ground at the bend in the track, about ten yards below the scrub jungle, we went down the hill for a hundred and fifty yards to where there were some big rocks, behind which we concealed ourselves. The goat was one of the best callers I have ever heard, and while his shrill and piercing bleat continued there was no necessity for us to watch him, for he had been very securely tied and there was no possibility of the leopard carrying him away.

The sun—a fiery red ball—was a hand's breadth from the snow mountains above Kedarnath when we took up our position behind the rocks, and half an hour later, when we had been in shadow for a few minutes, the goat suddenly stopped calling. Creeping to the side of the rock and looking through a screen of grass, I saw the goat with ears cocked, looking up towards the bushes; as I watched, the goat shook his head, and backed to the full length of the rope.

The leopard had undoubtedly come, attracted by the calling of the goat, and that he had not pounced before the goat became aware of his presence was proof that he was suspicious. Ibbotson's aim would be more accurate than mine, for his rifle was fitted with a telescopic sight, so I made room for him, and as he lay down and raised his rifle I whispered to him examine carefully the bushes in the direction in which the goat was looking, for I felt sure that if the goat could see the leopard—and all the indications were that it could—Ibbotson should also be able to see it through his powerful telescope. For minutes Ibbotson kept his eye to the telescope and then shook his head, laid down the rifle, and made room for me.

The goat was standing in exactly the same position in which I had last seen it, and taking direction from it I fixed the telescope on the same bush at which it was looking. The flicker of an eyelid, or the very least movement of ear or even whiskers, would have been visible through the telescope, but though I also watched for minutes I too could see nothing.

When I took my eye away from the telescope I noted that the light was rapidly fading, and that the goat now showed as a red-and-white blur on the hillside. We had a long way to go and waiting longer would be both useless and dangerous, so getting to my feet I told Ibbotson it was time for us to make a move.

Going up to the goat—who from the time he had stopped bleating had not made a sound—we freed it from the peg, and with the man leading it we set off for the village. The goat quite evidently had never had a rope round its neck before and objected violently to being led, so I told the man to take the rope off—my experience being that when a goat is freed after having been tied up in the jungle, through fear or for want of companionship it follows at heel like a dog. This goat, however, had ideas of its own, and no sooner had the man removed the rope from its neck, than it turned and ran up the track.

It was too good a calling goat to abandon—it had attracted the leopard once, and might do so again. Moreover, we had only a few hours previously paid good money for it, so we in turn ran up the track in hot pursuit. At the bend, the goat turned to the left, and we lost sight of it. Keeping to the track, as the goat had done, we went to the shoulder of the hill where a considerable extent of the hill, clothed in short grass, was visible, and as the goat was nowhere in sight we decided it had taken a short cut back to the village, and started to retrace our steps. I was leading, and as we got half-way along the hundred yards of track, bordered on the upper side by scattered bushes and on the steep lower side by short grass, I saw something white on the track in front of me. The light had nearly gone, and on cautiously approaching the white object I found it was the goat—laid head and tail on the narrow track, in the only position in which it could have been laid to prevent it from rolling down the steep hillside. Blood was oozing from its throat, and when I placed my hand on it the muscles were still twitching.

It was as though the man-eater—for no other leopard would have killed the goat and laid it on the track—had said, 'Here, if you want your goat so badly, take it; and as it is now dark and you have a long way to go, we will see which of you lives to reach the village.'

I do not think all three of us would have reached the village alive if I had not, very fortunately, had a full box of matches with me (Ibbotson at that time was a non-smoker). Striking a match and casting an anxious look all round and taking a few hurried steps, and then again striking another match, we stumbled down the rough track until we got to within calling distance of the village. Then, at our urgent summons, men with lanterns and pine torches came up to meet us.

We had left the goat lying where the leopard had placed it, and when I returned at daybreak next morning I found the pug-marks of the man-eater where he had followed us down to the village, and I found the goat untouched and lying just as we had left it.

# CYANIDE POISONING

**AS I WAS RETURNING TO THE** Inspection Bungalow after visiting the goat that had been killed the previous night, I was informed in the village that my presence was urgently needed at Rudraprayag, for news had just been received that the man-eater had killed a human being the previous night. My informants were unable to give me any particulars as to where the kill had taken place, but as the pug-marks of the man-eater showed that, after following us to the village, it had gone back up the goat track and turned right at the bend, I assumed—rightly, as I later found— that the leopard, after failing to bag one of us, had secured a victim farther up the mountain-side.

At the bungalow I found Ibbotson in conversation with a man by the name of Nand Ram. Nand Ram's village was about four miles from where we had sat the previous evening. Half a mile above this village and on the far side of a deep ravine, a man of the depressed class, named Gawiya, had cleared a small area of forest land and built himself a house in which he lived with his mother, wife, and three children. At daybreak that morning, Nand Ram had heard the wailing of women from the direction of Gawiya's house and, on his shouting out and asking what was wrong, he had been informed that 'the man of the house' had been carried off by the man-eater half an hour previously. With this information Nand Ram had come hot-foot to the Inspection Bungalow.

Ibbotson had had the Arab and the English mare saddled, and after we had eaten a good meal we set out, with Nand Ram to show us the way. There were no roads on the hill, only goat and cattle tracks, and as the big English mare found the hairpin bends on these tracks difficult to negotiate we sent the horses back and did the rest of the hot and steep climb on foot.

Arrived at the little isolated clearing in the forest, the two distracted women—who appeared to be nursing the hope that the 'man of the house' might still be alive—showed us where Gawiya had been sitting near the door of the house when the leopard had seized him. The leopard had caught the unfortunate man by the throat, thus preventing him from making any sound, and after dragging him for a hundred yards had killed him. Then he had carried him for four hundred yards to a little hollow surrounded by dense brushwood. The wailing of the women and the shouting of Nand Ram had evidently disturbed the leopard at his meal, for he had only eaten the throat and jaw, and a small portion of one shoulder and thigh.

There were no trees within sight of the kill on which we could sit, so we poisoned the kill with cyanide at the three places where the leopard had eaten, and as it was now getting towards evening we took up position on a hill several hundred yards away, from where we could over look the hollow in which the kill was lying. The leopard was undoubtedly in the dense brushwood, but though we lay in our concealed position and watched for two hours, we saw nothing of him. At dusk we lit the lantern we had provided ourselves with, and went back to the bungalow.

We were up very early next morning, and it was just getting light when we again sat down on the hill over-looking the hollow. We saw and heard nothing, and when the sun had been up an hour, we went to the kill; the leopard had not touched the three places where we had buried the poison, but had eaten the other shoulder and leg, and had then carried the body away for a short distance and hidden it under some bushes.

Again there were no trees overlooking the kill on which we could sit, and after a prolonged discussion we eventually decided that while Ibbotson went down the hill for a mile to a village where there was a big mango-tree, in which he could make himself a *machan* and spend the night, I would sit about four hundred yards from the kill, over a village path on which the previous day we had seen the pug-marks of the man-eater.

The tree I selected to sit in was a rhododendron which many years previously had been cut about fifteen feet above ground. Stout branches had grown out from the cut, and sitting on the old stump surrounded by the branches I had a perfect seat and perfect concealment.

Facing me was a steep well-wooded hill with a dense undergrowth of bracken and dwarf bamboo. Running across the face of the hill east and west was a well-used footpath; the rhododendron tree was growing about ten feet below this footpath.

From my seat in the tree I had an uninterrupted view of a length of about ten yards of the path, which to my left crossed a ravine and carried on at the same level on the far side, and to my right, and some three hundred yards farther on, passed a little below the bushes where the kill was lying. There was no water in the ravine where the path crossed it, but thirty yards lower down and immediately below, and three or four yards from, the root of my tree, there were several small pools—the start of a little spring which lower down became a stream providing drinking water to the villagers and irrigation for their crops.

The ten yards of path of which I had an uninterrupted view was joined at right-angles by a path coming down the hill from the house three hundred yards above me where Gawiya had been killed. Thirty yards up this path there was a bend, and from this point a small depression ran down to the lower path—the points where the depression started on the upper path and ended on the lower were not in my view.

There was no need for a torch, for it was a brilliant moonlit night, and if the leopard came along the level path or down the path from the house—as its pug-marks showed it had done the previous day—I should get an easy shot at a range of from twenty to forty feet.

I had gone down the hill a short distance with Ibbotson, and then a little before sunset had taken up my position on the tree. A few minutes later three *kalege* pheasants—a cock and two hens—came down the hill, and after drinking at the spring went back the way they had come. On both occasions they had passed under my tree, and that they had not seen me was proof that my hide was a good one.

The early part of the night was silent, but at eight o'clock a *kakar* started barking in the direction of the kill. The leopard had arrived, and I was convinced he had not gone to the kill along either of the paths I was watching. After barking for a few minutes the *kakar* stopped, and thereafter the night was again silent up to ten o'clock, when the *kakar* again barked. The leopard had been at the kill for two hours—sufficient time for him to have had a good meal, and for him to have poisoned himself several times over. And there was a good chance of his having done so, for on this second night the kill had been very effectively poisoned, the cyanide having been buried deep in the victim's flesh.

Without closing an eye I sat watching the hill in front of me, where the moonlight was so brilliant that I could clearly see every blade of grass, and at 2 a.m. I heard the leopard coming down the path from the direction of the house. I had scattered dry leaves on this path, and also on the lower path, with the object of getting some warning of the leopard's approach, and that he was now walking carelessly over these leaves, and not making any attempt at silence, filled me with hope—though I expected within the next few seconds to put a bullet into him—that all was not well with him.

At the bend in the path the leopard made a short pause, and then leaving the path entered the little depression and followed it down to the lower path, on reaching which he again paused.

I had sat without movement for hours with my hands on the rifle lying across my knees, and as I was convinced that he would come along the path, I decided to let him pass in front of me, and when there was no longer any danger of his seeing the movement raise the rifle to my shoulder, and hit him where I wanted to. For seconds I watched the path, expecting to see his head appear from behind the screen of branches, and then, when tension was becoming unbearable, I heard him jump down off the path and come diagonally across the hill towards my tree. For a moment I thought he had in some mysterious way become aware of my presence on the tree and, not liking the flavour of his last kill, was intent on securing another human victim. His object, however, in leaving the path was not to try to get at me but to take a short cut down to the spring, for he passed the foot of the tree without a pause, and next second I heard him eagerly and noisily lapping water.

From the leopard's behaviour on the hill, and from the way he was now drinking, I was convinced he had poisoned himself, but not having had any previous experience of the effect of cyanide, I did not know how long the poison would take to act. For ten minutes after the leopard had stopped drinking, and just as I was beginning to hope that he had died at the spring, I heard him going up the hill on the far side of the ravine, all sound ceasing when he regained the path which carried on round the shoulder of the hill.

At no time, either when the leopard was coming down the path, coming down the depression, coming across the hill to the foot of my tree, when drinking, or going up the hill on the far side of the ravine, had I seen him, for either by accident or intent he had kept under cover to which not a glint of moonlight had penetrated.

There was now no hope of my getting a shot, but this was not of much account if the poison was as potent as the doctor in Naini Tal had claimed that it was.

I sat on for the rest of the night, watching the path and listening for sounds. At daylight Ibbotson returned, and while we brewed ourselves a very welcome cup of tea I told him of the night's happenings.

On visiting the kill we found that the leopard had eaten the leg from which he had taken a small portion two nights previously, and in which we had buried a full dose of poison, and that he had in addition eaten two other doses of poison, one from the left shoulder and the other from the back.

It was now necessary to make a search for the leopard, and for this purpose the *patwari*, who had returned with Ibbotson, set off to collect men. At about midday the *patwari* returned with two hundred men, and with these we made a line and beat the whole side of the hill in the direction in which the leopard had gone.

Half a mile from where the leopard had quenched his thirst, and in the direct line in which I had heard him going away, there were some big rocks at the foot of which there was a cave extending far into the hill, with an opening large enough to admit a leopard. Near the mouth of this cave the leopard had scratched up the ground, and rid himself of his victim's toes—which he had swallowed whole.

Willing hands brought loose stones from the hillside, and when we left the cave we had sealed it beyond all possibility of any leopard that might be lurking in it escaping.

Next morning I returned with a roll of one-inch wire-netting nd a number of iron tent-pegs, and, after removing the stones, ery effectively wired up the mouth of the cave. Thereafter for he following ten days I visited the cave morning and evening, nd as during this period no news of the man-eater came in from ny village on the left bank of the Alaknanda, my hopes each day rew stronger that on my next visit I would surely get some ndication that the leopard had died in the cave.

On the tenth morning, when I returned from my visit to the ave—where I had found the netting undisturbed—Ibbotson reeted me with the news that a woman had been killed the revious night in a village five miles away, and about a mile above he Rudraprayag–Badrinath pilgrim road.

Quite evidently cyanide was not the right poison for an animal hat had the reputation of thriving on, and being stimulated by, rsenic and strychnine. That the leopard had eaten the cyanide here could be no doubt whatever, nor was there any doubt that e had entered the cave, for his hairs were adhering to the rock vhere his back had come in contact with it when entering the ave.

An overdose might account for the poison not having had the lesired effect and a second opening somewhere farther up the ill might account for his escape from the cave. Even so, it was o longer any matter of surprise to me—who had only been cquainted with the leopard for a few short months—that the eople of Garhwal, who had lived in close and intimate association vith him for eight long years, should credit him—animal or spirit— vith supernatural powers, and that they should cling to the belief hat nothing but fire would rid them of this evil spirit.

# TOUCH AND GO

**NEWS THAT IS OF IMPORTANCE TO** every individual travel
fast, and during the past ten days everyone in Garhwal had heard
of the poisoning of the man-eater, and of our hope that we had
sealed it up in a cave. It was natural therefore for risks to have been
taken, and quite evidently the leopard, having recovered from the
effects of the poison and found a way out of the cave, had found
the first person who was taking a risk.

We had the day before us, for I had returned early from my
visit to the cave, and after breakfast, mounted on Ibbotson's
surefooted horses and carrying our rifles, we set out for the village
where the woman was reported to have been killed.

After a fast ride up the pilgrim road we took a track that went
diagonally across the hill, and a mile along this track, where the
path from the village joined it, there were signs of a struggle and a
big pool of blood.

The headman, and relatives of the victim, were waiting for us at
the village, and they showed us where the leopard had seized the
woman as she was in the act of closing the door of her house behind
her. From this point the leopard had dragged the woman along on
her back for a hundred yards to the junction of the tracks, where

ιe had released his hold, and after a violent struggle had killed her. The people in the village had heard the woman's screams as she was ɔeing dragged along the ground and as she was struggling for her iife with the leopard, but had been too frightened to render any help.

When the woman was dead, the leopard had picked her up and carried her over some waste land, across an open ravine a hundred yards wide, and up the hill on the far side for another two hundred yards. There were no drag marks, but the blood trail was easy to follow, and it led us to a flat bit of ground, four feet wide and twenty feet long. On the upper side of this narrow strip of ground there was a perpendicular bank eight feet high with a stunted medlar-tree growing on it, and on the lower side of the narrow strip the hill fell steeply away, and growing on it was a wild rose-bush, which had reached up and smothered the medlar-tree. Lying huddled up between the steep bank and the rose-bush, with her head against the bank, with every vestige of clothing stripped from her, and with her naked body flecked with white rose-petals that had fallen from above was the kill—an old grey-haired lady, seventy years of age.

For this pitiful kill the leopard would have to pay with his life, and after a short council of war, Ibbotson, leading the spare horse, returned to Rudraprayag for the things we needed, while I set off with my rifle to see whether it was possible to make contact with the man-eater in daylight.

This part of the country was new to me, and the first thing to do was to reconnoitre the ground. I had already noted while at the village that the hill went steeply up from the ravine to a height of four to five thousand feet; that about two thousand feet of the top of the hill was clothed with dense oak and pine forest, below which was an open stretch of short grass about half a mile wide, and that below the grass was scrub jungle.

Keeping now to the edge of the grass and scrub jungle I went round the shoulder of the hill, and found in front of me a wide depression, extending for half a mile down to the pilgrim road, and evidently caused in the days of long ago by a landslide. Beyond this depression, which was about a hundred yards wide at the upper end and about three hundred yards wide where it met the road the ground was open. The ground in the depression was damp and growing on this damp ground were a number of big trees and under the tree a dense growth of scrub jungle. At the upper end of the depression was a cliff of overhanging rock, varying in height from twenty to forty feet, and about a hundred yards long half-way along the cliff was a deep cleft a few feet wide, down which a tiny stream was trickling. Above the rocks was a narrow belt of scrub jungle, and above that again, open grassland.

I had reconnoitred the ground with care, for I did not want the leopard—which I was convinced was lying up in the depression—to be aware of my presence before it suited me. It was now necessary to find approximately where the leopard was most likely to be lying up, and to gain this information I went back to the kill.

We had been told in the village that it had got light shortly after the woman had been killed, and as it must have taken the leopard some little time to effect the kill, carry his victim four hundred yards, and eat a portion of it, it was reasonable to assume that he had left the spot where he had hidden the kill when day was fully established.

The hill on which the kill was lying was in full view of the village, in which at this hour there must had been considerable movement; the leopard therefore on leaving the kill would very naturally have kept to cover as far as was possible, and working on this assumption, and also because the ground was too hard to show pug-marks, I set out to follow him along the line I assumed he had taken.

When I had covered half a mile and was out of view of the village and was approaching the depression, I was gratified to find that I had followed on the leopard's tracks foot by foot, for in the lee of a bush where there was some loose earth, I found where he had been lying for several hours. His pug-marks when leaving this spot showed that he had entered the depression about fifty yards below the cliff of rock.

For half an hour I lay where the leopard had lain, watching the small area of tree and scrub jungle in front of me in the hope that the leopard would make some slight movement and give away his position.

After I had been watching for a few minutes a movement among the dead leaves attracted my attention, and presently two scimitar babblers came into view industriously turning over the leaves, looking for grubs. Where carnivores are concerned, these birds are among the most reliable informants in the jungle, and I hoped later to make use of this pair to help in locating the leopard.

No movement had been visible and no sound had come to indicate that the leopard was in the depression; but that he was there I was still convinced, and having failed to get a shot in one way I decided to try another way.

Without coming out into the open, there were two natural lines of retreat for the leopard, one down the hill towards the pilgrim road, and the other up the hill. To move him down the hill would not profit me, but if I moved him up the hill he would for a certainty go up the cleft in the rock cliff to gain the shelter of the bushes above the cliff, and while he was doing so, there was a reasonable chance of my getting a shot.

Entering the depression a little below where I thought the leopard was, I started to zigzag very slowly across it, gaining a few feet in height at each turn. There was as yet no need for me to keep an eye on the cleft, for the babblers were on the ground a few feet below it, and they would let me know when the leopard was on the move. I had gained about forty yards in height in my movements forward and backwards across the depression and was about ten yards from, and a little to the left of, the cleft, when the babblers rose in alarm and, flying into a small oak tree and hopping about excitedly on the branches, started to give their clear and ringing alarm call, which can in the hills be heard for a distance of half a mile. Holding the rifle ready to take a snap shot, I stood perfectly still for a minute, and then started slowly moving forward.

The ground here was wet and slippery and, with my eyes fixed on the cleft, I had only taken two steps when my rubber-soled shoes slipped on the wet surface; and while I was endeavouring to regain my balance, the leopard sprang up the cleft, and in the bushes above put up a covey of *kalege* pheasants, which came sailing down over my head.

My second attempt had failed, and though it would have been quite easy for me to have moved the leopard back to where he had started from, it would have been of no use for me to do so, for, from above, the cleft in the rock was not visible until one was right up to it, and long before I gained the position the leopard would have been far down the depression.

Ibbotson and I had arranged to meet in the open ravine at 2 p.m., and a little before that hour he returned from Rudraprayag, accompanied by several men carrying the things he had gone to fetch. These consisted of food, and drink—in the way of tea—our old friend the petromax lamp—which on this occasion I decided I would carry myself, if the necessity arose—two spare rifles and ammunition, my fishing-reel, a liberal supply of cyanide, and the gin-trap.

Sitting in the ravine by a clear stream of water, we had our lunch and brewed ourselves cups of tea, and then went over to the kill.

I will give a description of the
position of the kill, to enable you
to follow our movements and the
subsequent happenings.

The kill was lying about five
feet from the near or ravine
end of the flat strip of
ground, which was four
feet wide and about twenty feet
long. The upper side of this strip of ground was protected by a
high bank, and the lower side by a steep drop and a spreading
rose-bush. The stunted medlar tree on the bank was too small to
allow a *machan* being made in it, so we decided to depend entirely
on a gun-trap, poison, and the gin-trap; having come to this decision
we set about our preparations.

First we poisoned the kill, of which the leopard had—for want
of time—only eaten a small portion; hoping that on this occasion
he would only consume sufficient to poison himself effectively.
Then, while I bent over the kill in the position we anticipated the
leopard would assume when eating, Ibbotson sighted and securely
lashed his ·256 Mannlicher—which had a hair trigger—and my
·450 high-velocity rifle to two saplings, fifteen yards on our
approach side of the kill.

There were no insuperable obstacles to the leopard getting at
the kill from any side he might wish to, but his most natural line
of approach from where I had left him was along the fifteen feet
or so of flat ground, and on this strip of flat ground we proceeded
to bury the huge gin-trap, first removing from the ground every
dead leaf, bit of stick, and blade of grass that were lying on it.

After we had dug a hole sufficiently long, wide, and deep—
removing the displaced earth to a distance—we put the gin-trap
in it, and when the powerful springs that closed the jaws had been
depressed, and the plate that constituted the trigger adjusted as
delicately as we dared set it, we covered the whole trap with a layer
of green leaves, over which we sprinkled earth, and blades of grass

in the position we had found them. So carefully had the trap been set in the ground that we who had set it found it difficult to determine its exact position.

My fishing-reel was now produced and one end of the dressed silk line was tied to the trigger of one rifle, looped round the butt-end, and taken to within ten feet of the kill, from where it was taken back, looped round the butt-end of the second rifle, and tied to the trigger. The line was then cut—much to my regret, for it was a new and very good line—and after the end had been tied round the woman's waist, the line was passed through the loop, the lines to the triggers pulled taut, and a secure knot was tied. The line was then cut for the second time.

As we cast a final look over our handiwork—which appeared to us very good—it struck us that if the leopard was to wander round and approach the kill from our side, and not from the side we expected him to come, he *might* avoid both the guns and the gin-trap, and to prevent his doing so we sent to the village for a crowbar, while we cut five thornbushes from some little distance away. With the crowbar we made five holes a foot deep, on our side of the flat strip of ground, and into these holes we planted the bushes, stamping the earth round them and making them almost as secure and quite as natural to look at as when they were growing on the hillside. We were now quite satisfied that no animal bigger than a rat could approach the kill and eat any portion of it without meeting death in one form or another, so throwing off the safety-catches of the rifles, we returned to the village.

Fifty yards from the village, and close to where we had on our arrival found the pool of blood, there was a big wide-spreading mango tree. In this tree we made a *machan* from planks procured from the village, and on it we piled a lot of sweet-smelling rice straw, for it was our intention to spend the night on it, in anticipation of having to finish off the leopard if he was caught in the gin-trap.

Near sundown we took our position on the *machan*, which was long enough for us to lie on at length and wide enough for us to lie side by side. The distance from the *machan* to the kill across the ravine was two hundred yards, and the kill was on a higher level than the *machan* by about a hundred feet.

Ibbotson feared that his aim with the telescopic sight fitted to his rifle would not be quite accurate, so while he took a pair of powerful field-glasses from their case, I loaded my ·275 rifle. Our plan was that while Ibbotson concentrated on the portion of the hill along which we expected the leopard to come, I would keep a general look-out all over the hill, and if we saw the leopard, I would risk taking a shot, even if the shot had to be taken at the extreme range to which my rifle was sighted, which was three hundred yards.

While Ibbotson dozed, I smoked and watched the shadows cast by the hills in the west slowly creep up the hill in front of us, and when the rays from the setting sun were gilding the crest of the hill red, Ibbotson awoke and picked up his field-glasses, and I picked up my rifle, for the time had now come when we could expect the leopard to make his appearance. There was still some forty five-minutes of daylight left, and during the time we intently scanned— I with a pair of eyes that few are blessed with, and Ibbotson with his field-glasses—every foot of the considerable expanse of hill visible from our *machan*, without seeing the movement of a bird or animal.

When there was no longer sufficient light to shoot by, I put down my rifle, and a little later Ibbotson returned his field-glasses to their case. One chance of killing the leopard had gone, but there were still three chances left, so we were not unduly depressed.

Shortly after dark it came on to rain, and I whispered to Ibbotson that I feared it would prove our undoing, for if the additional weight of rain-water on the delicately set gin-trap did not set it off, the contracting of the fishing-line due to

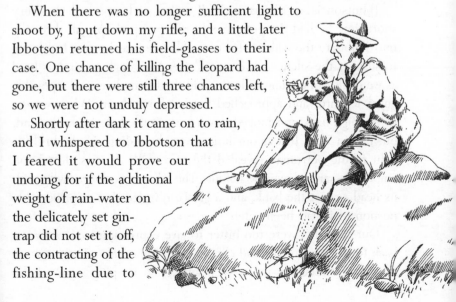

getting wet, no matter how slight it might be, would to a certainty fire off his hair-trigger rifle. Some time later, and while it was still raining, Ibbotson asked me what time it was. I had a luminous wrist-watch, and I had just told him it was a quarter to eight when a succession of savage and angry roars came from the direction of the kill—the leopard, the much-famed man-eating leopard of Rudraprayag, was at long last in the gin-trap.

Ibbotson took a flying leap from the *machan* while I swung down from a branch, and that neither of us broke limbs in the descent can only be attributed to luck. The petromax lamp hidden in a nearby yam field was found, and while Ibbotson proceeded to light it, I gave expression to my fears and doubts, and admit I deserved Ibbotson's rejoinder, 'You are a rotten pessimist. First you think a few drops of rain are going to spring the trap and fire off my rifle, and now you think because the leopard is not making a noise that it has got out of the trap.' That was just what I was thinking, and fearing, for on that other occasion when we had trapped a leopard it had roared and growled continuously, whereas this one, after that one expression of rage which had brought us tumbling out of the *machan*, had been ominously silent.

Ibbotson is an expert with all makes of lamps and in a very short time he had the petromax lit and pumped up, and throwing our doubts to the winds—for even Ibbotson was by now beginning to suspect the silence—we set off over the rough ground as hard as we could go, circling wide to avoid the fishing-lines and a possible angry leopard, and approached the kill from above. When we got to the high bank and looked down we saw the hole in the ground, but no gin-trap. Just as our hopes were bounding up, the brilliant light of the petromax revealed the trap; with its jaws closed and empty, ten yards down the hillside. The kill was no longer lying with its head against the bank, and a glance revealed that a considerable portion of it had been eaten.

Our thoughts were too bitter to give expression to as we went back to the mango tree and climbed into the *machan*. There was no longer any need for us to keep awake, so heaping some of the straw over ourselves, for we had no bedding and the night was cold, we went to sleep.

At the first streak of dawn a fire was built near the mango tree and water heated, and after we had drunk several cups of tea and warmed ourselves at the fire, we set off for the kill, accompanied by the *patwari* and several of Ibbotson's and my men, together with a number of men from the village.

I mention the fact that there were two of us, and that we had the *patwari* and a number of men with us, for had I been alone I would have hesitated to relate what I am now going to tell you.

Fiend or animal, had the slayer of the old woman been present and watched our overnight preparations it would even then have been difficult to understand how it had, on a dark and rainy night, avoided capture of death in one form or another. The rain, though light, had been sufficient to soften the ground, and we were able to reconstruct and to follow his every movement of the previous night.

The leopard had come from the direction from which we had expected him to come, and on arrival at the flat strip of ground, had skirted round and below it, and had then approached the kill from the side where we had firmly planted the thornbushes. Three of these bushes he had pulled up, making a sufficiently wide gap to go through, and then, getting hold of the kill, he had drawn it a foot or so towards the rifles, thus slackening off the fishing-lines. Having done this he had started to eat, avoiding while doing so contact with the fishing-line that was tied round the woman's body. We had not thought it necessary to poison either the head or the neck. These he had eaten first, and then—very carefully—he had eaten all that portion of the body between the many doses of poison we had inserted in different places.

After satisfying his hunger the leopard left the kill with the intention of seeking shelter from the rain and, while he was doing so, what I feared would happen actually happened. The weight of rainwater on the very finely set trap had depressed the plate that constituted the trigger, and released the springs just as the leopard was stepping over the trap, and the great jaws had met on either side of the stifle, or knee-joint, of his hind leg. And here was the greatest tragedy of all, for when bringing the trap up from Rudraprayag the men carrying it had let it fall, and one of the three-inch-long teeth had been broken off, and the stifle of the leopard's left hind leg had been caught by the jaws exactly where this missing tooth formed a gap in the otherwise perfectly fitting set of teeth. But for this missing tooth the leopard would have been fixed to the trap without any possibility of getting free, for the grip on his leg had been sufficiently good for him to lift the eighty-pound trap out of the hole in which we had buried it, and carry it ten yards down the hillside. And now, instead of the leopard, the jaws of the trap only held a tuft of hair and a small piece of skin, which we later—much later—had the great satisfaction of fitting back into position.

However unbelievable the actions of the leopard may appear to have been, they were in fact just what one would have expected from an animal that had been a man-eater for eight years. Avoiding the open ground, and approaching the kill under cover; removing the thorn obstruction we had erected across the blood trail he had left that morning; pulling the kill towards him into a convenient position for his meal, and rejecting those portions of the kill that we had poisoned—cyanide, of which he now had experience, has a very strong smell—were all quite normal and natural actions.

The explanation I have given for the springing of the trap is, I am convinced, correct. It was just a coincidence that the leopard happened to be directly over the trap the very moment that the additional weight of water set it off.

Having dismantled the gin-trap, and waited until the relatives had removed what remained of the old woman for cremation, we set out to walk back to Rudraprayag, leaving our men to follow us. Some time during the night the leopard had come to the mango tree, for we found his pug-marks near the tree where the pool of blood—now washed away by the rain—had been, and we followed these pug-marks down the track to the pilgrim road and four miles along the road to the gate of the Inspection Bungalow where, after scratching up the ground at the base of one of the pillars of the gate, he had gone on down the road for another mile to where my old friend the packman was camped, one of whose goats he had wantonly killed.

I need not tell those of you who have carried a sporting rifle in any part of the world that all these many repeated failures and disappointments, so far from discouraging me, only strengthened my determination to carry on until that great day or night came when, having discarded poisons and traps, I would get an opportunity of using my rifle as rifles were intended to be used, to put a bullet truly and accurately into the man-eater's body.

# A LESSON IN CAUTION

**I HAVE NEVER AGREED WITH** those sportsmen who attribute all their failures in big-game hunting to their being Jonahs.

The thoughts of a sportsman, whether they be pessimistic or whether they be optimistic, sitting waiting for an animal, cannot in any conceivable way influence the actions of the animal he is endeavouring to shoot or, maybe, to photograph.

We are apt to forget that the hearing and sight of wild animals, and especially of those animals that depend exclusively on these senses not only for food but also for self-preservation, are on a plane far and away above that of civilized human beings, and that there is no justification for us to assume that because we cannot hear or see the movements of our prospective quarry, our quarry cannot hear or see our movements. A wrong estimation of the intelligence of animals, and the inability to sit without making any sound or movement for the required length of time, is the cause of all failures when sitting up for animals. As an example of the acute sense of hearing of carnivores, and the care it is necessary to exercise when contact with one of them is desired, I will relate one of my recent experiences.

On a day in March, when the carpet of dry leaves on the ground recorded the falling of every dead leaf and the movements of the smallest of the birds that feed on the ground, I located in some very heavy undergrowth the exact position of a tiger I had long wished to photograph, by moving a troop of *langurs* in the direction in which I suspected the tiger to be lying up. Seventy yards from the tiger there was an open glade, fifty yards long and thirty yards wide. On the edge of the glade, away from the tiger, there was a big tree overgrown with creepers that extended right up to the topmost branches; twenty feet from the ground the tree forked in two. I knew that the tiger would cross the glade in the late afternoon, for the glade lay directly between him and his *sambhar* kill which I had found early that morning. There was no suitable cover near the kill for the tiger to lie up in during the day, so he had gone to the heavy undergrowth where the *langurs* had located him for me.

It is often necessary, when shooting or photographing tigers and leopards on foot, to know the exact position of one's quarry, whether it be a wounded animal that one desires to put out of its misery or an animal that one wants to photograph, and the best way of doing this is by enlisting the help of birds or animals. With patience, and with a knowledge of the habit of the bird or animal the sportsman desires to use, it is not difficult to get a particular bird or animal to go in the required direction. The birds most suitable for this purpose are red jungle-fowl, peafowl, and white-capped babblers, and of animals the most suitable are *kakars* and *langurs*.

The tiger I am telling you about was unwounded and it would have been quite easy for me to go into the undergrowth and find him myself, but in doing so I should have disturbed him and defeated my own purposes, whereas by using the troop of *langurs* and knowing what their reactions would be on sighting the tiger—if he happened to be in the undergrowth—I was able to get the information I wanted without disturbing the tiger.

Very carefully I stalked the tree I have referred to, and avoiding contact with the creepers, the upper tendrils and leaves of which might have been visible from where the tiger was lying, I climbed to the fork, where I had a comfortable seat and perfect concealment. Getting out my 16-mm ciné-camera I made an opening in the screen of leaves in front of me just big enough to photograph through, and having accomplished all this without having made a sound, I sat still. My field of vision was confined to the glade and to the jungle immediately beyond it.

After I had been sitting for an hour, a pair of bronzewing doves rose out of the jungle and went skimming over the low brushwood, and a minute or two later, and a little closer to me, a small flight of upland pipits rose off the ground and, after daintily tripping along the branches of a leafless tree, rose above the tree-tops and went off. Neither of these two species of birds has any alarm call, but I knew from their behaviour that the tiger was afoot and that they had been disturbed by him. Minutes later I was slowly turning my eyes from left to right scanning every foot of ground visible to me, when my eyes came to rest on a small white object, possibly an inch or two square, immediately in front of me, and about ten feet from the edge of the glade. Focusing my eyes on this stationary object for a little while, I then continued to scan the bushes to the limit of my field of vision to the right, and then back again to the white object.

I was now convinced that this object had not been where it was for more than a minute or two before I had first caught sight of it, and that it could not be anything other than a white mark on the tiger's face. Quite evidently the tiger had heard me when I was approaching or climbing the tree, though I had done this in thin rubber shoes without making as far as I was aware any sound, and when the time had come for him to go to his kill he had stalked, for a distance of seventy yards over dry leaves, the spot he had pin-pointed as the source of some suspicious sound. After lying for half an hour without making any movement, he stood up, stretched himself, yawned, and, satisfied that he had nothing to fear, walked out into the glade. Here he stood, turning his head first to the right and then to the left, and then crossed the glade, passing right under my tree on his way to his kill.

When in my wanderings through the jungles I see the *machans* that have been put up for the purpose of shooting carnivores, and note the saplings that have been felled near by to make the platform, the branches that have been cut to give a clear view, and see the litter and debris left lying about, and consider the talking and noise that must have accompanied these operations, I am not surprised when I hear people say they have sat up hundreds of times for tigers and leopards without ever having seen one of these animals, and attribute their failures to their being Jonahs.

Our failure to bag the man-eater up to that date was not due to our having done anything we should not have done, or left undone anything we should have done. It could only be attributed to sheer bad luck. Bad luck that had prevented my receiving the electric light in time; that had given Ibbotson cramps in both legs; that had made the leopard eat an overdose of cyanide; and, finally, that had made the men drop the gin-trap and break the one tooth that mattered. So when Ibbotson returned to Pauri, after our failure to kill the leopard over the body of his seventy-year-old victim, I was full of hope, for I considered my chances of shooting the leopard as good as they were on the first day I arrived at Rudraprayag, and in fact better than they had then been, for I now knew the capabilities of the animal I had to deal with.

One thing was causing me a lot of uneasiness and much heart-searching, and that was confining the man-eater to one bank of the river. However I looked at it, it did not appear to be right that the people on the left bank of the Alaknanda should be exposed to attacks by the leopard, while the people on the right bank were free from the risk of such attacks.

Including the boy killed two days before our arrival, three people had recently lost their lives on the left bank, and others might meet with a like fate, and yet to open the two ridges and let the leopard cross over to the right bank would add an hundredfold to my difficulties, which were already considerable, and would not benefit Garhwal as a whole, for the lives of the people on the right bank of the river were just as valuable as the lives of the people on the left bank; so, very reluctantly, I decided to keep the bridges closed. And here I should like to pay my tribute to the people— numbering many thousands—living on the left bank of the river who, knowing that the closing of the bridges was confining the activities of the dread man-eater to their area, never once, during the months I closed the bridges, removed the barriers themselves, or asked me to do so.

Having decided to keep the bridges closed, I sent a man to warn the villagers of their danger, and myself carried the warning to as many villages as time and my ability to walk permitted of my doing. No one whom I talked with on the roads and in the villages ever expressed one word of resentment at the leopard having been confined to their area, and everywhere I went I was offered hospitality and speeded on my way with blessings, and I was greatly encouraged by the assurances from both men and women—who did not know but what they might be the man-eater's next victim—that it was no matter for regret that the leopard had not died yesterday, for surely it would die today or, maybe, tomorrow.

# A WILD BOAR HUNT

**THE OLD PACKMAN HAD ARRIVED** at the thorn enclosure late the previous evening. He was packing salt and *gur* from the bazaar at Hardwar to the villages beyond Badrinath, and as his flock of sheep and goats was heavily laden and the last march had been a long one, he had arrived too late at the thorn enclosure to repair the weak places in it, with the result that several of the goats had strayed out of the enclosure and one of them the leopard had killed, close to the road, during the early hours of the morning. The barking of his dogs had awakened him, and when it got light, he saw his best goat—a beautiful steel-grey animal nearly as large as a Shetland pony—lying dead near the road, wantonly killed by the man-eater.

The behaviour of the man-eater during the previous night showed the extent to which the habits of a leopard change when it has become a man-eater and has lived in close association with human beings over a long period of years.

It was reasonable to assume that the man-eater had received a great shock, and a great fright, by being caught in the gin-trap; his having carried the heavy trap for ten yards and the angry way in which he had roared were in fact proof of this; and one would have expected him, the moment he got out of the trap, to have retired to some secluded spot as far removed from human habitation as possible, and to have remained there until he was again hungry, which he would not be for several days. But, so far from doing this, he had quite evidently remained in the vicinity of the kill, and after watching us climb into the *machan* and giving us time to go to sleep, had come to investigate; fortunately for us, Ibbotson had taken the precaution to protect the *machan* by putting wire-netting all round it, for it is not an unheard-of thing for man-eating leopards to kill people who are sitting up trying to shoot them. At the present time there is a man-eating leopard in the Central Provinces that has—at different times—killed and eaten four Indian sportsmen who were trying to shoot him; up to the time I last heard of this animal he had killed forty human beings, and owing to his habit of eating his would-be slayers, he was living a very peaceful and undisturbed life, varying his human diet with game and domestic animals.

After his visit to the mango tree, our man-eater went along the village path to its junction with the track. Here, where we had found the pool of blood, he had turned to the right and gone down the track for a mile, and then along the pilgrim road for another four miles and into the most densely populated part of the area in which he was operating. On arrival at Rudraprayag, he had gone through the main street of the bazaar, and half a mile farther on had scratched up the ground at the gate of the Inspection Bungalow. The rain of the previous night had softened the clay surface of the road, and on the soft clay the pug-marks of the leopard showed up clearly, and from them it was possible to see that the leopard's encounter with the gin-trap had not resulted in injury to any of his limbs.

After breakfast I took up the tracks at the gate and followed them to the packman's camp. From a bend in the road, a hundred yards from the camp, the leopard had caught sight of the goats that had strayed from the enclosure, and crossing from the outer to the inner edge of the road and creeping along under shelter of the hill he had stalked the grazing animals and, after killing the steel-grey goat but without even troubling to drink its blood, had returned to the road.

In the thorn enclosure, guarding the dead goat and the neatly stacked pile of packs, were the packman's two sheep-dogs, tethered to stout pegs with short lengths of heavy chain. These big, black, and powerful dogs that are used by packmen throughout our hills are not accredited sheep-dogs in the same sense that sheep-dogs in Great Britain and in Europe are. On the march the dogs keep close to heel, and their duties—which they perform very efficiently—start when camp is made. At night they guard the camp against wild animals—I have known two of them to kill a leopard—and during the day and while the packmen are away grazing the flock they guard the camp against all intruders. A case is on record of one of these dogs having killed a man who was attempting to remove a pack from the camp it had been left to guard.

I picked up the tracks of the leopard where he returned to the road after killing the goat, and followed them through Golabrai and for a mile farther on, to where a deep ravine crosses the road, up which he had gone. The distance the leopard had covered from the mango tree to the ravine was about eight miles. This long and seemingly aimless walk away from a kill was in itself a thing no ordinary leopard would under any circumstances have undertaken, nor would an ordinary leopard have killed a goat when he was not hungry.

A quarter of a mile beyond the ravine the old packman was sitting on a rock by the side of the road, spinning wool and watching his flock, which were grazing on the open hillside. When he had dropped his spinning-stick and wool into the capacious pocket in his blanket robe and accepted a cigarette, he asked if I had come past his camp. When I told him I had done so and that I had seen what the evil spirit had done, and added that it would be wise to sell his dogs to camelmen on his next visit to Hardwar, for it was quite evident that they were lacking in courage, he nodded his head as one in agreement with what he heard. Then he said, 'Sahib, even we old hands are apt at times to make mistakes, and suffer for them, even as I have this night suffered by losing my best goat. My dogs have the courage of tigers, and are the best dogs in all Garhwal, and it is an insult to them for you to say they are only fit to be sold to camelmen. My camp as you doubtless observed, is very close to the road, and I feared that if by chance anyone came along the road by night, my dogs might do him an injury, so I chained them up outside the thorn enclosure instead of leaving them loose, as is my wont. You have seen the result; but do not blame the dogs, sahib, for in their efforts to save my goat their collars have bitten deep into their necks, and made wounds that will take many days to heal.'

While we were talking, an animal appeared on the crest of the hill on the far side of the Ganges. From its colour and size, I at first thought it was a Himalayan bear, but when it started to come down the hill towards the river, I saw it was a big wild boar. The pig was followed by a pack of village pye dogs, who in turn were followed by a rabble of boys and men, all armed with sticks of varying size. Last of all came a man carrying a gun. As this man crested the hill he raised his piece and we saw a puff of smoke, and a little later heard the dull report of a muzzle-loading gun. The only living things within range of the gun were the boys and men, but as none of them dropped out of the race, the sportsman appeared to have missed them.

The pig had a long grassy slope before him, with an odd bush dotted here and there, and below the grass slope was some broken ground, and below that again a dense belt of brushwood which

extended right down to the river.

On the rough broken ground the pig lost his lead, and pig and pye dogs disappeared into the brushwood together. Next minute all the dogs, with the exception of the big light-coloured animal that had been leading the pack, dashed back out of the brushwood. When the boys and men arrived they appeared to urge the dogs to re-enter the cover, but this—after apparently having recently seen what the pig could do with his tusks—they were unwilling to do. The man with the gun then arrived, and was immediately surrounded by the boys and men.

To us sitting on our elevated grandstand with the river flowing between, the scene being enacted on the farther hill was a silent picture, for the noise of the water deadened sound and all we had heard was the dull report of the muzzle-loader.

The sportsman was apparently as reluctant to enter the cover as the dogs were, for presently he broke away from his companions and sat down on a rock, as if to say, 'I have done my bit, now you do yours'. Confronted with this double dilemma—for the dogs, even after some of them had been beaten, stoutly refused to face the pig—first the boys and then the men started to throw stones into the brushwood.

While this was going on, we saw the pig emerge from the lower end of the brushwood on to a narrow strip of sand. With a few quick steps he came out into the open, stood perfectly still for a few seconds, took a few more steps, stopped again, and then with a little run plunged into the river. Pigs—the wild variety—are exceptionally good swimmers, and they do not cut their throats with their hooves while swimming, as is generally believed.

The current in the river was strong, but there is no bigger-hearted animal than our wild pig, and when I last saw the old boar he had been washed down the river a quarter of a mile, but was swimming strongly and was nearing our bank, which I have no doubt he reached safely.

'Was the pig within range of your rifle, sahib?' asked the packman.

'Yes I replied, 'the pig was within range, but I have not brought a rifle to Garhwal to shoot pigs that are running for their lives, but to shoot what you think is an evil spirit, and what I know is a leopard.'

'Have it your own way,' he rejoined; 'and now, as you are going, and we may never meet again, take my blessings with you, and time will prove whether you or I am right.'

I regret I never saw the packman again, for he was a grand old man, as proud as Lucifer, and as happy as the day was long, when leopards were not killing his best goats and when the courage of his dogs was not being questioned.

# VIGIL ON A PINE TREE

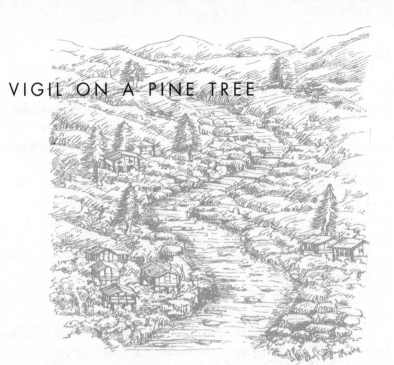

**IBBOTSON RETURNED TO PAURI NEXT DAY,** and the following morning, when I was visiting the villages on the hill to the east of Rudraprayag, I found the tracks of the man-eater on a path leading out of a village in which the previous night he had tried to break open the door of a house in which there was a child suffering from a bad cough. On following the tracks for a couple of miles they led me to the shoulder of the mountain where, some days previously, Ibbotson and I had sat up over the calling goat which the leopard had later killed.

It was still quite early, and as there was a chance of finding the leopard basking on one of the rocks in this considerable area of broken ground, I lay on a projecting rock that commanded an extensive view. It had rained the previous evening—thus enabling me to track the leopard—and washed the haze out of the atmosphere. Visibility was at its best and the view from the projecting rock was as good as could be seen in any part of the world where mountains rise to a height of twenty-three thousand feet. Immediately below me was the beautiful valley of the Alaknanda, with the river showing as a gleaming silver ribbon winding in and out of it. On the hill beyond the river, villages were dotted about, some with only a single thatched hut, and others with long rows of slate-roofed houses. These row buildings are in fact individual homesteads, built one against the other to save expense and to economize space, for the people are poor and every foot of workable land in Garhwal is needed for agriculture.

Beyond the hills were rugged rock cliffs, down which avalanches roar in winter and early spring, and beyond and above the cliffs were the eternal snows, showing up against the intense blue sky as clear as if cut out of white cardboard. No more beautiful or peaceful scene could be imagined, and yet when the sun, now shining on the back of my head, set on the far side of the snow mountains, terror—terror which it is not possible to imagine until experienced—would grip, as it had done for eight long years, the area I was now overlooking.

I had been lying on the rock for an hour when two men came down the hill, on their way to the bazaar. They were from a village about a mile farther up the hill that I had visited the previous day, and they informed me that a little before sunrise they had heard a leopard calling in this direction. We discussed the possibilities of my getting a shot at the leopard over a goat, and as at that time I had no goats of my own, they offered to bring me one from their village and promised to meet me where we were standing, two hours before sunset.

When the men had gone I looked round for a place where I could sit. The only tree on the whole of this part of the mountain was a solitary pine. It was growing on the ridge close to the path down which the men had come, and from under it a second path took off and ran across the face of the mountain skirting the upper edge of the broken ground, where I had recently been looking for the leopard. The tree commanded an extensive view, but it could be difficult to climb, and would afford little cover. However, as it was the only tree in the area, I had no choice, so decided I would try it.

The men were waiting for me with a goat when I returned at about 4 p.m., and when, in reply to their question where I intended sitting, I pointed to the pine, they started laughing. Without a rope ladder, they said, it would not be possible to climb the tree; and further, if I succeeded in climbing the tree without a ladder, and carried out my intention of remaining out all night, I should have no protection against the man-eater, to whom the tree would offer no obstacle. There were two white men in Garhwal—Ibbotson was one of them—who had collected birds' eggs when boys, and both of whom could climb the tree; and as there is no exact equivalent in Hindustani for 'waiting until you come to a bridge before crossing it', I let the second part of the men's objection go unanswered, contenting myself by pointing to my rifle.

The pine was not easy to climb, for there were no branches for twenty feet, but once having reached the lowest branch, the rest was easy. I had provided myself with a long length of cotton cord, and when the men had tied my rifle to one end of it, I drew it up and climbed to the top of the tree, where the pine-needles afforded most cover.

The men had assured me that the goat was a good caller, and after they tied it to an exposed root of the tree they set off for their village promising to return early next morning. The goat watched the men out of sight, and  then started to nibble the short

grass at the foot of the tree. The fact that it had not up to then called once did not worry me, for I felt sure that it would presently feel lonely and that it would then do its share of the business of the evening, and if it did it while it was still night, from my elevated position I should be able to kill the leopard long before it got anywhere near the goat.

When I climbed the tree the shadows cast by the snow mountains had reached the Alaknanda. Slowly these shadows crept up the hill and passed me, until only the top of the mountain glowed with red light. As this glow faded, long streamers of light shot up from the snow mountains where the rays of the setting sun were caught and held on a bank of clouds as soft and as light as thistledown. Everyone who has eyes to see a sunset—and the number, as you might have observed, is regrettably few—thinks that the sunsets in his particular part of the world are the best ever. I am no exception, for I too think that there are no sunsets in all the world to compare with ours, and a good second are the sunsets in northern Tanganyika, where some quality in the atmosphere makes snow-capped Kilimanjaro, and the clouds that are invariably above it, glow like molten gold in the rays of the setting sun. Our sunsets in the Himalayas are mostly red, pink, or gold. The one I was looking at the evening from my seat on the pine tree was rose pink, and the white shafts of light, starting as spear-points from valleys in the cardboard snows, shot through the pink clouds and, broadening, faded out in the sky overhead.

The goat, like many human beings, had no interest in sunsets, and after nibbling the grass within reach, scratched a shallow hole for itself, lay down, curled up, and went to sleep. Here was a dilemma. I had counted on the animal now placidly sleeping below me to call up the leopard, and not once since I had first seen it had it opened its mouth, except to nibble grass, and now, having made itself comfortable, it would probably sleep throughout the night. To have left the tree at that hour in an attempt to return to the bungalow would have added one more to the number who deliberately commit suicide, and as I had to be doing something to kill the man-eater, and as—in the absence of a kill—one place was as good as another, I decided to stay where I was, and try to call up the leopard myself.

If I were asked what had contributed most to my pleasure during all the years that I have spent in Indian jungles, I would unhesitatingly say that I had derived most pleasure from a knowledge of the language, and the habits, of the jungle-folk. There is no universal language in the jungles; each species has its own language, and though the vocabulary of some is limited, as in the case of porcupines and vultures, the language of each species is understood by all the jungle-folk. The vocal chords of human beings are more adaptable than the vocal chords of any of the jungle-folk, with the one exception of the crested wire-tailed drongo, and for this reason it is possible for human beings to hold commune with quite a big range of birds and animals. The ability to speak the language of the jungle-folk, apart from adding hundredfold to one's pleasure in the jungle, can, if so desired, be put to great use. One example will suffice.

Lionel Fortescue—up till recently a housemaster at Eton—and I were on a photographing and fishing tour in the Himalayas shortly after 1918, and we arrived one evening at a Forest Bungalow at the foot of a great mountain, on the far side of which was our objective, the Vale of Kashmir. We had been marching over hard ground for many days, and as the men carrying our luggage needed a rest, we decided to halt for a day at the bungalow. Next day, while Fortescue wrote up his notes, I set out to explore the mountain and try for a Kashmir stag. I had been informed by friends who had shot in Kashmir that it was not possible to shoot one of these stags without the help of an experienced *shikari*, and this was confirmed by the *chowkidar* in charge of the Forest Bungalow. With the whole day before me I set out alone, after breakfast, without having the least idea at what elevation the red deer lived, or the kind of ground on which they were likely to be found. The mountain, over which there is a pass into Kashmir, is about twelve thousand feet high, and after I had climbed to a height of eight thousand a storm came on.

From the colour of the clouds I knew I was in for a hailstorm, so I selected with care a tree under which to shelter. I have seen both human beings and animals killed by hail, and by the lightning that invariably accompanies hailstorms, so rejecting the big fir trees with tapering tops I selected a small tree with a rounded top and dense foliage, and collecting a supply of dead wood and fir-cones, I built a fire, and for the hour that the thunder roared overhead and the hail lashed down, I sat at the foot of my tree safe and warm.

The moment the hail stopped the sun came out, and from the

shelter of the tree I stepped into fairyland, for the hail that carpeted the ground gave off a million points of light to which every glistening leaf and blade of grass added its quota. Continuing up for another two or three thousand feet, I came on an outcrop of rock, at the foot of which was a bed of blue mountain poppies. The stalks of many of these, the most beautiful of all wild flowers in the Himalayas, were broken, even so these sky-blue flowers standing in a bed of spotless white were a never-to-be-forgotten sight.

The rocks were too slippery to climb, and there appeared to be no object in going to the top of the hill, so keeping to the contours I went to the left, and after half a mile through a forest of giant fir trees I came to a grassy slope which, starting from the top of the hill, extended several thousand feet down into the forest. As I came through the trees towards this grassy slope I saw on the far side of it an animal standing on a little knoll, with its tail towards me. From illustrations seen in game books I knew the animal was a red Kashmir deer, and when it raised its head, I saw it was a hind.

On my side of the grassy slope, and about thirty yards from the edge of the forest, there was a big isolated rock some four feet high; the distance between this rock and the knoll was about forty yards. Moving only when the deer was cropping the grass, and remaining still each time she raised her head, I crept up to the shelter of the rock. The hind was quite obviously a sentinel, and from the way she looked to her right each time she raised her head, I knew she had companions, and the exact direction in which these companions were. To approach any nearer over the grass without being seen was not possible. To re-enter the forest and work down from above would not have been difficult but would have defeated my purpose, for the wind was blowing down the hill. There remained the alternative of re-entering the forest and skirting round the lower end of the grass slope, but this would take time and entail a stiff climb. I therefore finally decided to remain where I was and see if these deer—which I was seeing for the first time— would react in the same way as *cheetal* and *sambhar* do to the call of a leopard, of which I knew there was at least one on the mountain, for I had seen its scratch-marks earlier in the day. With only one eye showing, I waited until the hind was cropping the grass, and then gave the call of a leopard.

At the first sound of my voice the hind swung round and, facing me, started to strike the ground with her forefeet. This was a warning to her companions to be on the alert, but those companions whom I wanted to see would not move until the hind called, and this she would not do until she saw the leopard. I was wearing a brown tweed coat, and projecting a few inches of my left shoulder beyond the rock I moved it up and down. The movement was immediately detected by the hind, who, taking a few quick steps forward, started to call; the danger she had warned her companions of was in sight, and it was now safe for them to join her. The first to come was a yearling, which, stepping daintily over the hail-covered ground, ranged itself along side the hind; the yearling was followed by three stags, who in turn were followed by an old hind. The entire herd, numbering six in all, were now in full view at a range of thirty-five yards. The hind was still calling, while the others, with ears alternately held rigid or feeling forward and backward for sound and wind direction, were standing perfectly still and gazing into the forest behind me. My seat on the melting hail was uncomfortable and wet, and to remain inactive longer would possibly result in a cold. I had seen a representative herd of the much-famed Kashmir deer, and I had heard a hind call, but there was one thing more that I wanted. That was, to hear a stag call; so I again projected a few inches of my shoulder beyond the rock, and had the satisfaction of hearing the stags, the hinds, and the yearling calling in different pitched keys.

My pass permitted me to shoot one stag, and for all I knew one of the stags might have carried a record head, but though I had set out that morning to look for a stag, and procure meat for the camp, I now realized that I was in no urgent need of a trophy. In any case the stag's meat would probably be tough so, instead of using the rifle, I stood up, and six of the most surprised deer in Kashmir vanished out of sight, and a moment later I heard them crashing through the undergrowth on the far side of the knoll.

It was now time for me to retrace my steps to the bungalow, and I decided to go down the grassy slope and work through the lighter forest at the foot of the mountain. The slope was at an angle that lent itself to an easy lope, provided care was taken to see that every step was correctly placed. I was running in the middle of the hundred-yard open ground and had gone about six hundred yards when I caught sight of a white object, standing on a rock at the edge of the forest on the left-hand side of the slope, and about three hundred yards below me. A hurried glance convinced me that the white object was a goat, that had probably been lost in the forest. We had been without meat for a fortnight and I had promised Fortescue that I would bring something back with me, and there was my opportunity. The goat had seen me, and if I could disarm suspicion would possibly let me pass close enough to catch it by the legs; so as I loped along I edged to the left, keeping the animal in sight out of the corner of my eyes. Provided the animal stayed where it was, no better place on all the mountain could have been found on which to catch it, for the flat rock, at the very edge of which it was standing, jutted out into the slope, and was about five feet high. Without looking directly at it, and keeping up a steady pace, I ran past the rock and, as I did so, made a sweep with my left hand for its forelegs. With a sneeze of alarm the animal reared up, avoiding my grasp, and when I pulled up clear of the rock and turned round, I saw to my amazement that the animal I had mistaken for a white goat was an albino musk-deer. With only some ten feet between us the game little animal was standing its ground and sneezing defiance at me. Turning away I walked down the hill for fifty yards, and when I looked back, the deer was still standing on the rock, possibly congratulating itself on having frightened me away. When some weeks later I related the occurrence to the Game Warden of Kashmir he expressed great regret at my not having shot the deer, and was very anxious to know the exact locality in which I had seen it, but as my memory for places, and my description of localities, is regrettably faulty, I do not think that particular albino musk-deer is gracing any museum.

Male leopards are very resentful of intrusion of others of their kind in the area they consider to be their own. True, the man-eater's territory extended over an area of five hundred square miles in which there were possibly many other male leopards; still, he had been in this particular area for several weeks, and might very reasonably consider it his own. And again, the mating season was only just over, and the leopard might mistake my call for the call of a female in search of a mate, so waiting until it was quite dark I called and, to my surprise and delight, was immediately answered by a leopard some four hundred yards below and a little to the right.

The ground between us was strewn with great rocks and overgrown with matted thornbushes, and I knew the leopard would not come in a straight line towards me, and that he would probably skirt round the broken ground and come up a subsidiary ridge to the one my tree was on; this I found, when next he called, that he was doing. Five minutes later I located his call as coming from the path that, starting from my tree, ran across the face of the hill, about two hundred yards away. This call I answered, to give the leopard direction. Three, or it may have been four, minutes later, he called again from a distance of a hundred yards.

It was a dark night and I had an electric torch lashed to the side of my rifle, and my thumb on the push button. From the root of the tree the path ran in a straight line for fifty yards, to where there was a sharp bend in it. It would not be possible for me to know when or where to direct the beam of the torch on this part of the path, so I should have to wait until the leopard was on the goat.

Just beyond the bend, and only sixty yards away, the leopard again called, and was answered by another leopard far up the mountain-side. A complication as unexpected as it was unfortunate, for my leopard was too close now for me to call, and as he had last heard me from a distance of two hundred yards he would naturally assume that the coy female had removed herself farther up the hill and was calling to him to join her there. There was, however, just a possibility of his continuing along the path to its junction with the path coming down the hill, in which case he would be sure to kill the goat, even if he had no use for it. But the goat's luck was in, and mine out, for the leopard cut across the angle formed by the two paths, and the next time he called he was a hundred yards farther from me, and a hundred yards nearer his prospective coaxing mate. The calling of the two leopards drew nearer and nearer together, and finally stopped. After a long period of silence the caterwauling of these two giant cats came floating down to me from where I judged the grassland ended and the dense forest began.

The leopard's luck was unfortunately in, in more ways than one, not least of all because it was dark, for leopards when courting are very easy to shoot. The same can be said of tigers, but the sportsman who goes on foot to look for courting tigers should be quite sure that he wants to see them, for a tigress—never a tiger—is very sensitive at these times, and quite understandably so, for males of the cat tribe are rough in their courting, and do not know how sharp their claws are.

The leopard had not died, nor would he die that night, but may be he would die the next day, or the day after, for his sands were running out; and so for a long moment I thought were mine, for without any warning a sudden blast of wind struck the tree, and my heels and my head changed their relative position with the land of Garhwal. For seconds I thought it impossible for the tree to regain its upright position, or for me to retain contact with it. When the pressure eased, the tree and I got back to where we were before the wind struck us, and fearing that worse might follow, I hurriedly tied the rifle to a branch, to have the use of both hands. The pine had possibly withstood many wind-storms equally bad, if not worse, but never with a human being on it to add weight and increase wind-pressure. When the rifle was safe, I climbed out on to one branch after another, and broke off all the tassels of pine-needles that I could reach. It may only have been my imagination, but after I had lightened the tree it did not appear to heel over as dangerously as it had at first done. Fortunately the pine was comparatively young and supple, and its roots firm set, for it was tossed about like a blade òf grass for an hour and then, as suddenly as it had started, the wind died down. There was no possibility of the leopard returning, so, after I had smoked a cigarette, I followed the goat into the land of dreams.

As the sun was rising a cooee brought me back to within fifty feet of earth, and under the tree were my two companions of the previous evening, reinforced by two youths from their village. When they saw that I was awake they asked whether I had heard the leopards during the night, and what had happened to the tree, and were hugely amused when I told them I had had a friendly conversation with the leopards, and that having nothing else to do I had amused myself by breaking the branches of the tree. I then asked them if by chance they had noticed that there had been some little wind during the night, on which one of the youths answered, 'A little wind, sahib! Such a big wind has never been known, and it has blown away my hut!' To which his companion rejoined, 'That is no matter for regret, sahib, for Sher Singh has long been threatening to rebuild his hut, and the wind has saved him the trouble of dismantling the old one.'

# MY NIGHT OF TERROR

**FOR SEVERAL DAYS AFTER MY EXPERIENCE** on the pine tree I lost touch with the man-eater. He did not return to the broken ground and I found no trace of him, or of the female who had saved his life, in the miles of forest I searched on the high ground above the cultivated land. In these forests I was more at home, and if the leopards had been anywhere in them I should have been able to find them, for there were birds and animals in the forest that would have helped me.

The female, being restless, was quite evidently straying far from her home when she heard me call from the top of the pine tree, and on being joined by the male had gone back to her own area, accompanied by the mate I had helped her to find. The male would presently return alone, and as the precautions now being taken by the people on the left bank were making it difficult for him to procure a human kill, he would probably try to cross over to the right bank of the Alaknanda, so for the next few nights I mounted guard on the Rudraprayag bridge.

Of the approaches to the bridge on the left bank, the one from the south passed close to the bridge *chowkidar's* house, and on the fourth night I heard the leopard killing the *chowkidar's* dog; a friendly nondescript little beast that used to run out and greet me every time I passed that way. The dog seldom barked, but that night it had been barking for five minutes when suddenly the bark ended in a yelp, followed by the shouting of the *chowkidar* from inside his house, after which there was silence. The thornbushes had been removed from the archway and the bridge was open, yet though I lay with finger on trigger for the rest of the night the leopard did not try to cross.

After killing the dog and leaving it lying on the road, the leopard, as I found from his tracks next morning, came to the tower. Five more steps in the direction in which he was going would have brought him out on the bridge, but those five steps he did not take. Instead he turned to the right, and after going a short distance up the footpath towards the bazaar, he returned and went up the pilgrim road to the north. A mile up the road I lost his tracks.

Two days later I received a report that a cow had been killed the previous evening, seven miles up the pilgrim road. It was suspected that the cow had been killed by the man-eater, for the previous night—the night the dog had been killed—the leopard had tried to break open the door a house close to where, the next evening, the cow had been killed.

On the road I found a number of men waiting for me who, knowing that the walk up from Rudraprayag would be a hot one, had very thoughtfully provided a dish of tea. While we sat in the shade of a mango-tree and smoked, and I drank the dish of tea, they told me that the cow had not returned with the herd the previous evening, and that it had been found between the road and the river when a search had been made for it that morning. They also told me of the many hairbreadth escapes each of them had had from the man-eater during the past eight years. I was very interested to learn from them that the leopard had only adopted his present habit of trying—and in many cases succeeding—to break open the doors of houses three years previously, and that before he had been content to take people who were outside their houses, or from houses the doors of which had been left open. 'Now,' they said, 'the *shaitan* has become so bold that sometimes when he has not been able to break down the door of a house, he has dug a hole through the mud wall, and got at his victims in the way.'

To those who do not know our hill-people, or understand their fear of the supernatural, it will seem incredible that a people renowned for their courage, and who have won the highest awards on the field of battle, should permit a leopard to break open a door, or to dig a hole in a wall of a house, in which in many cases there must have been men with axes, *kukris*, or, even in some cases, firearms at hand. I know of only one case in all those eight long years in which resistance was offered to the man-eater, and in that case the resister was a woman. She was sleeping alone in a house, the door of which she had left unfastened; this door, as in the case of the door of the house occupied by the woman who escaped with a lacerated arm, opened inwards. On entering the room the leopard seized the woman's left leg, and as it dragged her across the room, the woman's hand came in contact with a *gandesa*—a tool used for chopping chaff for cattle—and with this the woman dealt the leopard a blow. The leopard did not release his hold, but backed out of the room, and as it did so either the woman pushed the door, or else this happened accidentally. Whichever it may have been, with the woman on one side of the door and the leopard on the other, the leopard exerted its great strength and tore the limb from the woman's body. Mukandi Lal, at that time Member for Garhwal in the United Provinces Legislative Council, who was on an electioneering tour, arrived in the village the following day and spent a night in the room, but the leopard did not return. In a report to the Council, Mukandi Lal stated that seventy-five human beings had been killed by the leopard in the course of that one year, and he asked the Government to launch a vigorous campaign against the man-eater.

Accompanied by one of the villagers to show me the way, and

by Madho Singh, I went down to the kill. The cow had been killed in a deep ravine a quarter of a mile from the road and a hundred yards from the river. On one side of the ravine there were big rocks with dense brushwood between, and on the other side of the ravine there were a few small trees, none of which was big enough to sit in. Under the trees, and about thirty yards from the kill, there was a rock with a little hollow at the base of it, so in the hollow I decided to sit.

Both Madho Singh and the villager objected very strongly to my sitting on the ground, but as this was the first animal kill I had got since my arrival at Rudraprayag in a place where it was reasonable to expect the leopard to come at an early hour—about sundown— I overruled their objections, and sent them back to the village.

My seat was dry and comfortable, and with my back to the rock and a small bush to conceal my legs I was confident the leopard would not see me, and that I should be able to kill it before it was aware of my presence. I had provided myself with a torch and a knife, and with my good rifle across my knees I felt that in this secluded spot my chances of killing the leopard were better than any I had yet had.

Without movement and with my eyes on the rocks in front of me I sat through the evening, each second bringing the time nearer when the undisturbed and unsuspecting leopard would for a certainty return to his kill. The time I had been waiting for had come, and was passing. Objects near at hand were beginning to get blurred and indistinct. The leopard was a little later in coming than I had expected him to be, but that was not worrying me, for I had a torch, and the kill was only thirty yards from me, and I would be careful over my shot and make quite sure that I did not have a wounded animal to deal with.

In the deep ravine there was absolute silence. The hot sun of the past few days had made the dead leaves on the bank on which I was sitting as dry as tinder. This was very reassuring, for it was now dark and whereas previously I had depended on my eyes for protection I now had to depend on my ears, and with thumb on the button of the torch and finger on trigger I was prepared to shoot in any direction in which I heard the slightest sound.

The non-appearance of the leopard was beginning to cause me uneasiness. Was it possible that from some concealed place among the rocks he had been watching me all these hours, and was he now licking his lips in anticipation of burying his teeth in my throat?—for he had long been deprived of human flesh. In no other way could I account for his not having come, and if I were to have the good fortune to leave the ravine on my feet, my ears would have to serve me now as they had never served me before.

For what seemed like hours I strained my ears and then, noticing it was getting darker than it should have been, I turned my eyes up to the sky and saw that a heavy bank of clouds was drifting across the sky, obscuring the stars one by one. Shortly thereafter big drops of rain started to fall, and where there had been absolute and complete silence there was now sound and movement all round— the opportunity the leopard had been waiting for had come. Hastily taking off my coat I wound it round my neck, fastening it securely in place with the sleeves. The rifle was now useless but might help to cause a diversion, so transferring it to my left hand I unsheathed my knife and got a good grip of it with my right hand. The knife was what is called an Afridi stabbing knife, and I devoutly hoped it would serve me as well as it had served its late owner, for when buying it from the Government store at Hangu on the North-west Frontier, the Deputy Commissioner had drawn my attention to a label attached to it and to three notches on the handle, and said it had figured in three murders. Admittedly a gruesome relic, but I was glad to have it in my hand, and I clutched it tight while the rain lashed down.

Leopards, that is ordinary forest leopards, do not like rain and invariably seek shelter, but the man-eater was not an ordinary leopard, and there was no knowing what his likes or dislikes were, or what he might or might not do.

When Madho Singh was leaving he asked how long I intended sitting up, and I had answered 'Until I have shot the leopard,' so I could expect no help from him, and of help I was at that time in urgent need. Should I go or should I remain were the questions that were troubling me, and one option was as unattractive as the other. If the leopard up to then had not seen me it would be foolish to give my position away, and possibly fall across him on the difficult ground I should have to negotiate on my way up to the pilgrim road. On the other hand to remain where I was for another six hours—momentarily expecting to have to fight for my life with an unfamiliar weapon—would put a strain on my nerves which they were not capable of standing; so getting to my feet and shouldering the rifle, I set off.

I had not far to go, only about five hundred yards, half of which was over wet clay and the other half over rocks worn smooth by bare feet and the hooves of cattle. Afraid to use the torch for fear of attracting the man-eater, and with one hand occupied with the rifle and the other with the knife, my body made as many contacts with the ground as my rubber-shod feet. When I eventually reached the road I sent a full-throated cooee into the night, and a moment later I saw a door in the village far up the hillside open and Madho Singh and his companion emerge, carrying a lantern.

When the two men joined me Madho Singh said he had had no uneasiness about me until the rain started, and that he had then lit the lantern, and sat with his ear against the door listening. Both men were willing to accompany me back to Rudraprayag, so we set out on our seven-mile walk, Bachi Singh leading, Madho Singh carrying the lantern following, and I bringing up the rear. When I returned next day I found the kill had not been touched, and on the road I found the tracks of the man-eater. What time had elapsed between our going down the road and the man-eater following us, it was not possible to say.

When I look back on that night, I look back on it as my night of terror. I have been frightened times without number, but never have I been frightened as I was that night when the unexpected rain came down and robbed me of all my defences, and left me for protection a murderer's knife.

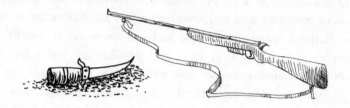

# LEOPARD FIGHTS LEOPARD

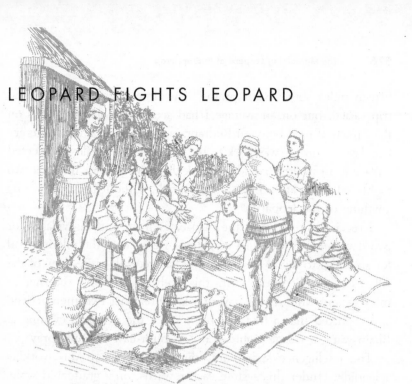

**AFTER FOLLOWING US TO RUDRAPRAYAG THE** leopard went down the pilgrim road through Golabrai, past the ravine up which he had gone a few days previously, and then up a rough track which the people living on the hills to the east of Rudraprayag use as a short cut on their way to and from Hardwar.

The pilgrimage to Kedarnath and Badrinath is seasonal, and the commencement of the pilgrimage and its duration depend in the one case on the melting and in the other on the falling of snow in the upper reaches of the high mountains in which these two shrines are situated. The High Priest of Badrinath temple had a few days previously sent the telegram that is eagerly awaited by good Hindus throughout the length and breadth of India, announcing that the road was open, and for the past few days pilgrims in small numbers had been passing through Rudraprayag.

During the past few years the man-eater had killed several pilgrims on the road, and it appeared to be his more or less regular habit while the pilgrim season lasted to go down the road to the extent of his beat, and then circle round through the villages on the hills to the east of Rudraprayag, and rejoin the Road anything up to fifteen miles above Rudraprayag. The time taken for this round trip varied, but on an average I had seen the leopard's tracks on the stretch of road between Rudraprayag and Golabrai once in every five days, so on my way back to the Inspection Bungalow I selected a place from where I could overlook the road, and for the next two nights sat in great comfort on a hayrick, without however seeing anything of the leopard.

I received no news of the man-eater from outlying villages for two days, and on the third morning I went down the pilgrim road for six miles to try to find out if he had recently visited any of the villages in the direction. From this twelve-mile walk I returned at midday, and while I was having a late breakfast two men arrived and reported that a boy had been killed the previous evening at Bhainswara, a village eighteen miles south-east of Rudraprayag.

The intelligence system introduced by Ibbotson was working splendidly. Under this system cash rewards, on a graduated scale, were paid for information about all kills in the area in which the man-eater was operating. These rewards, starting with two rupees for a goat and working up to twenty rupees for a human being, were keenly contested for, and so ensured our receiving information about all kills in the shortest time possible.

When I put ten rupees into the hands of each of the men who had brought me news about the boy, one of them offered to acccompany me back to Bhainswara to show me the way, while the other said he would stay the night at Rudraprayag as he had recently had fever and could not do another eighteen miles that day. I finished breakfast while the men were telling me their tale, and a little before 1 p.m. I set off, taking only my rifle, a few cartridges, and a torch with me. As we crossed the road near the Inspection Bungalow and started up the steep hill on the far side of it, my companion informed me we had a very long way to go, adding that it would not be safe for us to be out after dark, so I told him to walk ahead and set the pace. I never—if I can help it—walk uphill immediately after a meal, but here I had no option, and for the first three miles, in which we climbed four thousand feet, I had great difficulty in keeping up with my guide. A short stretch of comparatively flat ground at the end of the three miles gave me back my wind, and after that I walked ahead and set the pace.

On their way to Rudraprayag the two men had told the people in the villages they had passed through about the kill, and of their intention to try and persuade me to accompany them back to Bhainswara. I do not think that anyone doubted that I would answer to the call, for at every village the entire population were waiting for me, and while some gave me their blessings, others begged me not to leave the district until I had killed their enemy.

My companion had assured me that we had eighteen miles to go, and as we crested hill after hill with deep valleys between I realized I had undertaken to walk against time eighteen of the longest and hardest miles I had ever walked. The sun was near setting when, from the crest of one of these unending hills, I saw a number of men standing on a ridge a few hundred yards ahead of us. On catching sight of us some of the men disappeared over the ridge, while others came forward to meet us. The headman of Bhainswara was among the latter, and after he had greeted me, he cheered me by telling me that his village was just over the crest of the hill, and that he had sent his son back to get tea ready.

The 14th of April 1926 is a date that will long be remembered in Garhwal, for it was on that day that the man-eating leopard of Rudraprayag killed his last human victim. On the evening of that day a widow and her two children, a girl aged nine and a boy aged twelve, accompanied by a neighbour's son aged eight, went to a spring a few yards from Bhainswara village to draw water for the preparation of their evening meal.

The widow and her children occupied a house in the middle of a long row of homesteads. These homesteads were double-storied, the low-ceilinged ground floor being used for the storage of grain and fuel, and the first floor for residences. A veranda four feet wide ran the entire length of the building, and short flights of stone steps flanked by walls gave access to the veranda, each flight of steps being used by two families. A flagged courtyard, sixty feet wide and three hundred feet long, bordered by a low wall, extended along the whole length of the building.

The neighbour's son was leading as the party of four approached the steps used by the widow and her children, and as the boy started to mount the steps he saw an animal, which he mistook for a dog, lying in an open room on the ground floor adjoining the steps; he said nothing about the animal at the time, and the others apparently did not see it. The boy was followed by the girl, the widow came next, and her son brought up the rear. When she was half-way up the short flight of stone steps, the mother heard the heavy brass vessel her son was carrying crash on the steps and go rolling down them; reprimanding him for his carelessness, she set her own vessel down on the veranda and turned to see what damage her son had done. At the bottom of the steps she saw the overturned vessel. She went down and picked it up, and then looked round for her son. As he was nowhere in sight she assumed he had got frightened and had run away, so she started calling to him.

Neighbours in adjoining houses had heard the noise made by the falling vessel and now, hearing the mother calling to her son, they came to their doors and asked what all the trouble was about. It was suggested that the boy might be hiding in one of the ground-floor rooms, so as it was now getting dark in these rooms, a man lit a lantern and came down the steps towards the woman, and as he did so he saw drops of blood on the flagstones where the woman was standing. At the sound of the man's horrified ejaculation other people descended into the courtyard, among whom was an old man who had accompanied his master on many shooting expeditions. Taking the lantern from the owner's hand, this old man followed the blood trail across the courtyard and over the low wall. Beyond the wall was a drop of eight feet into a yam field; here in the soft earth were the splayed-out pug-marks of a leopard. Up to that moment no one suspected that the boy had been carried off by a man-eater, for though everyone had heard about the leopard it had never previously been within ten miles of their village. As soon as they realized what had happened the women began screaming and while some men ran to their houses for drums, others ran for guns—of which there were three in the village—and in a few minutes pandemonium broke out. Throughout the night drums were beaten and guns were fired. At daylight the boy's body was recovered, and two men were dispatched to Rudraprayag to inform me.

As I approached the village in company with the headman, I heard the wailing of a woman mourning her dead. It was the mother of the victim, and she was the first to greet me. Even to my unpractised eye it was apparent that the bereaved mother had just weathered one hysterical storm and was heading for another, and as I lack the art of dealing with people in this condition I was anxious to spare the woman a recital of the events of the previous evening; but she appeared to be eager to give me her version of the story, so I let her have her way. As the story unfolded itself it was apparent that her object in telling it was to ventilate her grievance against the men of the village for not having run after the leopard and rescued her son 'as his father would have done had he been alive'. In her accusation against the men I told her she was unjust, and in her belief that her son could have been rescued alive, I told her she was wrong. For when the leopard clamped his teeth round the boy's throat, the canine teeth dislocated the head from the neck and the boy was already dead before the leopard carried him across the courtyard, and nothing the assembled men—or anyone else—could have done would have been of any use.

Standing in the courtyard drinking the tea that had thoughtfully been provided for me, and noting the hundred or more people who were gathered round, it was difficult to conceive how an animal the size of a leopard had crossed the courtyard in daylight without being seen by any of the people who must have been moving about at that time, or how its presence had gone undetected by the dogs in the village.

I climbed down the eight-foot wall that the leopard carrying the boy had jumped down, and followed the drag across the yam field, down another wall twelve feet high, and across another field. At the edge of this second field there was a thick hedge of rambler roses, four feet high. Here the leopard had released his hold on the boy's throat, and after searching for an opening in the hedge and not finding one, he had picked the boy up by the small of the back and, leaping the hedge, gone down a wall ten feet high on the far side. There was a cattle track at the foot of this third wall and the leopard had only gone a short distance along it when the alarm was raised in the village. The leopard had then dropped the boy on the cattle track and gone down the hill. He was prevented from returning to his kill by the beating of drums and the firing of guns which had gone on all night in the village.

The obvious thing for me to have done would have been to carry the body of the boy back to where the leopard had left it, and to have sat over it there. But here I was faced with two difficulties—the absence of a suitable place in which to sit, and my aversion to sitting in an unsuitable place.

The nearest tree, a leafless walnut, was three hundred yards away, and was therefore out of the question, and quite frankly I lacked the courage to sit on the ground. I had arrived at the village at sundown; it had taken a little time to drink the tea, hear the mother's story, and trail the leopard, and there was not sufficient daylight left for me to construct a shelter that would have given me even the semblance of protection; therefore if I sat on the ground I should have to sit just anywhere, not knowing from which direction the leopard would come, and knowing full well that if the leopard attacked me I should get no opportunity of using the one weapon with which I was familiar, my rifle, for when in actual contact with an unwounded leopard or tiger it is not possible to use firearms.

When after my tour of inspection I returned to the courtyard, I asked the headman for a crowbar, a stout wooden peg, a hammer, and a dog chain. With the crowbar I prised up one of the flagstones in the middle of the courtyard, drove the peg firmly into the ground, and fastened one end of the chain to it. Then with the help of the headman I carried the body of the boy to the peg and chained it there.

The working of the intangible force which sets a period to life, which one man calls Fate and another calls *kismet*, is incomprehensible. During the past few days this force had set a period to the life of a breadwinner, leaving his family destitute; had ended in a very painful way the days of an old lady who after a lifetime of toil was looking forward to a few short years of comparative comfort; and now, had cut short the life of this boy who, by the look of him, had been nurtured with care by his widowed mother. Small wonder then that the bereaved mother should, in between her hysterical crying, be repeating over and over and over again, 'What crime, *Parmeshwar*, has my son, who was loved by all, committed that on the threshold of life he has deserved death in this terrible way?'

Before prising up the flagstone, I had asked for the mother and her daughter to be taken to a room at the very end of the row of buildings. My preparations completed, I washed at the spring and asked for a bundle of straw, which I laid on the veranda in front of the door of the house vacated by the mother.

Darkness had now fallen. Having asked the assembled people to be as silent during the night as it was possible for them to be and sent them to their respective homes, I took up my position on the veranda, where by lying prone on my side and heaping a little straw in front, I could get a clear view of the kill without much chance of being seen myself.

In spite of all the noise that had been made the previous night, I had a feeling that the leopard would return, and that when he failed to find his kill where he had left it, he would come to the village to try to secure another victim. The ease with which he had got his first victim at Bhainswara would encourage him to try again, and I started my vigil with high hopes.

Heavy clouds had been gathering all the evening, and at 8 p.m., when all the village sound—except the wailing of the woman—were hushed, a flash of lightning followed by a distant roll of thunder heralded an approaching storm. For an hour the storm raged, the lightning being so continuous and brilliant that had a rat ventured into the courtyard I should have seen and probably been able to shoot it. The rain eventually stopped but, the sky remaining overcast, visibility was reduced to a few inches. The time had now come for the leopard to start from wherever he had been sheltering from the storm, and the time of his arrival would depend on the distance of that place from the village.

The woman had now stopped wailing, and in all the world there appeared to be no sound. This was as I had hoped, for all I had to warn me that the leopard had come were my ears, and to help them I had used the dog chain instead of a rope.

The straw that had been provided for me was as dry as tinder and my ears, straining into the black darkness, first heard the sound when it was level with my feet—something was creeping, very stealthily creeping, over the straw on which I was lying. I was wearing an article of clothing called shorts, which left my legs bare in the region of my knees. Presently, against this bare skin, I felt the hairy coat of an animal brushing. It could only be the man-eater, creeping up until he could lean over and get a grip of my throat. A little pressure now on my left shoulder—to get a foothold—and then, just as I was about to press the trigger of the rifle to cause a diversion, a small animal jumped down between my arms and my chest. It was a little kitten, soaking wet, that had been caught out in the storm and, finding every door shut, had come to me for warmth and protection.

The kitten had hardly made itself comfortable inside my coat, and I was just beginning to recover from the fright it had given me,

when from beyond the terraced
fields there was some low growling
which gradually grew louder, and then
merged into the most savage fight
I have ever heard. Quite evidently
the man-eater had returned to
the spot where the previous
night he had left his kill, and
while he was searching for it, in not
too good a temper, another male leopard
who looked upon this particular area as his hunting-ground, had
accidentally come across him and set on him. Fights of the nature
of the one that was taking place in my hearing are very unusual, for
carnivores invariably keep to their own areas, and if by chance two
of a sex happen to meet, they size up each other's capabilities at a
glance, and the weaker gives way to the stronger.

The man-eater, though old, was a big and a very powerful male,
and in the five hundred square miles he ranged over there was
possibly no other male capable of disputing his rule, but here at
Bhainswara he was a stranger and a trespasser, and to get out of
the trouble he had brought on himself he would have to fight for
his life. And this he was undoubtedly doing.

My chance of getting a shot had now gone, for even if the man-
eater succeeded in defeating his attacker, his injuries would probably
prevent him from taking any interest in kills for some time to come.
There was even a possibility of the fight ending fatally for him, and
here would indeed be an unexpected end to his career: killed in an
accidental encounter by one of his own kind, when the combined
efforts of the Government and the public had failed, over a period
of eight years, to accomplish this end.

The first round, lasting about five minutes, was fought with
unabating savagery, and was inconclusive, for at the end of it I could
still hear both animals. After an interval of ten or fifteen minutes
the fight was resumed, but at a distance of two to three hundred

yards from where it had originally started; quite evidently the local champion was getting the better of the fight and was gradually driving the intruder out of the ring. The third round was shorter than the two that had preceded it, but was no less savage, and when after another long period of silence the fight was again resumed, the scene had receded to the shoulder of the hill, where after a few minutes it died out of hearing.

There were still six hours of darkness left; even so I knew my mission to Bhainswara had failed, and that my hope that the fight would be fought to a finish and would end in the death of the man-eater had been short-lived. In the running fight into which the contest had now degenerated the man-eater would sustain injuries, but they were not likely to reduce his craving for human flesh or impair his ability to secure it.

The kitten slept peacefully throughout the night, and as the first streak of dawn showed in the east I descended into the courtyard and carried the boy to the shed from where we had removed him, and covered him with the blanket which previously had been used for the purpose. The headman was still asleep when I knocked on his door. I declined the tea, which I knew would take some time to make, and assured him that the man-eater would never again visit his village; and when he had promised to make immediate arrangements to have the boy carried to the burning-ghat, I set off on my long walk back to Rudraprayag.

No matter how often we fail in any endeavour, we never get used to the feeling of depression that assails us after each successive failure. Day after day over a period of months I had left the Inspection Bungalow full of hope that on this particular occasion I would meet with success, and day after day I had returned disappointed and depressed. Had my failures only concerned myself they would not have mattered, but in the task I had undertaken those failures concerned others more than they concerned me. Bad luck—for to nothing else could I attribute my failures—was being meted out to me in ever-increasing measure, and the accumulated effect was beginning to depress me and give me the feeling that I was not destined to do what I had set out to do. What but bad luck had made the man-eater drop his kill where there were no trees? And what but bad luck had made a leopard who possibly had thirty square miles in which to wander, arrive at a particular spot in those thirty miles just as the man-eater, not finding his kill where he had left it, was quite conceivably on his way to the village where I was waiting for him?

The eighteen miles had been long yesterday but they were longer today, and the hills were steeper. In the villages I passed through the people were eagerly awaiting me, and though I only had bad news they did not show their disappointment. Their boundless faith in their philosophy, a faith strong enough to move mountains and very soothing to depressed feelings, that no human beings and no animals can die before their appointed time, and that the man-eater's time had not yet come, called for no explanation, and admitted of no argument.

Ashamed of the depression and feeling of frustration that I had permitted to accompany me throughout the morning, I left the last village—where I had been made to halt and drink a cup of tea—greatly cheered, and as I swung down the last four miles to Rudraprayag I became aware that I was treading on the pug-marks of the man-eater. Strange how one's mental condition can dull, or sharpen, one's powers of observation. The man-eater had quite possibly joined the track many miles farther back, and now, after my conversation with the simple village-folk—and a drink of tea—I was seeing his pug-marks for the first time that morning. The track here ran over red clay which the rain had softened, and the pug marks of the man-eater showed that he was walking at his accustomed pace. Half a mile farther on he started to quicken his pace, and this pace he continued to maintain until he reached the head of the ravine above Golabrai; down this ravine the leopard had gone.

When a leopard or tiger is walking at its normal pace only the

imprints of the hind feet are seen, but when the normal pace is for any reason exceeded, the hind feet are placed on the ground in advance of the forefeet, and thus the imprints of all four feet are seen. From the distance between the imprints of the fore and the hind feet it is possible to determine the speed at which an animal of the cat tribe was travelling. The coming of daylight would in this instance have been sufficient reason for the man-eater to have quickened his pace.

I had previously had experience of the man-eater's walking capabilities, but only when ranging his beat in search of food. Here he had a better reason for the long walk he had undertaken, for he was anxious to put as great a distance as possible between himself and the leopard who had given him a lesson in the law of trespass; how severe that lesson had been will be apparent from a description given later.

# A SHOT IN THE DARK

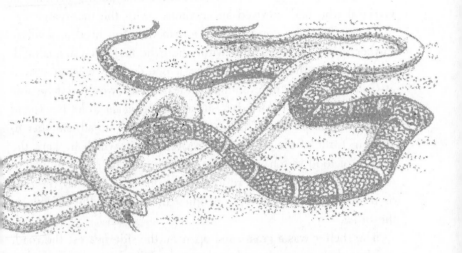

**MEALTIMES IN INDIA VARY ACCORDING TO** the season of the year and individual tastes. In most establishments the recognized times for the three principal meals are: breakfast, 8 to 9; lunch, 1 to 2; and dinner, 8 to 9. During all the months I was at Rudraprayag my mealtimes were very erratic, and contrary to the accepted belief that health depends on the composition and regularity of meals, my unorthodox and irregular meals kept me fighting fit. Porridge supped at 8 p.m., soup taken at 8 a.m., one combined meal in the day or no meal at all, appeared to have no injurious effect beyond taking a little flesh off my bones.

I had eaten nothing since my breakfast the previous day, so as I intended spending the night out I had a nondescript meal on my return from Bhainswara, and after an hour's sleep and a bath set off for Golabrai to warn the *pundit* who owned the pilgrim shelter of the presence in his vicinity of the man-eater.

I had made friends with the *pundit* on my first arrival at Rudraprayag and I never passed his house without having a few words with him, for in addition to the many interesting tales he had to tell about the man-eater and the pilgrims who passed through Golabrai, he was one of the only two people—the woman who escaped with the lacerated arm being the other—whom I met during my stay in Garhwal who had survived an encounter with the man-eater.

One of his tales concerned a woman who had lived in a village further down the road, and with whom he had been acquainted. After a visit to the Rudraprayag bazaar one day this woman arrived at Golabrai late in the evening, and fearing she would not be able to reach her home before dark she asked the *pundit* to let her spend the night in his shelter. This he permitted her to do advising her to sleep in front of the door of the storeroom in which he kept the articles of food purchased by the pilgrims, for, he said, she would then be protected by the room on the one side, and by the fifty or more pilgrims who were spending the night in the shelter on the other.

The shelter was a grass shed open on the side nearest the road, and boarded up on the side nearest the hill; the store-room was midway along the shed, but was recessed into the hill and did not obstruct the floor of the shed, so when the woman lay down at the door of the store-room there were rows of pilgrims between her and the road. Some time during the night one of the women pilgrims screamed out and said she had been stung by a scorpion. No lights were available, but with the help of matches the woman's foot was examined and a small scratch from which a little blood was flowing was found on her foot. Grumbling that the woman had made a lot of fuss about nothing, and that in any case blood did not flow from a scorpion sting, the pilgrims soon composed themselves and resumed their sleep.

In the morning, when the *pundit* arrived from his house on the hill above the mango tree, he saw a *sari* worn by hill-women lying on the road in front of the shelter, and on the *sari* there was blood. The pundit had given his friend what he considered to be the safest place in the shelter, and with fifty or more pilgrims lying all round her the leopard had walked over the sleeping people, killed the woman, and accidentally scratched the sleeping pilgrim's foot when returning to the road. The explanation given by the *pundit* as to why the leopard had rejected the pilgrims and carried off the hill-woman was that she was the only person in the shelter that night who was wearing a coloured garment. This explanation is not convincing, and but for the fact that leopards do not hunt by scent, my own explanation would have been that of all the people in the shelter the hill-woman was the only one who had a familiar smell. Was it just bad luck, or fate, or being the only one of all the sleepers who realized the danger of sleeping in an open shed? Had the victim's fear in some inexplicable way conveyed itself to the man-eater, and attracted him to her?

It was not long after this occurrence that the *pundit* had his own encounter with the man-eater. The exact date—which could if desired be ascertained from the hospital records at Rudraprayag— is immaterial, and for the purpose of my story it will be sufficient to say that it took place during the hottest part of the summer of 1921, that is four years before I met the *pundit*. Late one evening of that summer ten pilgrims from Madras arrived weary and footsore at Golabrai, and expressed their intention of spending the night in the pilgrim shelter. Fearing that if any more people were killed at Golabrai his shelter would get a bad reputation, the *pundit* tried to persuade them to continue on for another two miles to Rudraprayag, where they would be ensured of safe accommodation. Finding that nothing he could say had any effect on the tired pilgrims, he finally consented to give them accommodation in his house, which was fifty yards above the mango-tree to which I have already drawn attention.

The *pundit's* house was built on the same plan as the homesteads at Bhainswara; a low ground-floor room used for storage of fuel, and a first-floor room used as a residence. A short flight of stone steps gave access to a narrow veranda, the door of the residential room being opposite to the landing at the top of the steps.

After the *pundit* and the ten guests that had been forced on him had eaten their evening meal, they locked themselves into the room, which was not provided with any means of ventilation. The heat in the room was stifling, and fearing that he would be suffocated the *pundit* some time during the night opened the door, stepped outside, and stretched his hands to the pillars on either side of the steps supporting the roof of the veranda. As he did so and filled his lungs with the night air, his throat was gripped as in a vice. Retaining his hold on the pillars, he got the soles of his feet against the body of his assailant and with a desperate kick tore the leopard's teeth from his throat, and hurled it down the steps. Then, fearing that he was going to faint, he took a step sideways and supported himself by putting both hands on the railing of the veranda, and the moment he did so the leopard sprang up from below and buried its claws in his left forearm. The downward pull was counteracted by the railing on which the *pundit* had the palm of his hand, and the weight of the leopard caused its sharp claws to rip through the flesh of his arm until they tore free at his wrist. Before the leopard was able to spring a second time, the pilgrims, hearing the terrifying sounds the *pundit* was making in his attempts to breathe through the gap torn in his throat, dragged him into the room and bolted the door. For the rest of that long hot night the *pundit* lay gasping for breath and bleeding profusely, while the leopard growled and clawed at the frail door, and the pilgrims screamed with terror.

At daylight the pilgrims carried the *pundit*, now mercifully unconscious, to a Kalakamli hospital at Rudraprayag, where for three months he was fed through a silver tube inserted in his throat. After an absence of over six months he returned to his home in Golabrai, broken in health and with his hair turned grey. Photographs were taken five years later, and scarcely show the leopard's teeth-marks on the left side of the *pundit's* face and in his throat, and its claw-marks on his left arm, though they were still clearly visible.

In his conversations with me the *pundit* always referred to the man-eater as an evil spirit, and after the first day, when he had asked me what proof I could give him in face of his own experience that evil spirits could not assume material form, I also, to humour him, referred to the man-eater as 'the evil spirit'.

On arrival at Golabrai that evening I told the *pundit* of my fruitless visit to Bhainswara, and warned him to take extra precautions for his safety and for the safety of any pilgrims who might be staying in his shelter; for the evil spirit, after its long excursion into the hills, had now returned to the vicinity.

That night, and for the following three nights, I sat on the haystack, keeping a watch on the road; and on the fourth day Ibbotson returned from Pauri.

Ibbotson always infused new life into me, for his creed, like that of the locals, was that no one was to blame if the man-eater had not died yesterday, for surely it would died today or maybe tomorrow. I had a lot to tell him, for though I had corresponded with him regularly—extracts from my letters being embodied in his reports to the Government, and by them made available to the press—I had not been able to give him all the details which he was now eager to hear. On his part Ibbotson also had a lot to tell me; this concerned the clamour being made in the press for the destruction of the man-eater, and the suggestion that sportsmen from all parts of India be encouraged to go to Garhwal to assist in killing the leopard. This press campaign had resulted in Ibbotson receiving only one inquiry, and only one suggestion. The inquiry was from a sportsman who said that, if arrangements for his travel, accommodation, food, and so on, were made to his satisfaction, he would consider whether it was worth his while to come to Golabrai; and the suggestion was from a sportsman in whose opinion the speediest and easiest way of killing the leopard was to paint a goat over with arsenic, sew up its mouth to prevent it licking itself, and then tie it up in a place where the leopard would find and eat it, and so poison itself.

We talked long that day, reviewing my many failures in minutest detail, and by lunch-time, when I had told Ibbotson of the leopard's habit of going down the road between Rudraprayag and Golabrai on an average once in every five days, I convinced him that the only hope I now had of shooting the leopard was by sitting over the road for ten nights, for, as I pointed out to him, the leopard would be almost certain to use the road at least once during the period. Ibbotson consented to my plan very reluctantly, for I had already sat up many nights and he was afraid that another ten on end would be too much for me. However, I carried my point, and then told Ibbotson that if I did not succeed in killing the leopard within the stipulated time, I would return to Naini Tal and leave the field free for any new-comers who might consider it worth their while to take my place.

That evening Ibbotson accompanied me to Golabrai and helped me to put up a *machan* in the mango tree a hundred yards from the pilgrim shelter and fifty yards below the *pundit's* house. Immediately below the tree, and in the middle of the road, we drove a stout wooden peg, and to this peg we tethered a goat with a small bell round its neck. The moon was nearly at its full; even so, the high hill to the east of Golabrai only admitted of the moon lighting up the deep Ganges valley for a few hours, and if the leopard came while it was dark the goat would warn me of his approach.

When all our preparations had been made Ibbotson returned to the bungalow, promising to send two of my men for me early next morning. While I sat on a rock near the foot of the tree and smoked and waited for night to close in, the *pundit* came and sat down beside me; he was a *bhakti* and did not smoke. Earlier in the evening he had seen us building the *machan*, and he now tried to dissuade me from sitting all night in the tree when I could sleep comfortably in bed. Nevertheless, I assured him I would sit all that night in the tree, and for nine nights thereafter, for if I was not able to kill the evil spirit I could at least guard his house and the pilgrim shelter from attack by all enemies. Once during the night a *kakar* barked on the hill above me, but thereafter the night was silent. At sunrise next morning two of my men arrived, and I set off for the Inspection Bungalow, examining the road as I went for pug-marks, and leaving the men to follow with my rug and rifle.

During the following nine days my programme did not vary.

Leaving the bungalow accompanied by two men in the early evening, I took up my position in the *machan* and sent the men away in time for them to get back to the bungalow before dusk. The men had strict orders not to leave the bungalow before it was fully light, and they arrived each morning as the sun was rising on the hills on the far side of the river and accompanied me back to the bungalow.

During all those ten nights the barking of the *kakar* on the first night was all that I heard. That the man-eater was still in the vicinity we had ample proof, for twice within those ten nights it had broken into houses and carried off, on the first occasion, a goat and, on the second occasion, a sheep. I found both kills with some difficulty for they had been carried a long distance, but neither had been of any use to me as they had been eaten out. Once also during those ten nights the leopard had broken down the door of a house which, fortunately for the inmates, had two rooms, the door of the inner room being sufficiently strong to withstand the leopard's onslaught.

On return to the bungalow after my tenth night in the mango tree, Ibbotson and I discussed our future plans. No further communications had been received from the sportsman, no one else had expressed a desire to accept the Government's invitation, and no one had responded to the appeals made by the press. Neither Ibbotson nor I could afford to spend more time at Rudraprayag; Ibbotson because he had been away from his headquarters for ten days and it was necessary for him to return to Pauri to attend to urgent work; and I because I had work to do in Africa and had delayed my departure for three months and could not delay it any longer. Both of us were reluctant to leave Garhwal to the tender mercies of the man-eater and yet, situated as we were, it was hard to decide what to do. One solution was for Ibbotson to apply for leave, and for me to cancel my passage to Africa and cut my losses. We finally agreed to leave the decision over for that night, and to decide on our line of action next morning. Having come to this decision I told Ibbotson I would spend my last night in Garhwal in the mango tree.

Ibbotson accompanied me on that eleventh, and last, evening, and as we approached Golabrai we saw a number of men standing on the side of the road, looking down into a field a little beyond the mango tree; the men had not seen us and before we got up to them they turned and moved off towards the pilgrim shelter. One of them however looked back, and seeing me beckoning retraced his steps. In answer to our questions he said he and his companions had for an hour been watching a great fight between two big snakes down in the field. No crops appeared to have been grown there for a year or more, and the snakes had last been seen near the big rock in the middle of the field. There were smears of blood on this rock, and the man said they had been made by the snakes, which had bitten each other and were bleeding in several places. Having broken a stick from a nearby bush, I jumped down into the field to see if there were any holes near the rock, and as I did so I caught sight of the snakes in a bush just below the road. Ibbotson had in the meantime armed himself with a stout stick, and as one of the snakes tried to climb up on to the road he killed it. The other one disappeared into a hole in the bank from where we were unable to dislodge it. The snake Ibbotson had killed was about seven feet long and of a uniform light straw colour, and on its neck it had several bites. It was not a rat snake, and as it had very pronounced poison fangs we concluded it was some variety of hoodless cobra. Cold-blooded creatures are not immune to snake poison, for I have seen a frog bitten by a cobra die in a few minutes, but I do not know if snakes of the same variety can poison each other, and the one that escaped into the hole may have died in a few minutes or it may have lived to die of old age.

After Ibbotson left, the *pundit* passed under my tree on his way to the pilgrim shelter, carrying a pail of milk. He informed me that a hundred and fifty pilgrims, who had arrived during the day, were determined to spend the night in his shelter and that he was powerless to do anything about it. It was then too late for me to take any action, so I told him to warn the pilgrims to keep close together and not on any account to move about after dark. When he hurried back to his house a few minutes later, he said he had warned the pilgrims accordingly.

In a field adjoining the road, and about a hundred yards from my tree, there was a thorn enclosure in which a packman—not my old friend—earlier in the evening had penned his flock of goats and sheep. With the packman were two dogs who had barked very fiercely at us as we came down the road, and at Ibbotson after he left me to go back to the bungalow.

The moon was a few days past the full, and the valley was in darkness when, a little after 9 p.m., I saw a man carrying a lantern leave the pilgrim shelter and cross the road. A minute or two later, he recrossed the road and on gaining the shelter extinguished the lantern and at the same moment the packman's dogs started barking furiously. The dogs were unmistakably barking at a leopard, which quite possibly had seen the man with the lantern and was now coming down the road on its way to the shelter.

At first the dogs barked in the direction of the road, but after a little while they turned and barked in my direction. The leopard had now quite evidently caught sight of the sleeping goat and lain down out of sight of the dogs—which had stopped barking—to consider his next move. I knew that the leopard had arrived, and I also knew that he was using my tree to stalk the goat, and the question that was tormenting me as the long minutes dragged by was whether he would skirt round the goat and kill one of the pilgrims, or whether he would kill the goat and give me a shot.

During all the nights I had sat in the tree I adopted a position that would enable me to discharge my rifle with the minimum of movement and in the minimum of time. The distance between the goat and my *machan* was about twenty feet, but the night was so dark under the dense foliage of the tree that my straining eyes could not penetrate even this short distance, so I closed them and concentrated on my hearing.

My rifle, to which I had a small electric torch attached, was pointing in the direction of the goat, and I was just beginning to think that the leopard—assuming it was the man-eater—had reached the shelter and was selecting a human victim, when there was a rush from the foot of the tree, and the goat's bell tinkled sharply. Pressing the button of the torch I saw that the sights of the rifle were aligned on the shoulder of a leopard, and without having to move the rifle a fraction of an inch I pressed the trigger, and as I did so the torch went out.

Torches in those days were not in as general use as they are now, and mine was the first I had ever possessed. I had carried it for several months and never had occasion to use it, and I did not know the life of the battery, or that it was necessary to test it. When I pressed the button on this occasion the torch gave only one dim flash and then went out, and I was again in darkness without knowing what the result of my shot had been.

The echo of my shot was dying away in the valley when the *pundit* opened his door and called out to ask if I needed any help. I was at the time listening with all my ears for any sounds that might come from the leopard, so I did not answer him, and he hurriedly shut his door.

The leopard had been lying across the road with his head away from me when I fired, and I was vaguely aware of his having sprung over the goat and gone down the hillside, and just before the *pundit* had called I thought I heard what may have been a gurgling sound, but of this I could not be sure. The pilgrims had been aroused by my shot but, after murmuring for a few minutes, they resumed their sleep. The goat appeared to be unhurt, for from the sound of his bell I could tell that he was moving about and apparently eating the grass of which he was given a liberal supply each night.

I had fired my shot at 10 p.m. As the moon was not due to rise for several hours, and as there was nothing I could do in the meantime, I made myself comfortable, and listened and smoked.

Hours later the moon lit up the crest of the hills on the far side of the Ganges and slowly crept down into the valley, and a little later I saw it rise over the top of the hill behind me. As soon as it was overhead I climbed to the top of the tree, but found that the spreading branches impeded my view. Descending again to the *machan*, I climbed out on the branches spreading over the road, but from here also I found it was not possible to see down the hillside in the direction in which I thought the leopard had gone. It was then 3 a.m., and two hours later the moon began to pale. When nearby objects became visible in the light of the day that was being born in the east, I descended from the tree and was greeted by a friendly bleat from the goat.

Beyond the goat, and at the very edge of the road, there was a long low rock, and on this rock there was an inch-wide streak of blood; the leopard from which that blood had come could only have lived a minute or two, so dispensing with the precautions usually taken when following up the blood trail of carnivores, I scrambled down off the road and, taking up the trail on the far side of the rock, followed it for fifty yards, to where the leopard was lying dead. He had slid backwards into a hole in the ground, in which he was now lying crouched up, with his chin resting on the edge of the hole.

No marks by which I could identify the dead animal were visible, even so I never for one moment doubted that the leopard in the hole was the man-eater. But here was no fiend, who while watching me through the long night hours had rocked and rolled with silent fiendish laughter at my vain attempts to outwit him, and licked his lips in anticipation of the time when, finding me off my guard for one brief moment, he would get the opportunity he was waiting for of burying his teeth in my throat. Here was only an old leopard, who differed from others of his kind in that his muzzle was grey and his lips lacked whiskers; the best-hated and the most feared animal in all India, whose only crime—not against the laws of nature, but against the laws of man—was that he had shed human blood, with no object of terrorizing man, but only in order that he might live; and who now, with his chin resting on the rim of the hole and his eyes half-closed, was peacefully sleeping his long last sleep.

While I stood unloading my rifle, one bullet from which had more than cancelled my personal score against the sleeper, I heard a cough, and on looking up saw the *pundit* peering down at me from the edge of the road. I beckoned to him and he came gingerly down the hill. On catching sight of the leopard's head he stopped, and asked in a whisper whether it was dead, and what it was. When I told him it was dead, and that it was the evil spirit that had torn open his throat five years ago, and for fear of which he had hurriedly closed his door the previous night, he put his hands together and attempted to put his head on my feet. Next minute there was a call from the road above of, 'Sahib, where are you?' It was one of my men calling in great agitation, and when I sent an answering call echoing over the Ganges, four heads appeared, and catching sight of us four men came helter-skelter down the hill, one of them swinging a lighted lantern which he had forgotten to extinguish.

The leopard had got stiff in the hole and was extracted with some little difficulty. While it was being tied to the stout bamboo pole the men had brought with them, they told me they had been unable to sleep that night and that as soon as Ibbotson's *jemadar's* watch showed them it was 4.30 a.m., they lit the lantern, and arming themselves with a pole and a length of rope had come to look for me, for they felt that I was in urgent need of them. Not finding me in the *machan* and seeing the goat unhurt, and the streak of blood on the rock, they concluded the man-eater had killed me, and not knowing what to do they had in desperation called to me.

Leaving the *pundit* to retrieve my rug from the *machan*, and give the pilgrims who were now crowding round his version of the night's happenings, the four men and I, with the goat trotting alongside, set off for the Inspection Bungalow. The goat, who had escaped with very little injury owing to my having fired the moment the leopard caught him, little knew that his night's adventure was to make him a hero for the rest of his life, and that he was to wear a fine brass collar and be a source of income to the man from whom I had purchased him, and to whom I gave him back.

Ibbotson was still asleep when I knocked on the glazed door, and the moment he caught sight of me he jumped out of bed and dashing to the door flung it open, embraced me, and next minute was dancing round the leopard which the men had deposited on the veranda. Shouting for tea, and a hot bath for me, he called for his stenographer and dictated telegrams to the Government, the press, and my sister, and a cable to Jean. Not one question had he asked, for he knew that the leopard which I had brought home at that early hour was the man-eater, so what need was there for questions? On that previous occasion—in spite of all the evidence that had been produced—I had maintained that the leopard killed in the gin-trap was not the man-eater, and on this occasion I had said nothing.

Ibbotson had carried a heavy responsibility since October of the previous year, for to him was left the answering of questions of Councillors anxious to please their constituents, of Government officials who were daily getting more alarmed at the mounting death-roll, and of a press that was clamouring for results. His position had for a long time been like that of the head of a police force who, knowing the identity of a noted criminal, was unable to prevent his committing further crimes, and for this was being badgered on all sides. Little wonder then that Ibbotson on that 2nd of May 1926 was the happiest man I had even seen, for not only was he now able to inform all concerned that the criminal had been executed, but he was also able to tell the people from the bazaars, and from the surrounding villages, and the pilgrims, all of whom were swarming into the compound of the Inspection Bungalow, that the evil spirit that had tormented them for eight long years was now dead.

After emptying a pot of tea and having a hot bath I tried to

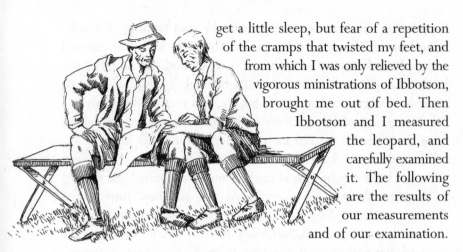

get a little sleep, but fear of a repetition of the cramps that twisted my feet, and from which I was only relieved by the vigorous ministrations of Ibbotson, brought me out of bed. Then Ibbotson and I measured the leopard, and carefully examined it. The following are the results of our measurements and of our examination.

## MEASUREMENTS

Length, between pegs       7 feet, 6 inches
Length, over curves        7 feet, 10 inches

[Note: these measurements were taken after the leopard had been dead twelve hours.]

## DESCRIPTION

*Colour*:  Light straw.
*Hair*:  Short and brittle.
*Whiskers*:  None.
*Teeth*:  Worn and discoloured, one canine tooth broken.
*Tongue and mouth*:  Black.
*Wounds*:  One fresh bullet-wound in right shoulder.

One old bullet-wound in pad of left hind foot, and part of one toe and one claw missing from same foot.
Several deep and partly-healed cuts on head.
One deep and partly-healed cut on right hind leg.
Several partly-healed cuts on tail.
One partly-healed wound on stifle of left hind leg.

I am unable to account for the leopard's tongue and mouth being black. It was suggested that this might have been caused by cyanide, but whether this was so or not I cannot say. Of the partly-healed wounds, those on the head, right hind leg, and tail were acquired in his fight at Bhainswara, and the one on the stifle of his left hind leg was the result of his having been caught in the gin-trap, for the piece of skin and tuft of hair we found in the trap fitted into this wound. The injuries on the left hind foot were the result of the bullet fired on the bridge by the young army officer in 1921. When skinning the leopard later, I found a pellet of buckshot embedded in the skin of his chest which an Indian Christian—years later—claimed he had fired at the leopard the year it became a man-eater.

After Ibbotson and I had measured and examined the leopard it was laid in the shade of a tree, and throughout the day thousands of men, women, and children came to see it.

When the people of our hills visit an individual for any particular purpose, as for instance to show their gratitude or to express their thanks, it is customary for them not to go on their mission empty-handed. A rose, a marigold, or a few petals of either flower, suffices, and the gift is proffered in hands cupped together. When the recipient has touched the gift with the tips of the fingers of his right hand, the person proffering the gift goes through the motion of pouring the gift on to the recipient's feet, in the same manner as if his cupped hands contained water.

I have on other occasions witnessed gratitude, but never as I witnessed it that day at Rudraprayag, first at the Inspection Bungalow and later at a reception in the bazaar.

'He killed our only son, sahib, and we being old, our house is now desolate.'

'He ate the mother of my five children, and the youngest is but a few months old, and there is none in the home now to care for the children, or to cook the food.'

'My son was taken ill at night and no one dared go to the hospital for medicine, and so he died.'

Tragedy upon pitiful tragedy, and while I listened, the ground around my feet was strewn with flowers.

# EPILOGUE

**THE EVENTS I HAVE NARRATED TOOK** place between 1925 and 1926. Sixteen years later, in 1942, I was doing a war job in Meerut and my sister and I were invited one day by Colonel Flye to help entertain wounded men at a garden party. The men, some fifty or sixty in number, and from all parts of India, were sitting round a tennis-court just finishing a sumptuous tea, and getting to the smoking stage, when we arrived. Taking opposite sides of the court, my sister and I started to go round the circle.

The men were all from the Middle East, and, after a rest, were to be sent to their homes, some on leave, and some on discharge.

Music, in the form of a gramophone with Indian records, had been provided by Mrs Flye, and as my sister and I had been requested to stay until the party gave over—which would be in about two hours' time—we had ample time to make our circuit of the wounded men.

I had got about half-way round the circle when I came to a boy sitting in a low chair; he had been grievously wounded, and on the ground near his chair were two crutches. At my approach he very painfully slid off his chair and attempted to put his head on my feet. He was woefully light, for he had spent many months in hospital, and when I had picked him up and made him comfortable in his chair, he said: 'I have been talking with your lady sister, and when I told her I was a Garhwali, she told me who you were. I was a small boy when you shot the man-eater, and as our village is far from Rudraprayag I was not able to walk there, and my father not being strong was unable to carry me, so I had to stay at home. When my father returned he told me he had seen the man-eater, and that with his own eyes he had seen the sahib who had shot it. He also told me of the sweets that had been distributed that day— his share of which he had brought back for me—and of the great crowds he had seen. And now, sahib, I will go back to my home with great joy in my heart, for I shall be able to tell my father that with my own eyes I have seen you and, may be, if I can get anyone to carry me to the fair that is held every year at Rudraprayag to commemorate the death of the man-eater, I shall tell all the people I meet there that I have seen and had speech with you.'

A cripple, on the threshold of manhood, returning from the wars with a broken body, with no thought of telling of brave deeds done, but only eager to tell his father that with his own eyes he had seen the man who years ago he had not had the opportunity of seeing, a man whose only claim to remembrance was that he had fired one accurate shot.

A typical son of Garhwal, of that simple and hardy hill-folk; and of that greater India, whose sons only those few who live among them are privileged to know. It is these big-hearted sons of the soil, no matter what their caste or creed, who will one day weld the contending factions into a composite whole, and make of India a great nation.

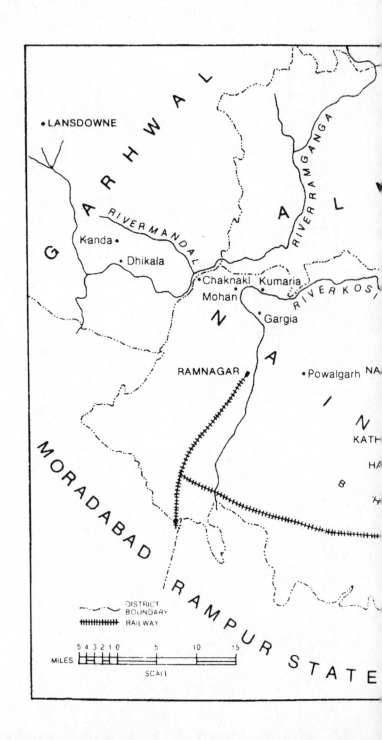

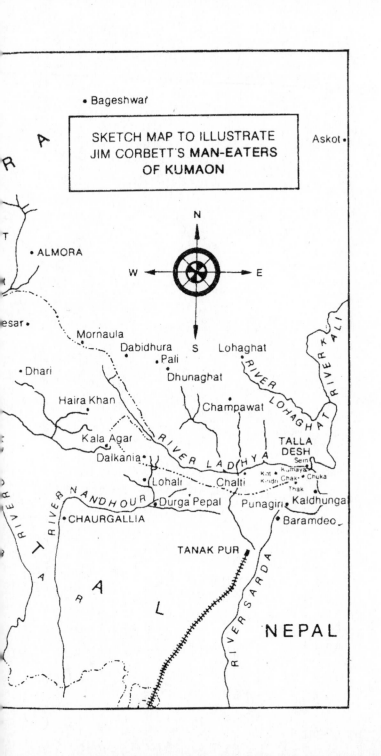